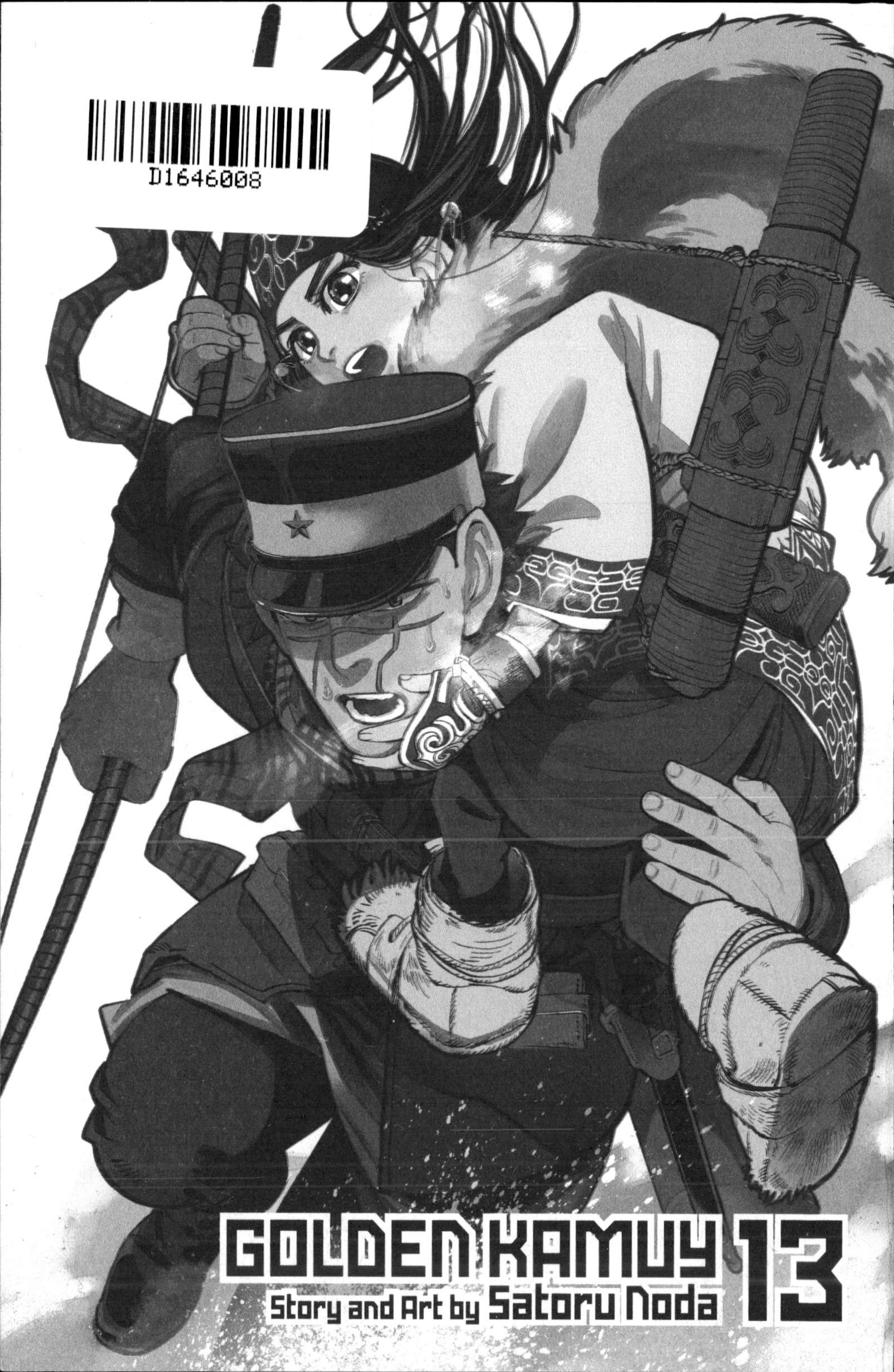

GOLDEN KAMUY 13

Story and Art by Satoru Noda

The Story So Far

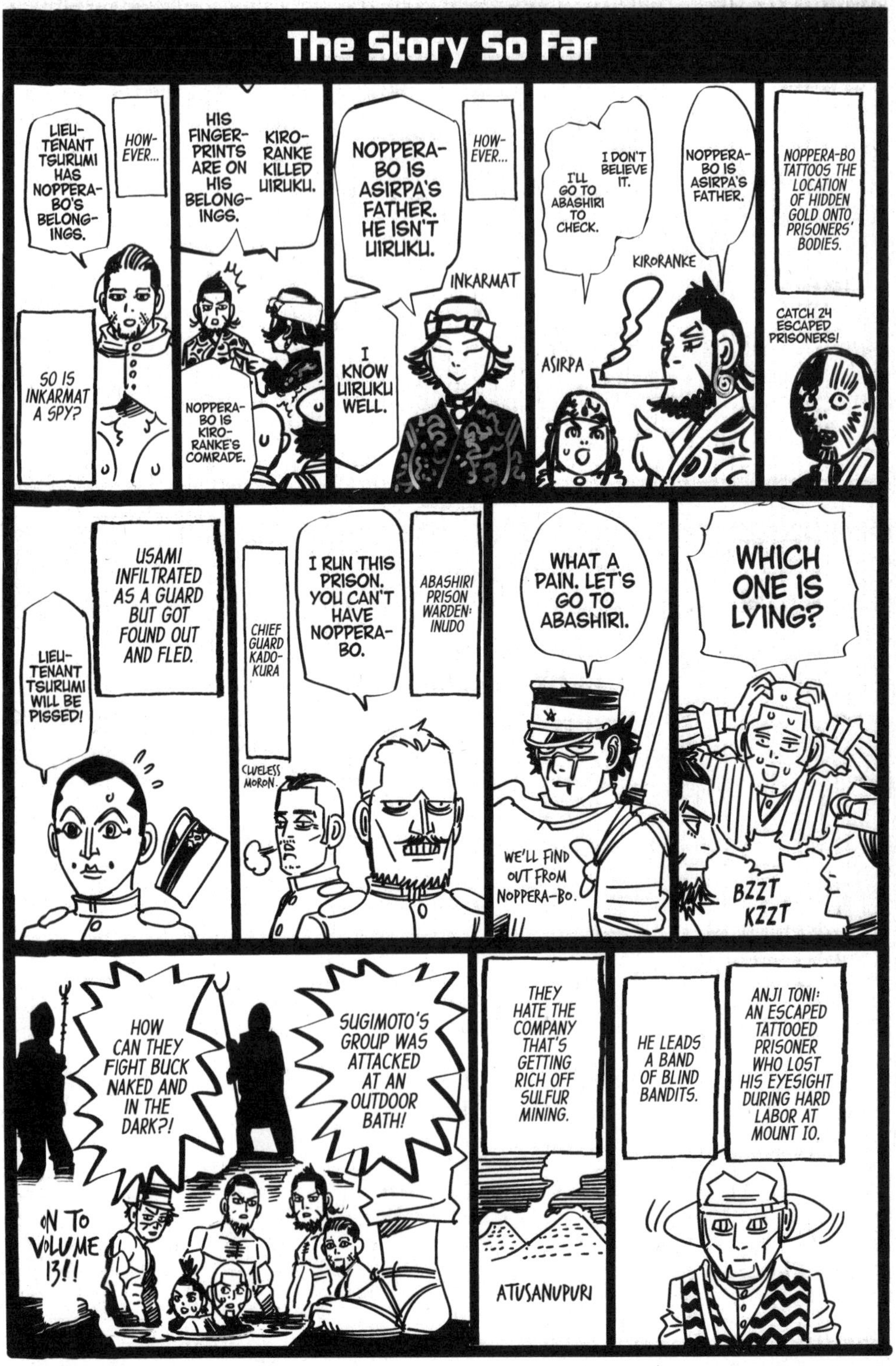
NOPPERA-BO TATTOOS THE LOCATION OF HIDDEN GOLD ONTO PRISONERS' BODIES.
CATCH 24 ESCAPED PRISONERS!
NOPPERA-BO IS ASIRPA'S FATHER.
KIRORANKE
I DON'T BELIEVE IT.
I'LL GO TO ABASHIRI TO CHECK.
ASIRPA
HOWEVER...
NOPPERA-BO IS ASIRPA'S FATHER. HE ISN'T UIRUKU.
INKARMAT
I KNOW UIRUKU WELL.
KIRORANKE KILLED UIRUKU.
HIS FINGERPRINTS ARE ON HIS BELONGINGS.
NOPPERA-BO IS KIRORANKE'S COMRADE.
HOWEVER...
LIEUTENANT TSURUMI HAS NOPPERA-BO'S BELONGINGS.
SO IS INKARMAT A SPY?
WHICH ONE IS LYING?
BZZT
KZZT
WHAT A PAIN. LET'S GO TO ABASHIRI.
WE'LL FIND OUT FROM NOPPERA-BO.
ABASHIRI PRISON WARDEN: INUDO
I RUN THIS PRISON. YOU CAN'T HAVE NOPPERA-BO.
CHIEF GUARD KADOKURA
CLUELESS MORON.
USAMI INFILTRATED AS A GUARD BUT GOT FOUND OUT AND FLED.
LIEUTENANT TSURUMI WILL BE PISSED!
ANJI TONI: AN ESCAPED TATTOOED PRISONER WHO LOST HIS EYESIGHT DURING HARD LABOR AT MOUNT IO.
HE LEADS A BAND OF BLIND BANDITS.
THEY HATE THE COMPANY THAT'S GETTING RICH OFF SULFUR MINING.
ATUSANUPURI
SUGIMOTO'S GROUP WAS ATTACKED AT AN OUTDOOR BATH!
HOW CAN THEY FIGHT BUCK NAKED AND IN THE DARK?!
ON TO VOLUME 13!!

CONTENTS

GOLDEN KAMUY

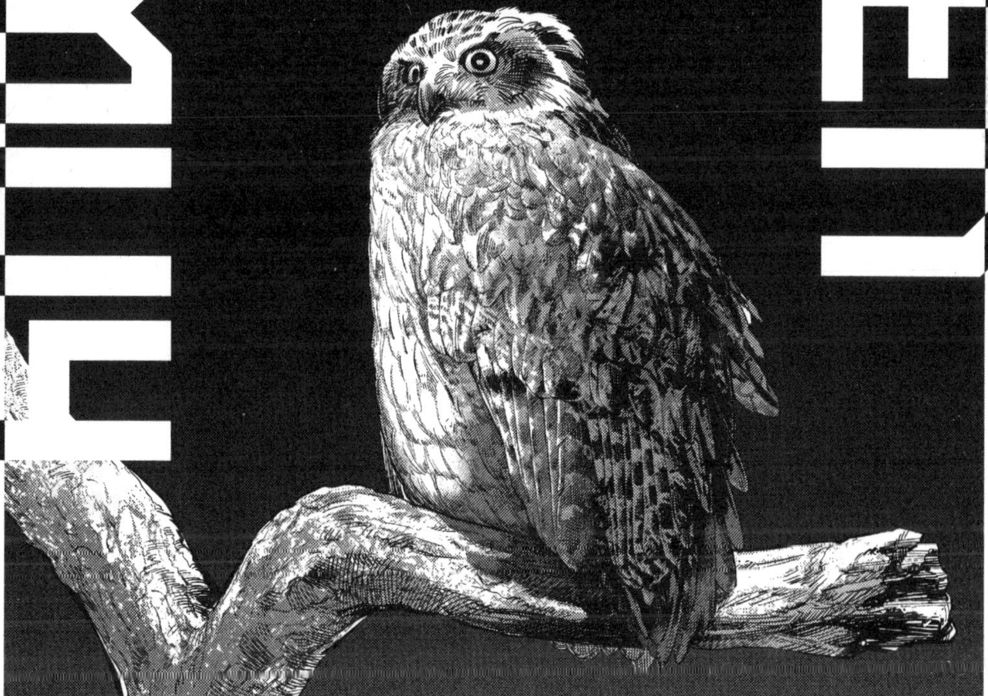

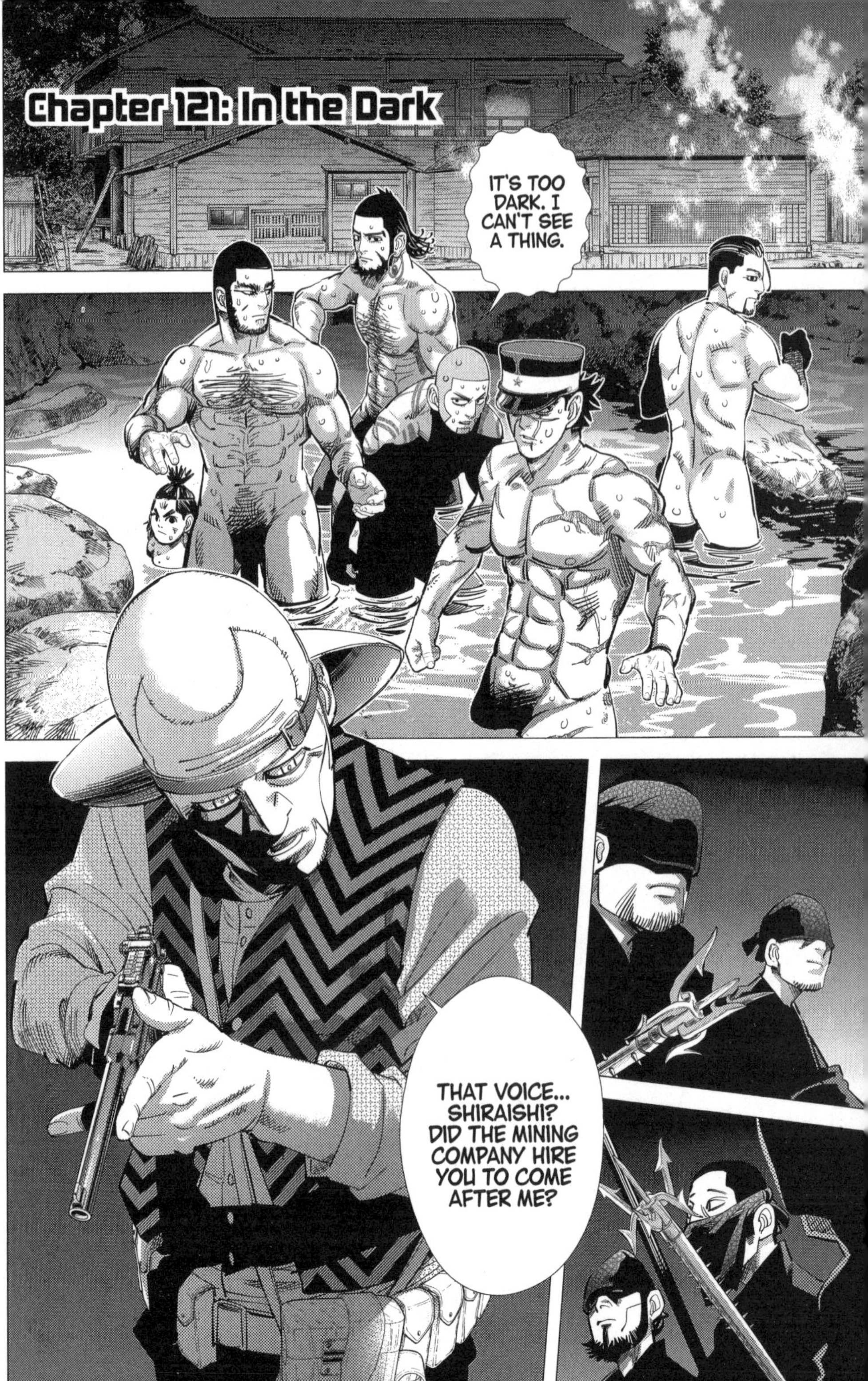
Chapter 121: In the Dark
IT'S TOO DARK. I CAN'T SEE A THING.
THAT VOICE... SHIRAISHI? DID THE MINING COMPANY HIRE YOU TO COME AFTER ME?

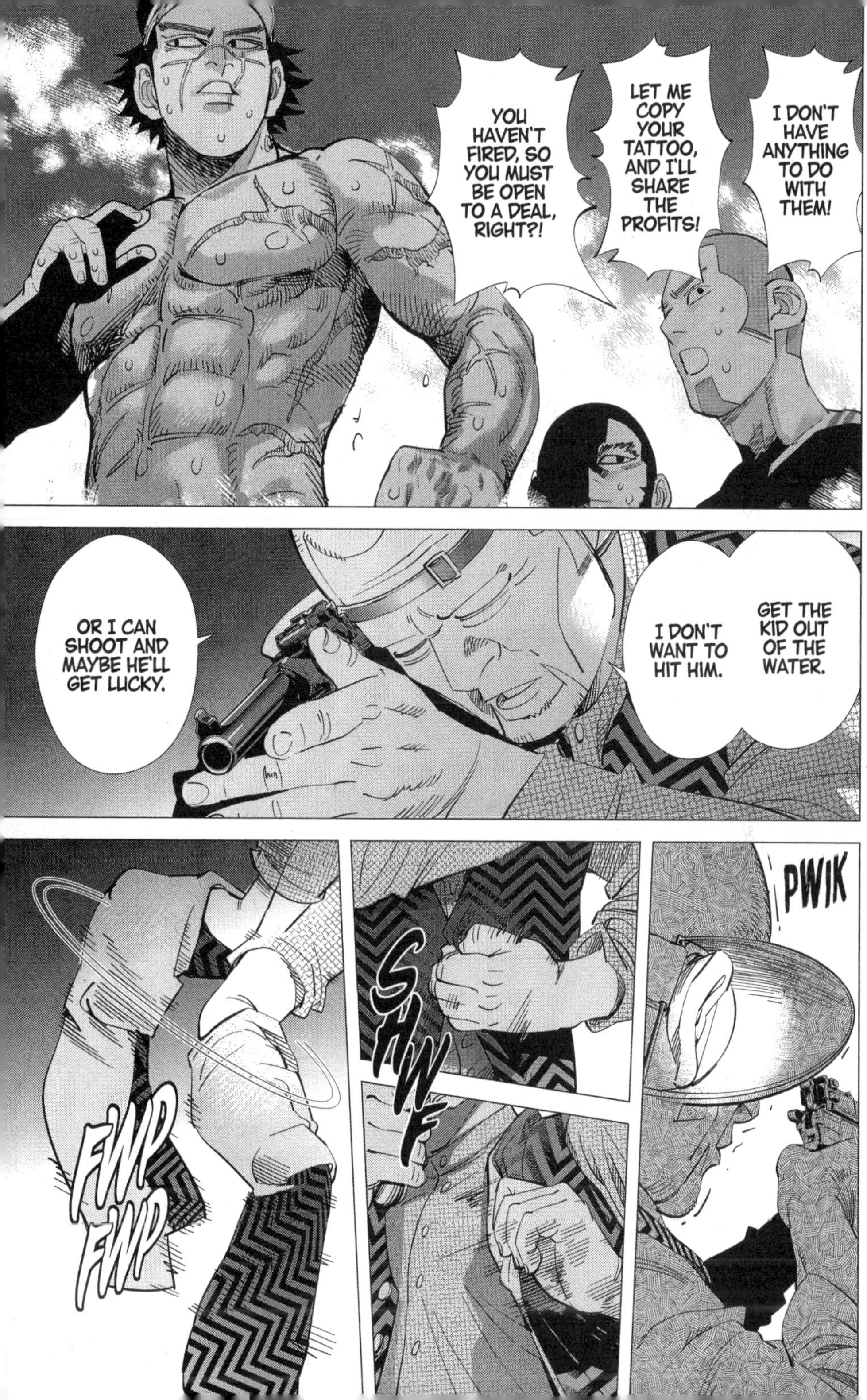
I DON'T HAVE ANYTHING TO DO WITH THEM!
LET ME COPY YOUR TATTOO, AND I'LL SHARE THE PROFITS!
YOU HAVEN'T FIRED, SO YOU MUST BE OPEN TO A DEAL, RIGHT?!
GET THE KID OUT OF THE WATER.
I DON'T WANT TO HIT HIM.
OR I CAN SHOOT AND MAYBE HE'LL GET LUCKY.
PWIK
SHWF
FWP FWP

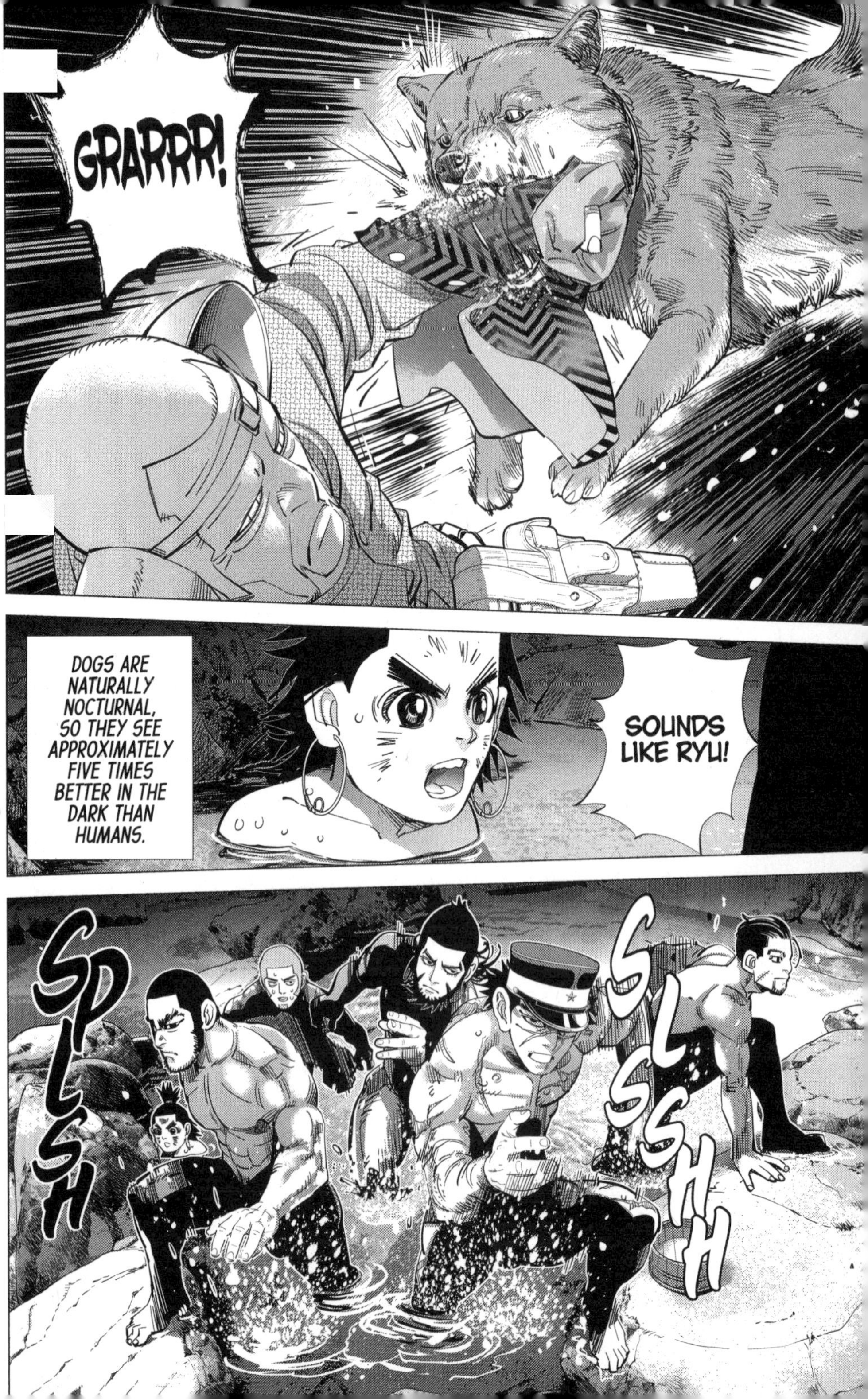
GRARRR!
SOUNDS LIKE RYU!
DOGS ARE NATURALLY NOCTURNAL, SO THEY SEE APPROXIMATELY FIVE TIMES BETTER IN THE DARK THAN HUMANS.
SLSSHH
SPLSH

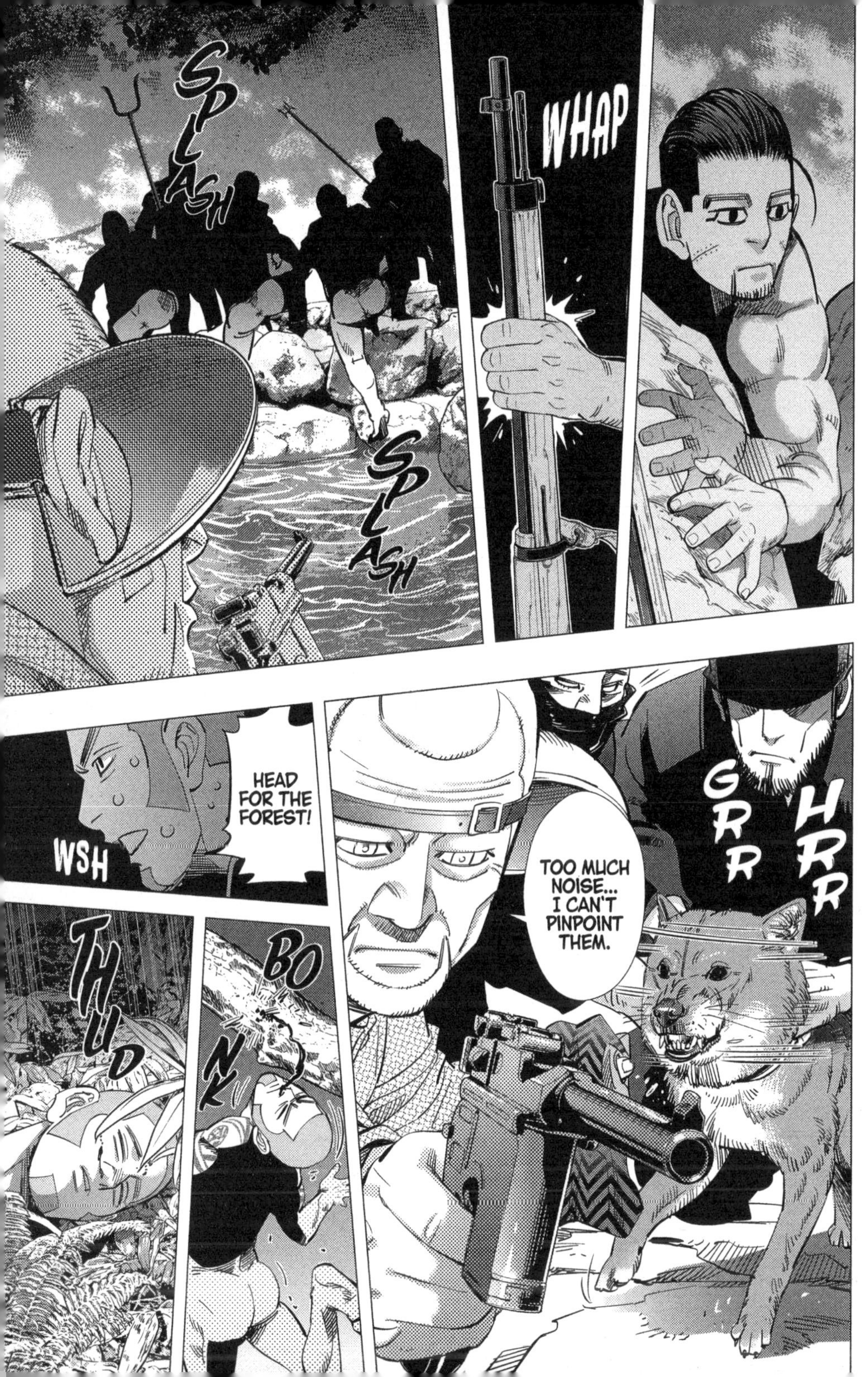
WHAP
SPLASH
SPLASH
HRRR
GRRR
TOO MUCH NOISE... I CAN'T PINPOINT THEM.
HEAD FOR THE FOREST!
WSH
BONK
THUD

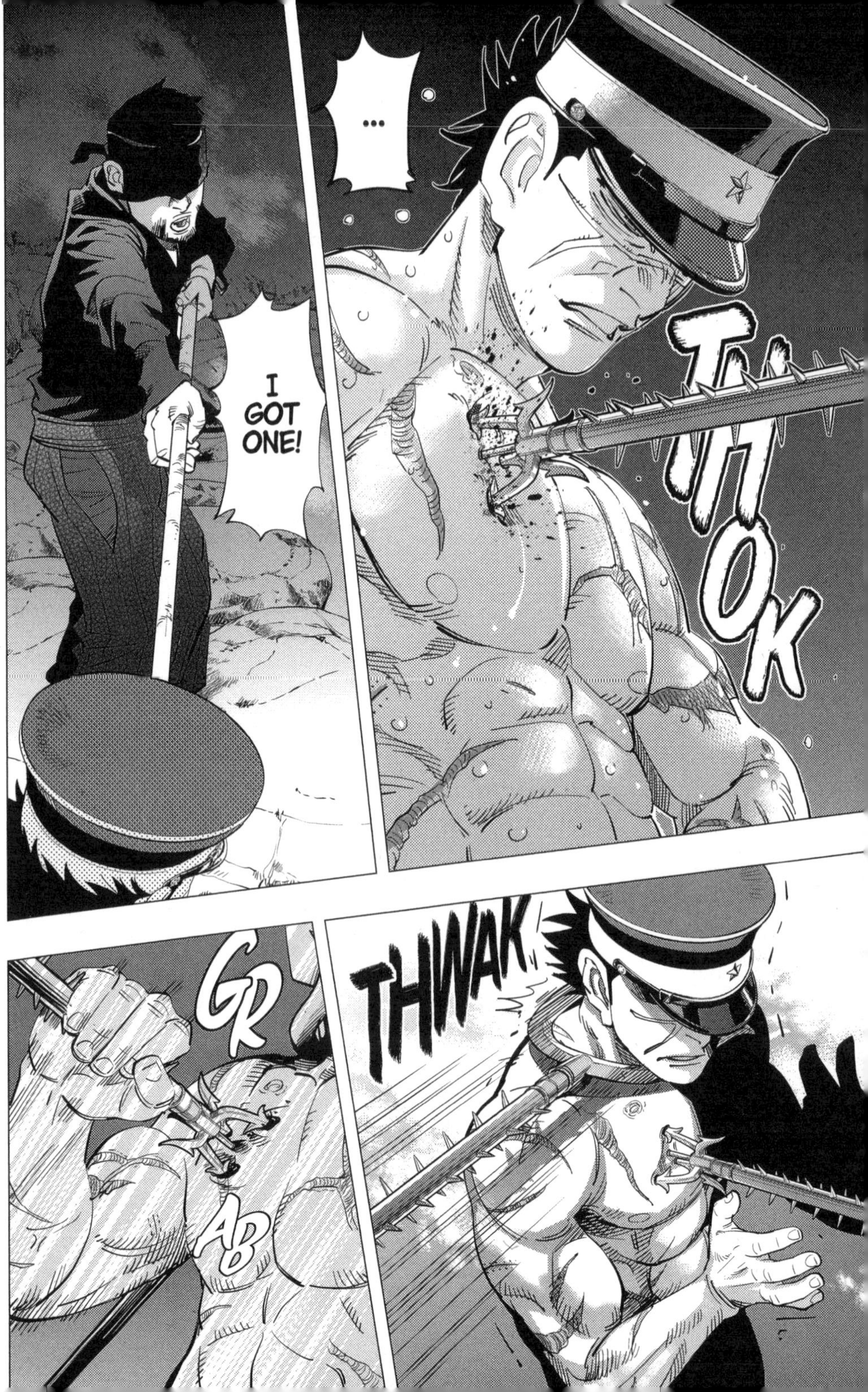
...
THOK
I GOT ONE!
THWAK
GR
AB

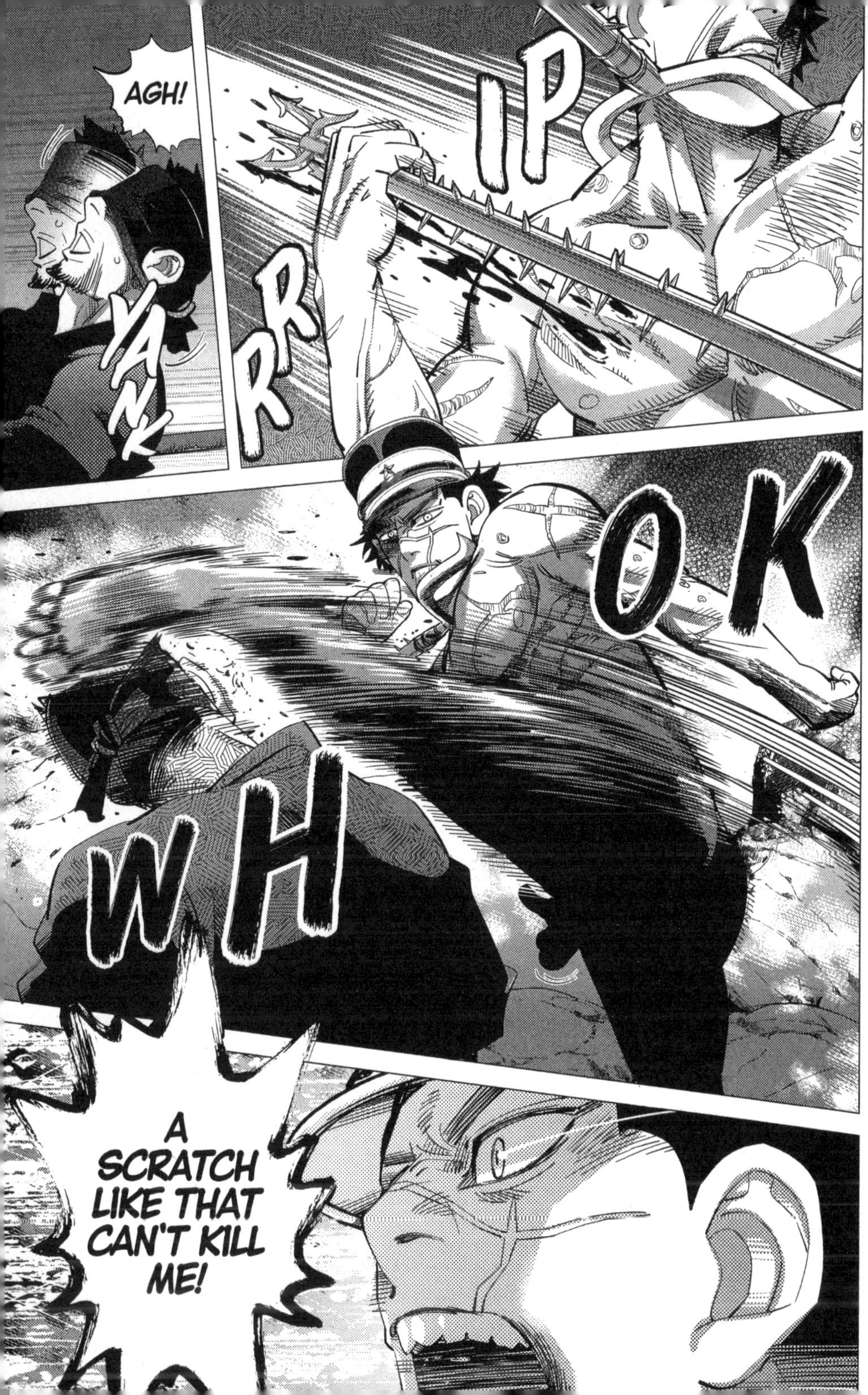
RRIP
AGH!
YANK
WHOK
A SCRATCH LIKE THAT CAN'T KILL ME!

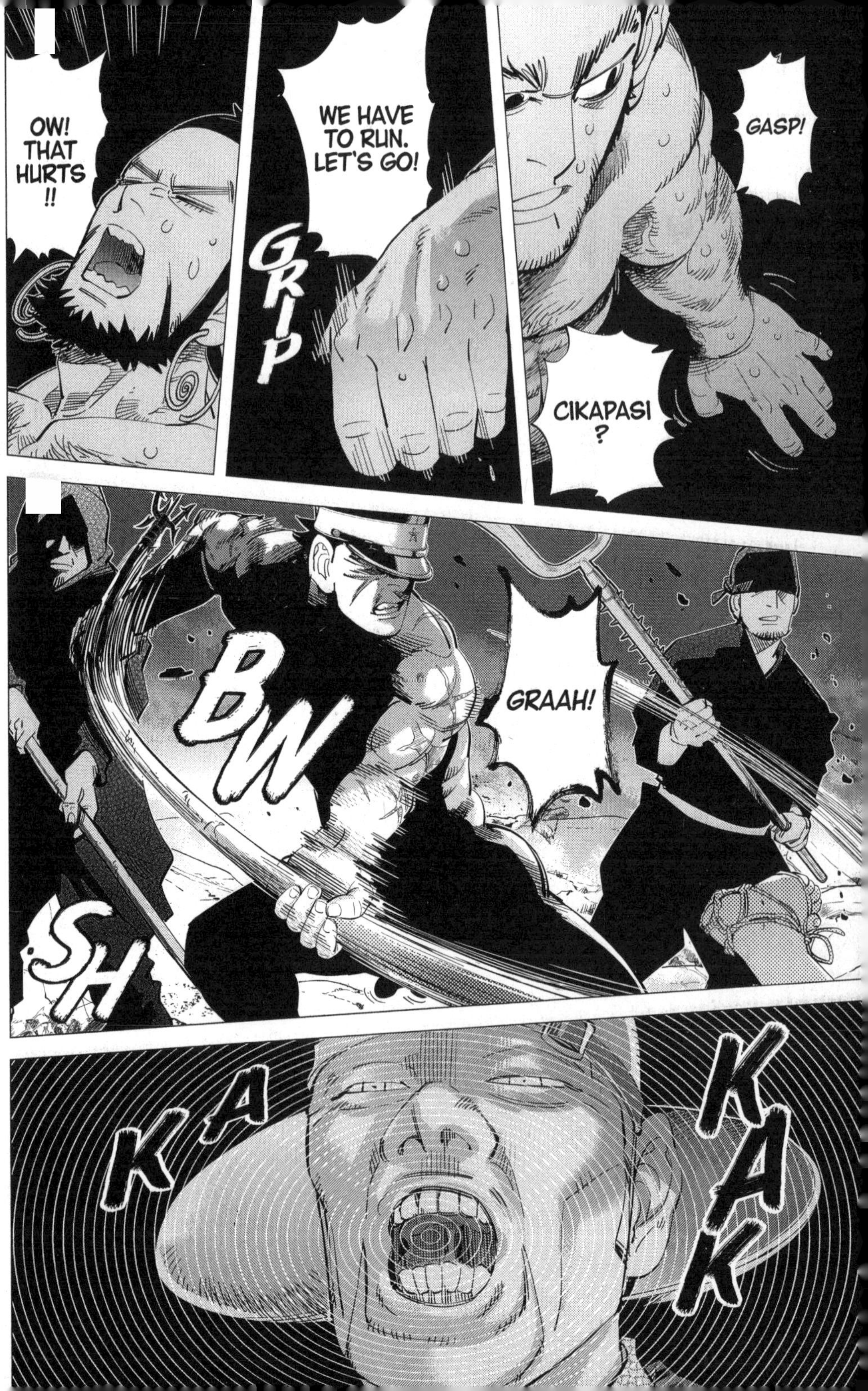
GASP!
CIKAPASI?
WE HAVE TO RUN. LET'S GO!
GRIP
OW! THAT HURTS!!
GRAAH!
BW
SH
KAK
KA

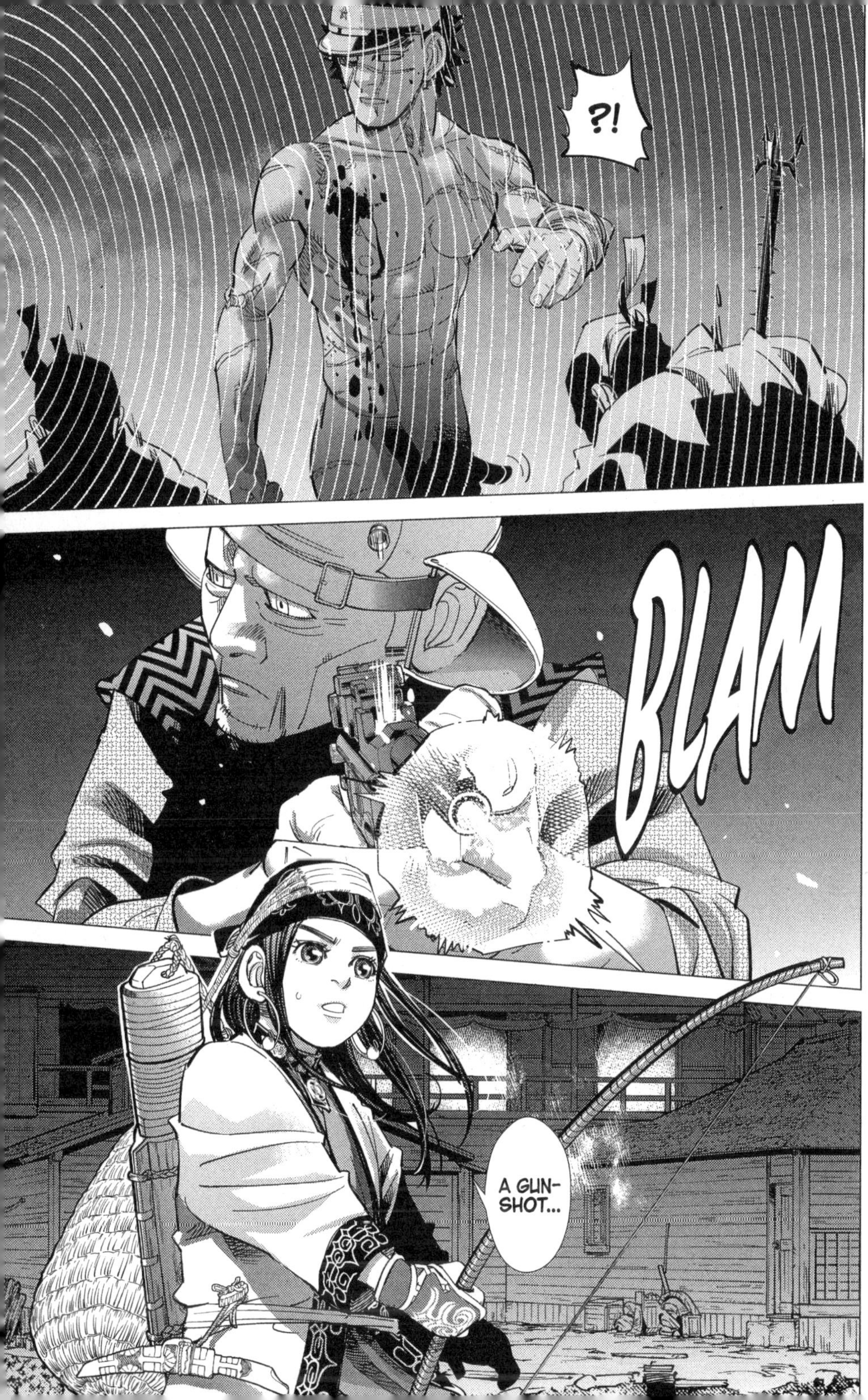
?!
BLAM
A GUN-SHOT...

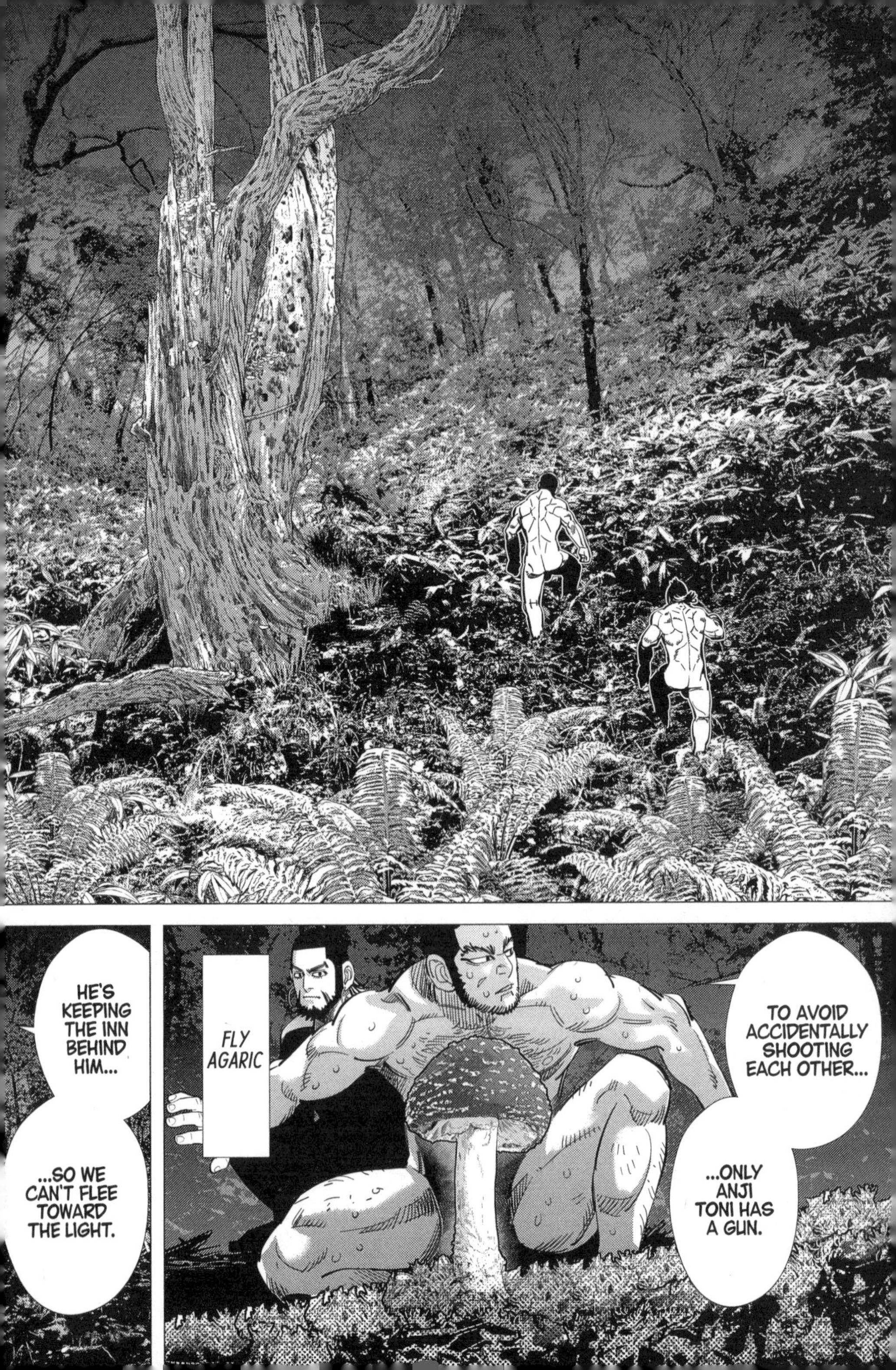
TO AVOID ACCIDENTALLY SHOOTING EACH OTHER...
...ONLY ANJI TONI HAS A GUN.
FLY AGARIC
HE'S KEEPING THE INN BEHIND HIM...
...SO WE CAN'T FLEE TOWARD THE LIGHT.

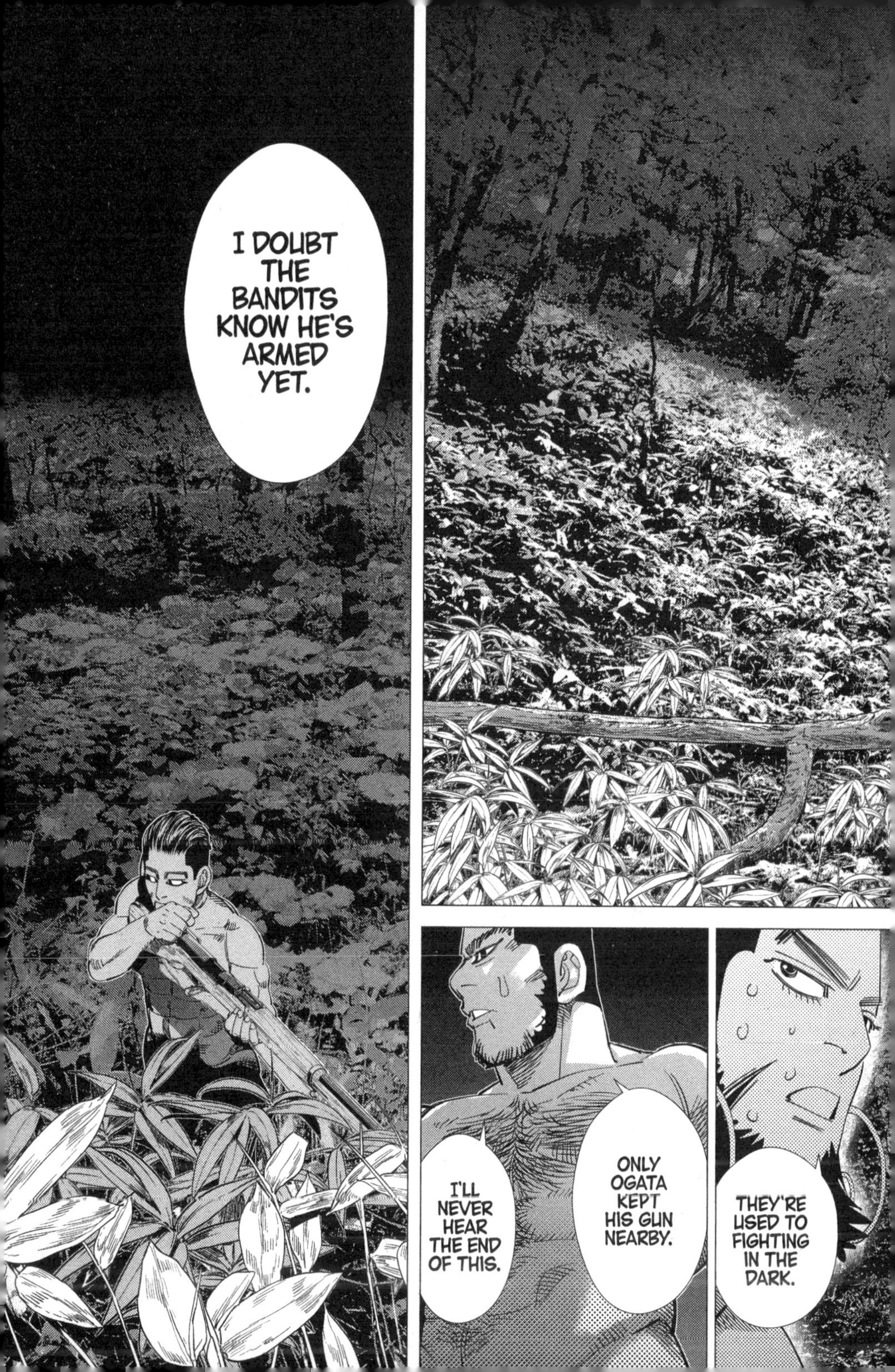
THEY'RE USED TO FIGHTING IN THE DARK.
ONLY OGATA KEPT HIS GUN NEARBY.
I'LL NEVER HEAR THE END OF THIS.
I DOUBT THE BANDITS KNOW HE'S ARMED YET.

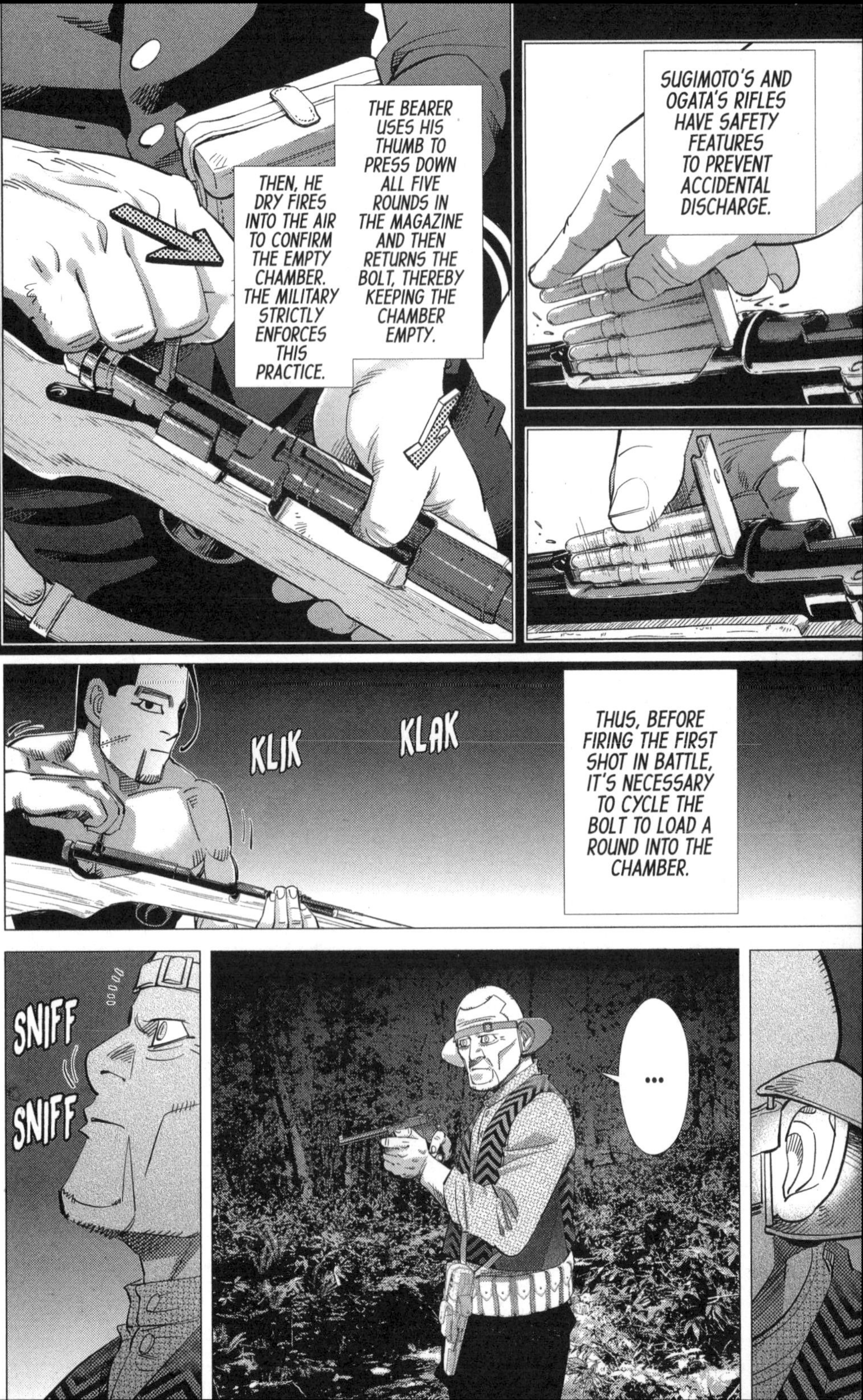
SUGIMOTO'S AND OGATA'S RIFLES HAVE SAFETY FEATURES TO PREVENT ACCIDENTAL DISCHARGE.
THE BEARER USES HIS THUMB TO PRESS DOWN ALL FIVE ROUNDS IN THE MAGAZINE AND THEN RETURNS THE BOLT, THEREBY KEEPING THE CHAMBER EMPTY.
THEN, HE DRY FIRES INTO THE AIR TO CONFIRM THE EMPTY CHAMBER. THE MILITARY STRICTLY ENFORCES THIS PRACTICE.
THUS, BEFORE FIRING THE FIRST SHOT IN BATTLE, IT'S NECESSARY TO CYCLE THE BOLT TO LOAD A ROUND INTO THE CHAMBER.
KLIK
KLAK
...
SNIFF
SNIFF

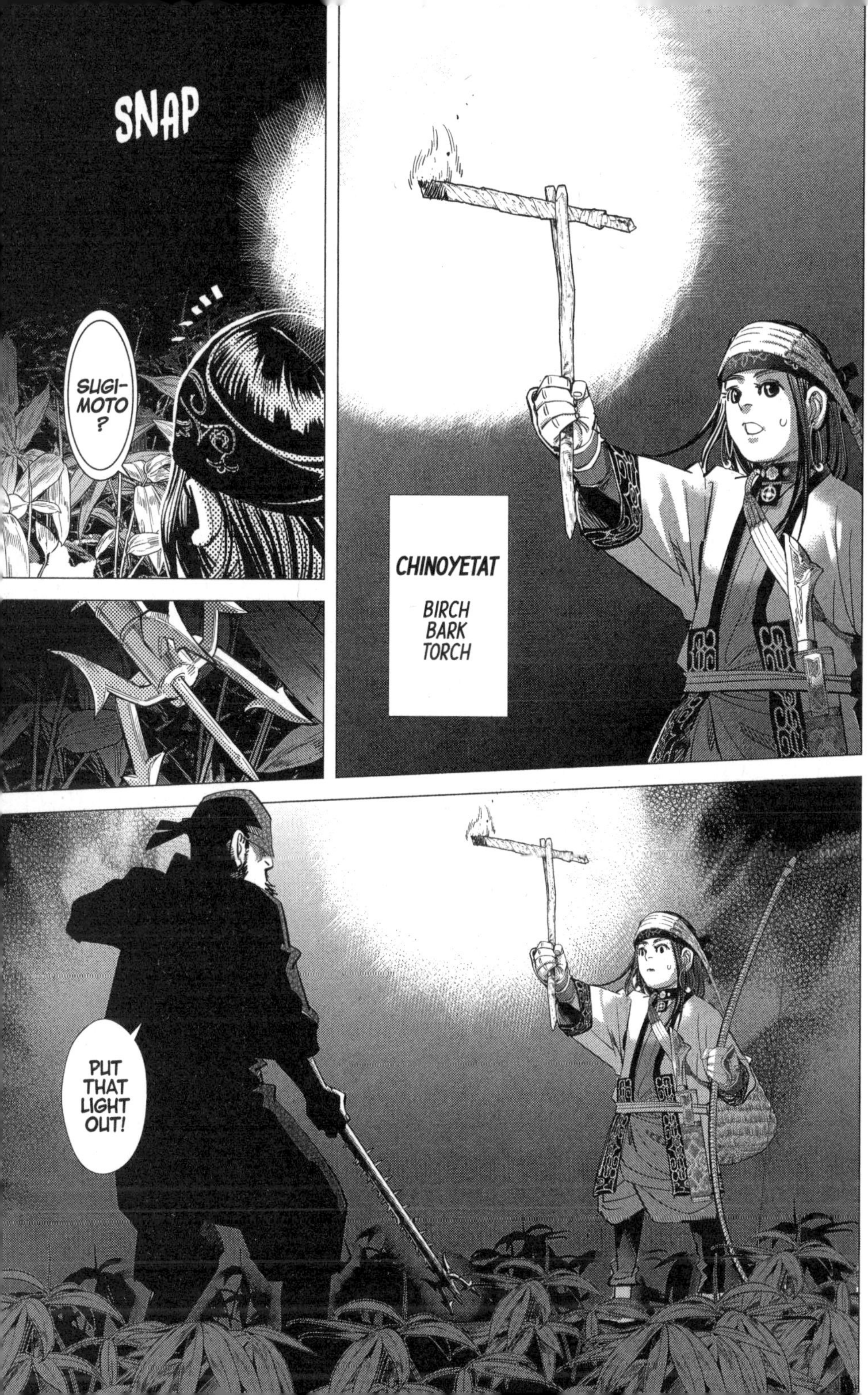
CHINOYETAT
BIRCH BARK TORCH
SNAP
SUGI-MOTO?
PUT THAT LIGHT OUT!

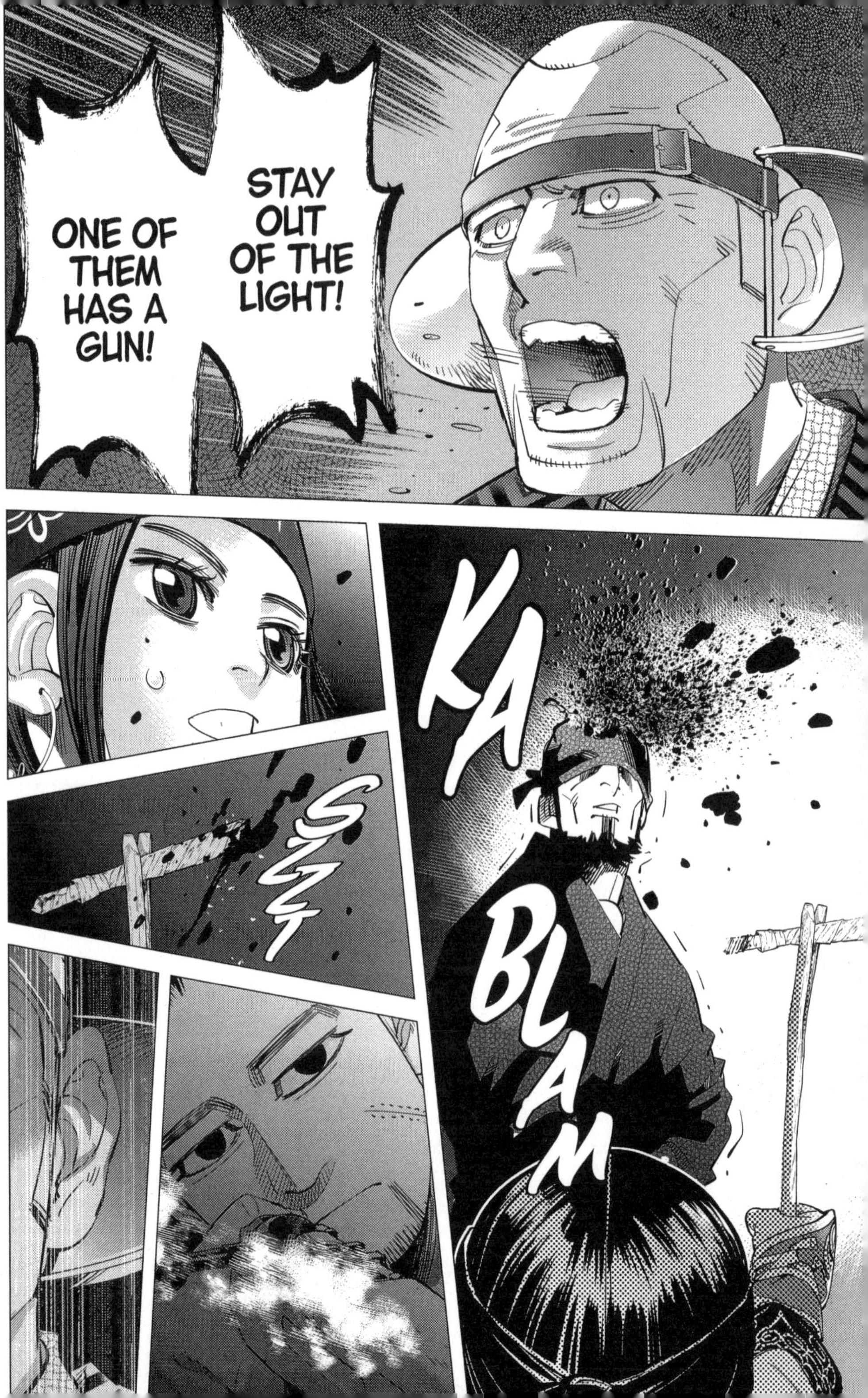
STAY OUT OF THE LIGHT!
ONE OF THEM HAS A GUN!
KABLAM
SZZZT

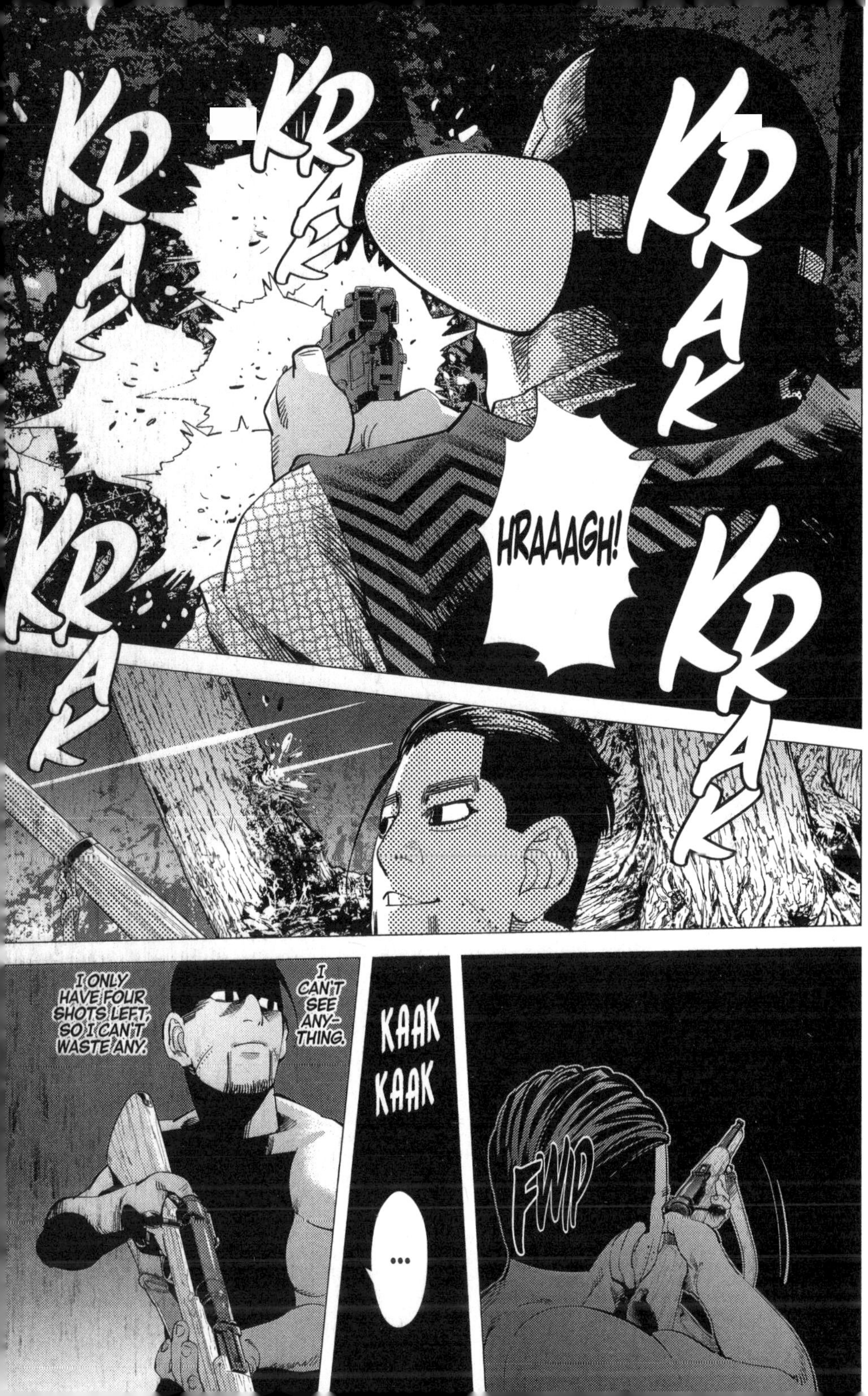
KRAK
HRAAAGH!
KRAK
KRAK
KRAK
KRAK
FWIP
KAAK KAAK
...
I CAN'T SEE ANYTHING.
I ONLY HAVE FOUR SHOTS LEFT, SO I CAN'T WASTE ANY.

ZSH
ZSH
ZSH

KCHIK

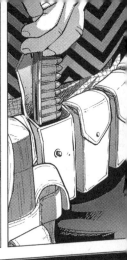

ZSH
ZSH
ZSH

GWUP

LET
ME—!

ASIRPA.
IT'S ME.

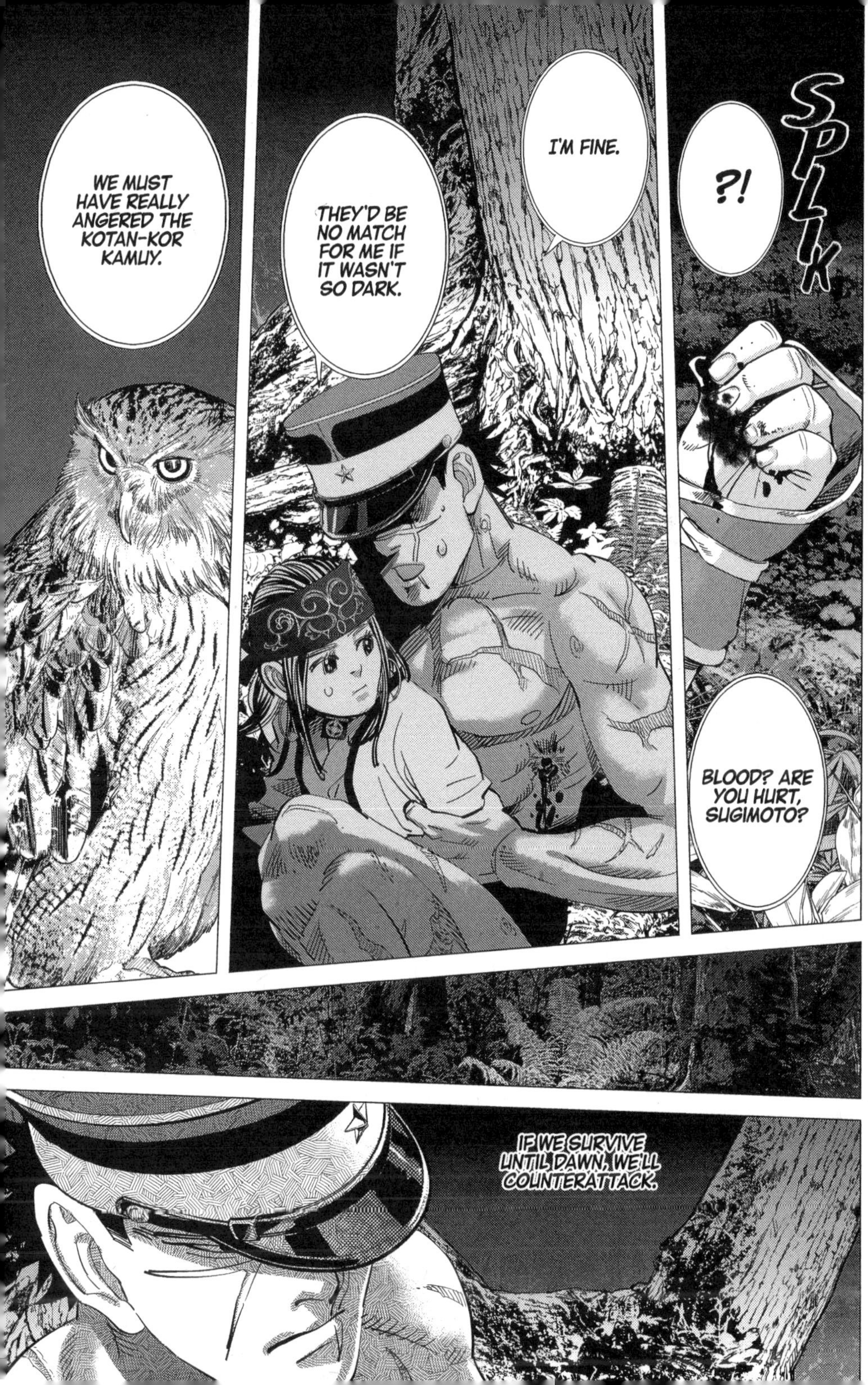
SPLIK
?!
BLOOD? ARE YOU HURT, SUGIMOTO?
I'M FINE.
THEY'D BE NO MATCH FOR ME IF IT WASN'T SO DARK.
WE MUST HAVE REALLY ANGERED THE KOTAN-KOR KAMUY.
IF WE SURVIVE UNTIL DAWN, WE'LL COUNTERATTACK.

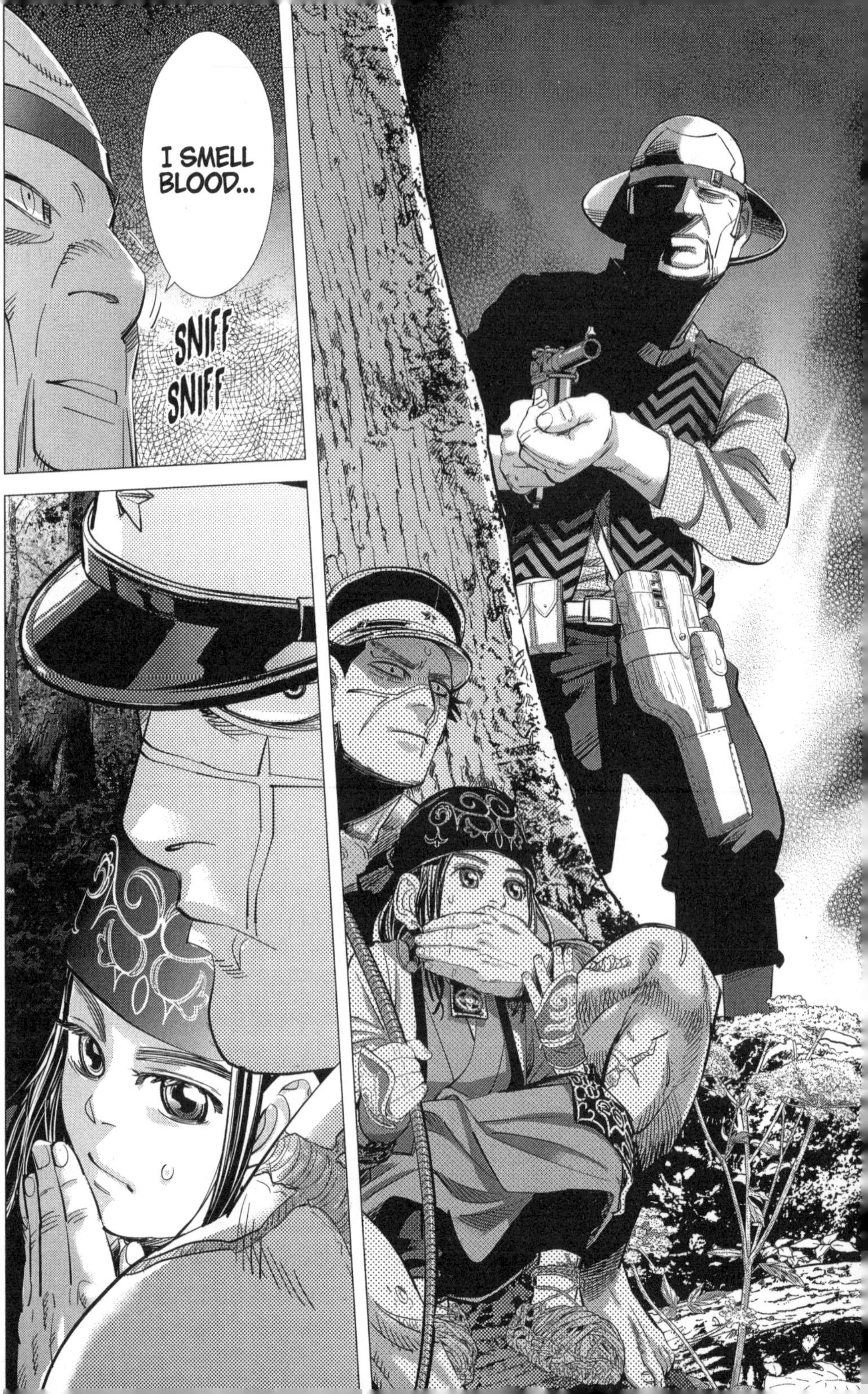
I SMELL BLOOD...
SNIFF SNIFF

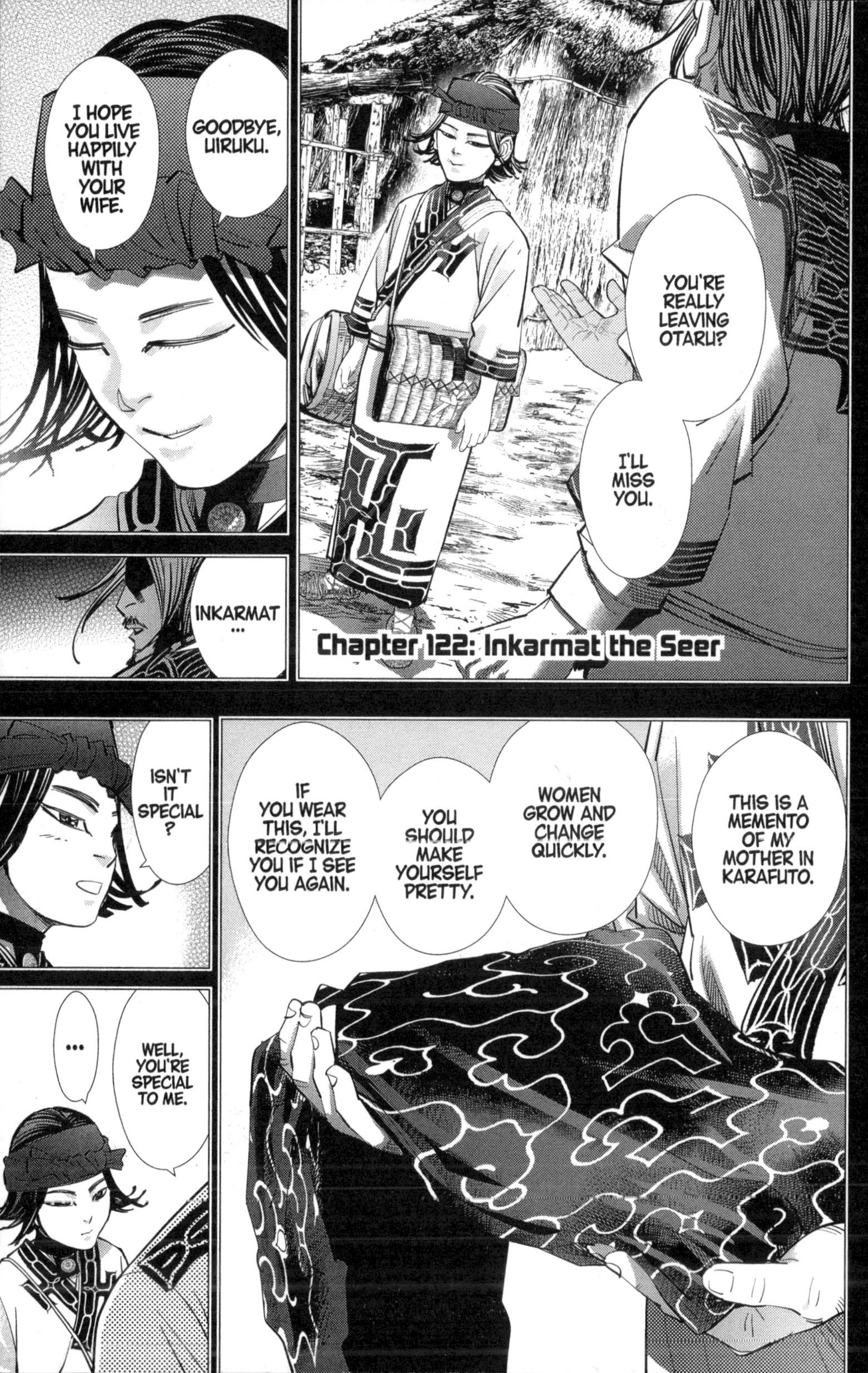
YOU'RE REALLY LEAVING OTARU?
I'LL MISS YOU.
Chapter 122: Inkarmat the Seer
GOODBYE, UIRUKU.
I HOPE YOU LIVE HAPPILY WITH YOUR WIFE.
INKARMAT...
THIS IS A MEMENTO OF MY MOTHER IN KARAFUTO.
WOMEN GROW AND CHANGE QUICKLY.
YOU SHOULD MAKE YOURSELF PRETTY.
IF YOU WEAR THIS, I'LL RECOGNIZE YOU IF I SEE YOU AGAIN.
ISN'T IT SPECIAL?
WELL, YOU'RE SPECIAL TO ME.
...

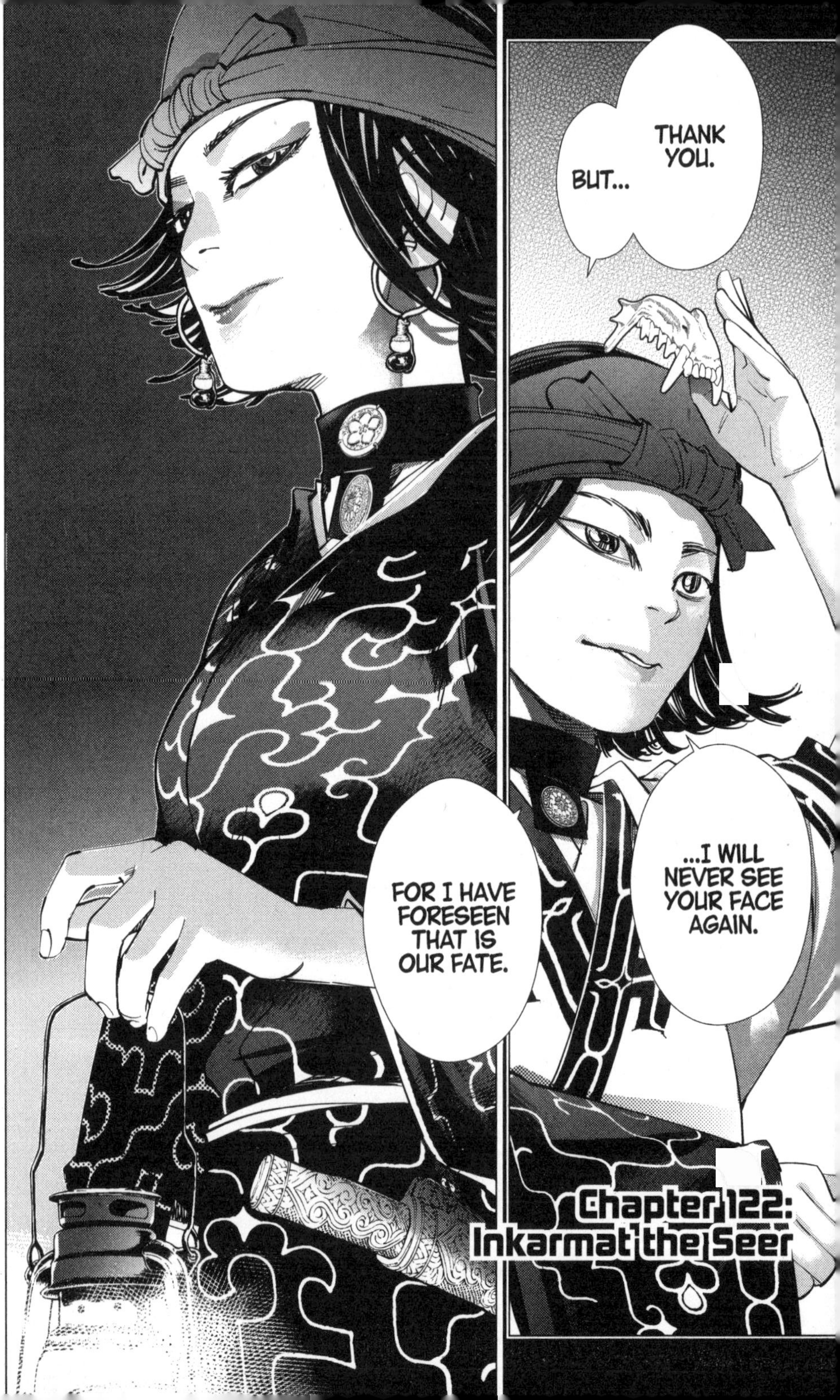
THANK YOU.
BUT...
...I WILL NEVER SEE YOUR FACE AGAIN.
FOR I HAVE FORESEEN THAT IS OUR FATE.

Chapter 122: Inkarmat the Seer

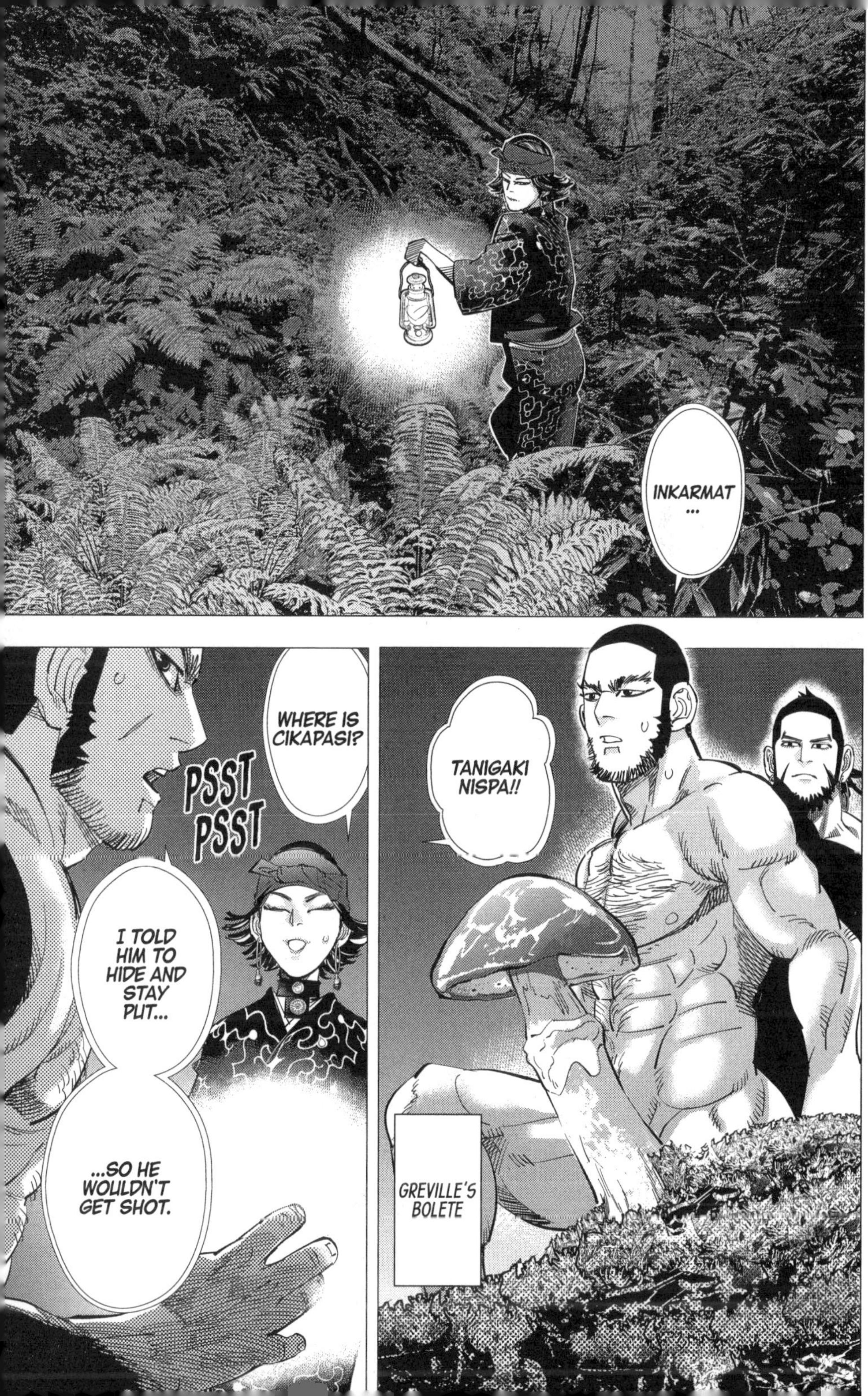
INKARMAT ...
TANIGAKI NISPA!!
GREVILLE'S BOLETE
WHERE IS CIKAPASI?
PSST PSST
I TOLD HIM TO HIDE AND STAY PUT...
...SO HE WOULDN'T GET SHOT.

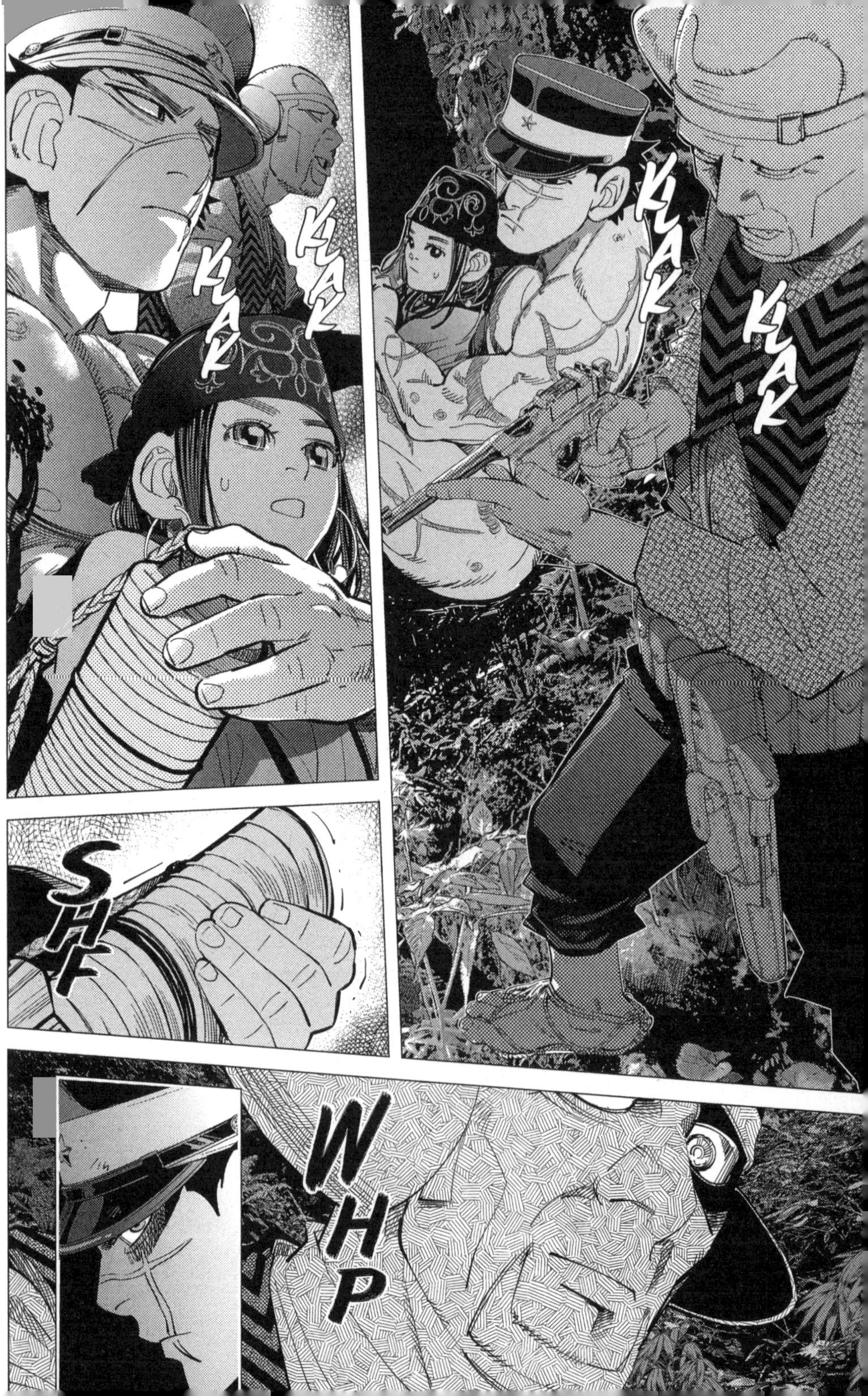
KLAK
KLAK
KLAK
KLAK
SHF
WHP

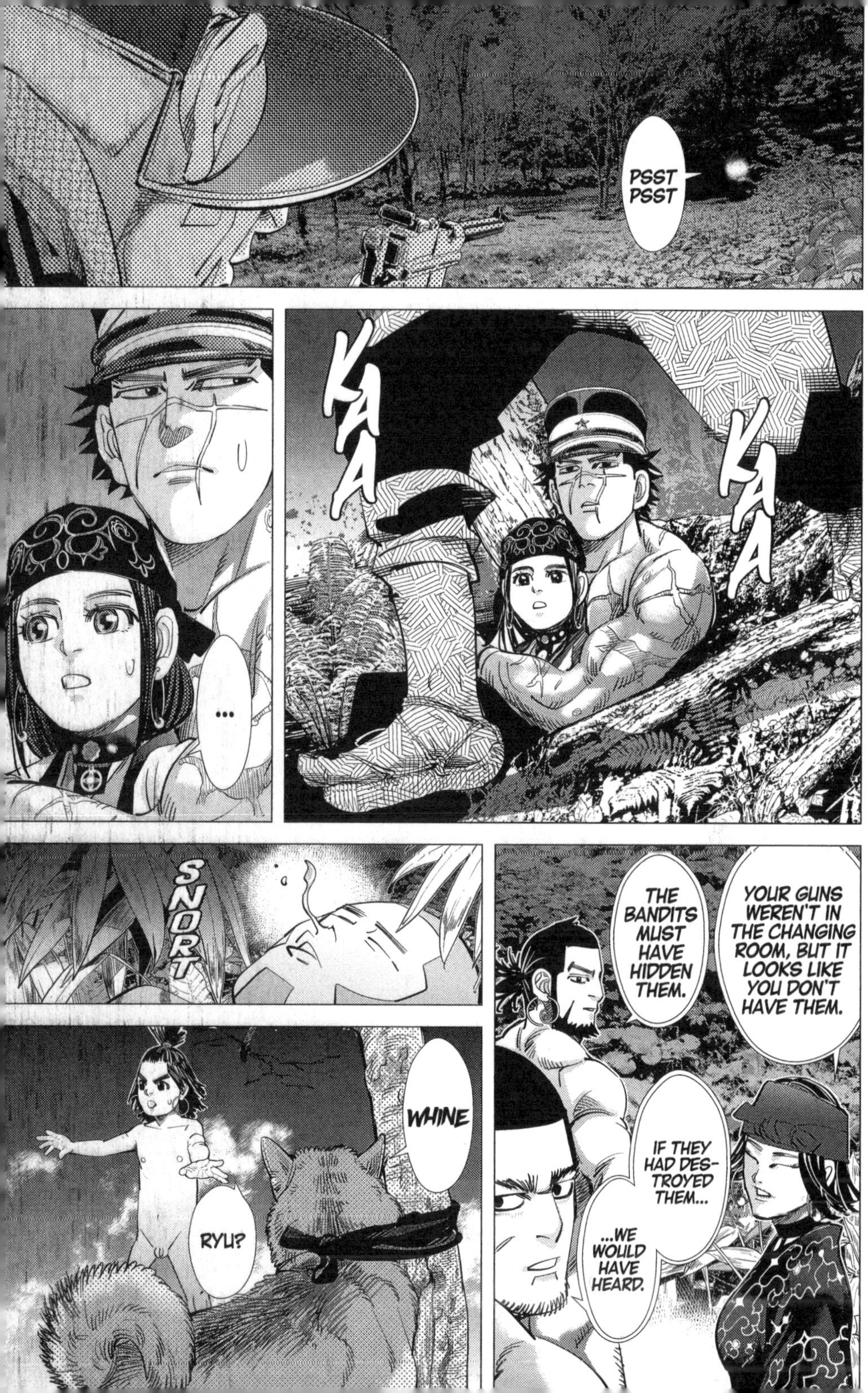
PSST PSST
KA KA
KA KA
...
YOUR GUNS WEREN'T IN THE CHANGING ROOM, BUT IT LOOKS LIKE YOU DON'T HAVE THEM.
THE BANDITS MUST HAVE HIDDEN THEM.
IF THEY HAD DES-TROYED THEM...
...WE WOULD HAVE HEARD.
SNORT
WHINE
RYU?

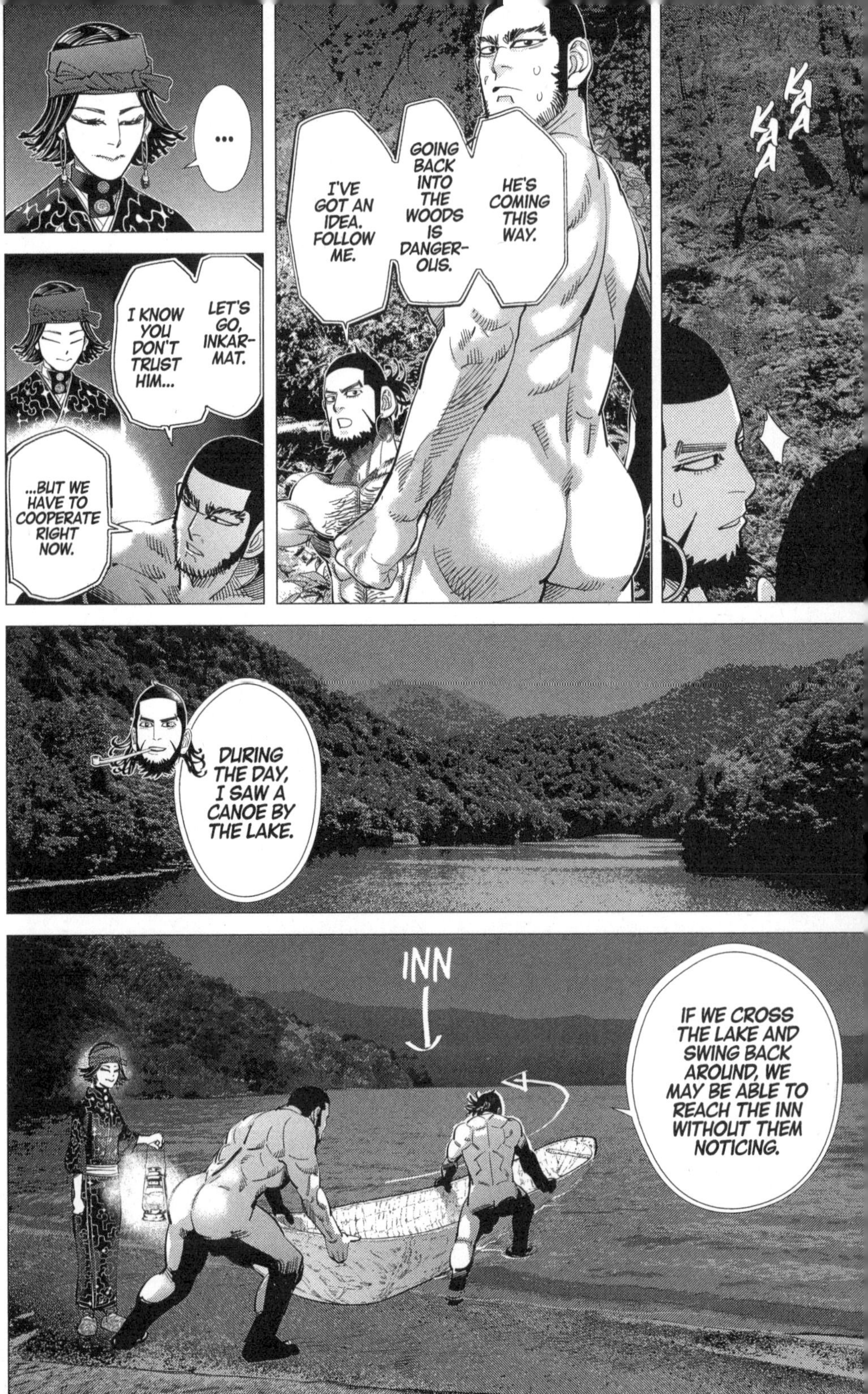
KAA KAA
HE'S COMING THIS WAY.
GOING BACK INTO THE WOODS IS DANGER-OUS.
I'VE GOT AN IDEA. FOLLOW ME.
...
LET'S GO, INKARMAT.
I KNOW YOU DON'T TRUST HIM...
...BUT WE HAVE TO COOPERATE RIGHT NOW.
DURING THE DAY, I SAW A CANOE BY THE LAKE.
INN
IF WE CROSS THE LAKE AND SWING BACK AROUND, WE MAY BE ABLE TO REACH THE INN WITHOUT THEM NOTICING.

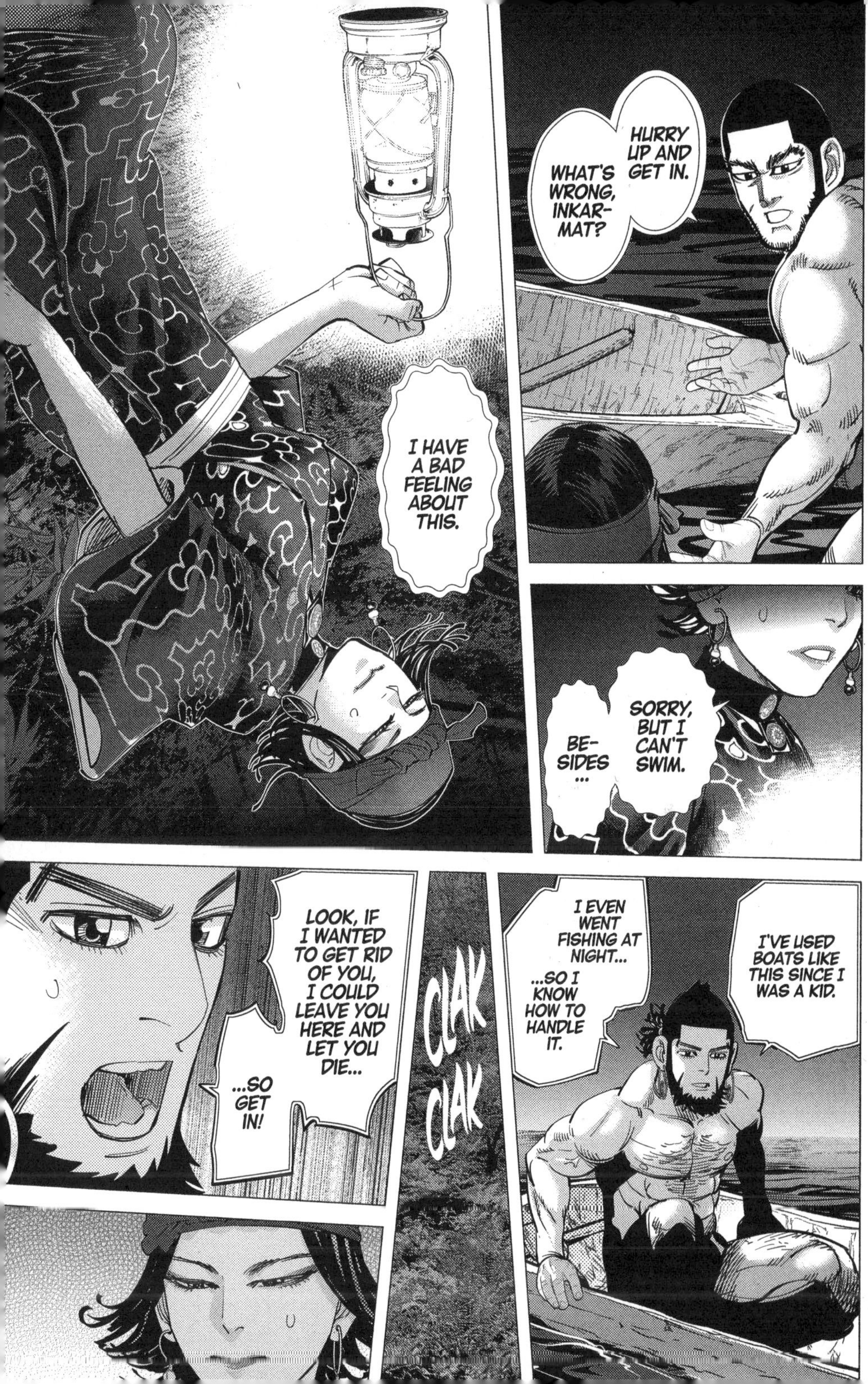
HURRY UP AND GET IN.
WHAT'S WRONG, INKARMAT?
SORRY, BUT I CAN'T SWIM.
BESIDES...
I HAVE A BAD FEELING ABOUT THIS.
I'VE USED BOATS LIKE THIS SINCE I WAS A KID.
I EVEN WENT FISHING AT NIGHT...
...SO I KNOW HOW TO HANDLE IT.
CLAK CLAK
LOOK, IF I WANTED TO GET RID OF YOU, I COULD LEAVE YOU HERE AND LET YOU DIE...
...SO GET IN!

PADDLE QUIETLY. DON'T MAKE A SOUND.

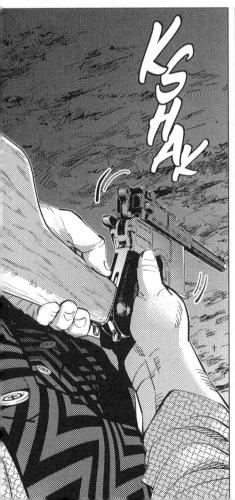

KSHAK

SHF

SPLISH

SPLOSH

A FISH?

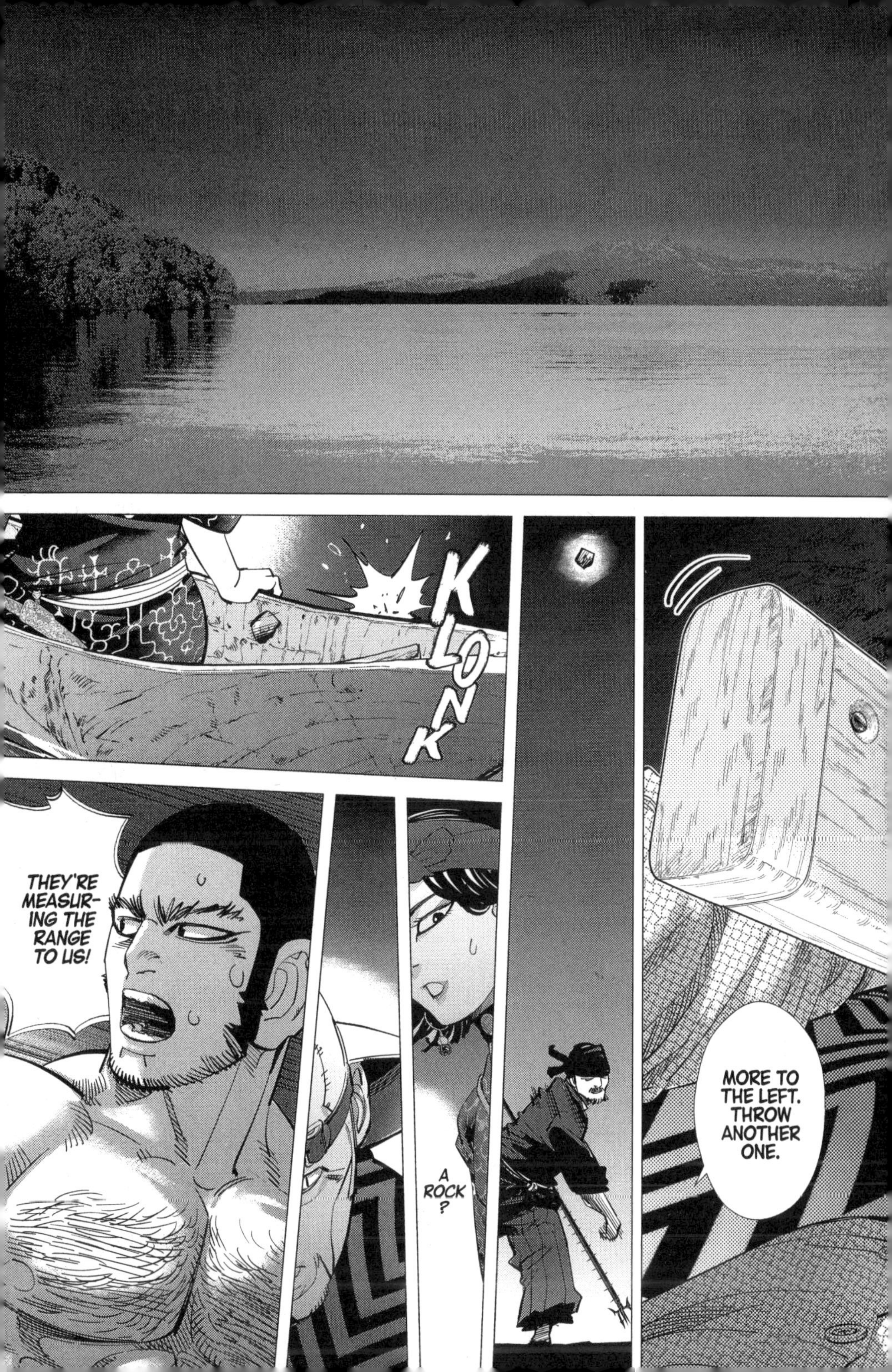
MORE TO THE LEFT. THROW ANOTHER ONE.
KLONK
A ROCK?
THEY'RE MEASURING THE RANGE TO US!

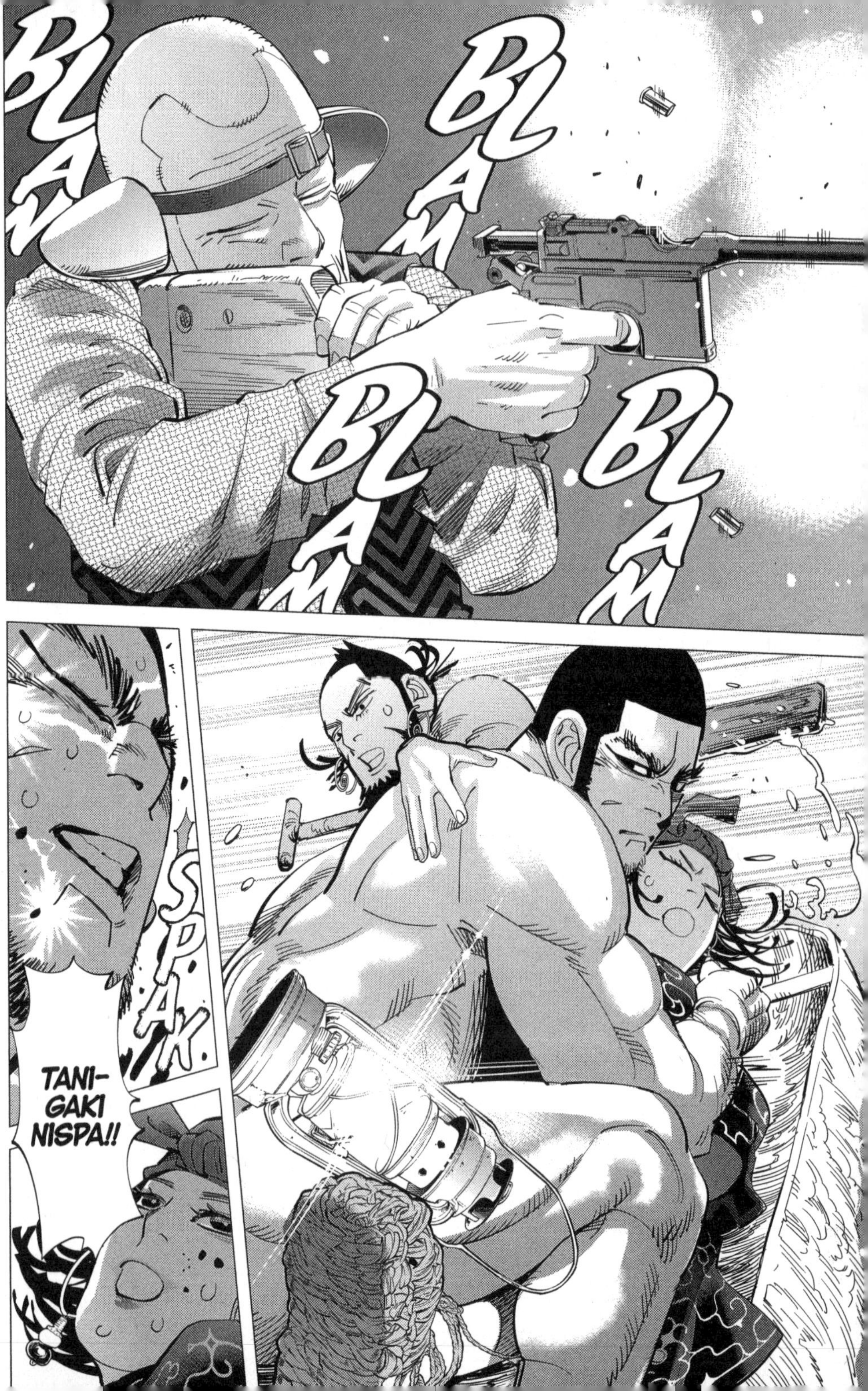
BLAM
BLAM
BLAM
BLAM
SPAK
TANI-GAKI NISPA!!

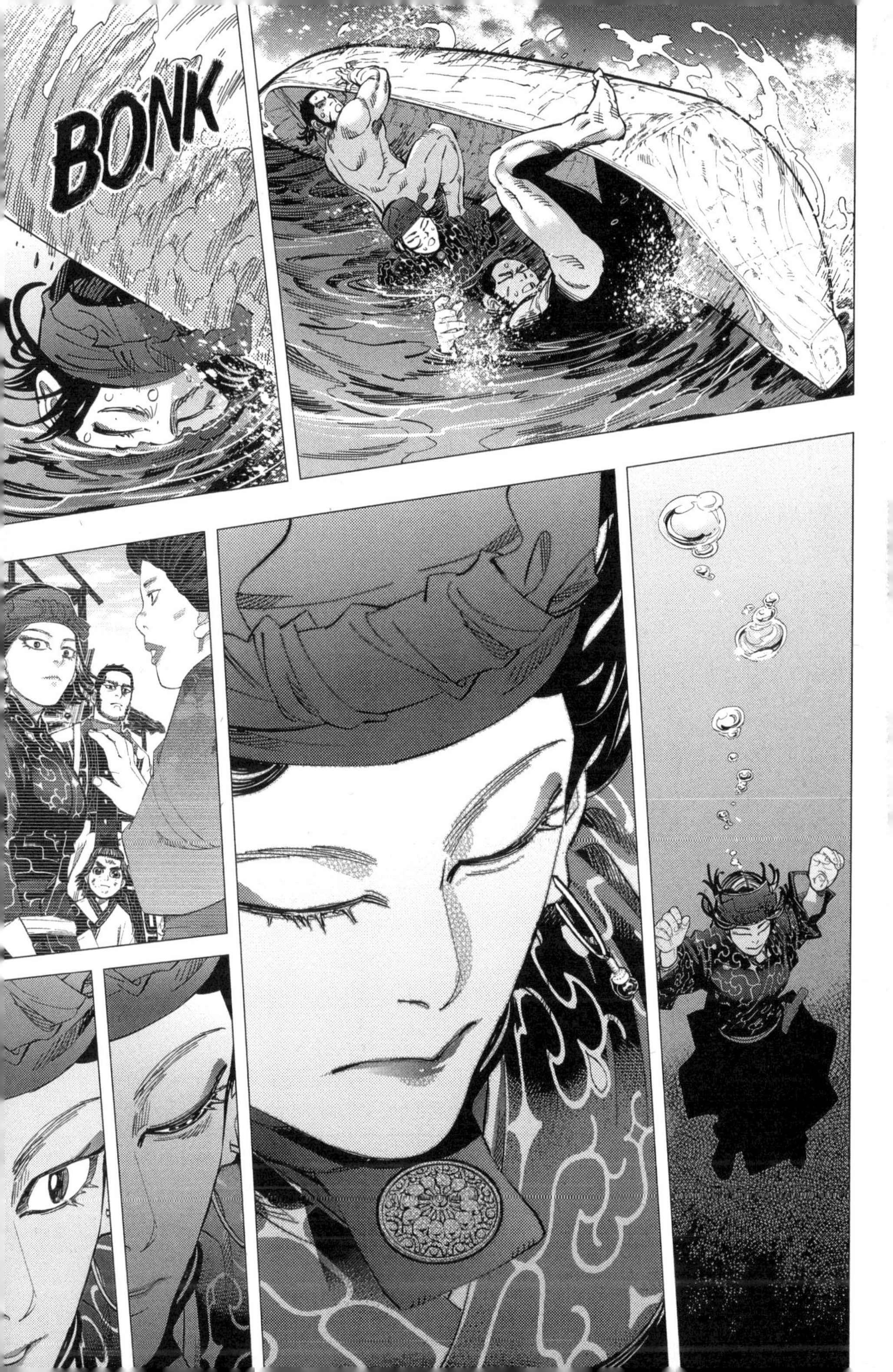
BONK

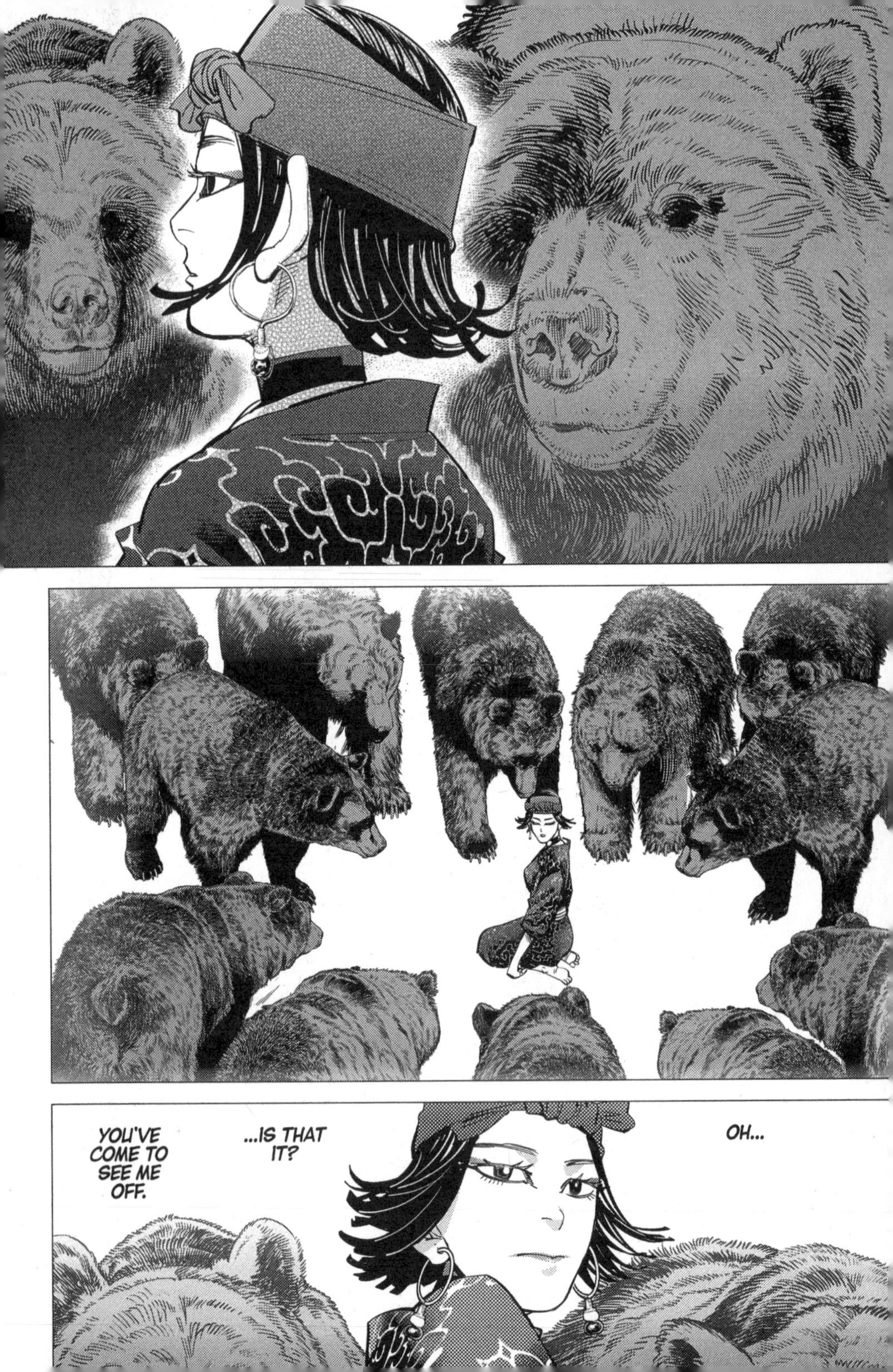
OH...
...IS THAT IT?
YOU'VE COME TO SEE ME OFF.

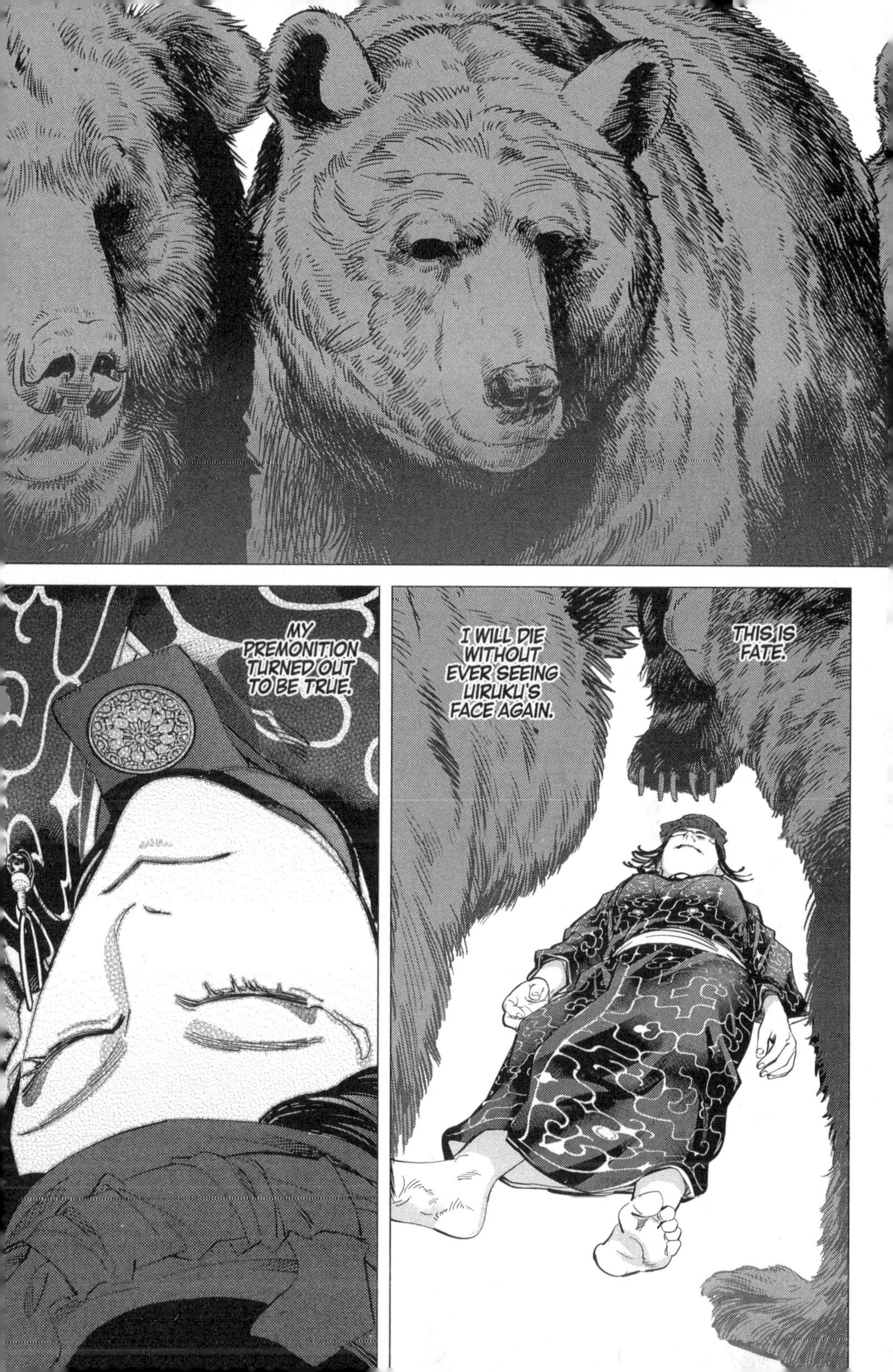
THIS IS FATE.
I WILL DIE WITHOUT EVER SEEING UIRUKU'S FACE AGAIN.
MY PREMONITION TURNED OUT TO BE TRUE.

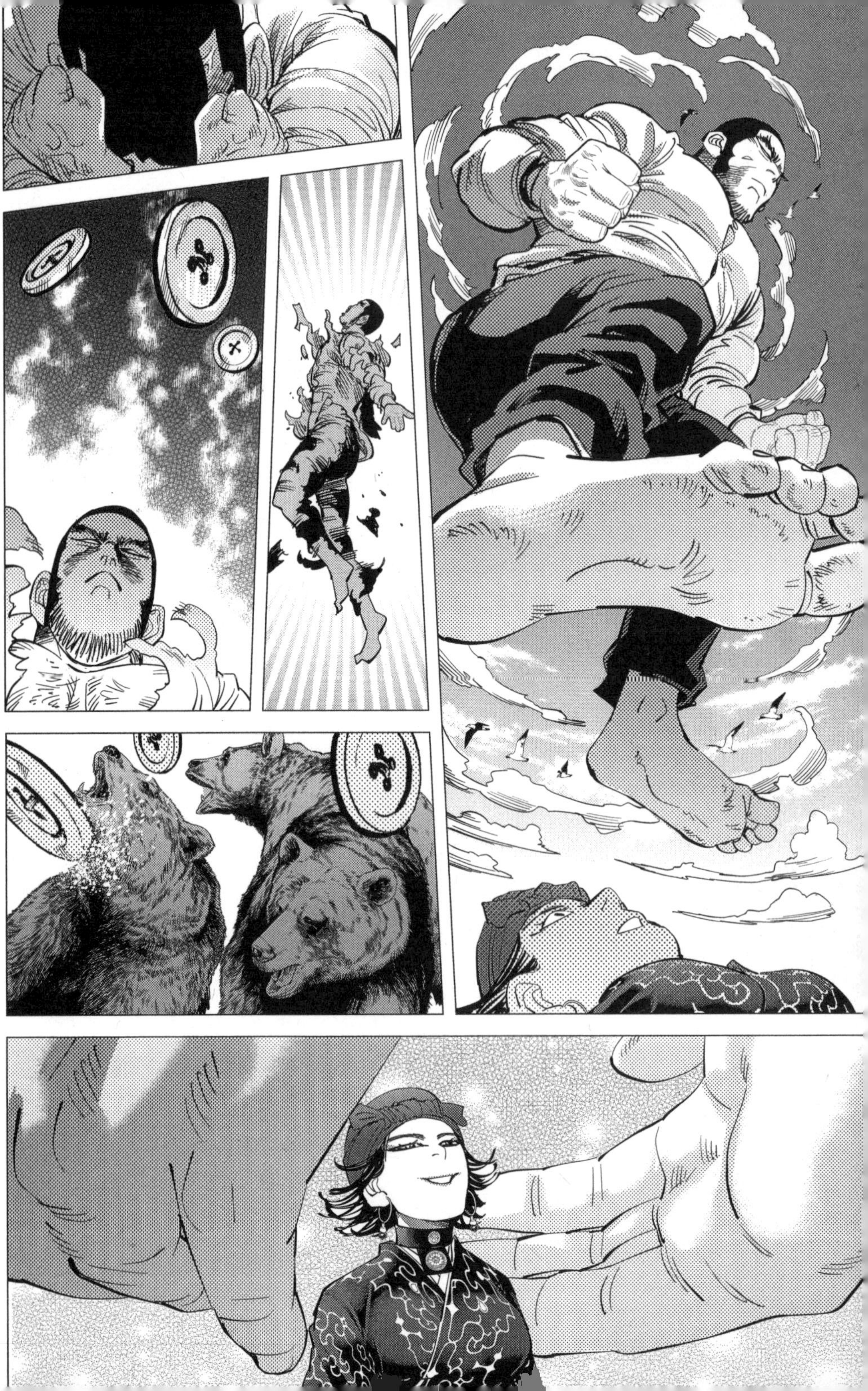

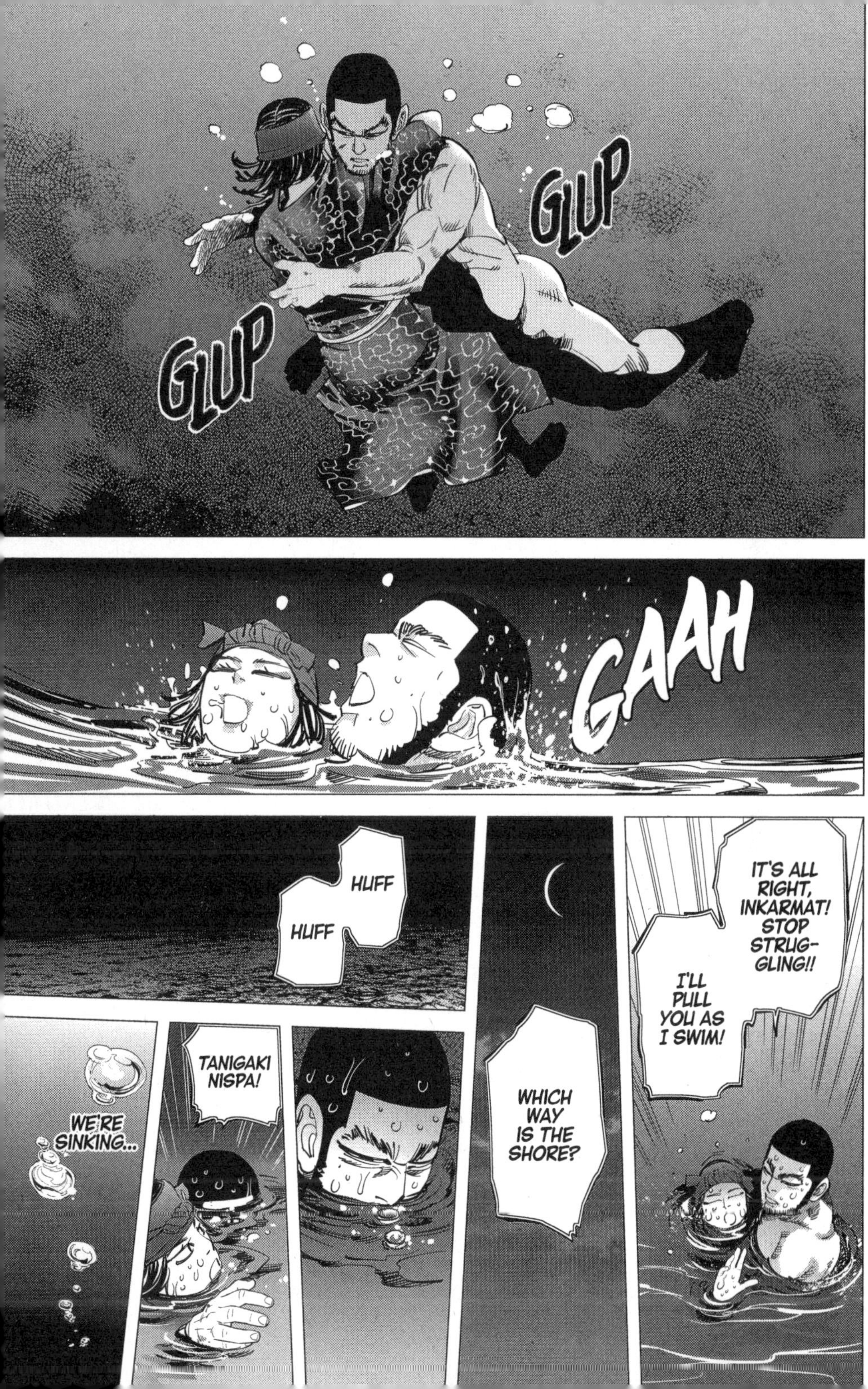
GLUP
GLUP
GAAH
IT'S ALL RIGHT, INKARMAT! STOP STRUG-GLING!!
I'LL PULL YOU AS I SWIM!
WHICH WAY IS THE SHORE?
HUFF
HUFF
TANIGAKI NISPA!
WE'RE SINKING...

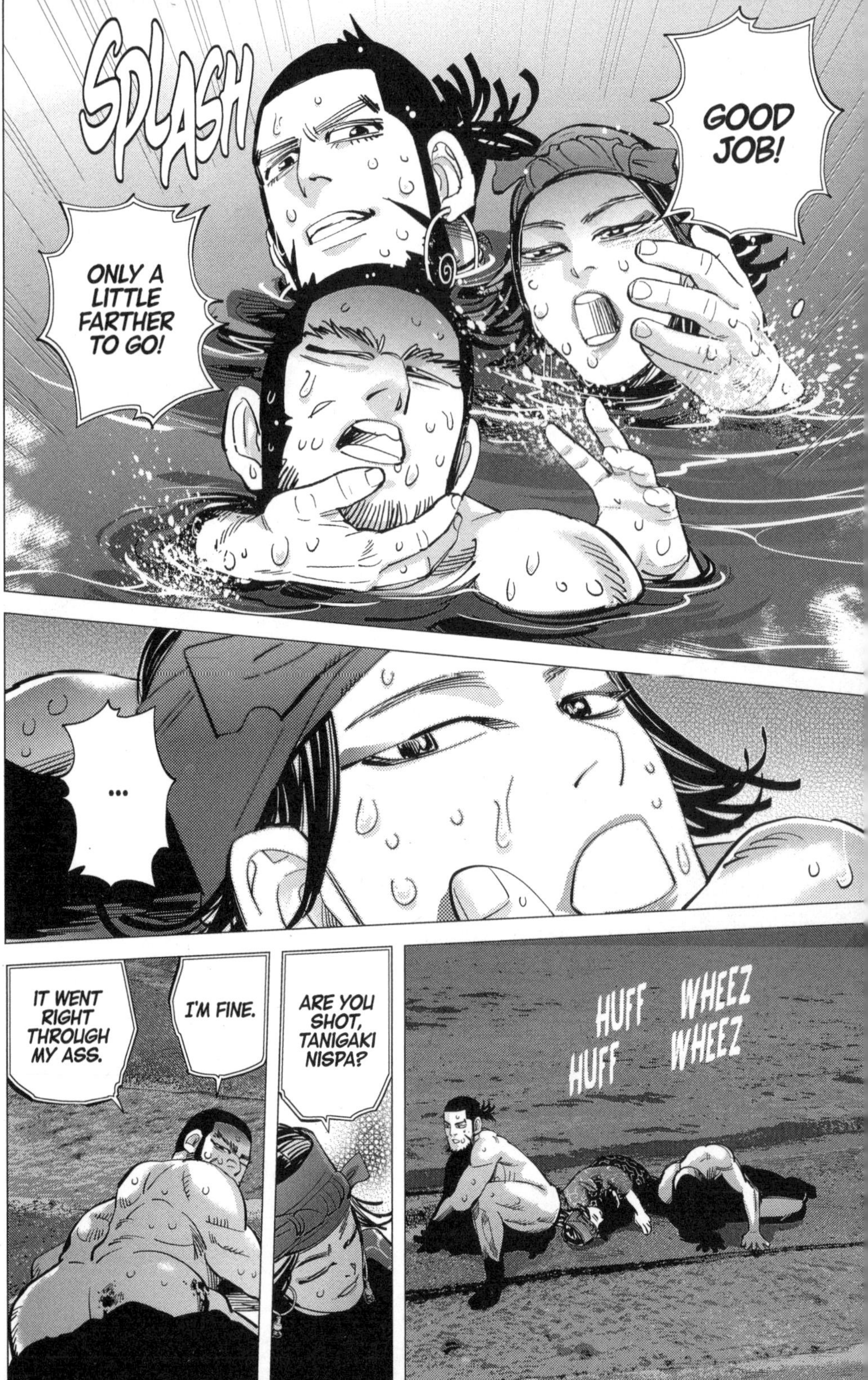
GOOD JOB!
SPLASH
ONLY A LITTLE FARTHER TO GO!
...
WHEEZ WHEEZ
HUFF HUFF
ARE YOU SHOT, TANIGAKI NISPA?
I'M FINE.
IT WENT RIGHT THROUGH MY ASS.

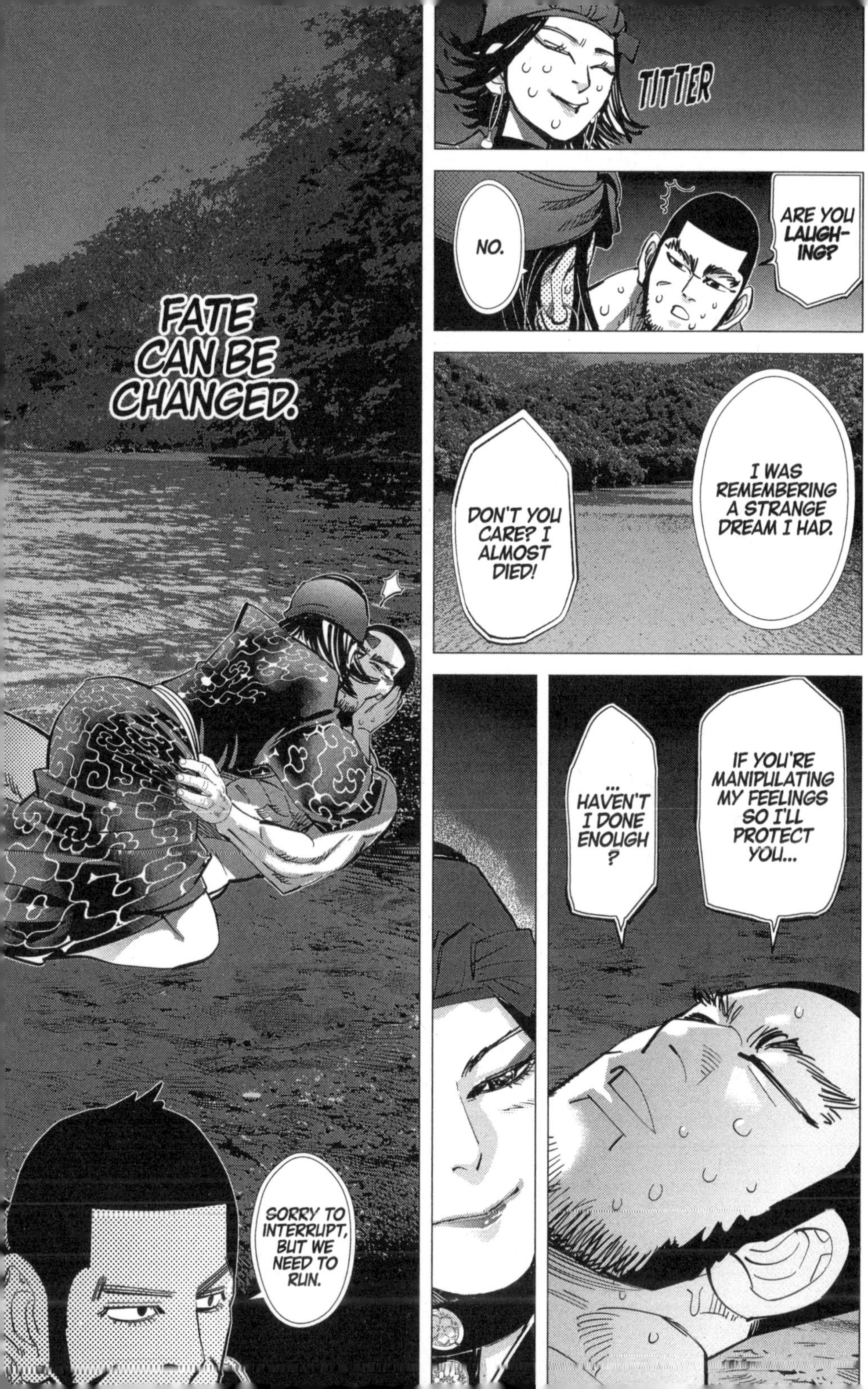
TITTER
ARE YOU LAUGHING?
NO.
I WAS REMEMBERING A STRANGE DREAM I HAD.
DON'T YOU CARE? I ALMOST DIED!
IF YOU'RE MANIPULATING MY FEELINGS SO I'LL PROTECT YOU...
...HAVEN'T I DONE ENOUGH?
FATE CAN BE CHANGED.
SORRY TO INTERRUPT, BUT WE NEED TO RUN.

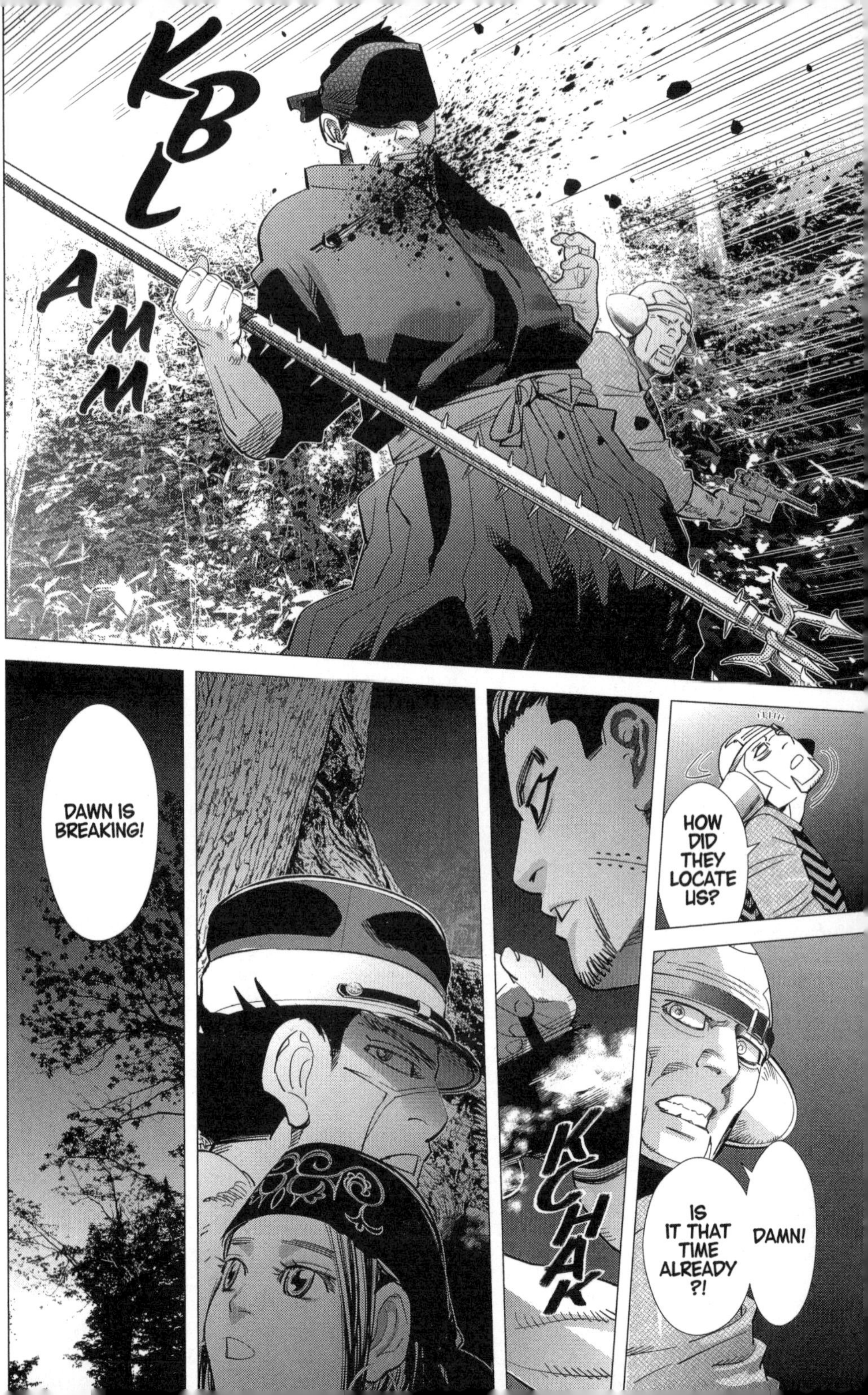
KBLAMM
HOW DID THEY LOCATE US?
DAMN!
IS IT THAT TIME ALREADY?!
KCHAK
DAWN IS BREAKING!

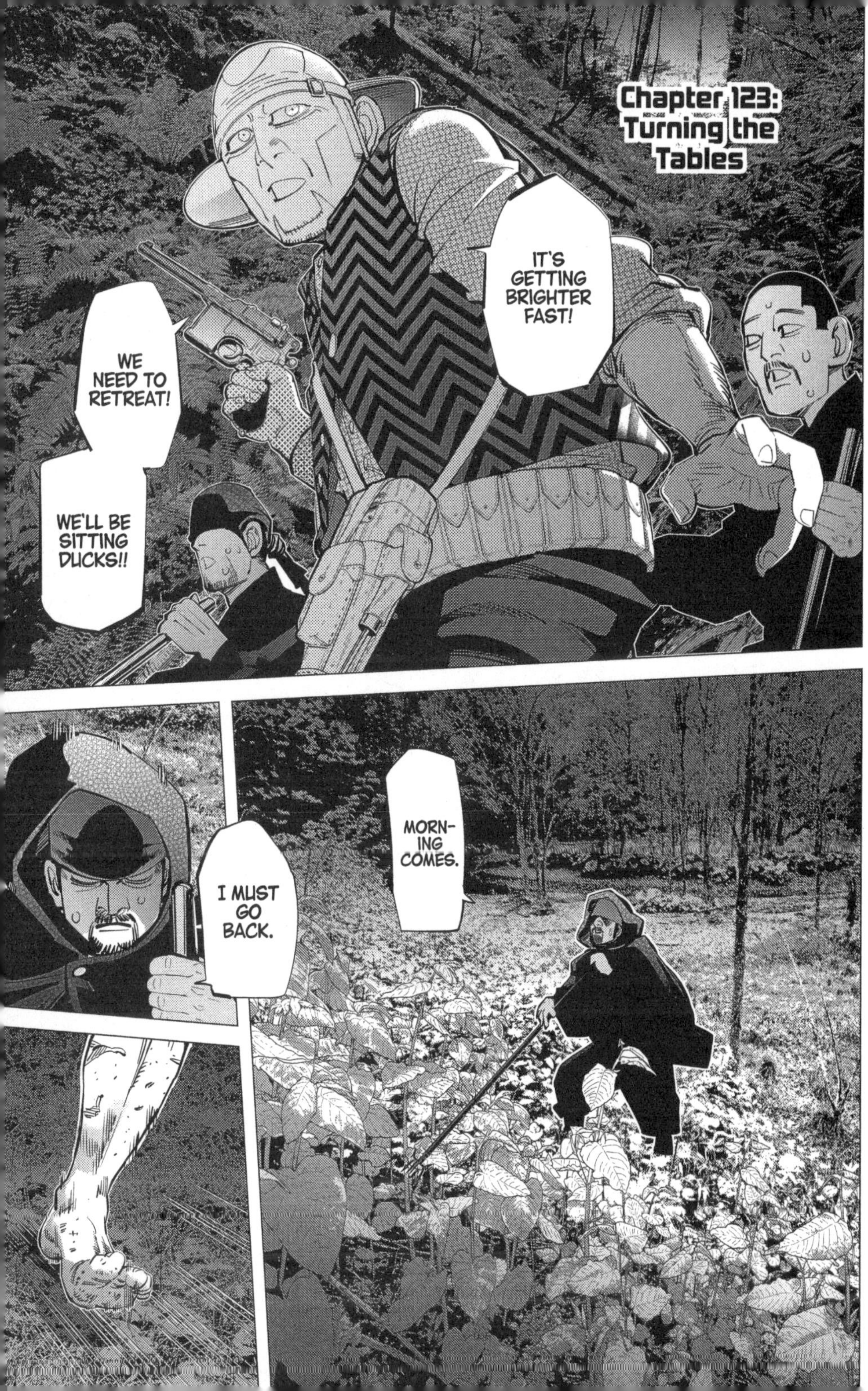
Chapter 123: Turning the Tables
IT'S GETTING BRIGHTER FAST!
WE NEED TO RETREAT!
WE'LL BE SITTING DUCKS!!
MORNING-ING COMES.
I MUST GO BACK.

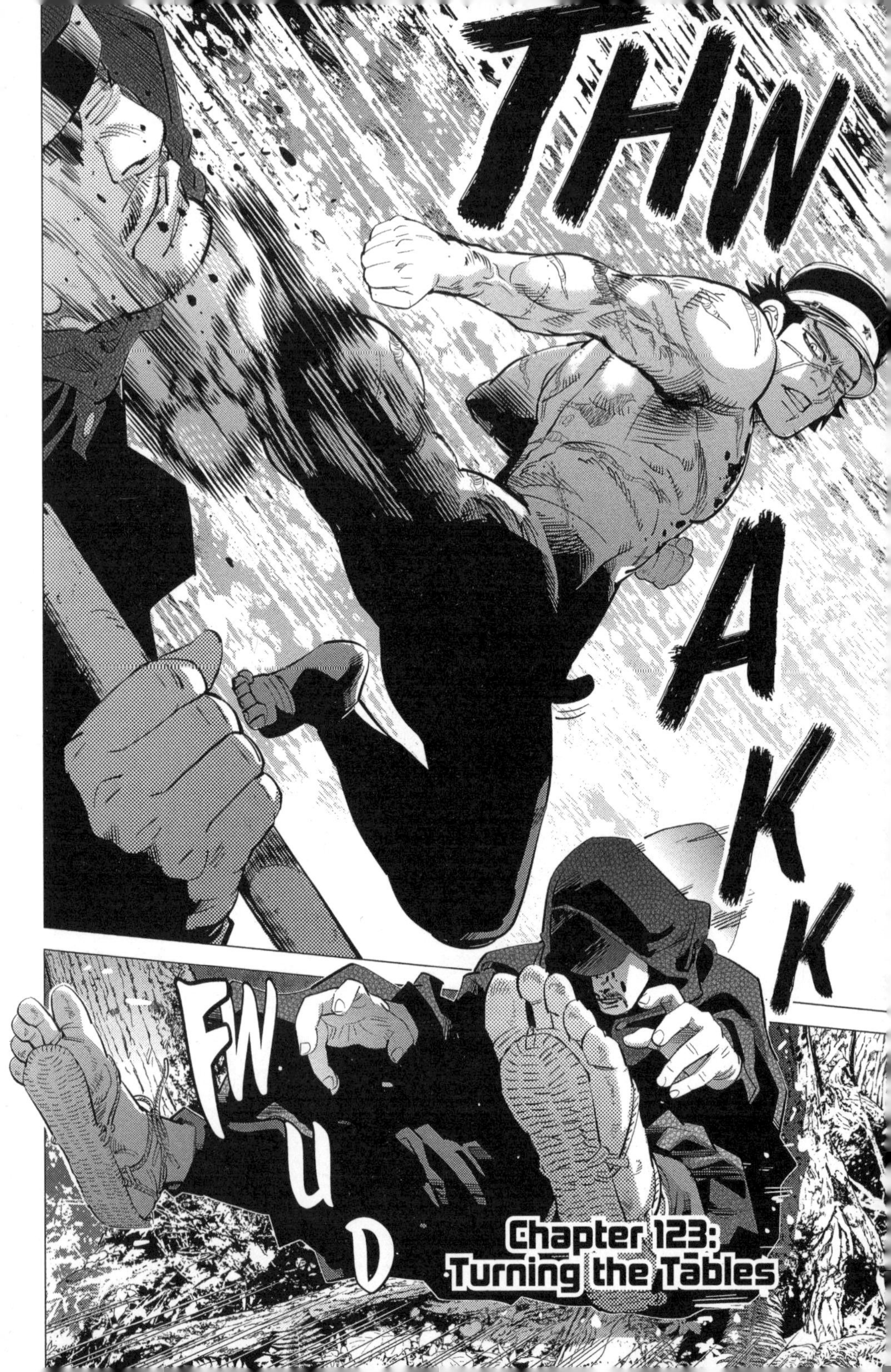
THWAKK
FWUD
Chapter 123:
Turning the Tables

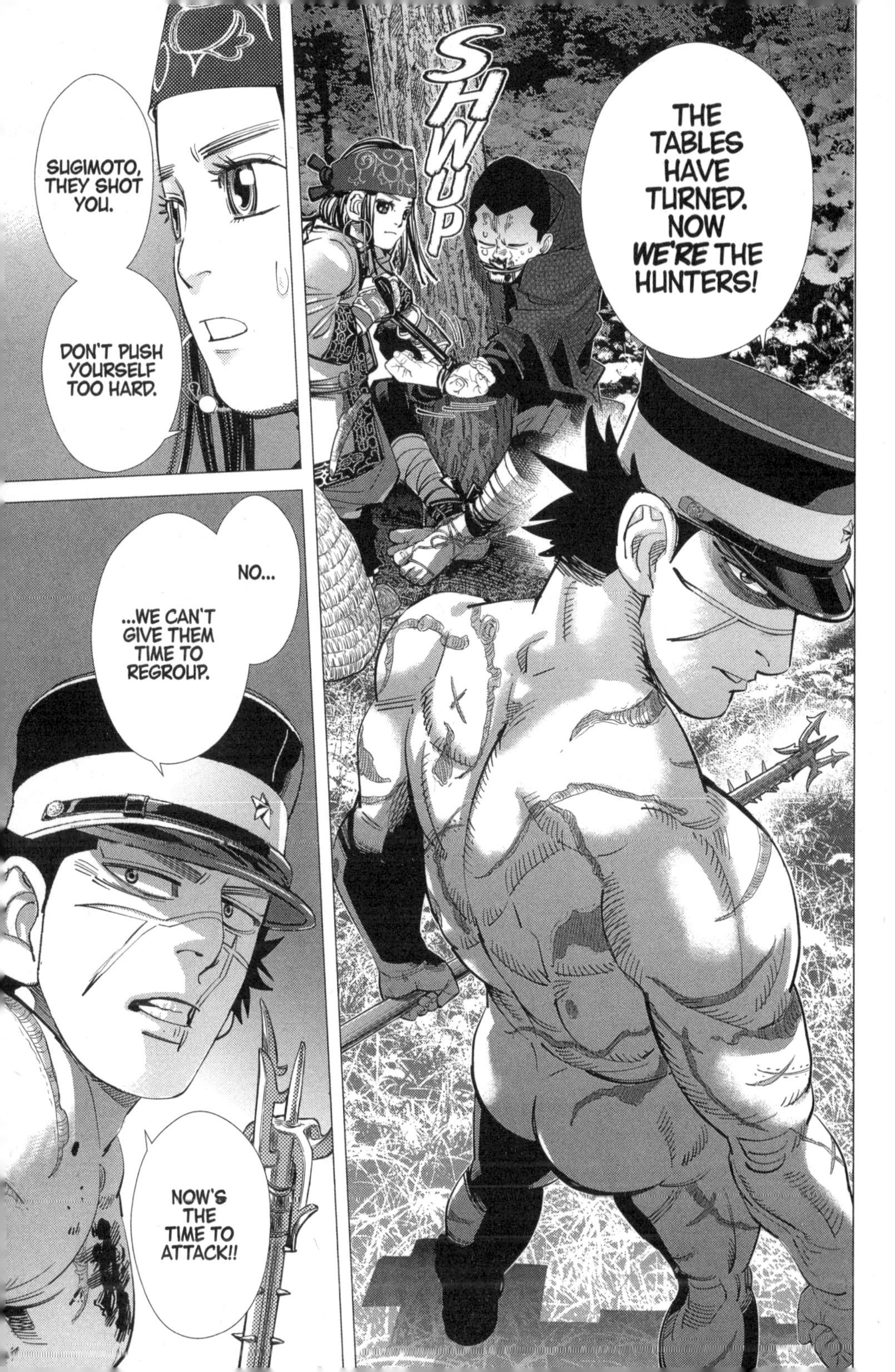
SHWUP
THE TABLES HAVE TURNED. NOW WE'RE THE HUNTERS!
SUGIMOTO, THEY SHOT YOU.
DON'T PUSH YOURSELF TOO HARD.
NO...
...WE CAN'T GIVE THEM TIME TO REGROUP.
NOW'S THE TIME TO ATTACK!!

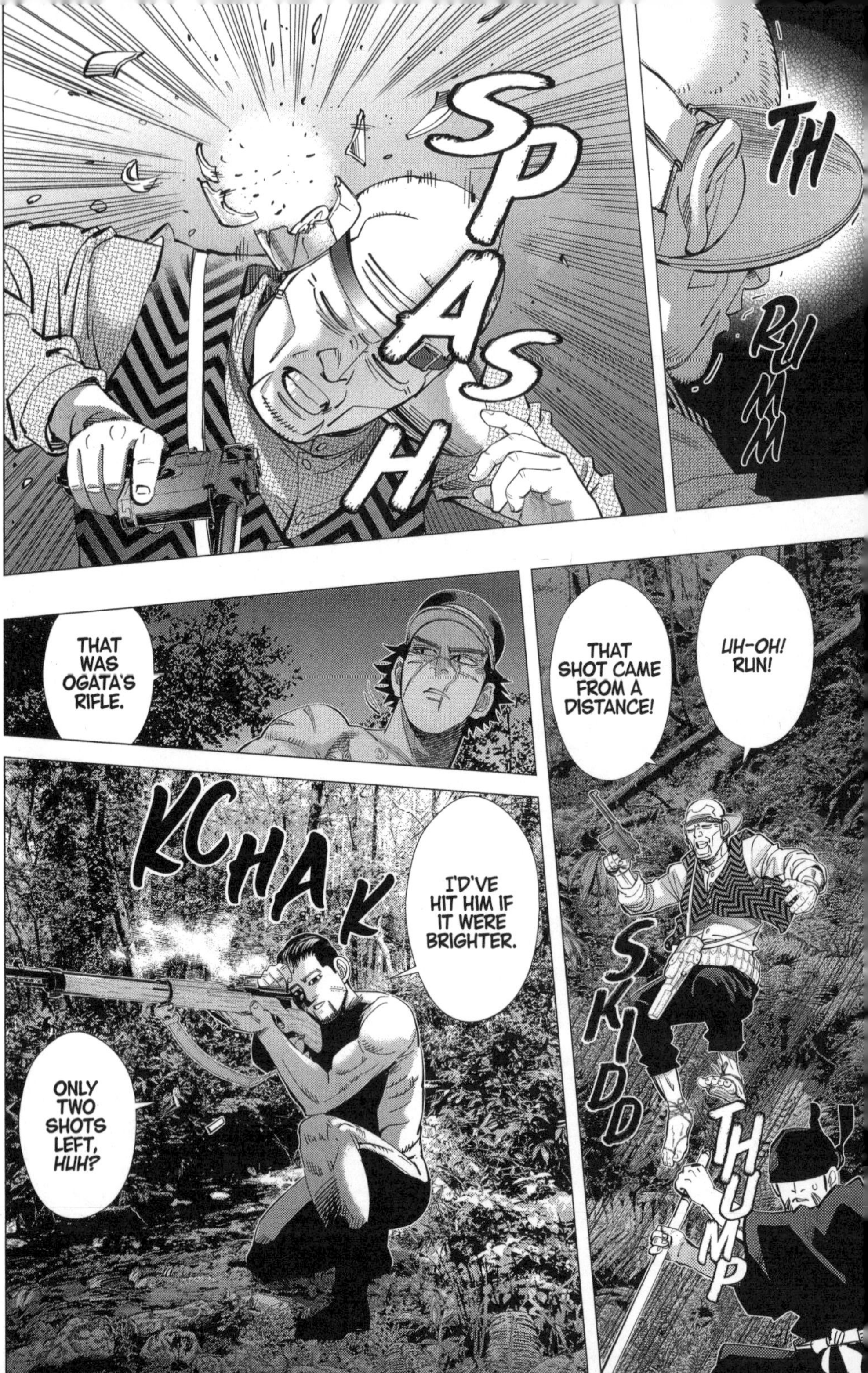
THRUMMM
SPASH
UH-OH! RUN!
THAT SHOT CAME FROM A DISTANCE!
SKIDD
THUMP
THAT WAS OGATA'S RIFLE.
KCHAK
I'D'VE HIT HIM IF IT WERE BRIGHTER.
ONLY TWO SHOTS LEFT, HUH?

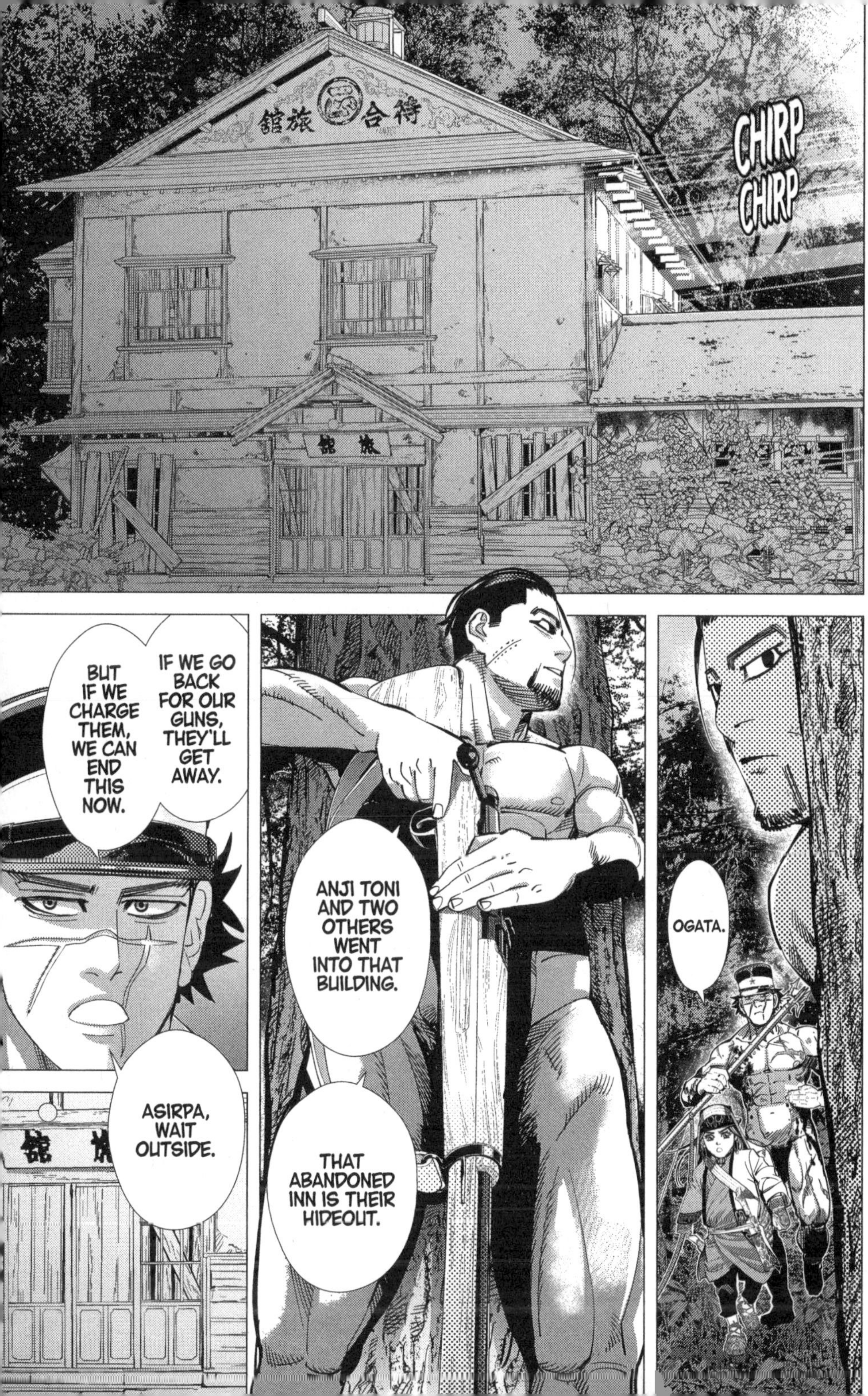
待合旅館
旅館
CHIRP CHIRP
OGATA.
ANJI TONI AND TWO OTHERS WENT INTO THAT BUILDING.
THAT ABANDONED INN IS THEIR HIDEOUT.
IF WE GO BACK FOR OUR GUNS, THEY'LL GET AWAY.
BUT IF WE CHARGE THEM, WE CAN END THIS NOW.
ASIRPA, WAIT OUTSIDE.

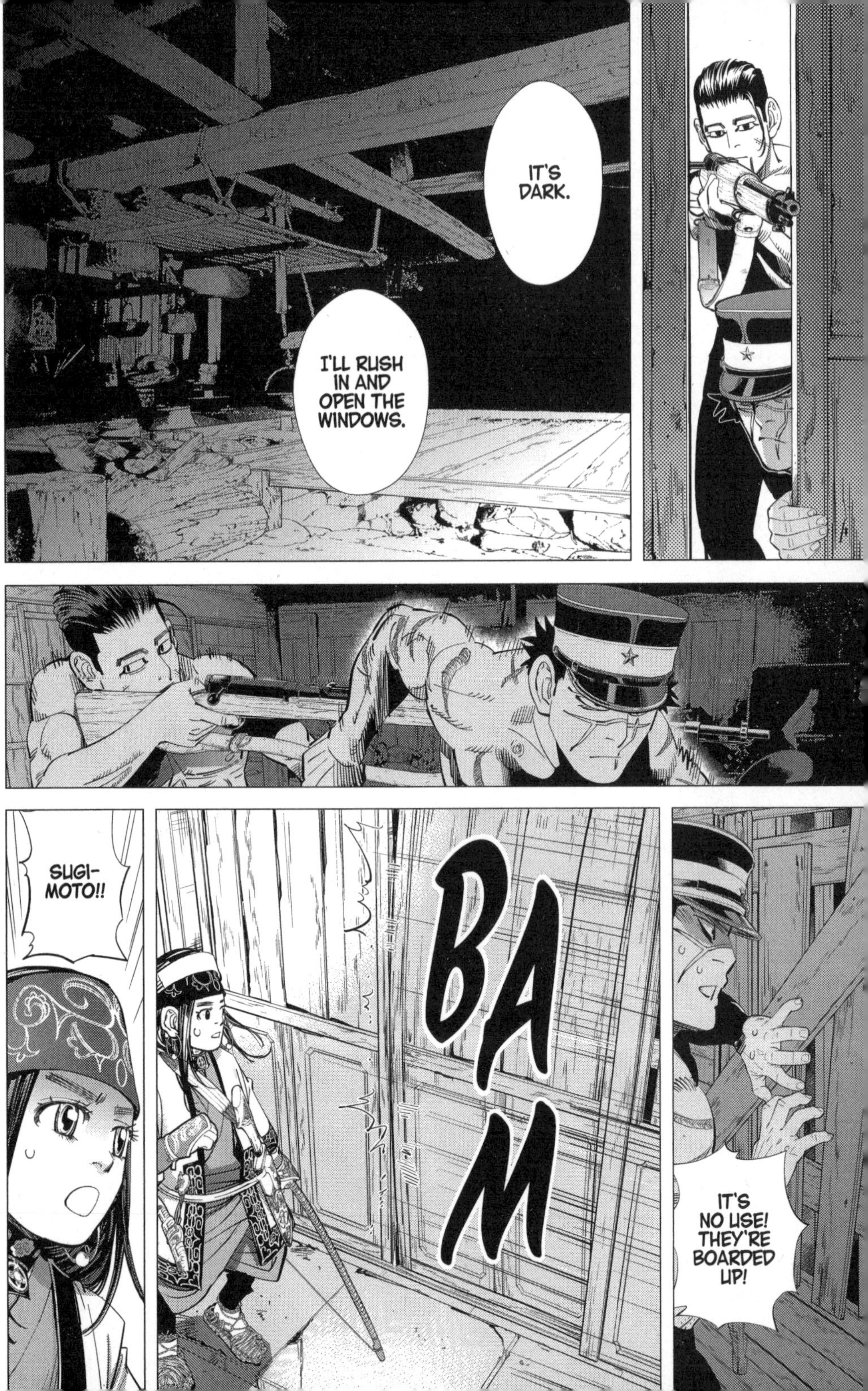
IT'S DARK.
I'LL RUSH IN AND OPEN THE WINDOWS.
IT'S NO USE! THEY'RE BOARDED UP!
BAM
SUGI-MOTO!!

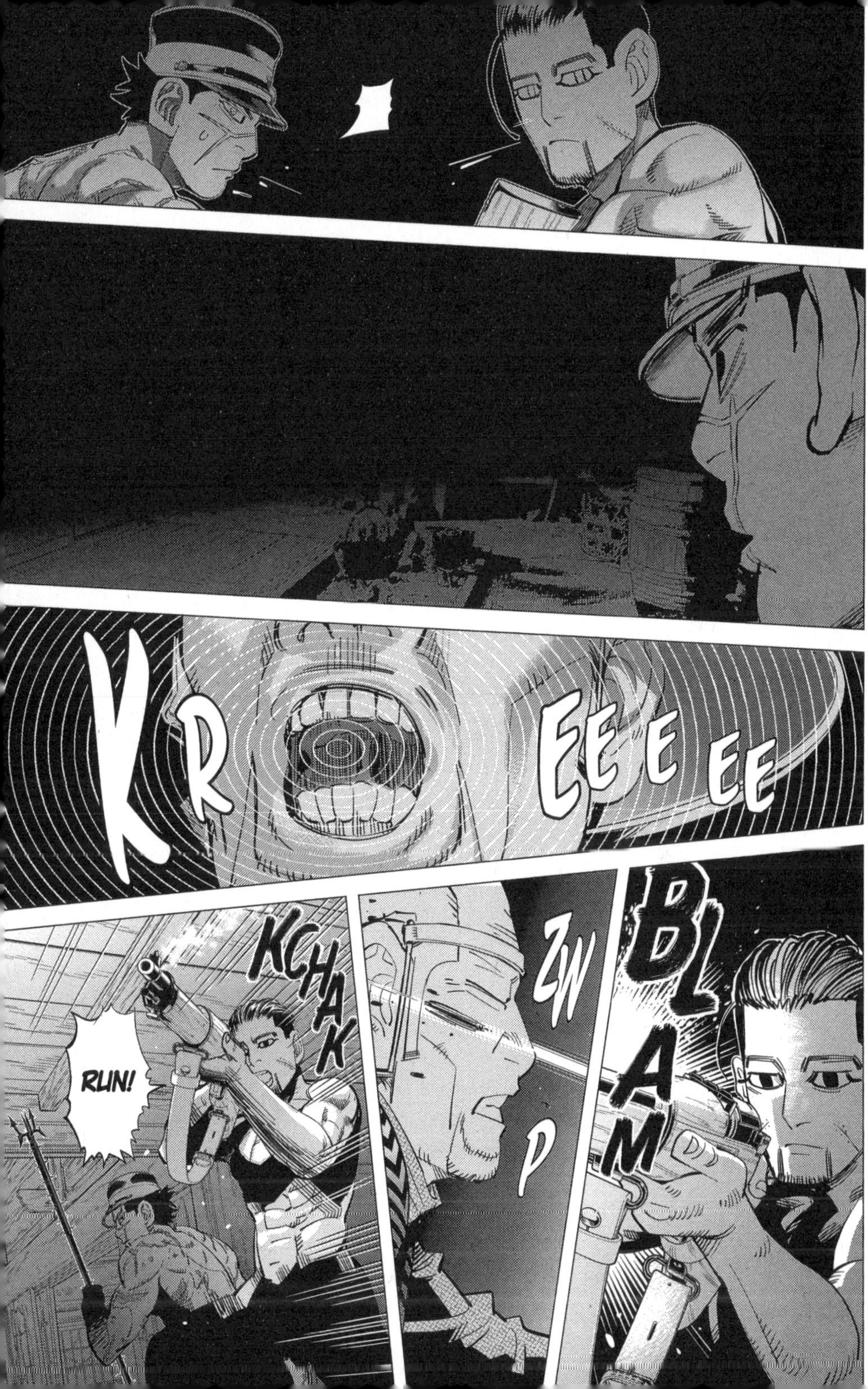
KREEEEE
BLAM
ZWP
KCHAK
RUN!

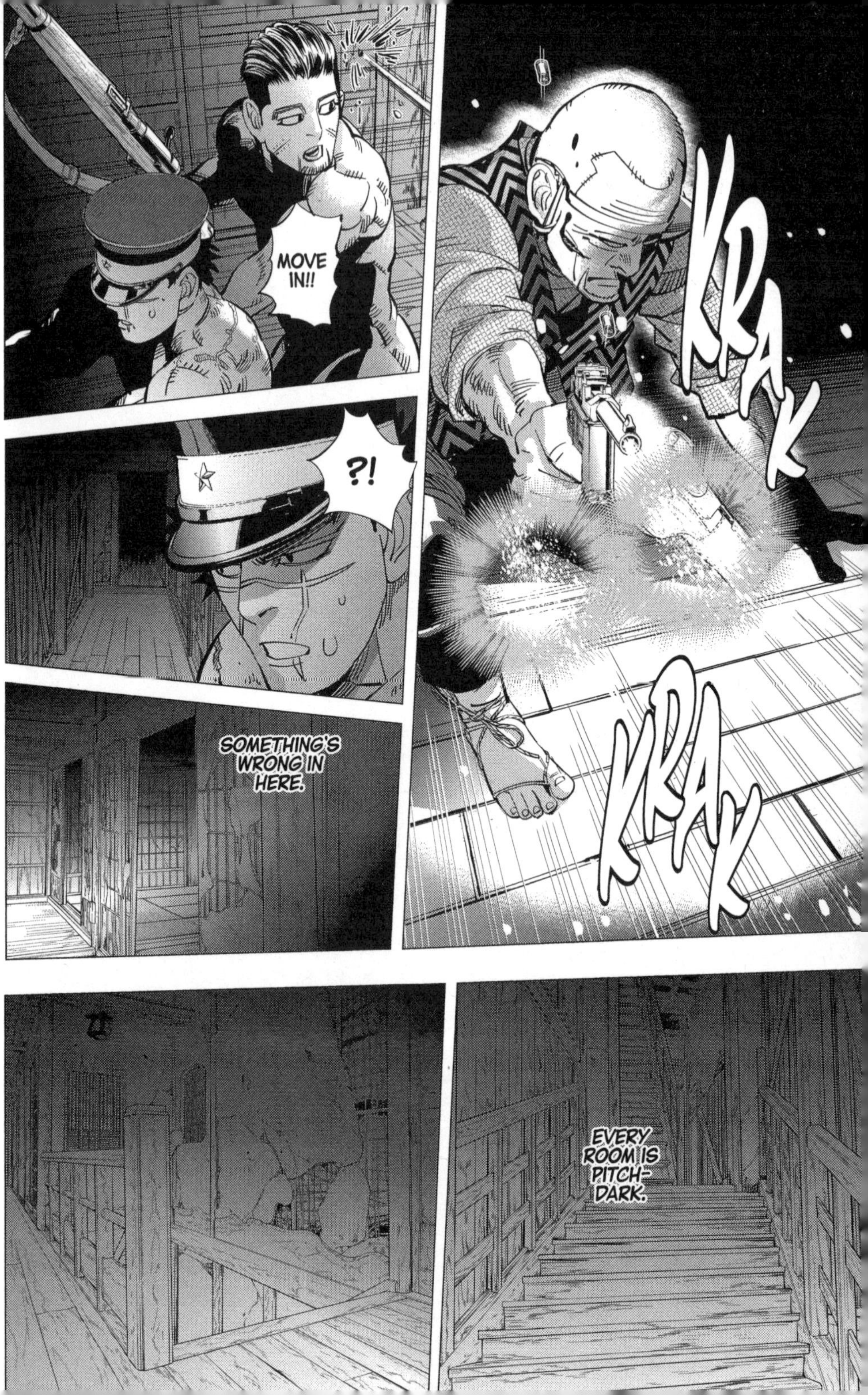
KRAK
KRAK
MOVE IN!!
?!
SOMETHING'S WRONG IN HERE.
EVERY ROOM IS PITCH-DARK.

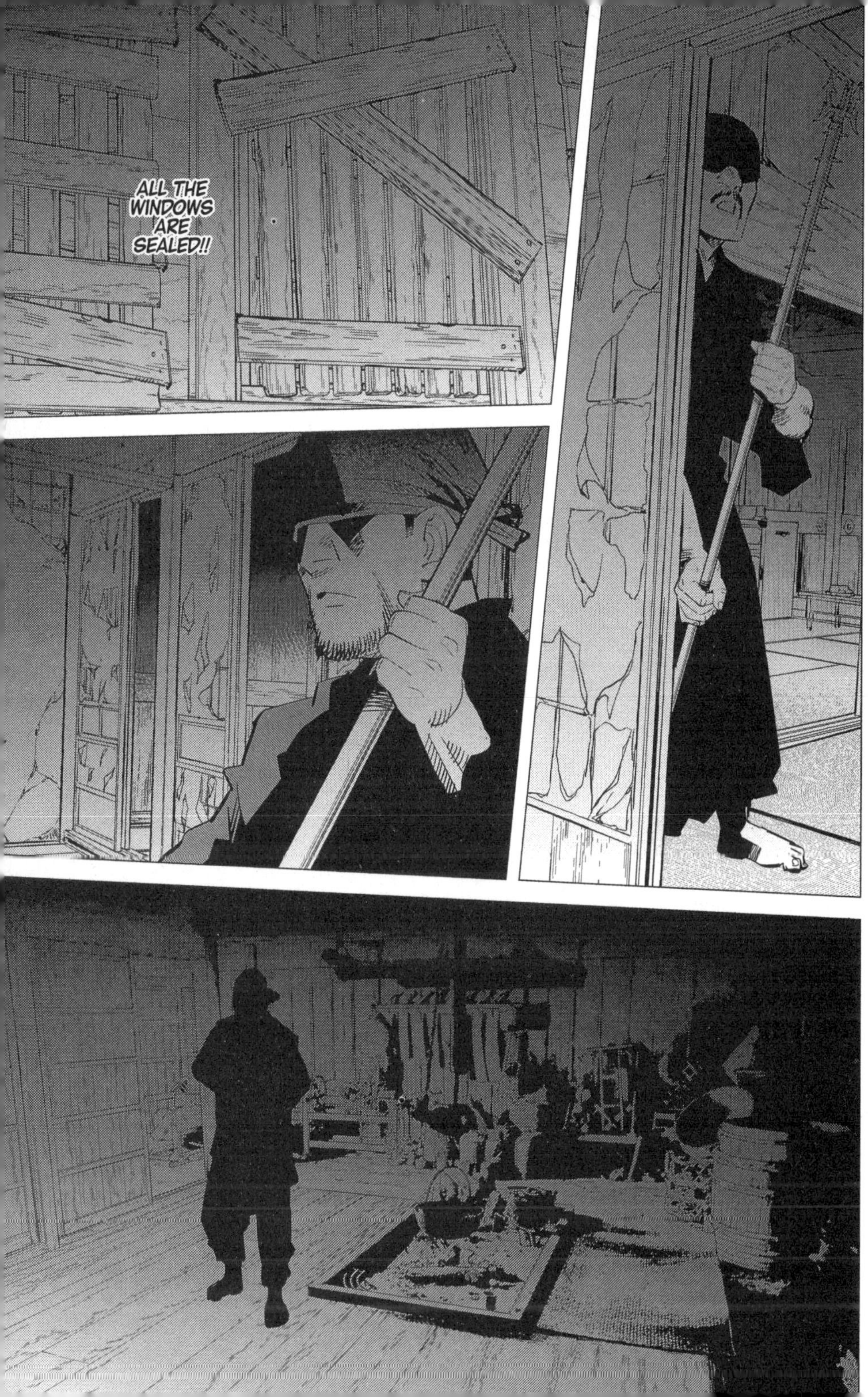
ALL THE WINDOWS ARE SEALED!!

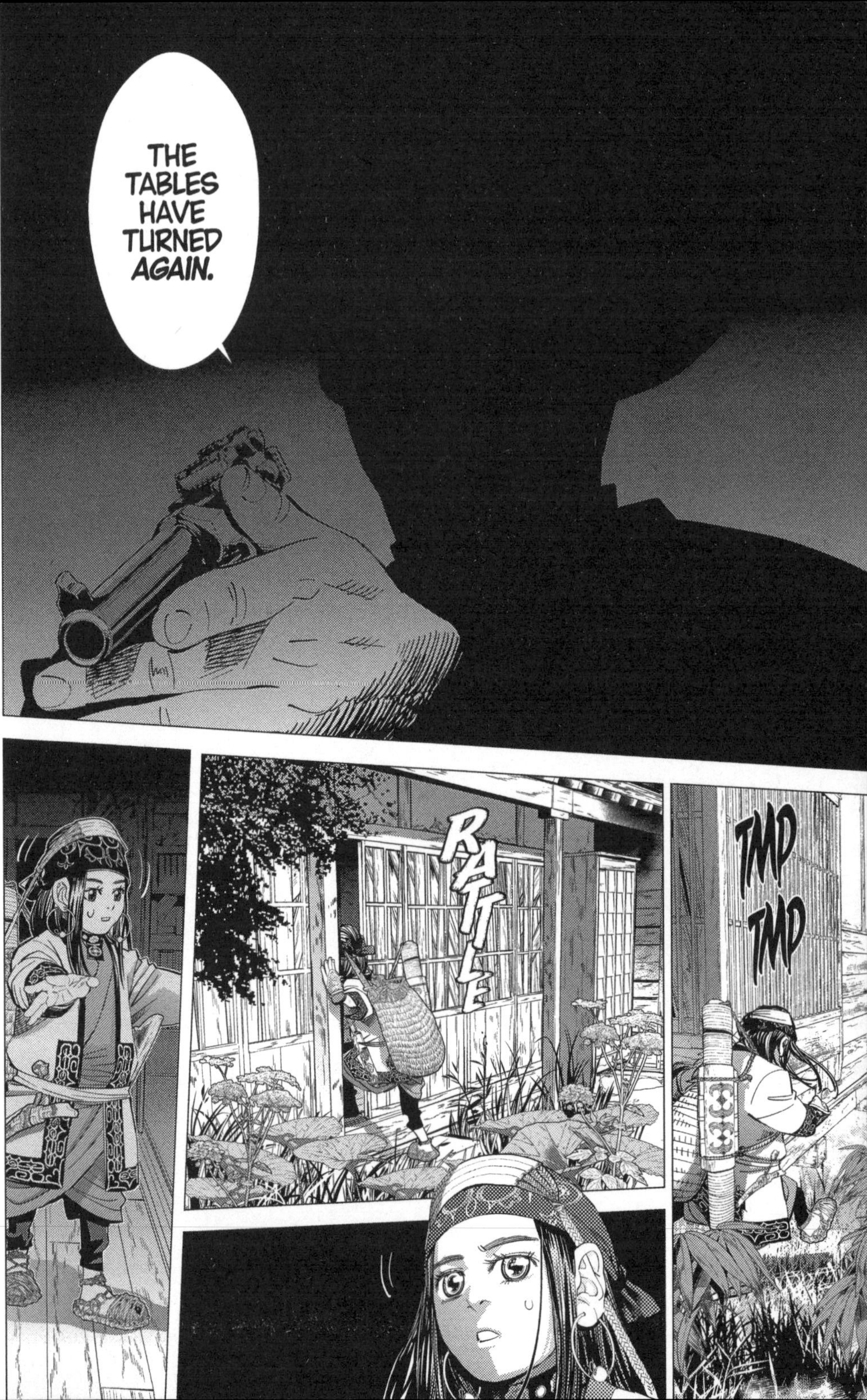
THE TABLES HAVE TURNED AGAIN.
TMP TMP
RATTLE

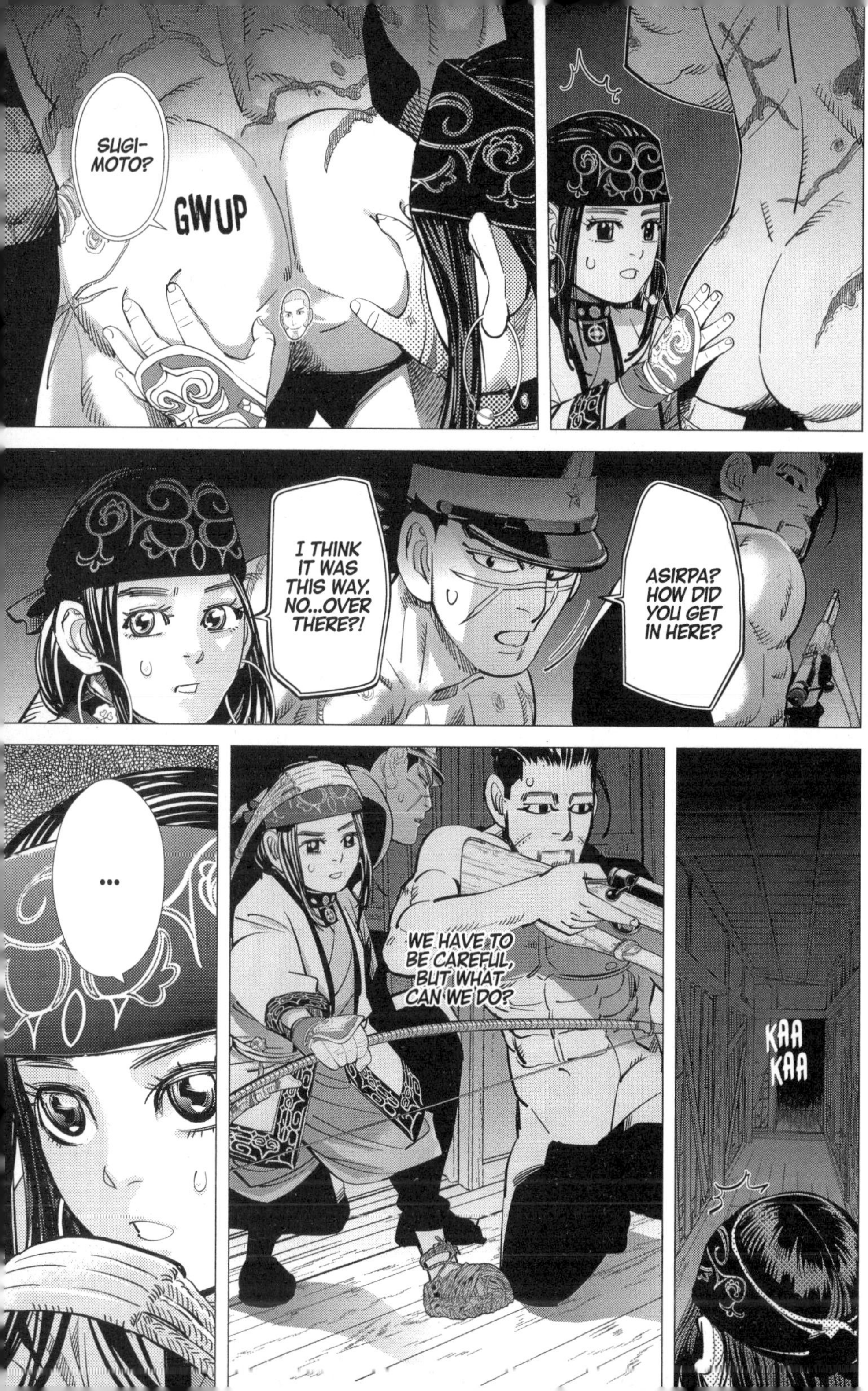
SUGI-MOTO?
GWUP
ASIRPA? HOW DID YOU GET IN HERE?
I THINK IT WAS THIS WAY. NO...OVER THERE?!
KAA KAA
WE HAVE TO BE CAREFUL, BUT WHAT CAN WE DO?
...

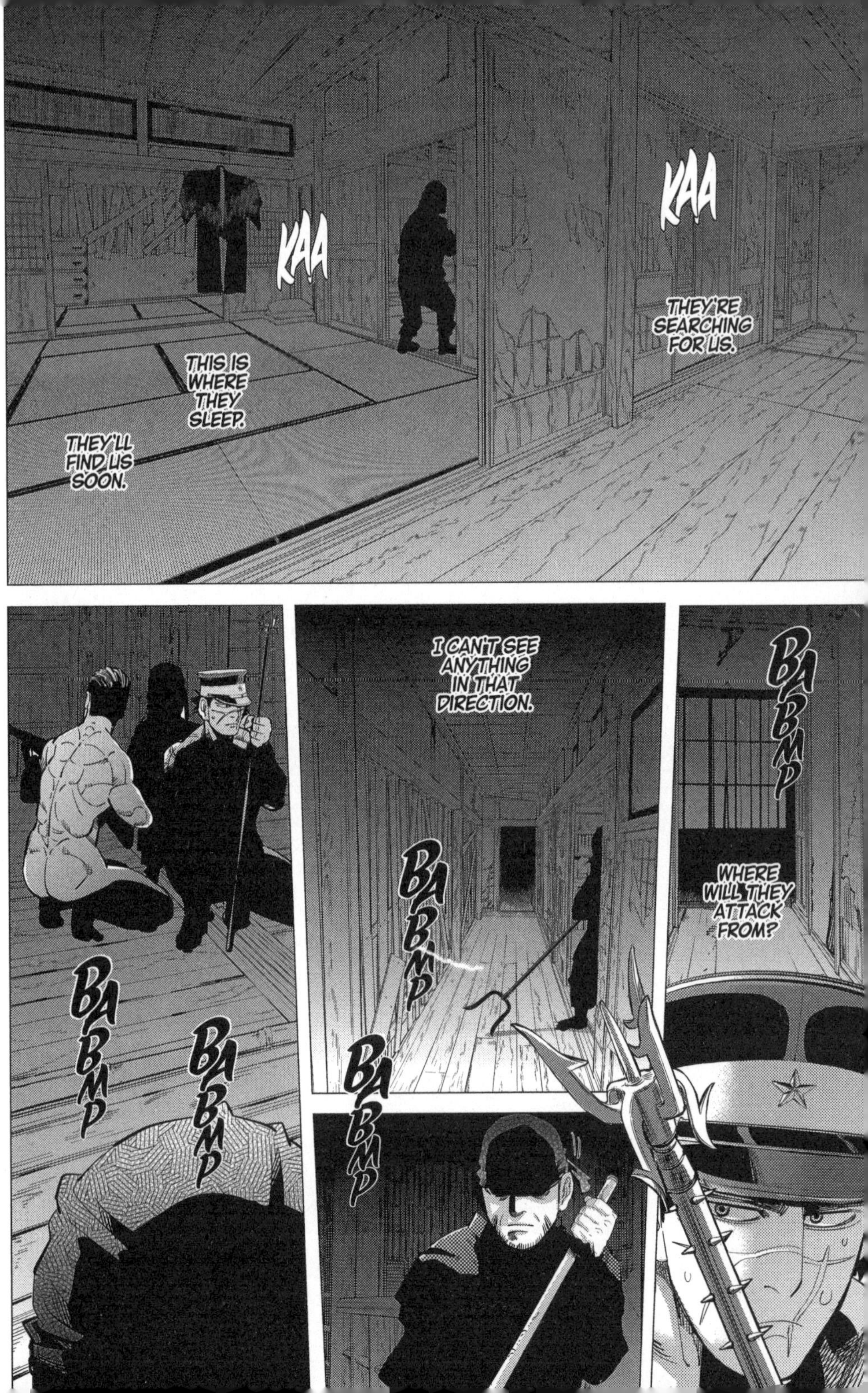
KAA
THEY'RE SEARCHING FOR US.
KAA
THIS IS WHERE THEY SLEEP.
THEY'LL FIND US SOON.
BABUMP
WHERE WILL THEY ATTACK FROM?
I CAN'T SEE ANYTHING IN THAT DIRECTION.
BABUMP
BABUMP
BABUMP
BABUMP

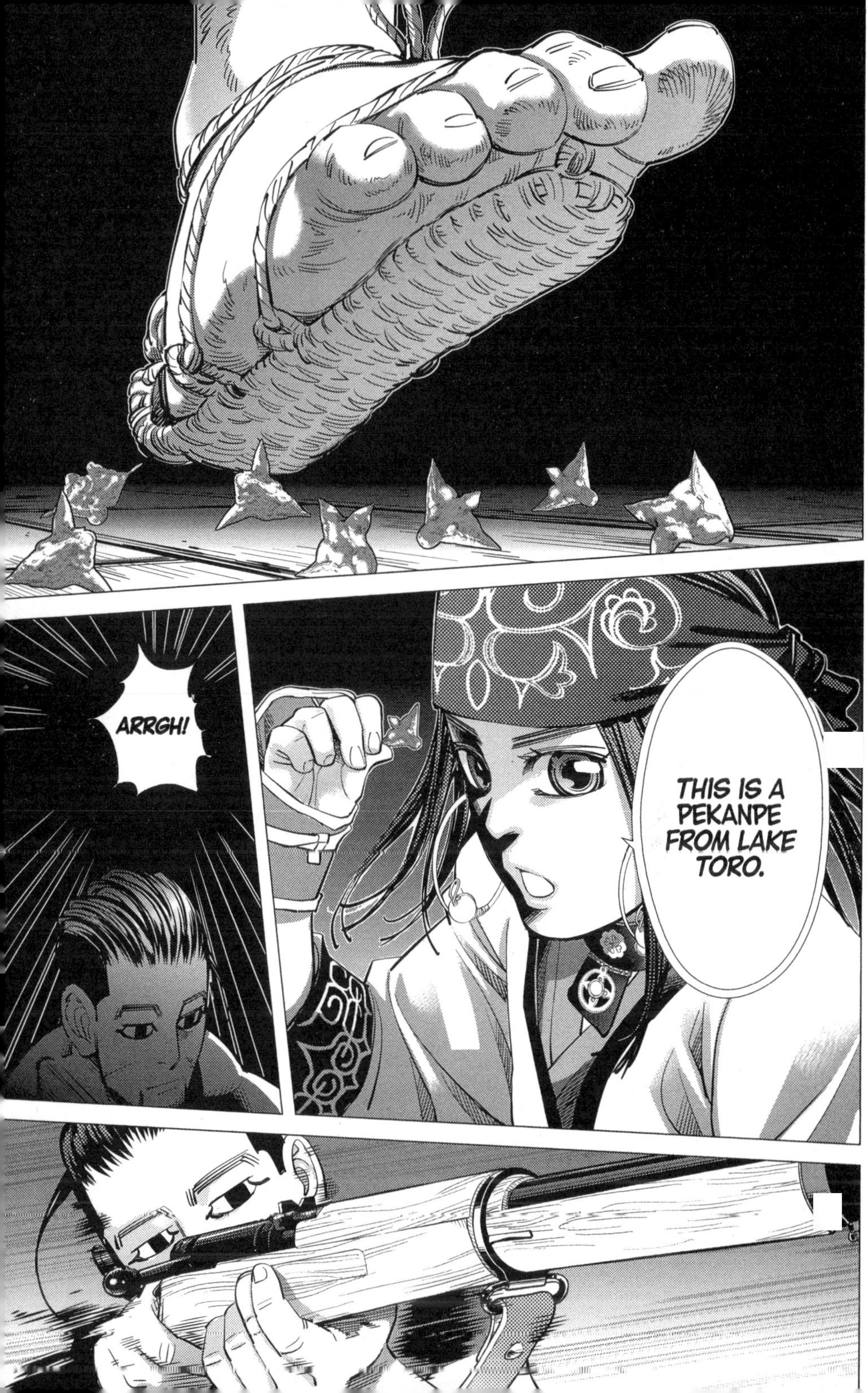
THIS IS A PEKANPE FROM LAKE TORO.
ARRGH!

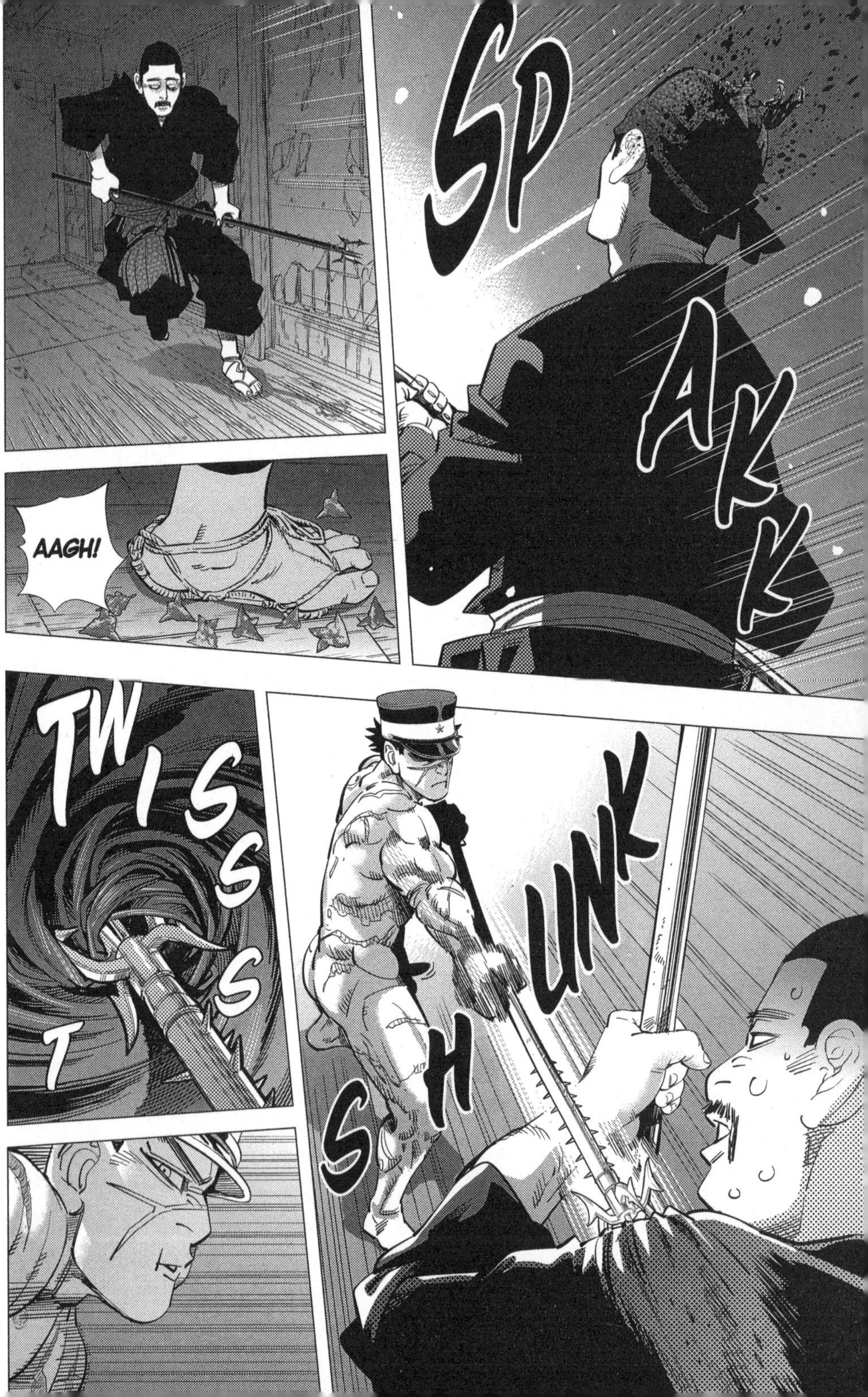
SPAKK
AAGH!
SHUNK
TWISST

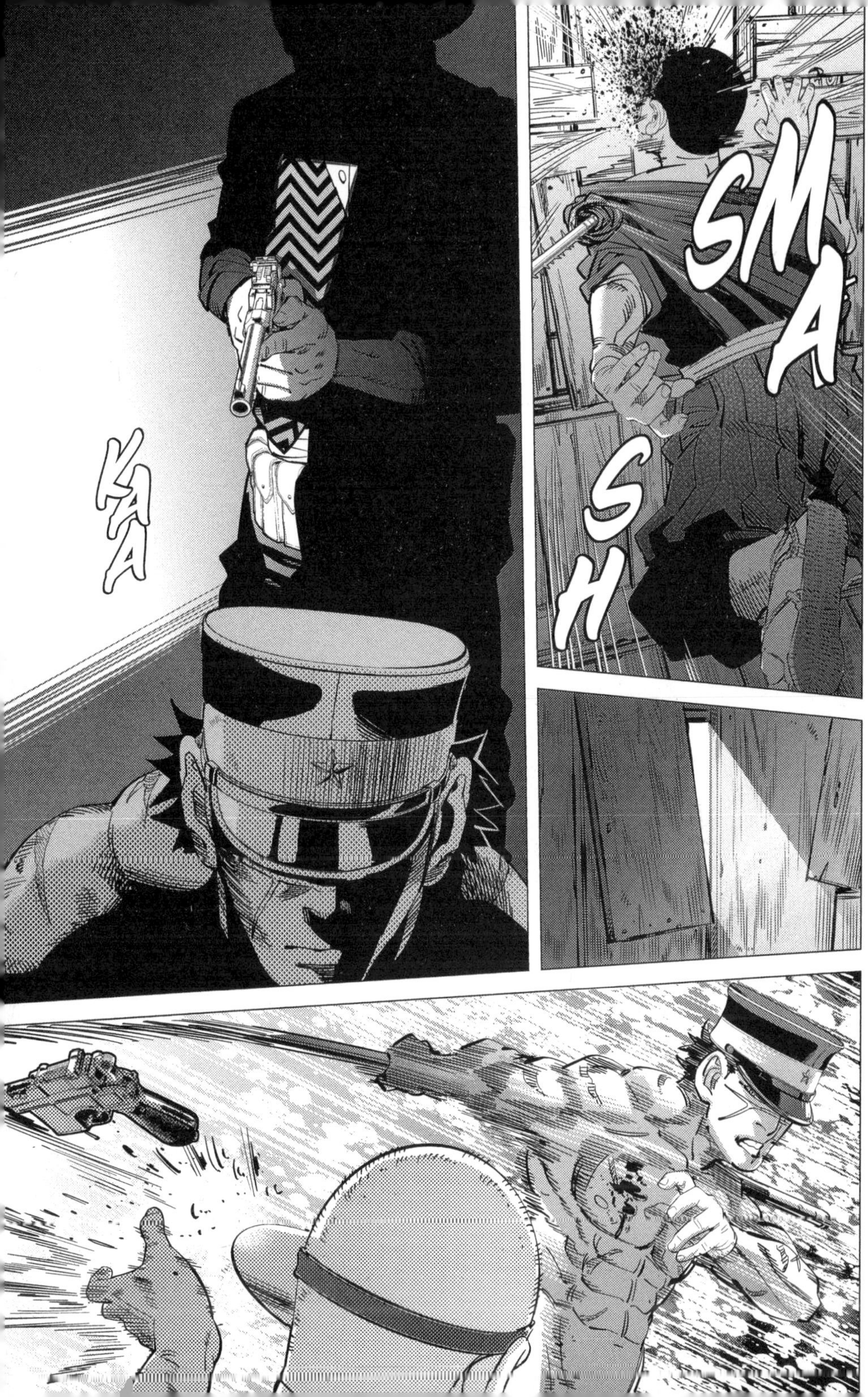
SMASH
KAA

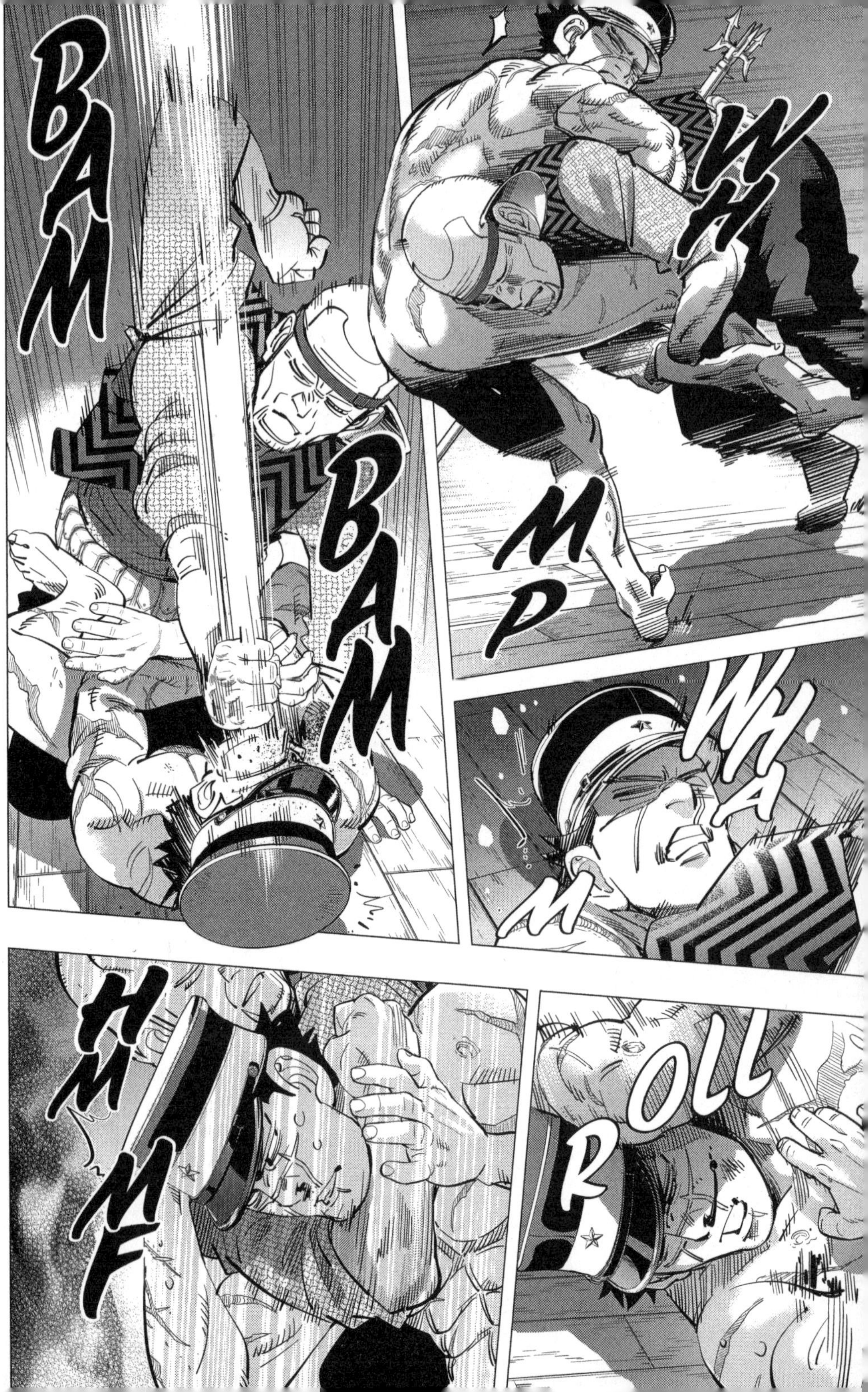

WH
MP
WHAM
BAM
BAM
ROLL
HMMMF

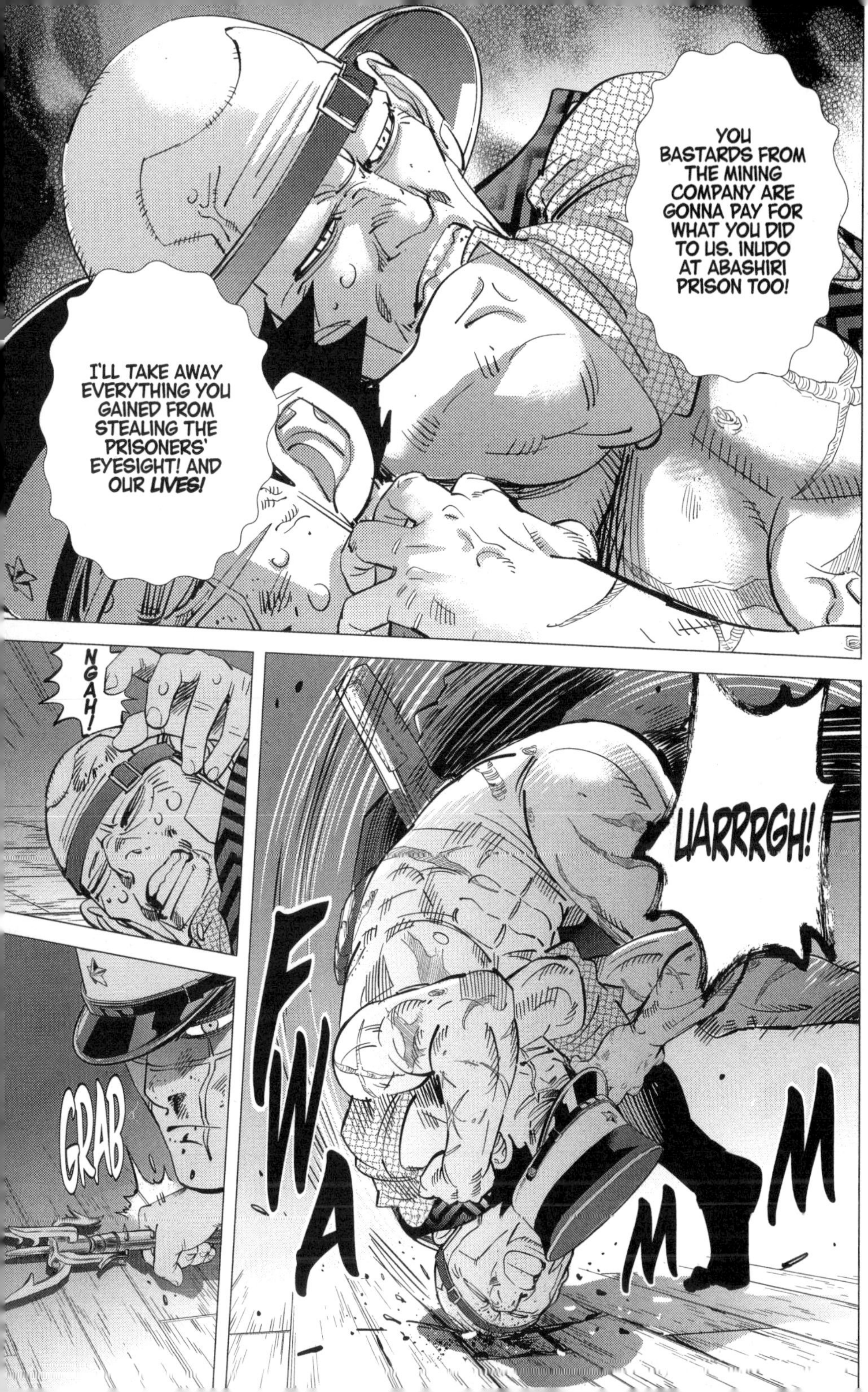
YOU BASTARDS FROM THE MINING COMPANY ARE GONNA PAY FOR WHAT YOU DID TO US. INUDO AT ABASHIRI PRISON TOO!
I'LL TAKE AWAY EVERYTHING YOU GAINED FROM STEALING THE PRISONERS' EYESIGHT! AND OUR *LIVES!*
UARRRGH!
FWAMMM
NGAH!
GRAB

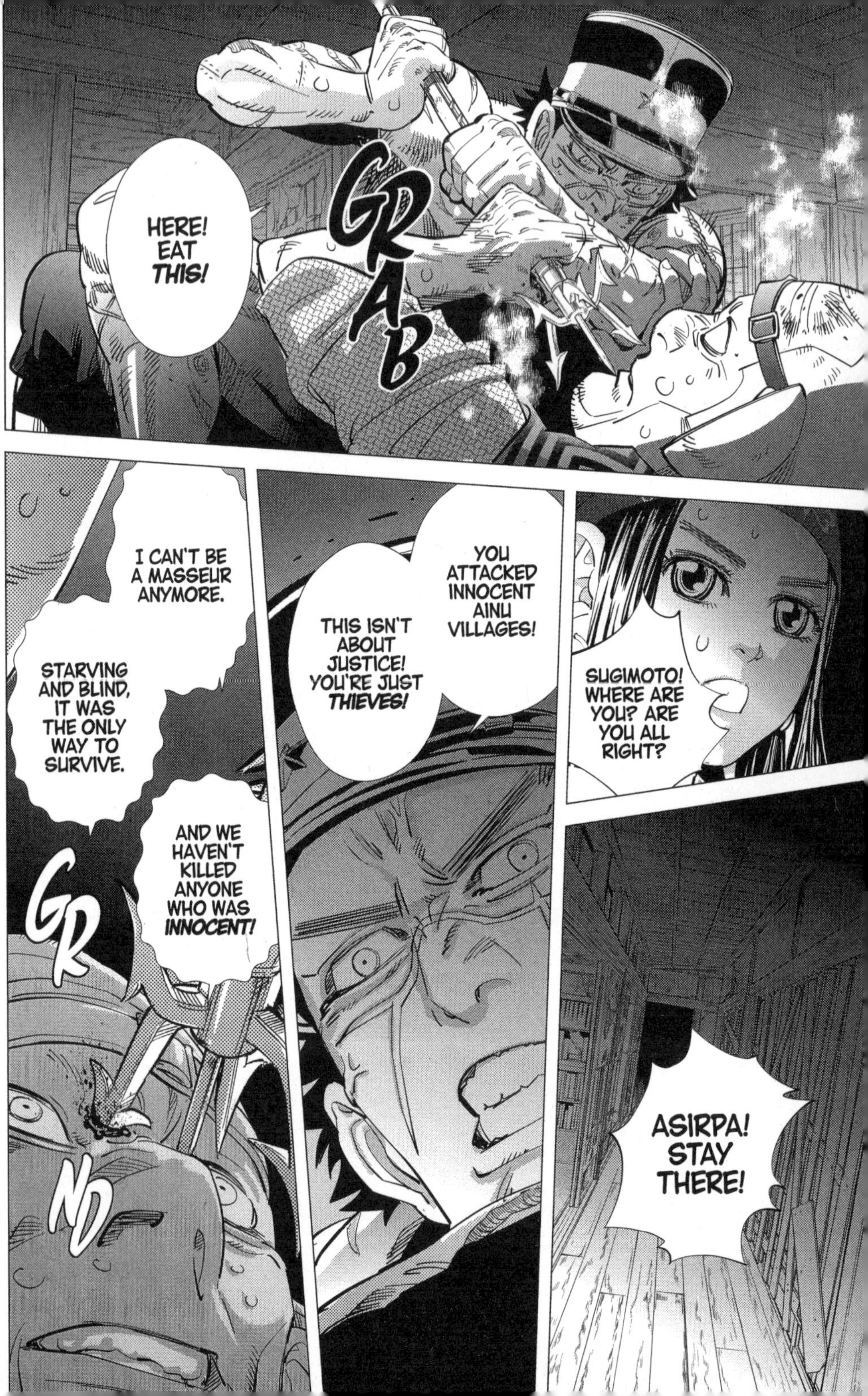
HERE! EAT THIS!
GRAB
SUGIMOTO! WHERE ARE YOU? ARE YOU ALL RIGHT?
ASIRPA! STAY THERE!
YOU ATTACKED INNOCENT AINU VILLAGES!
THIS ISN'T ABOUT JUSTICE! YOU'RE JUST THIEVES!
I CAN'T BE A MASSEUR ANYMORE.
STARVING AND BLIND, IT WAS THE ONLY WAY TO SURVIVE.
AND WE HAVEN'T KILLED ANYONE WHO WAS INNOCENT!
GR
ND

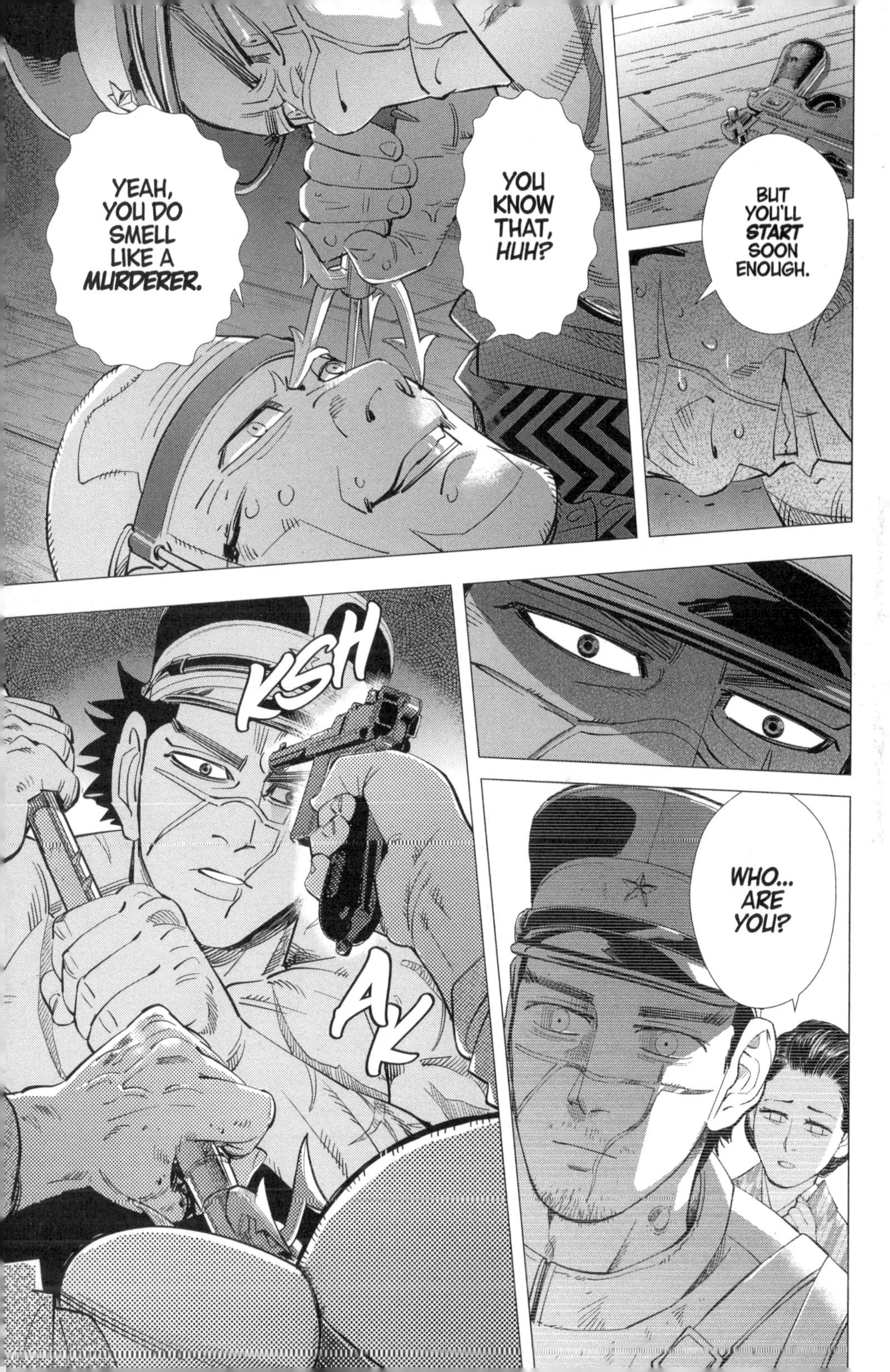
BUT YOU'LL START SOON ENOUGH.
YOU KNOW THAT, HUH?
YEAH, YOU DO SMELL LIKE A MURDERER.
WHO... ARE YOU?
KSH
AK

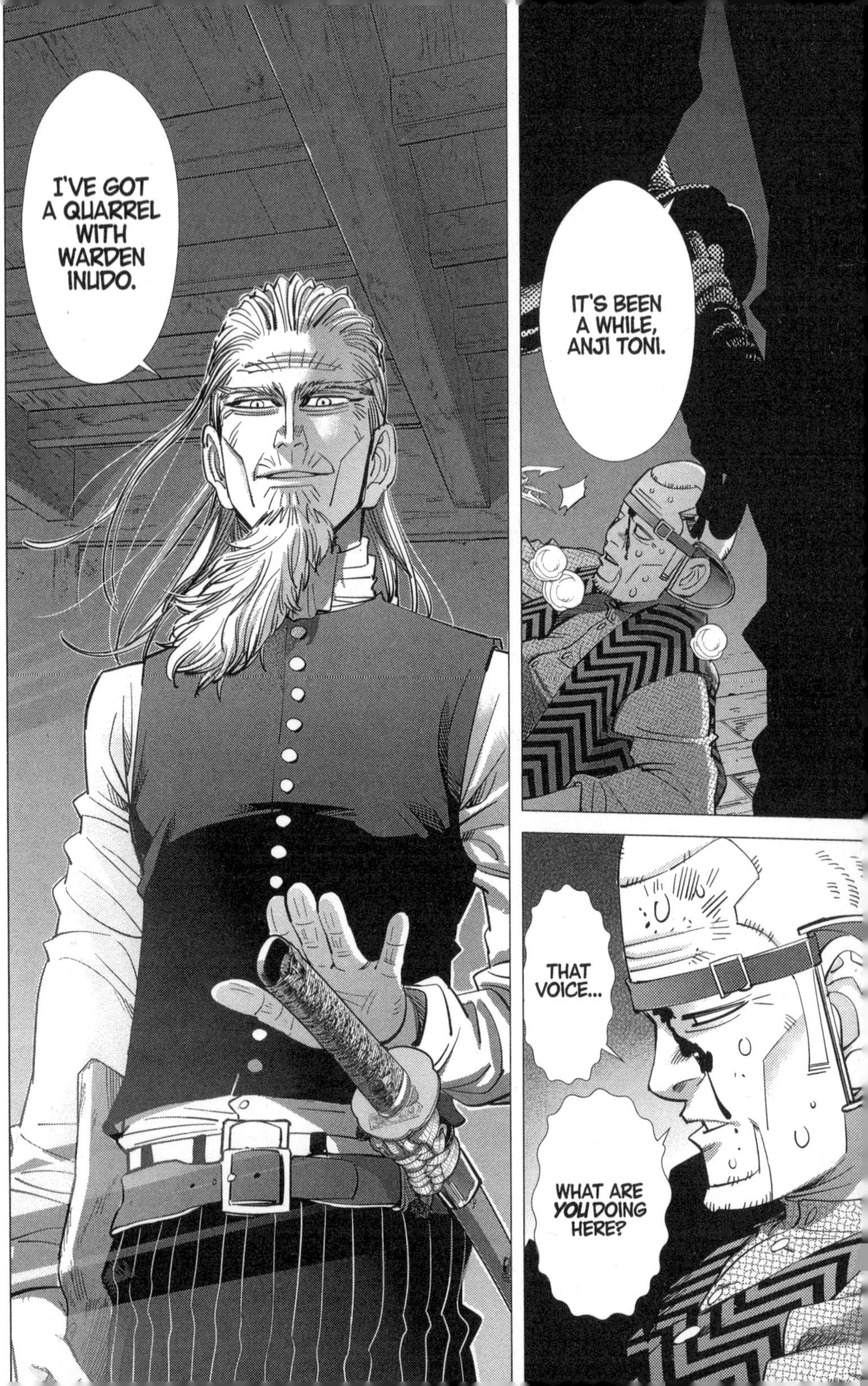
IT'S BEEN A WHILE, ANJI TONI.
THAT VOICE...
WHAT ARE YOU DOING HERE?
I'VE GOT A QUARREL WITH WARDEN INUDO.

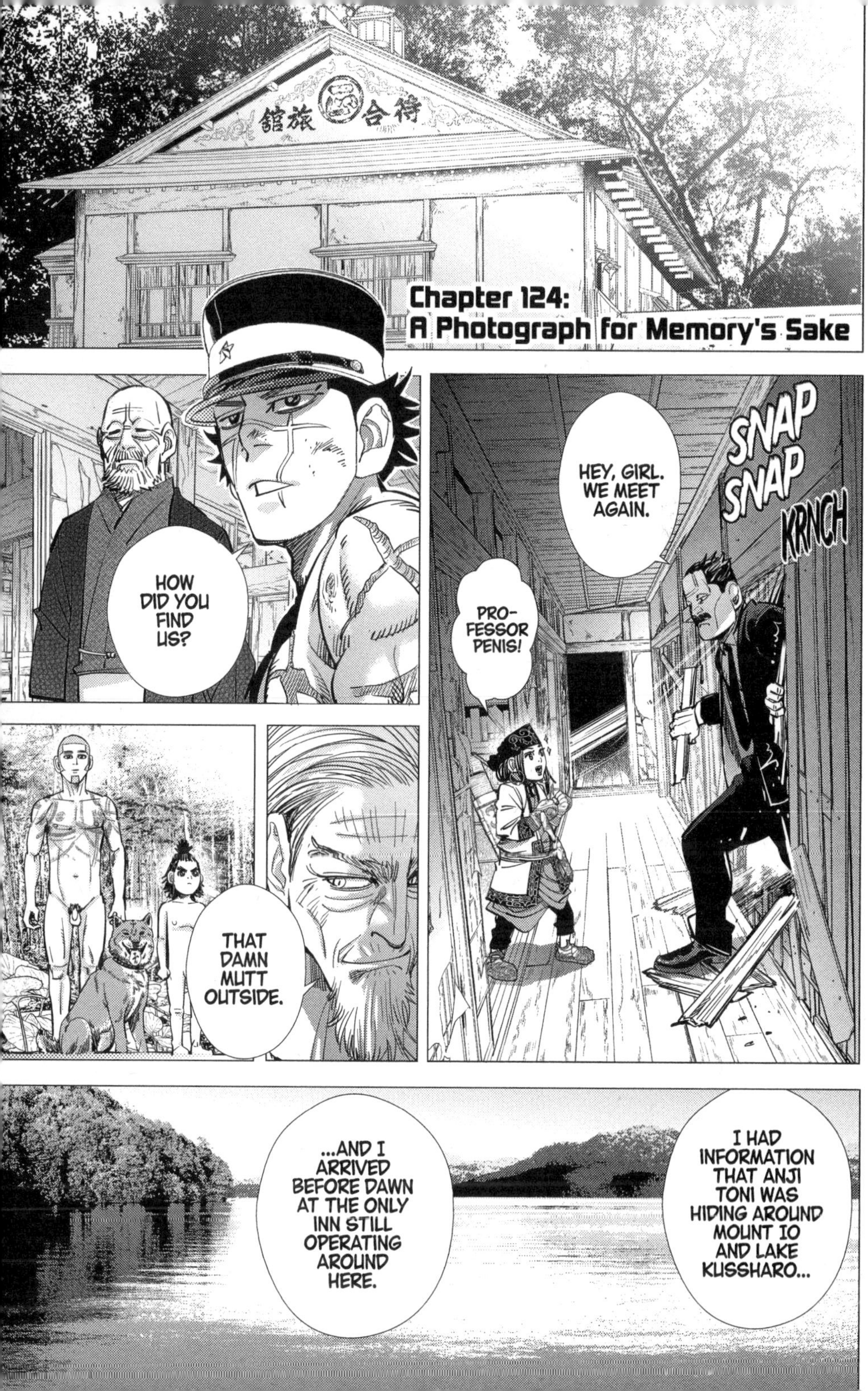

待合旅館
Chapter 124:
A Photograph for Memory's Sake
SNAP SNAP KRNCH
HEY, GIRL. WE MEET AGAIN.
PRO-FESSOR PENIS!
HOW DID YOU FIND US?
THAT DAMN MUTT OUTSIDE.
I HAD INFORMATION THAT ANJI TONI WAS HIDING AROUND MOUNT IO AND LAKE KUSSHARO...
...AND I ARRIVED BEFORE DAWN AT THE ONLY INN STILL OPERATING AROUND HERE.

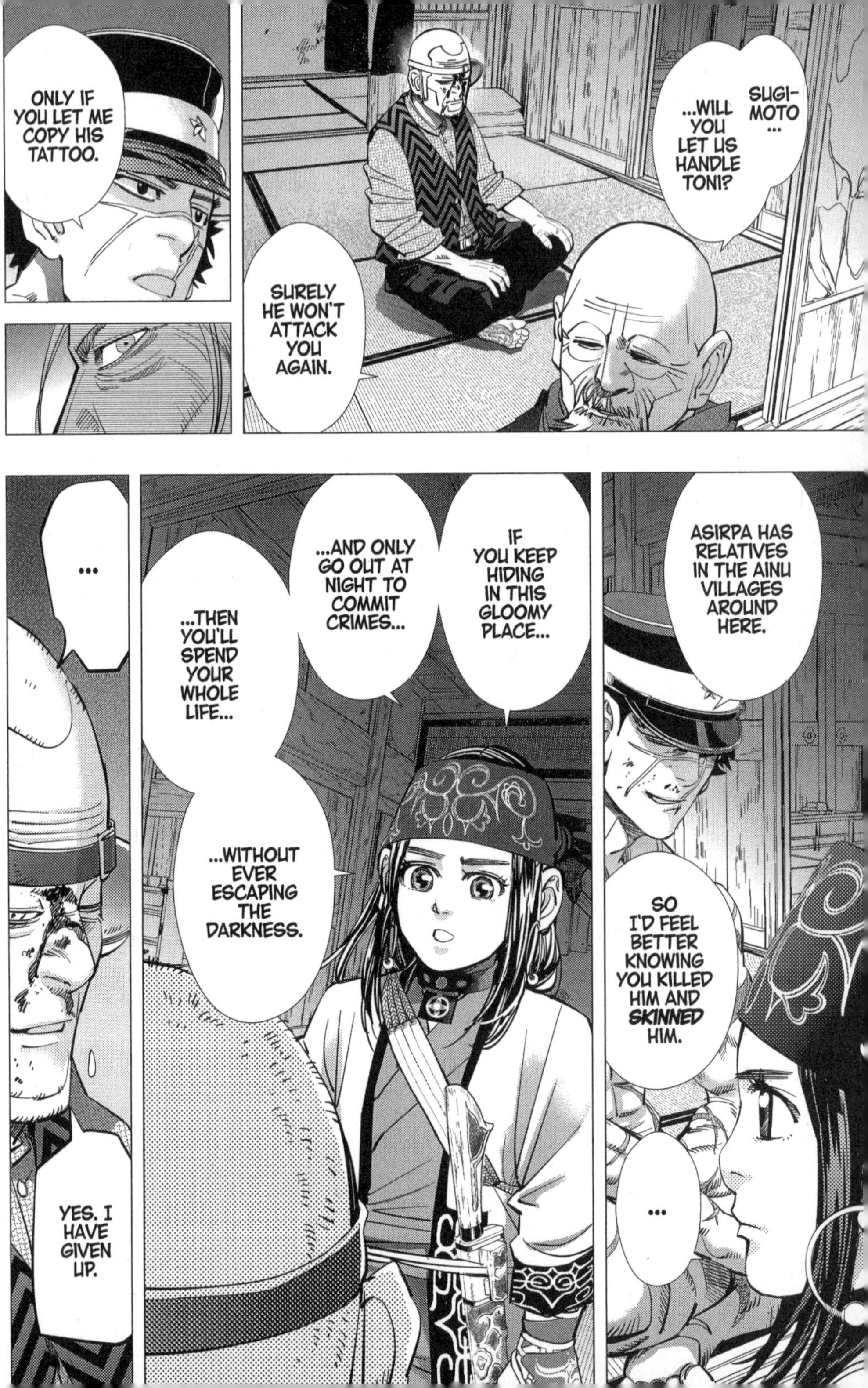
SUGI-MOTO ...
...WILL YOU LET US HANDLE TONI?
SURELY HE WON'T ATTACK YOU AGAIN.
ONLY IF YOU LET ME COPY HIS TATTOO.
ASIRPA HAS RELATIVES IN THE AINU VILLAGES AROUND HERE.
SO I'D FEEL BETTER KNOWING YOU KILLED HIM AND **SKINNED** HIM.
...
IF YOU KEEP HIDING IN THIS GLOOMY PLACE...
...AND ONLY GO OUT AT NIGHT TO COMMIT CRIMES...
...THEN YOU'LL SPEND YOUR WHOLE LIFE...
...WITHOUT EVER ESCAPING THE DARKNESS.
...
YES. I HAVE GIVEN UP.

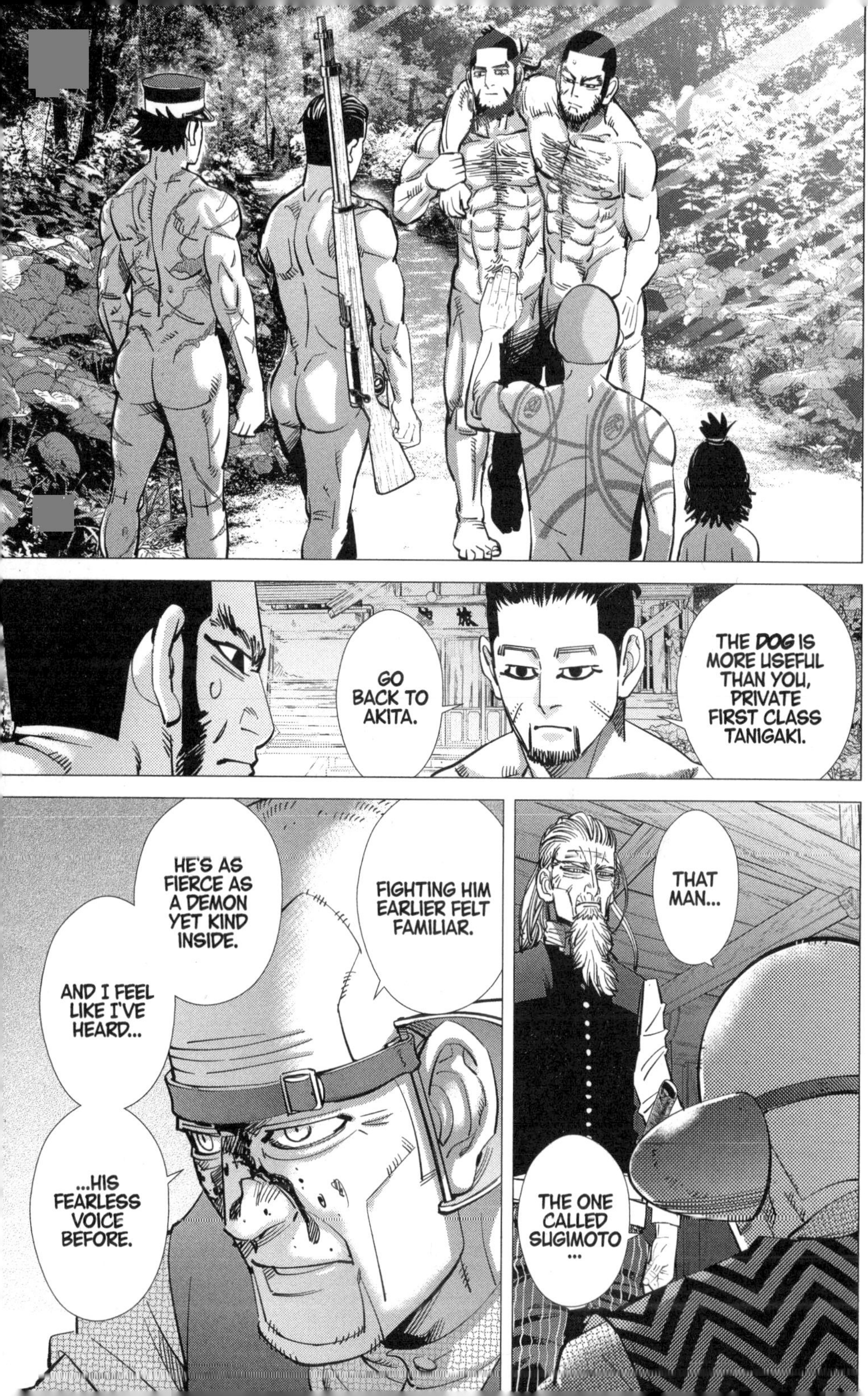
THE DOG IS MORE USEFUL THAN YOU, PRIVATE FIRST CLASS TANIGAKI.
GO BACK TO AKITA.
THAT MAN...
THE ONE CALLED SUGIMOTO ...
FIGHTING HIM EARLIER FELT FAMILIAR.
HE'S AS FIERCE AS A DEMON YET KIND INSIDE.
AND I FEEL LIKE I'VE HEARD...
...HIS FEARLESS VOICE BEFORE.

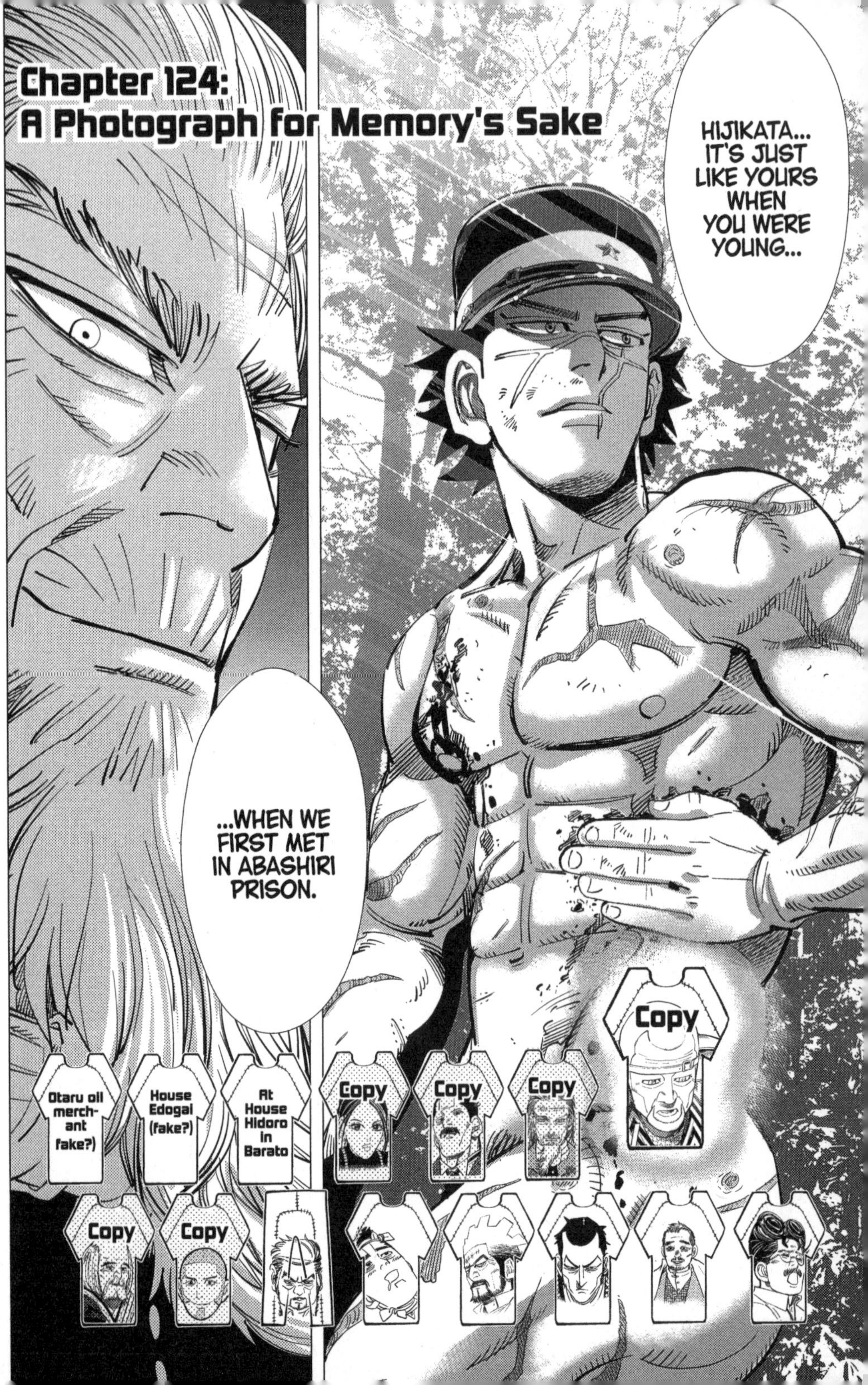
Chapter 124:
A Photograph for Memory's Sake
HIJIKATA... IT'S JUST LIKE YOURS WHEN YOU WERE YOUNG...
...WHEN WE FIRST MET IN ABASHIRI PRISON.
Copy
Copy
Copy
Copy
At House Hidoro in Barato
House Edogai (fake?)
Otaru oil merch-ant fake?)
Copy
Copy

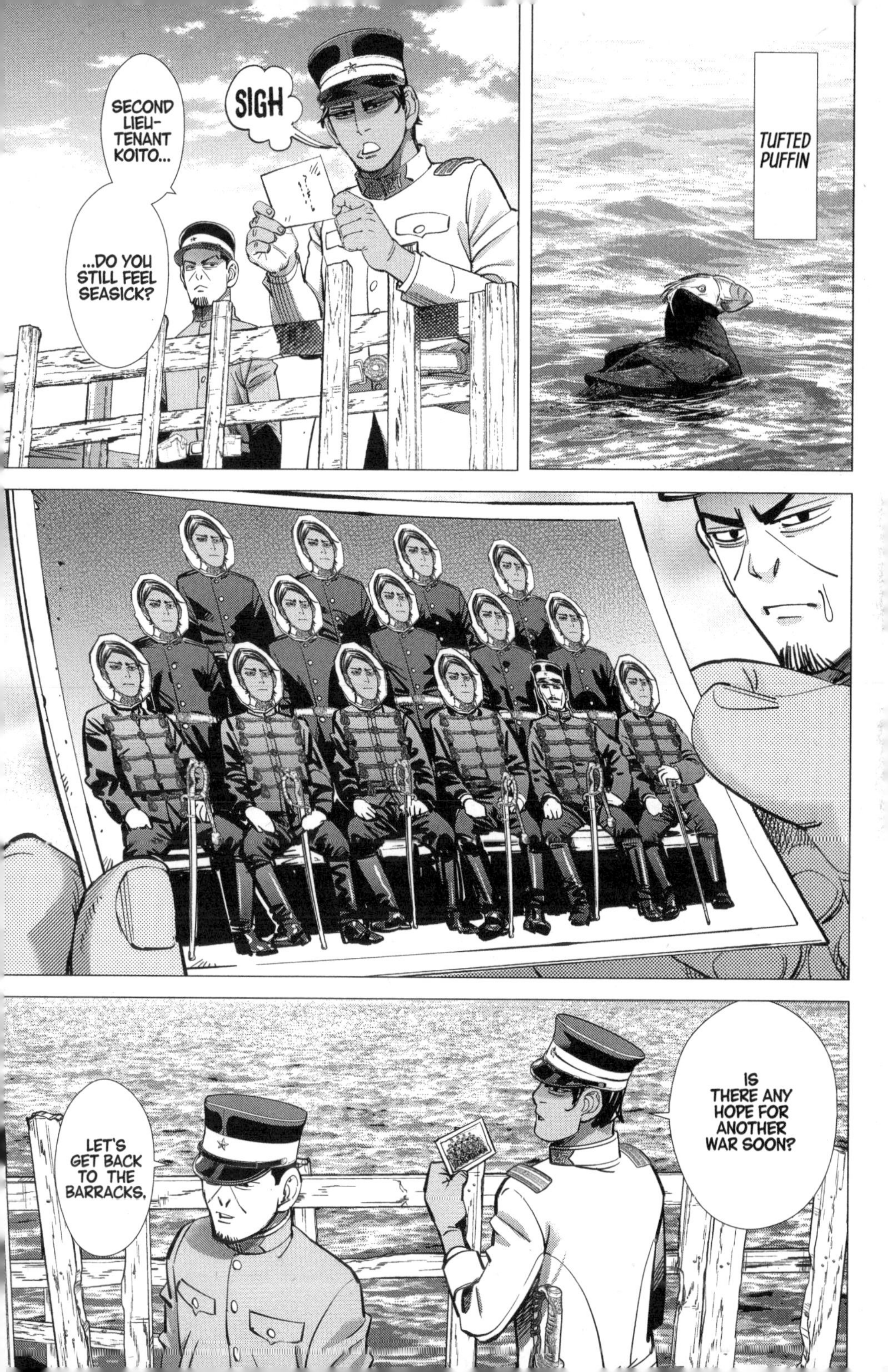
TUFTED PUFFIN
SIGH
SECOND LIEU-TENANT KOITO...
...DO YOU STILL FEEL SEASICK?
IS THERE ANY HOPE FOR ANOTHER WAR SOON?
LET'S GET BACK TO THE BARRACKS.

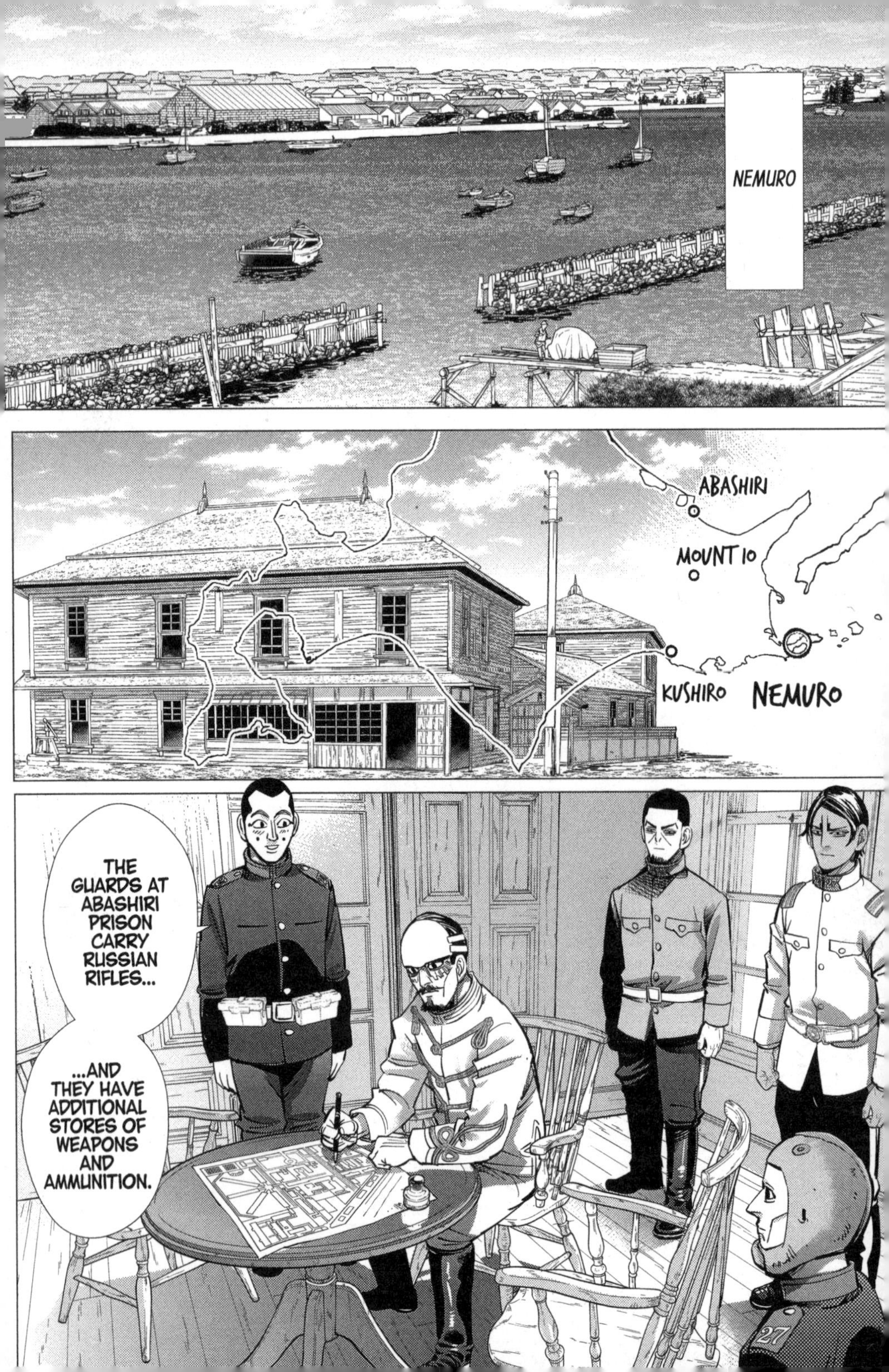
NEMURO
ABASHIRI
MOUNT IO
KUSHIRO
NEMURO
THE GUARDS AT ABASHIRI PRISON CARRY RUSSIAN RIFLES...
...AND THEY HAVE ADDITIONAL STORES OF WEAPONS AND AMMUNITION.

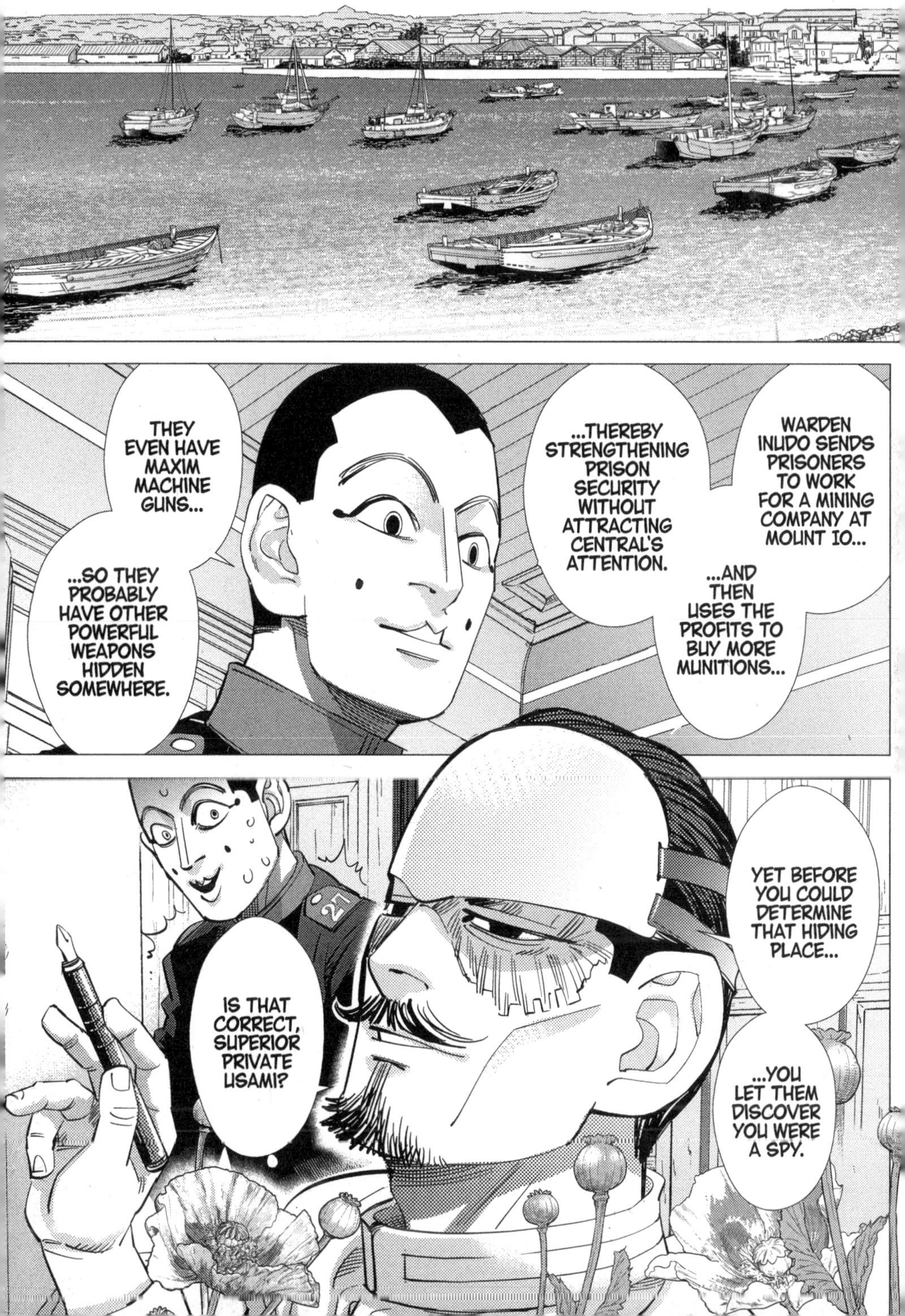
WARDEN INUDO SENDS PRISONERS TO WORK FOR A MINING COMPANY AT MOUNT IO...
...AND THEN USES THE PROFITS TO BUY MORE MUNITIONS...
...THEREBY STRENGTHENING PRISON SECURITY WITHOUT ATTRACTING CENTRAL'S ATTENTION.
THEY EVEN HAVE MAXIM MACHINE GUNS...
...SO THEY PROBABLY HAVE OTHER POWERFUL WEAPONS HIDDEN SOMEWHERE.
YET BEFORE YOU COULD DETERMINE THAT HIDING PLACE...
...YOU LET THEM DISCOVER YOU WERE A SPY.
IS THAT CORRECT, SUPERIOR PRIVATE USAMI?

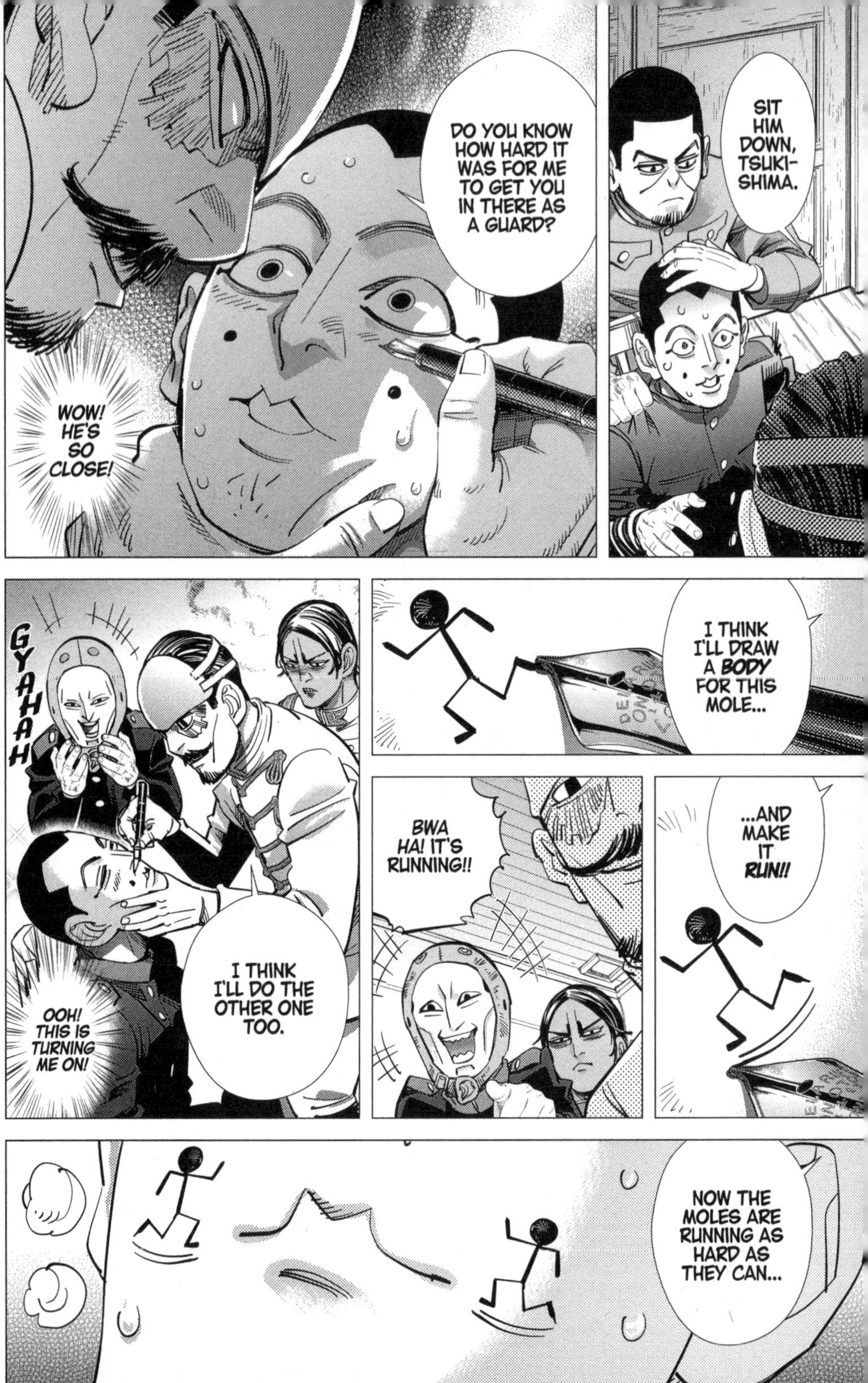
SIT HIM DOWN, TSUKI-SHIMA.
DO YOU KNOW HOW HARD IT WAS FOR ME TO GET YOU IN THERE AS A GUARD?
WOW! HE'S SO CLOSE!
I THINK I'LL DRAW A *BODY* FOR THIS MOLE...
...AND MAKE IT *RUN!!*
BWA HA! IT'S RUNNING!!
GYAHAH
I THINK I'LL DO THE OTHER ONE TOO.
OOH! THIS IS TURNING ME ON!
NOW THE MOLES ARE RUNNING AS HARD AS THEY CAN...

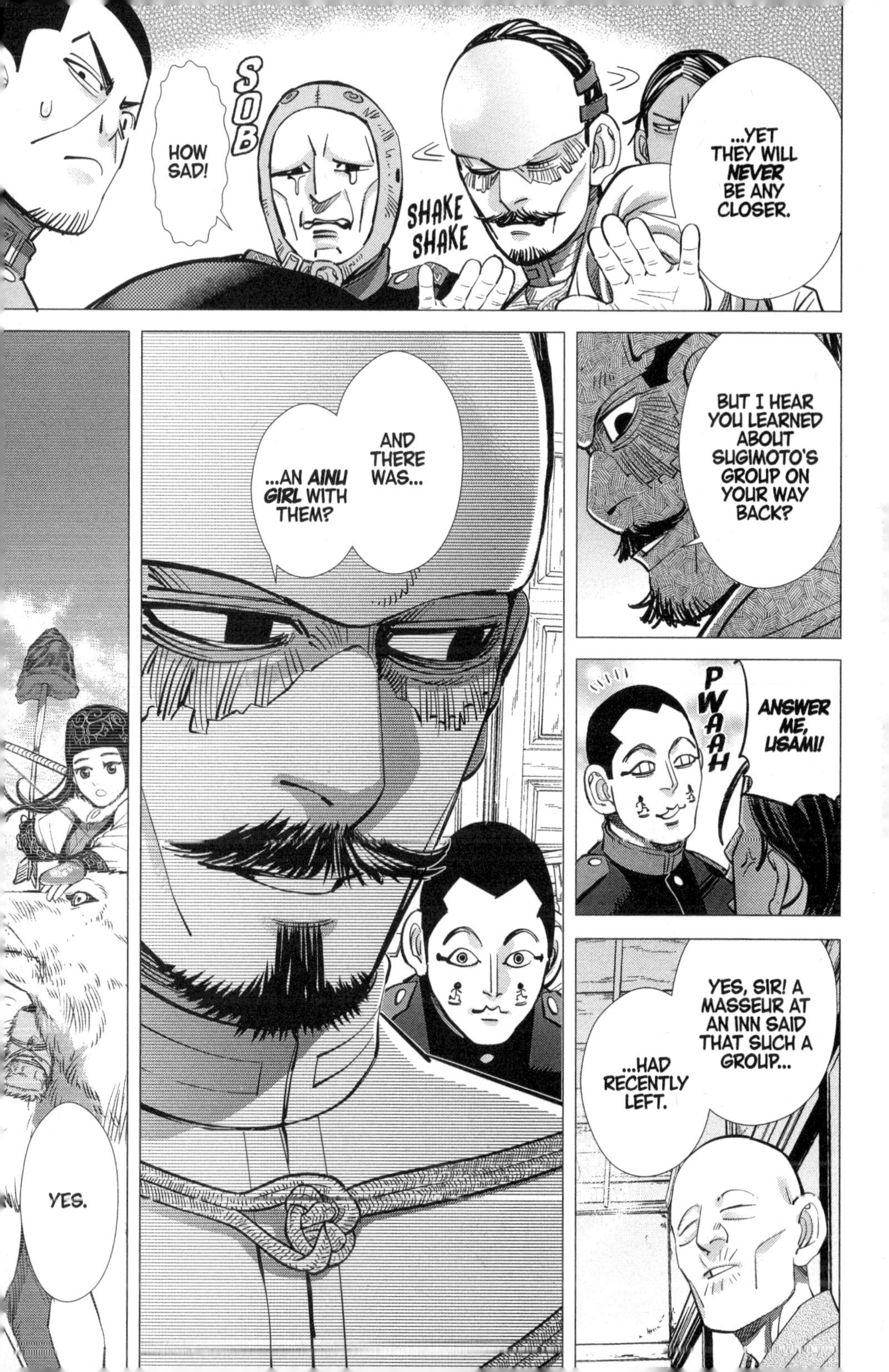
...YET THEY WILL NEVER BE ANY CLOSER.
SHAKE SHAKE
SOB
HOW SAD!
BUT I HEAR YOU LEARNED ABOUT SUGIMOTO'S GROUP ON YOUR WAY BACK?
PWAAH
ANSWER ME, USAMI!
YES, SIR! A MASSEUR AT AN INN SAID THAT SUCH A GROUP...
...HAD RECENTLY LEFT.
AND THERE WAS...
...AN AINU GIRL WITH THEM?
YES.

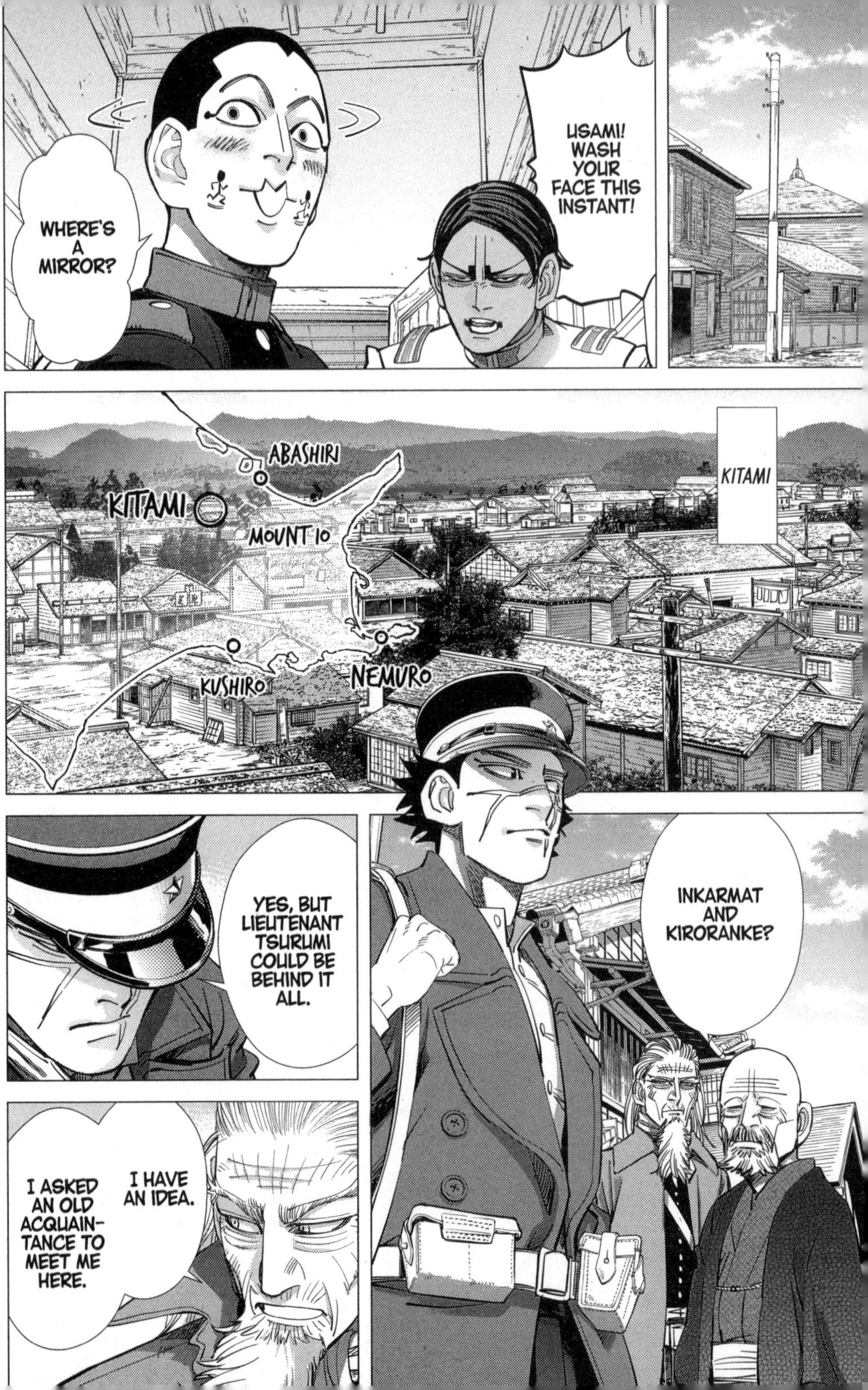
USAMI! WASH YOUR FACE THIS INSTANT!
WHERE'S A MIRROR?
KITAMI
ABASHIRI
KITAMI
MOUNT IO
NEMURO
KUSHIRO
INKARMAT AND KIRORANKE?
YES, BUT LIEUTENANT TSURUMI COULD BE BEHIND IT ALL.
I HAVE AN IDEA.
I ASKED AN OLD ACQUAINTANCE TO MEET ME HERE.

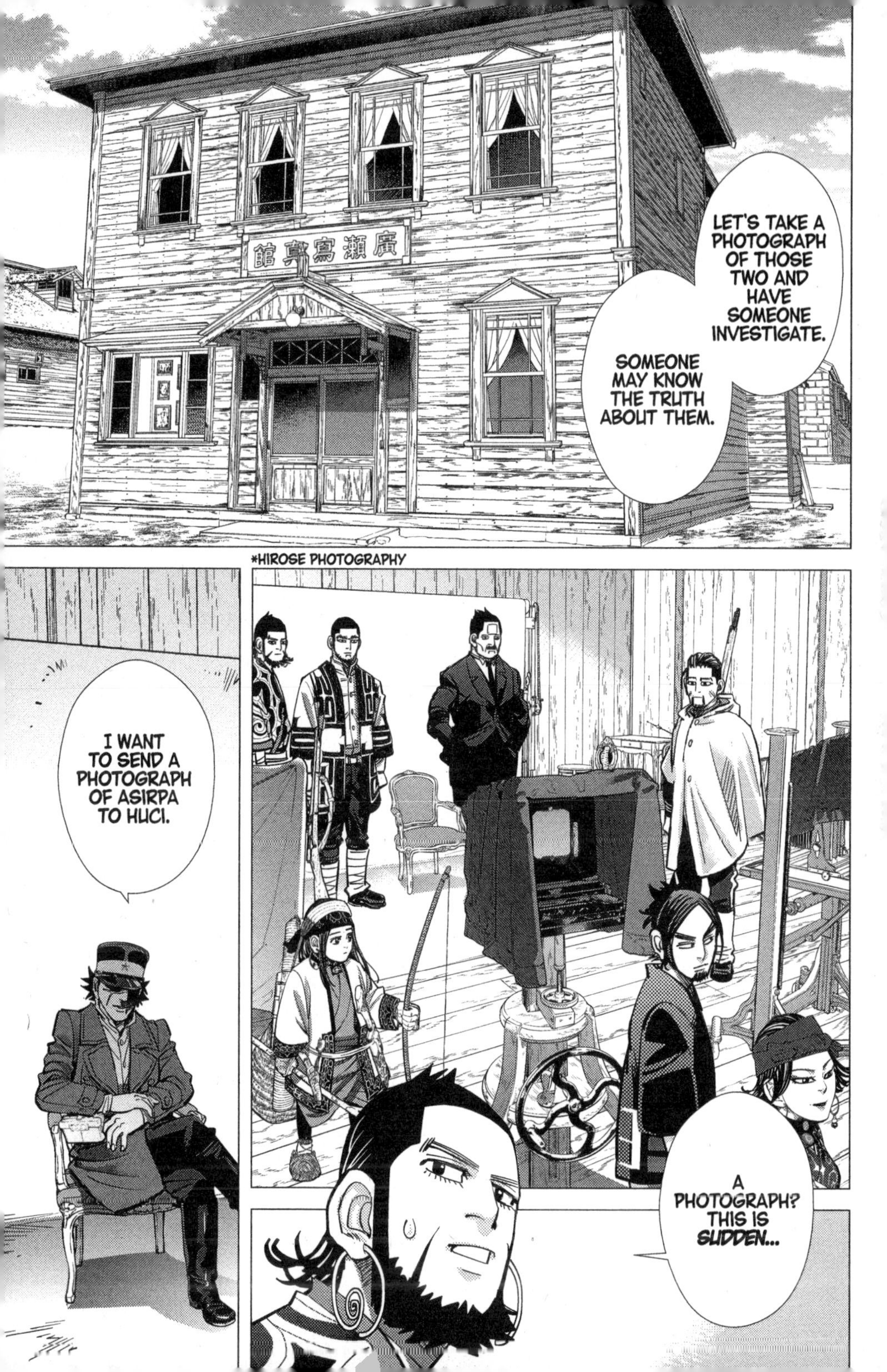
廣瀬寫眞館
LET'S TAKE A PHOTOGRAPH OF THOSE TWO AND HAVE SOMEONE INVESTIGATE.
SOMEONE MAY KNOW THE TRUTH ABOUT THEM.
*HIROSE PHOTOGRAPHY
I WANT TO SEND A PHOTOGRAPH OF ASIRPA TO HUCI.
A PHOTOGRAPH? THIS IS SUDDEN...

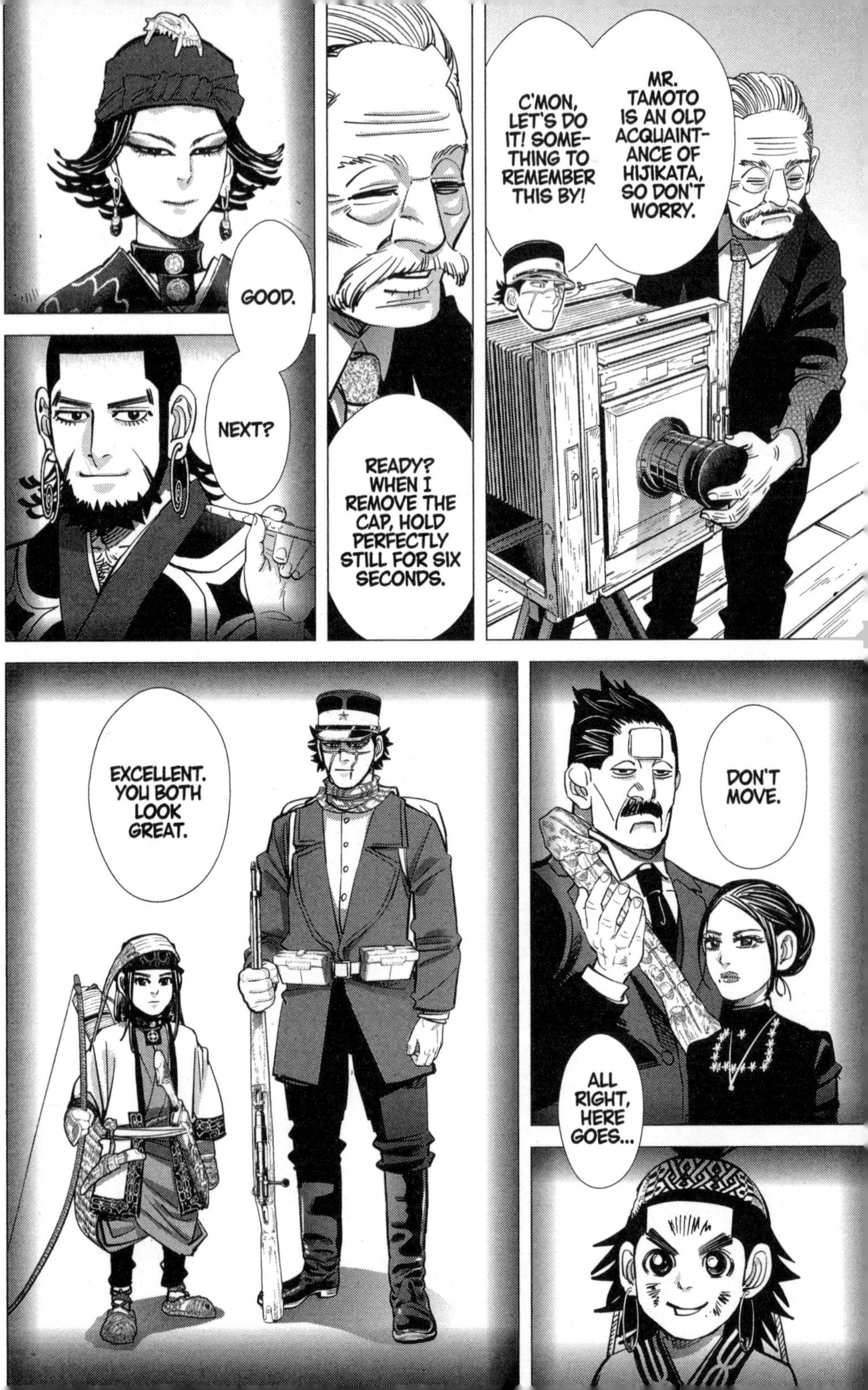
MR. TAMOTO IS AN OLD ACQUAINT-ANCE OF HIJIKATA, SO DON'T WORRY.
C'MON, LET'S DO IT! SOME-THING TO REMEMBER THIS BY!
READY? WHEN I REMOVE THE CAP, HOLD PERFECTLY STILL FOR SIX SECONDS.
GOOD.
NEXT?
DON'T MOVE.
ALL RIGHT, HERE GOES...
EXCELLENT. YOU BOTH LOOK GREAT.

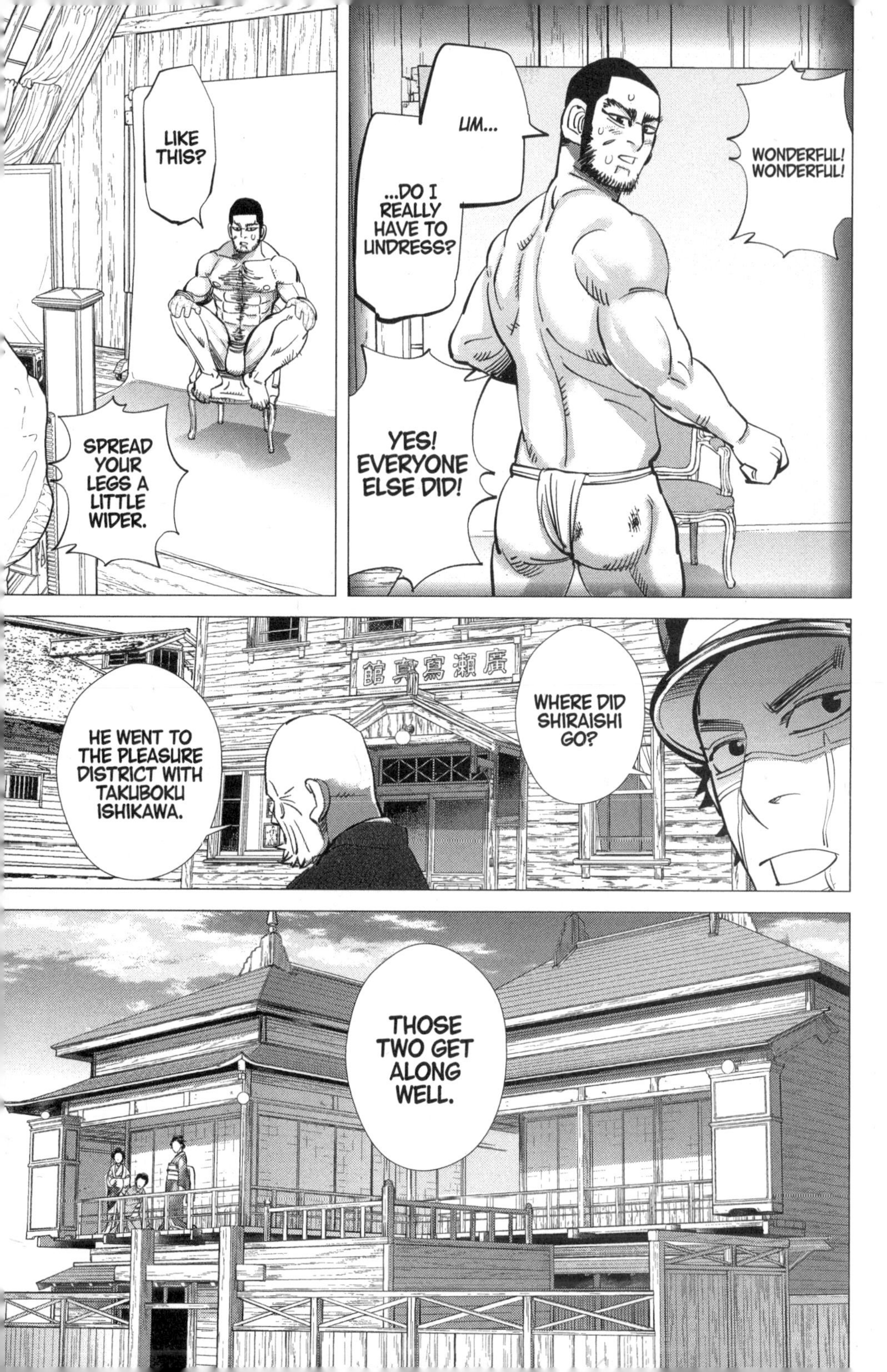
WONDERFUL! WONDERFUL!
UM...
...DO I REALLY HAVE TO UNDRESS?
YES! EVERYONE ELSE DID!
LIKE THIS?
SPREAD YOUR LEGS A LITTLE WIDER.
廣瀨寫真館
WHERE DID SHIRAISHI GO?
HE WENT TO THE PLEASURE DISTRICT WITH TAKUBOKU ISHIKAWA.
THOSE TWO GET ALONG WELL.

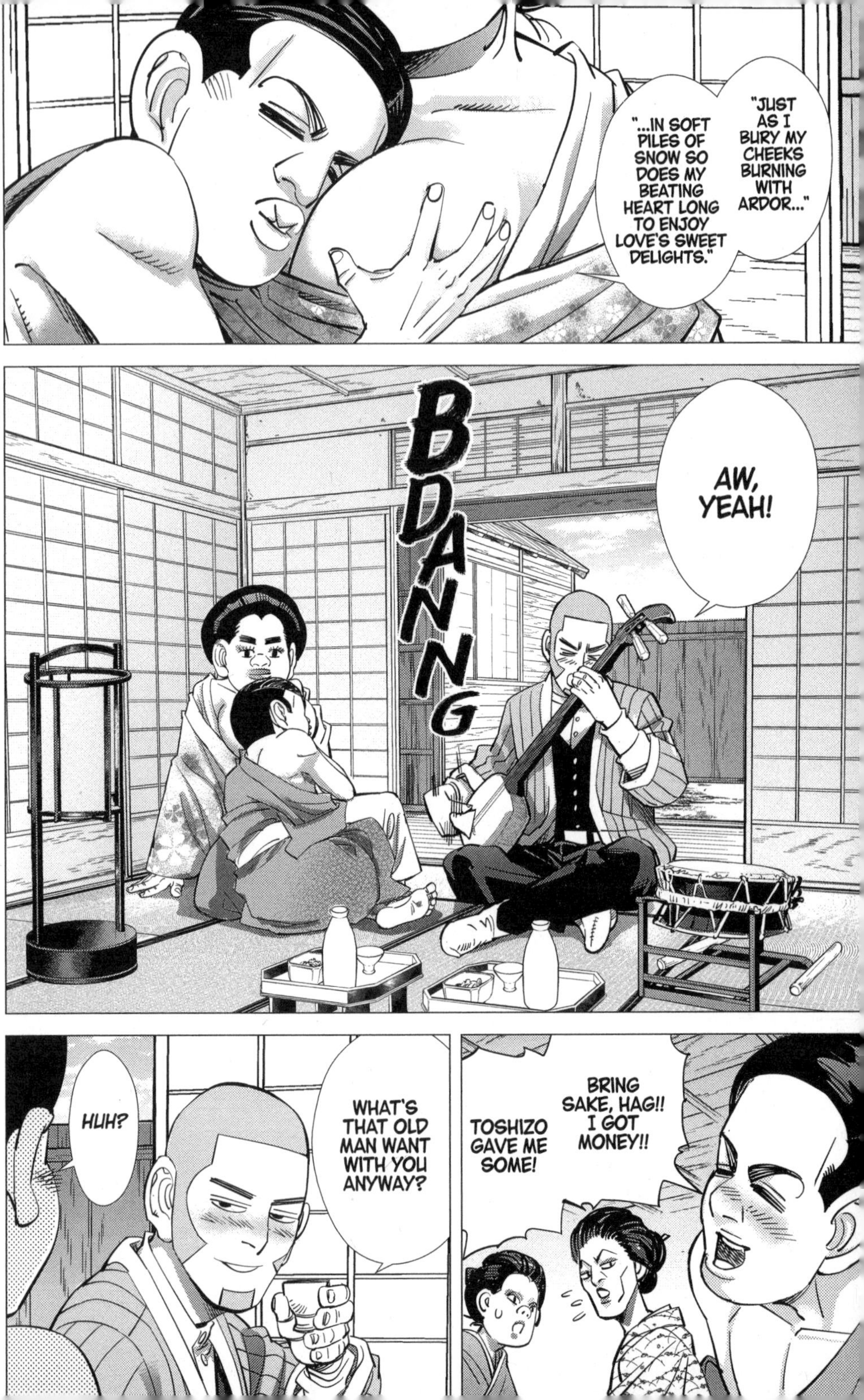
"JUST AS I BURY MY CHEEKS BURNING WITH ARDOR..."
"...IN SOFT PILES OF SNOW SO DOES MY BEATING HEART LONG TO ENJOY LOVE'S SWEET DELIGHTS."
AW, YEAH!
BDANNG
BRING SAKE, HAG!! I GOT MONEY!!
TOSHIZO GAVE ME SOME!
WHAT'S THAT OLD MAN WANT WITH YOU ANYWAY?
HUH?

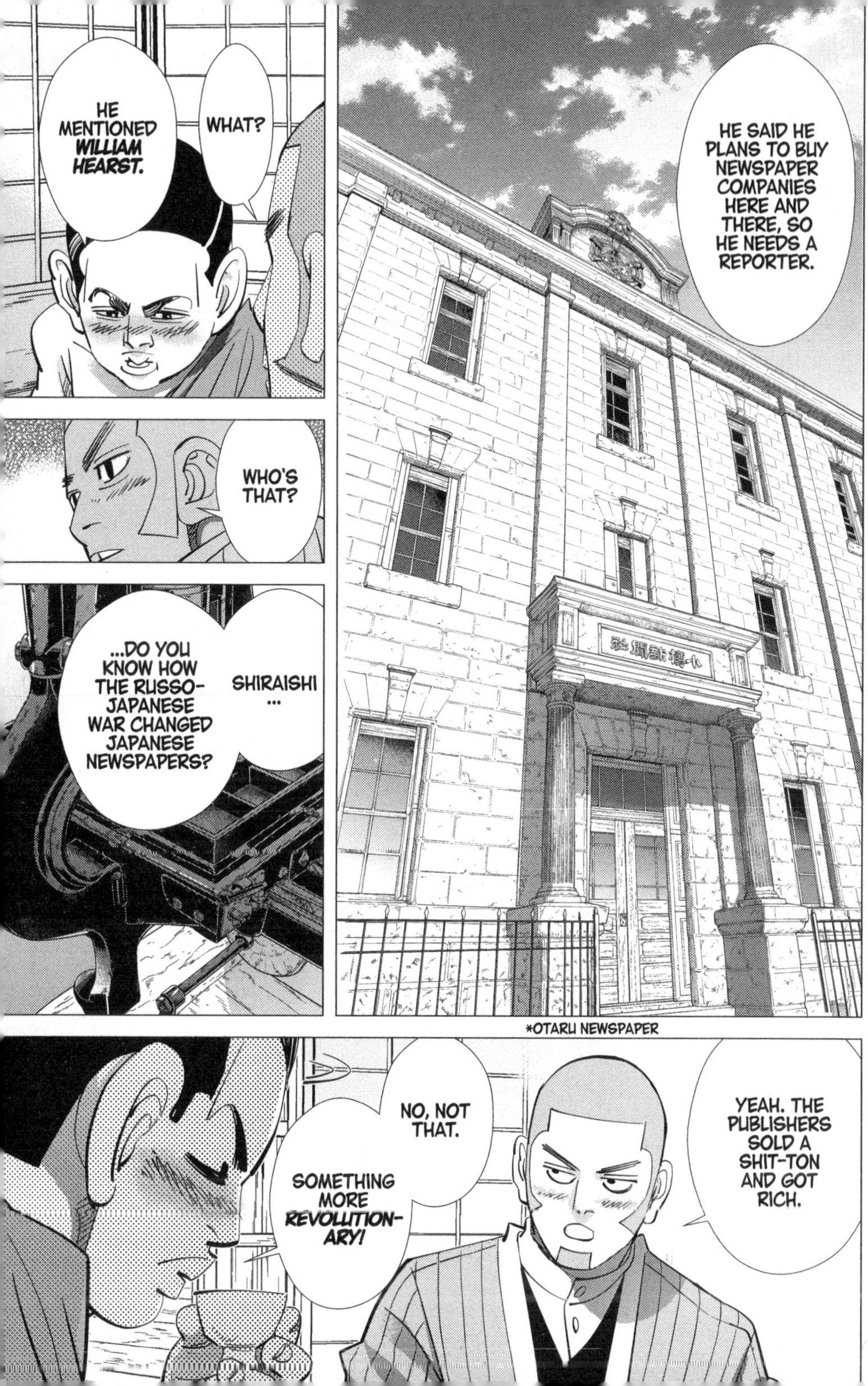
HE SAID HE PLANS TO BUY NEWSPAPER COMPANIES HERE AND THERE, SO HE NEEDS A REPORTER.
小樽新聞社
*OTARU NEWSPAPER
WHAT?
HE MENTIONED WILLIAM HEARST.
WHO'S THAT?
SHIRAISHI...
...DO YOU KNOW HOW THE RUSSO-JAPANESE WAR CHANGED JAPANESE NEWSPAPERS?
YEAH. THE PUBLISHERS SOLD A SHIT-TON AND GOT RICH.
NO, NOT THAT.
SOMETHING MORE REVOLUTIONARY!

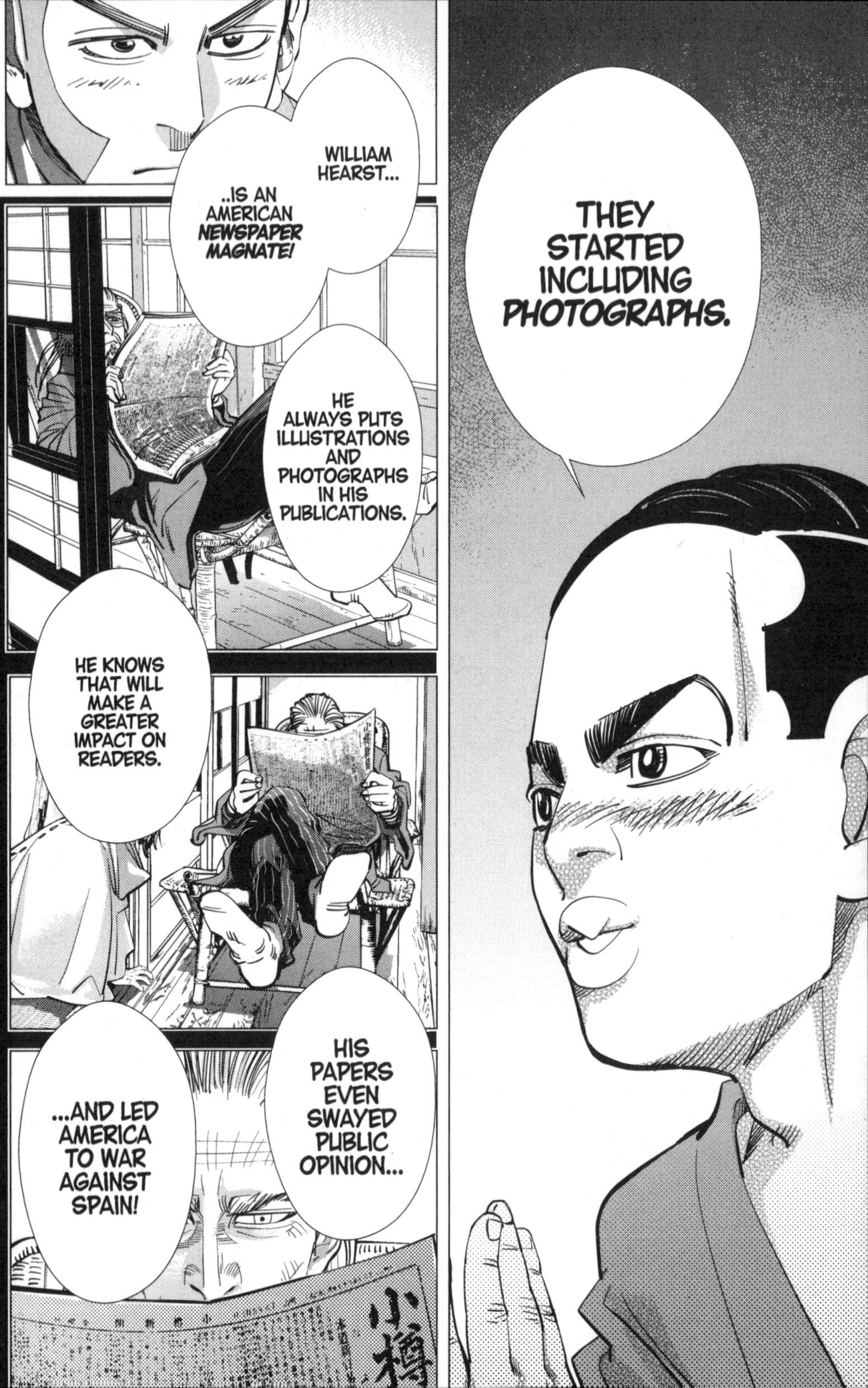
THEY STARTED INCLUDING PHOTOGRAPHS.
WILLIAM HEARST...
..IS AN AMERICAN NEWSPAPER MAGNATE!
HE ALWAYS PUTS ILLUSTRATIONS AND PHOTOGRAPHS IN HIS PUBLICATIONS.
HE KNOWS THAT WILL MAKE A GREATER IMPACT ON READERS.
HIS PAPERS EVEN SWAYED PUBLIC OPINION...
...AND LED AMERICA TO WAR AGAINST SPAIN!
小樽

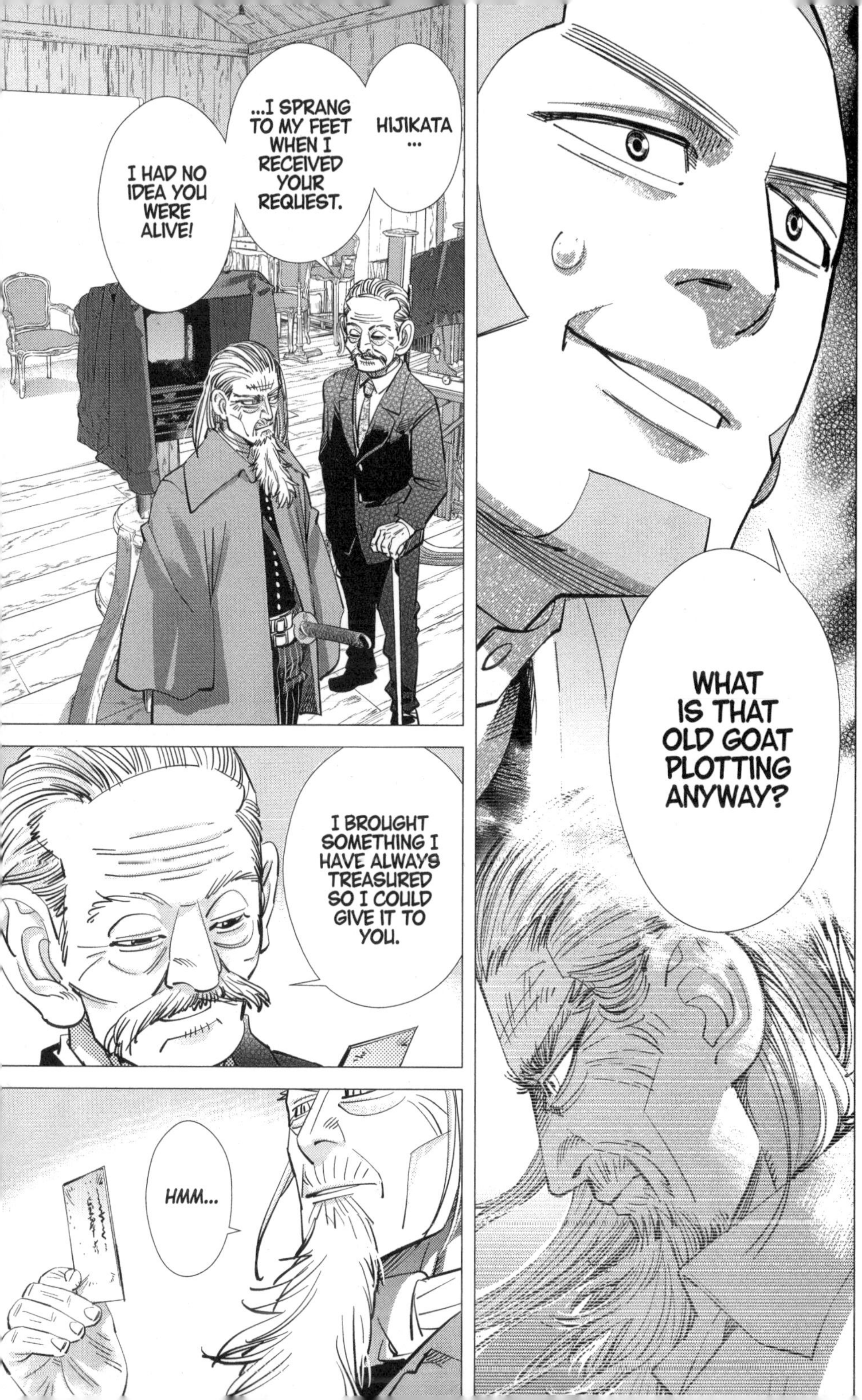
WHAT IS THAT OLD GOAT PLOTTING ANYWAY?
HIJIKATA...
...I SPRANG TO MY FEET WHEN I RECEIVED YOUR REQUEST.
I HAD NO IDEA YOU WERE ALIVE!
I BROUGHT SOMETHING I HAVE ALWAYS TREASURED SO I COULD GIVE IT TO YOU.
HMM...

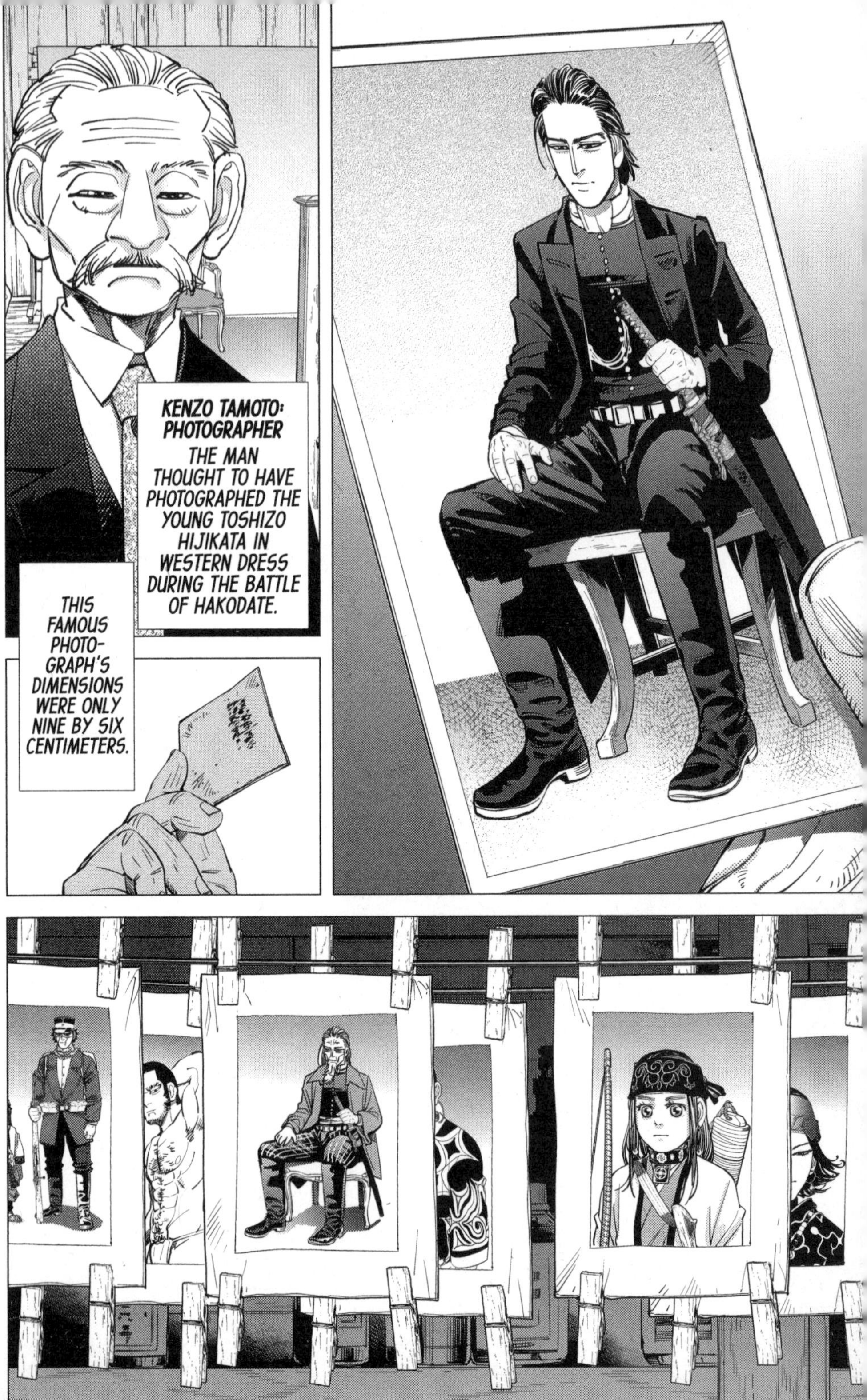
KENZO TAMOTO: PHOTOGRAPHER
THE MAN THOUGHT TO HAVE PHOTOGRAPHED THE YOUNG TOSHIZO HIJIKATA IN WESTERN DRESS DURING THE BATTLE OF HAKODATE.
THIS FAMOUS PHOTO-GRAPH'S DIMENSIONS WERE ONLY NINE BY SIX CENTIMETERS.

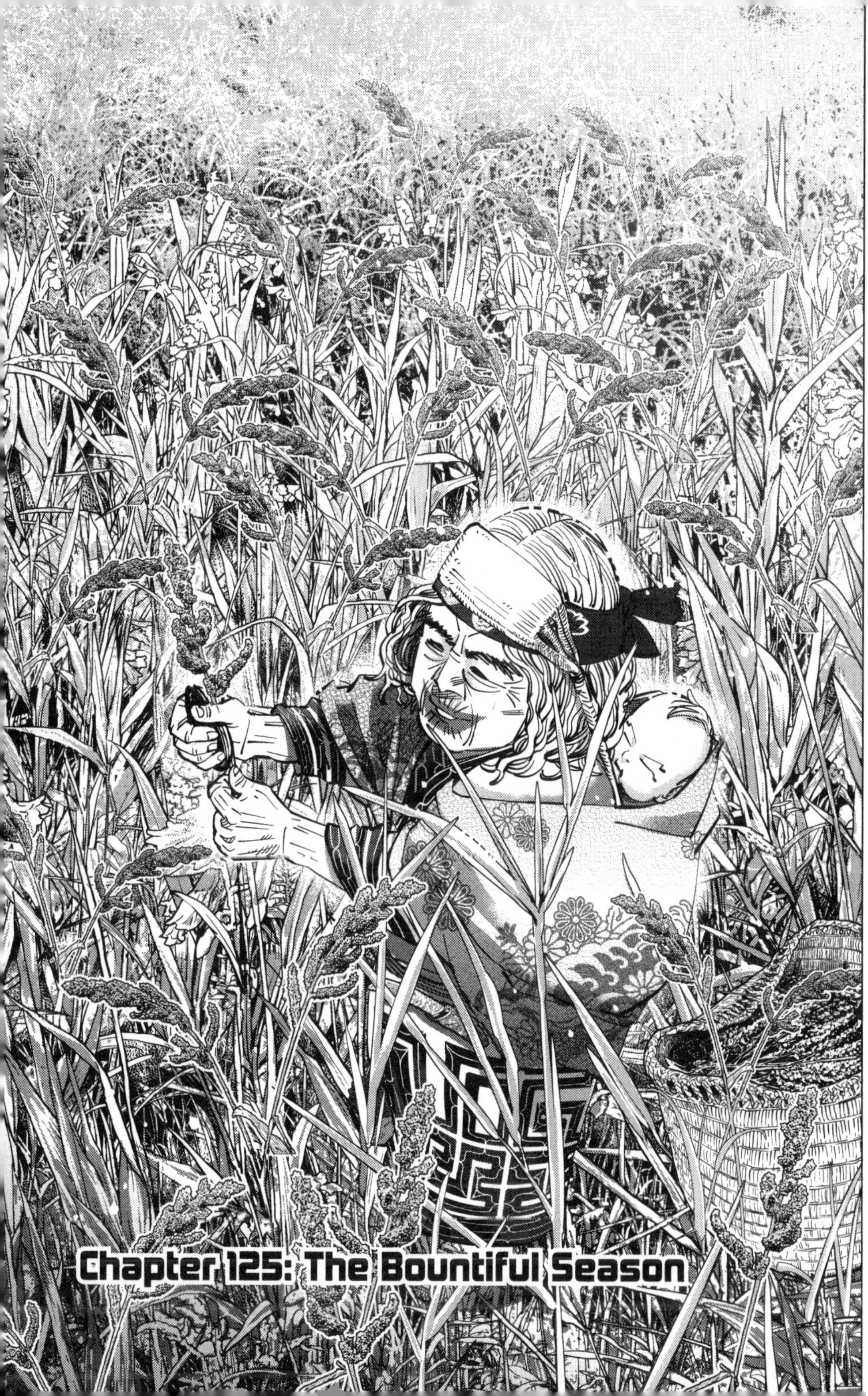
Chapter 125: The Bountiful Season

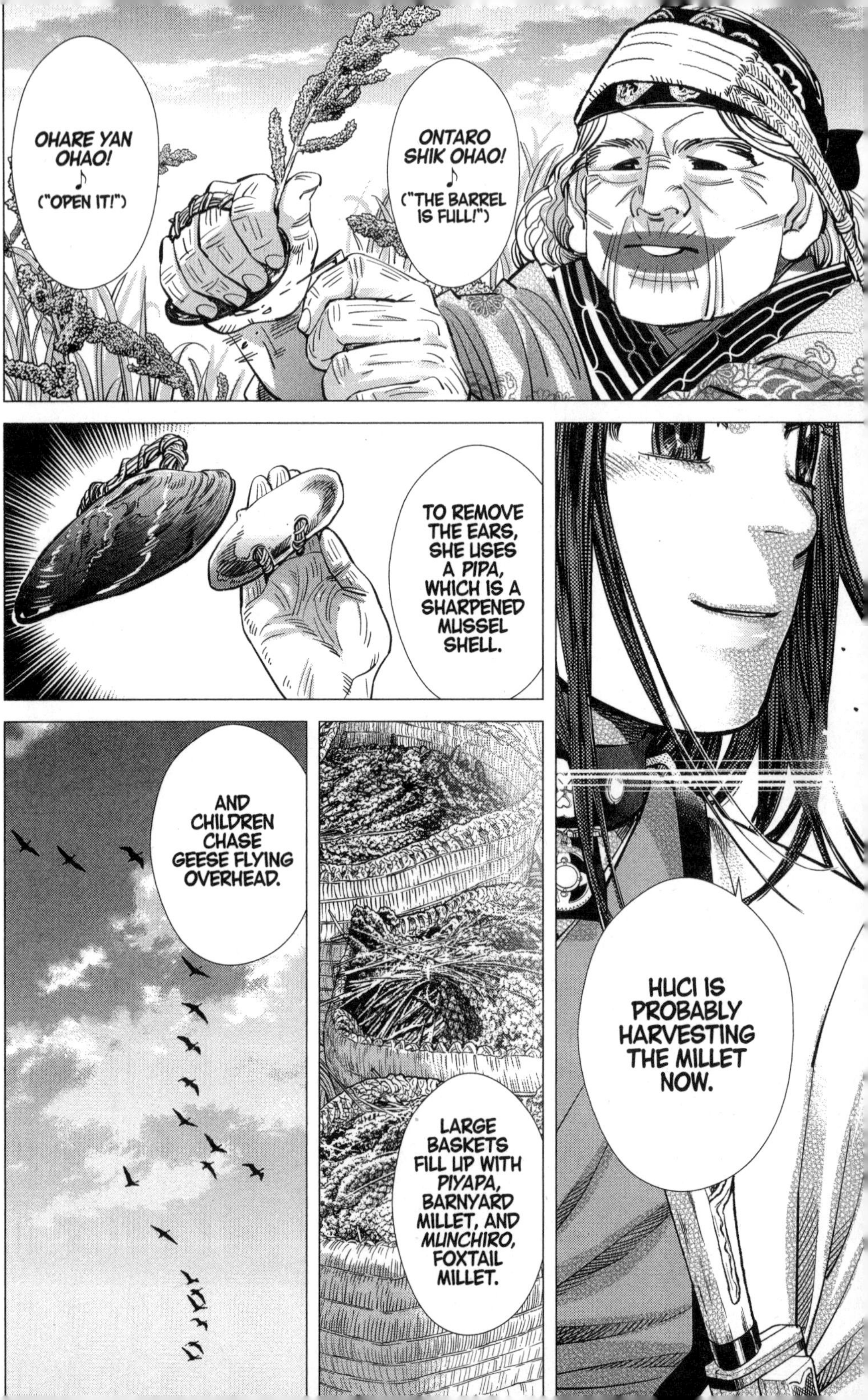
ONTARO SHIK OHAO! ♪ ("THE BARREL IS FULL!")
OHARE YAN OHAO! ♪ ("OPEN IT!")
HUCI IS PROBABLY HARVESTING THE MILLET NOW.
TO REMOVE THE EARS, SHE USES A PIPA, WHICH IS A SHARPENED MUSSEL SHELL.
LARGE BASKETS FILL UP WITH PIYAPA, BARNYARD MILLET, AND MUNCHIRO, FOXTAIL MILLET.
AND CHILDREN CHASE GEESE FLYING OVERHEAD.

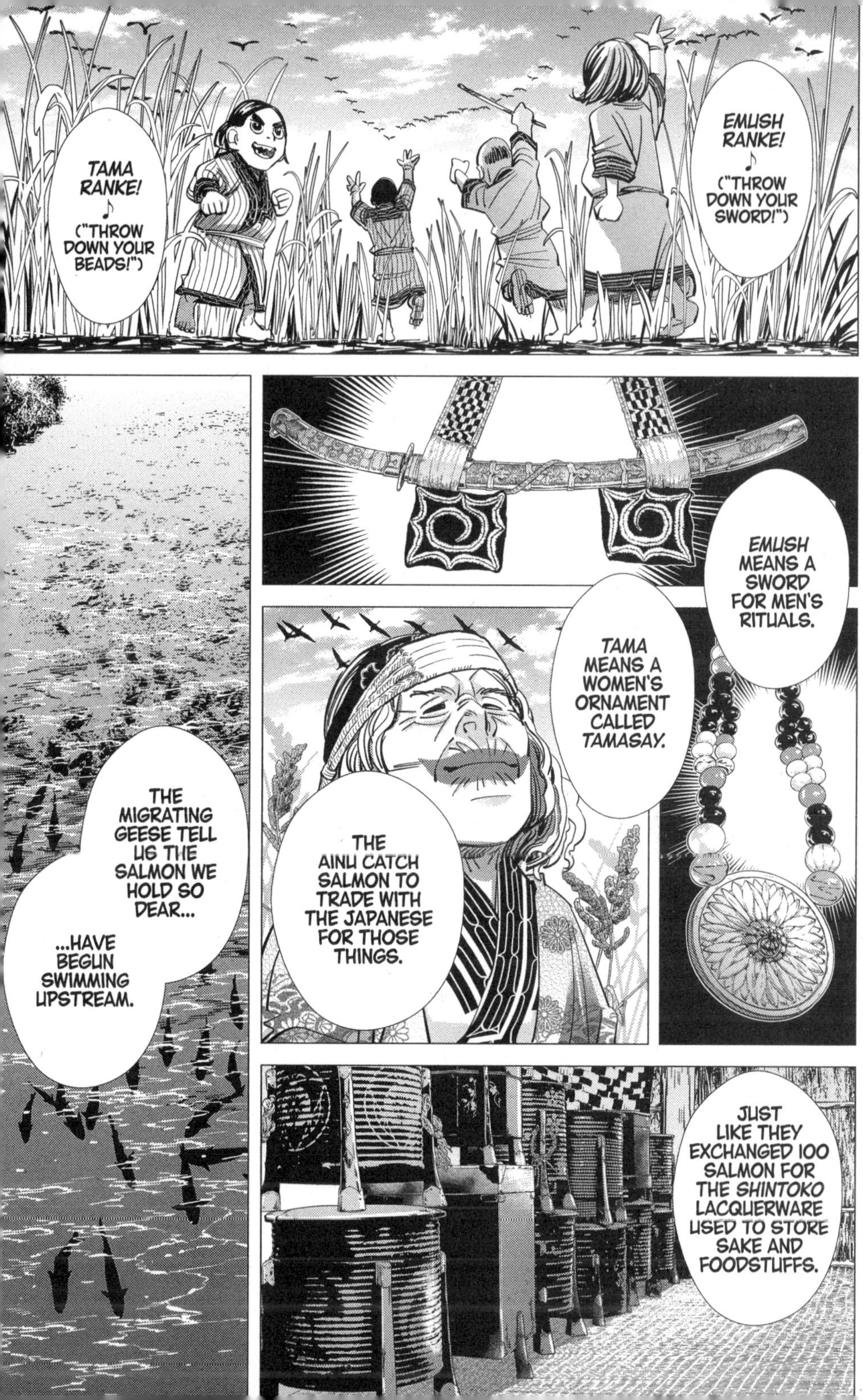
EMUSH RANKE! ♪
("THROW DOWN YOUR SWORD!")
TAMA RANKE! ♪
("THROW DOWN YOUR BEADS!")
EMUSH MEANS A SWORD FOR MEN'S RITUALS.
TAMA MEANS A WOMEN'S ORNAMENT CALLED TAMASAY.
THE AINU CATCH SALMON TO TRADE WITH THE JAPANESE FOR THOSE THINGS.
JUST LIKE THEY EXCHANGED 100 SALMON FOR THE SHINTOKO LACQUERWARE USED TO STORE SAKE AND FOODSTUFFS.
THE MIGRATING GEESE TELL US THE SALMON WE HOLD SO DEAR...
...HAVE BEGUN SWIMMING UPSTREAM.

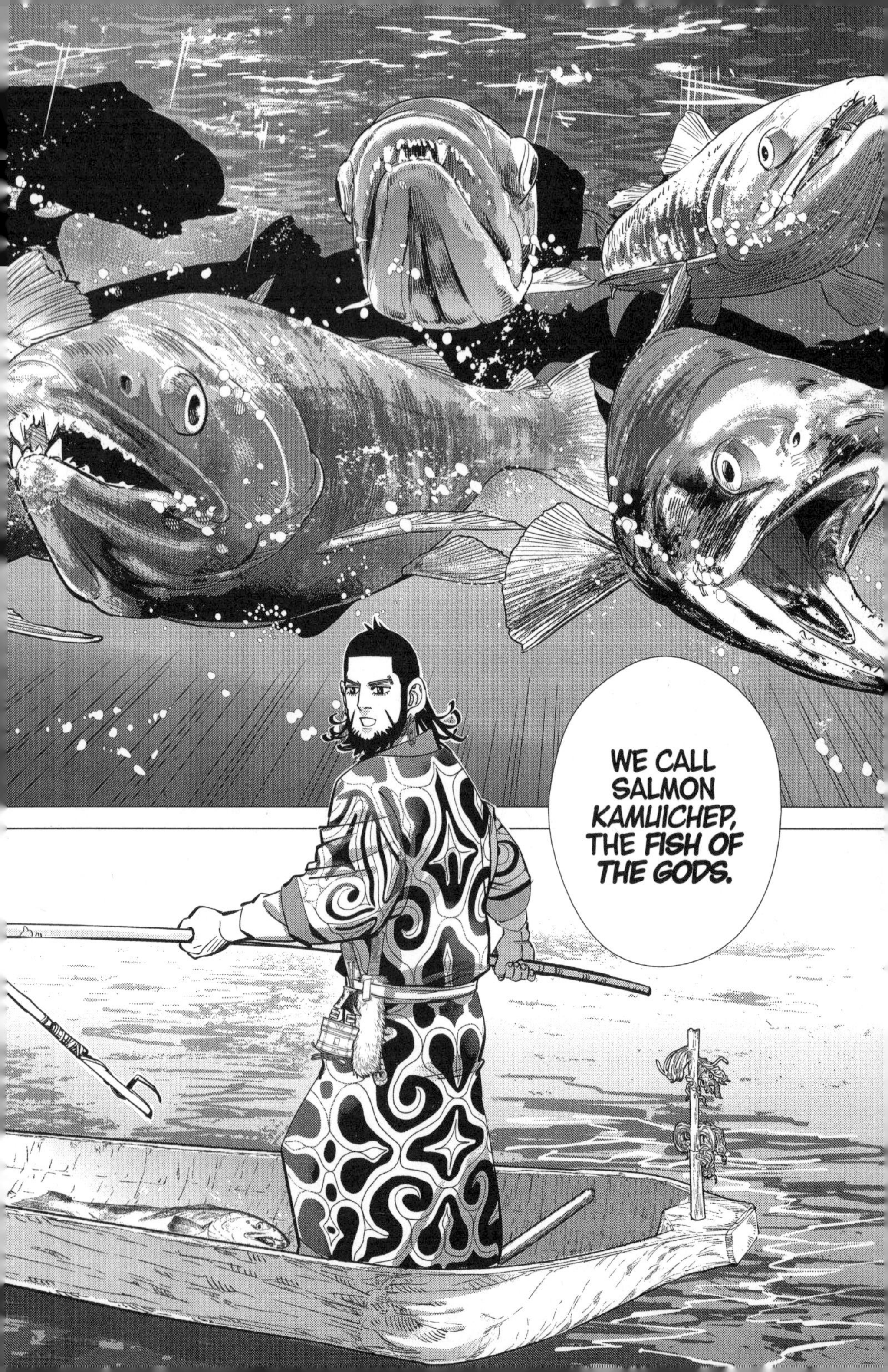
WE CALL SALMON KAMUICHEP, THE FISH OF THE GODS.

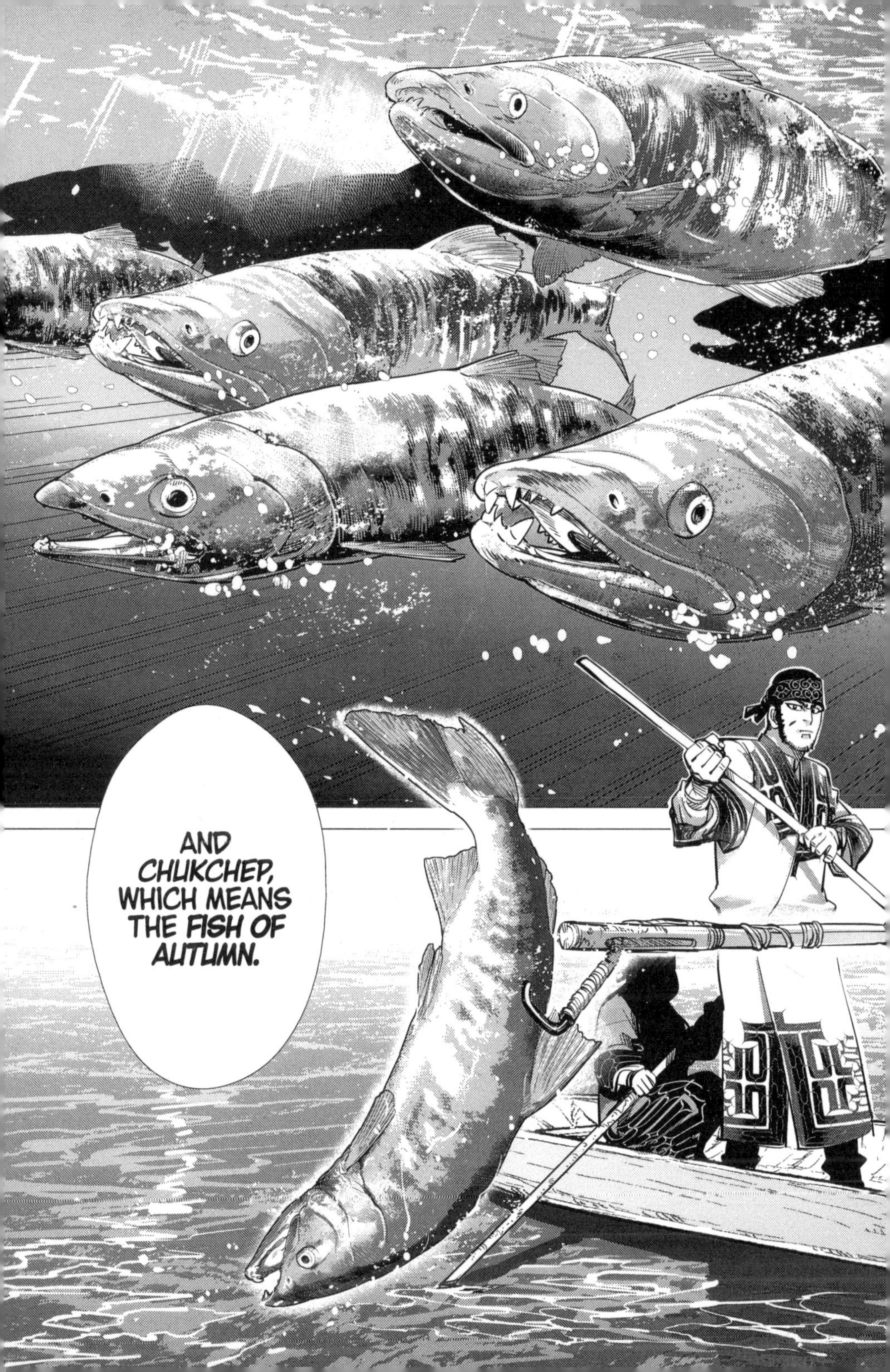
AND CHUKCHEP, WHICH MEANS THE FISH OF AUTUMN.

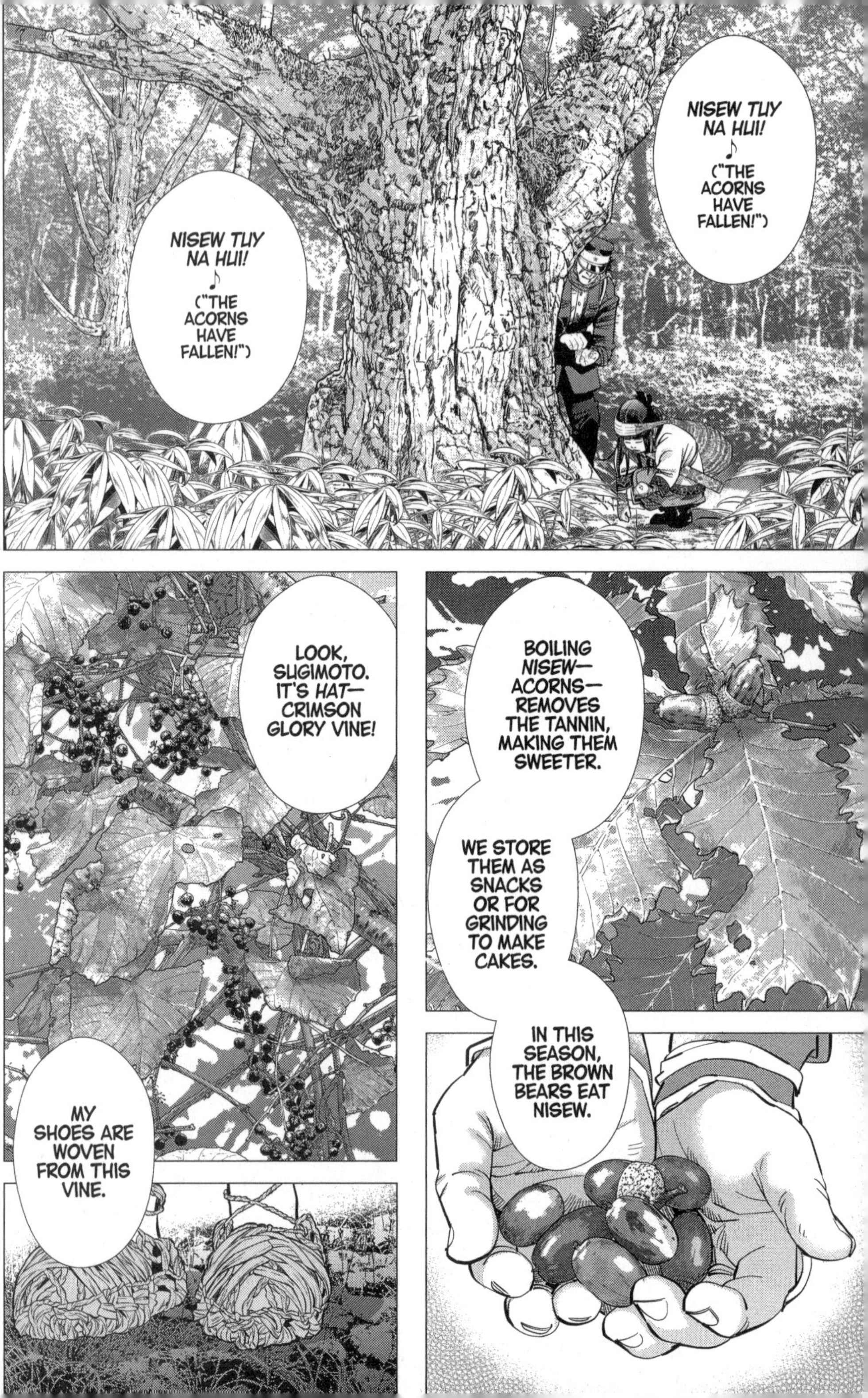
NISEW TUY NA HUI! ♪ ("THE ACORNS HAVE FALLEN!")
NISEW TUY NA HUI! ♪ ("THE ACORNS HAVE FALLEN!")
BOILING NISEW—ACORNS—REMOVES THE TANNIN, MAKING THEM SWEETER.
WE STORE THEM AS SNACKS OR FOR GRINDING TO MAKE CAKES.
LOOK, SUGIMOTO. IT'S HAT—CRIMSON GLORY VINE!
IN THIS SEASON, THE BROWN BEARS EAT NISEW.
MY SHOES ARE WOVEN FROM THIS VINE.

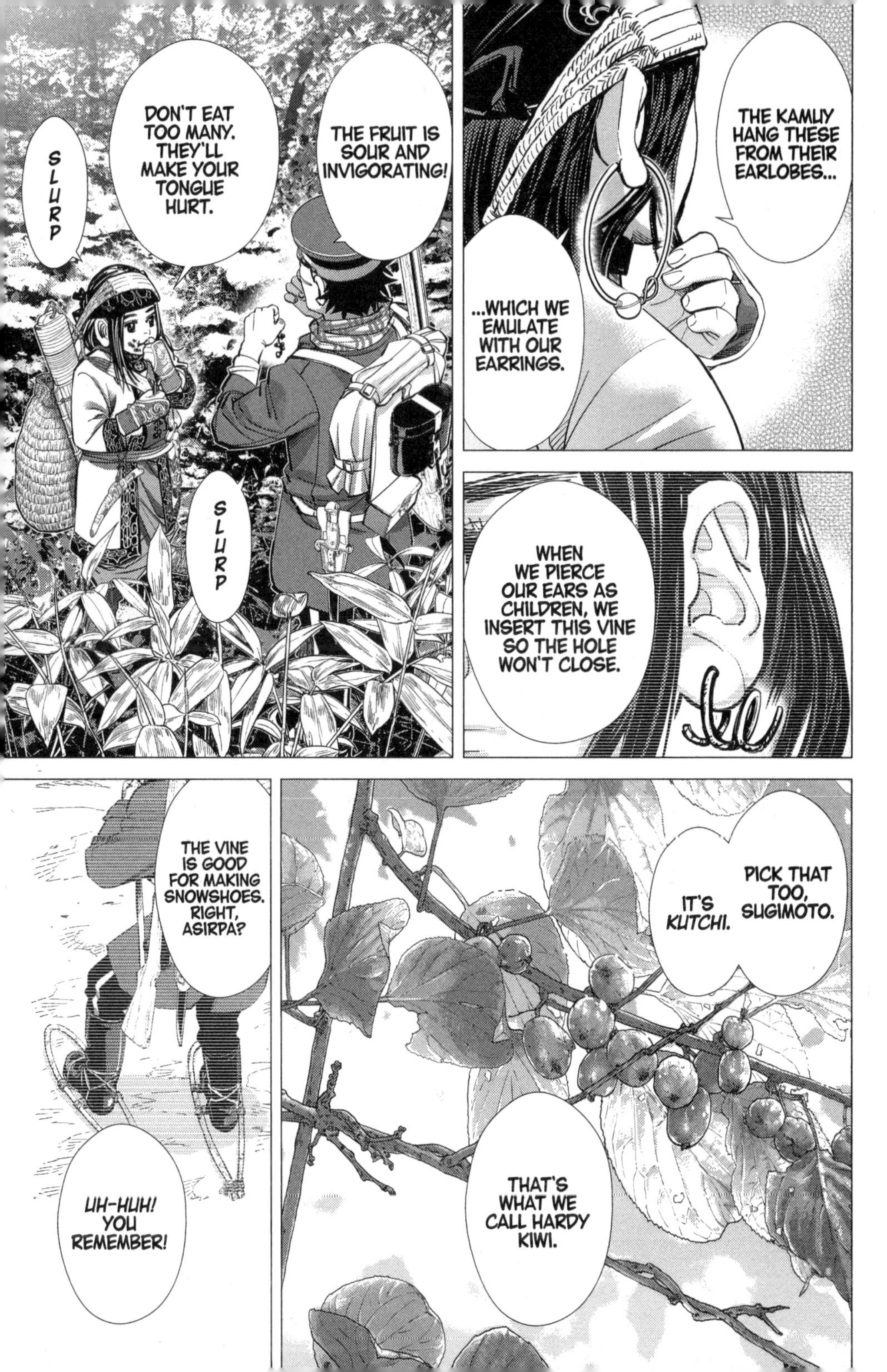
THE KAMUY HANG THESE FROM THEIR EARLOBES...
...WHICH WE EMULATE WITH OUR EARRINGS.
WHEN WE PIERCE OUR EARS AS CHILDREN, WE INSERT THIS VINE SO THE HOLE WON'T CLOSE.
THE FRUIT IS SOUR AND INVIGORATING!
DON'T EAT TOO MANY. THEY'LL MAKE YOUR TONGUE HURT.
SLURP
SLURP
PICK THAT TOO, SUGIMOTO.
IT'S KUTCHI.
THAT'S WHAT WE CALL HARDY KIWI.
THE VINE IS GOOD FOR MAKING SNOWSHOES. RIGHT, ASIRPA?
UH-HUH! YOU REMEMBER!

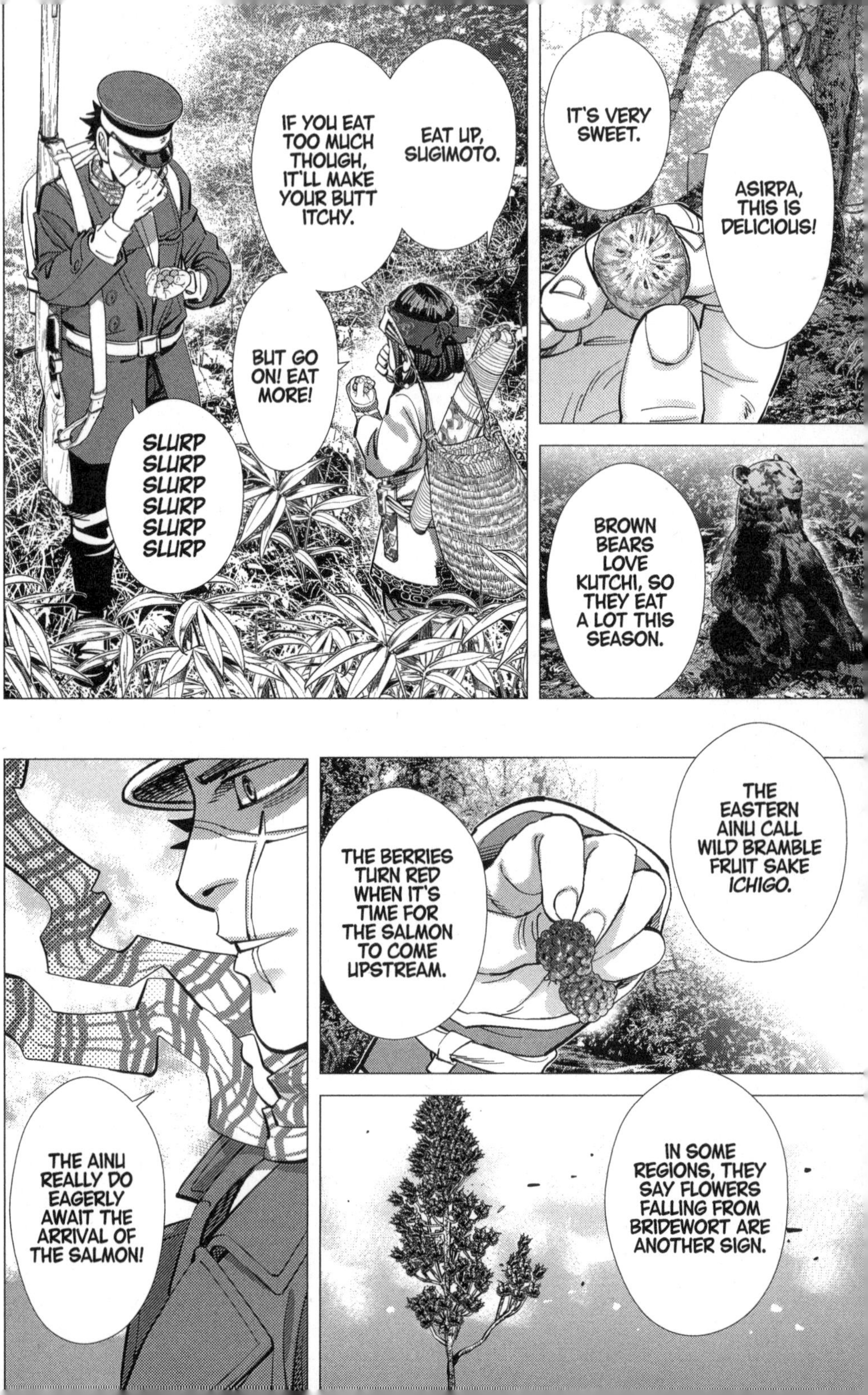
ASIRPA, THIS IS DELICIOUS!
IT'S VERY SWEET.
BROWN BEARS LOVE KUTCHI, SO THEY EAT A LOT THIS SEASON.
EAT UP, SUGIMOTO.
IF YOU EAT TOO MUCH THOUGH, IT'LL MAKE YOUR BUTT ITCHY.
BUT GO ON! EAT MORE!
SLURP SLURP SLURP SLURP SLURP SLURP
THE EASTERN AINU CALL WILD BRAMBLE FRUIT SAKE *ICHIGO*.
THE BERRIES TURN RED WHEN IT'S TIME FOR THE SALMON TO COME UPSTREAM.
IN SOME REGIONS, THEY SAY FLOWERS FALLING FROM BRIDEWORT ARE ANOTHER SIGN.
THE AINU REALLY DO EAGERLY AWAIT THE ARRIVAL OF THE SALMON!

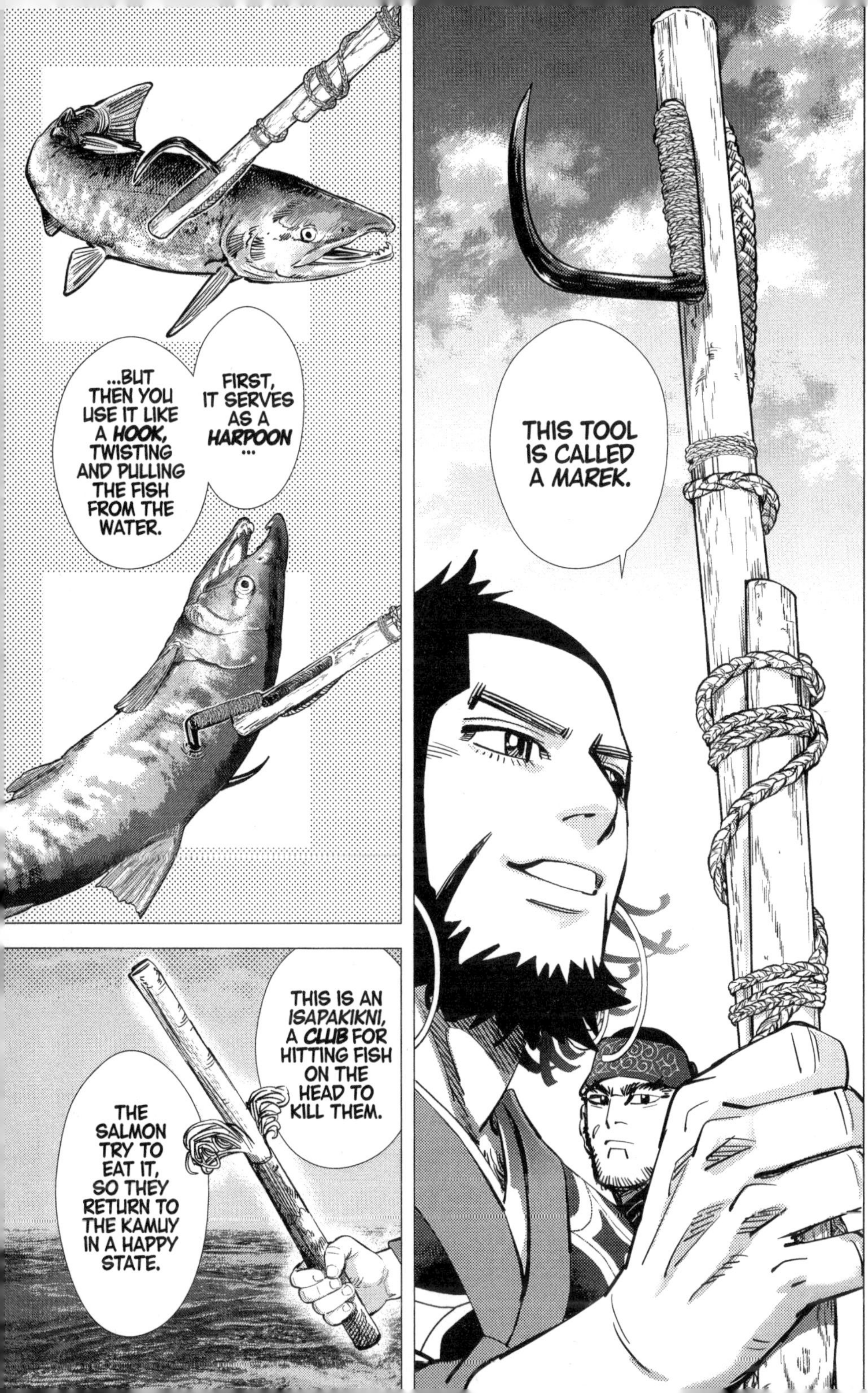
THIS TOOL IS CALLED A *MAREK*.
FIRST, IT SERVES AS A ***HARPOON***...
...BUT THEN YOU USE IT LIKE A ***HOOK***, TWISTING AND PULLING THE FISH FROM THE WATER.
THIS IS AN *ISAPAKIKNI*, A ***CLUB*** FOR HITTING FISH ON THE HEAD TO KILL THEM.
THE SALMON TRY TO EAT IT, SO THEY RETURN TO THE KAMUY IN A HAPPY STATE.

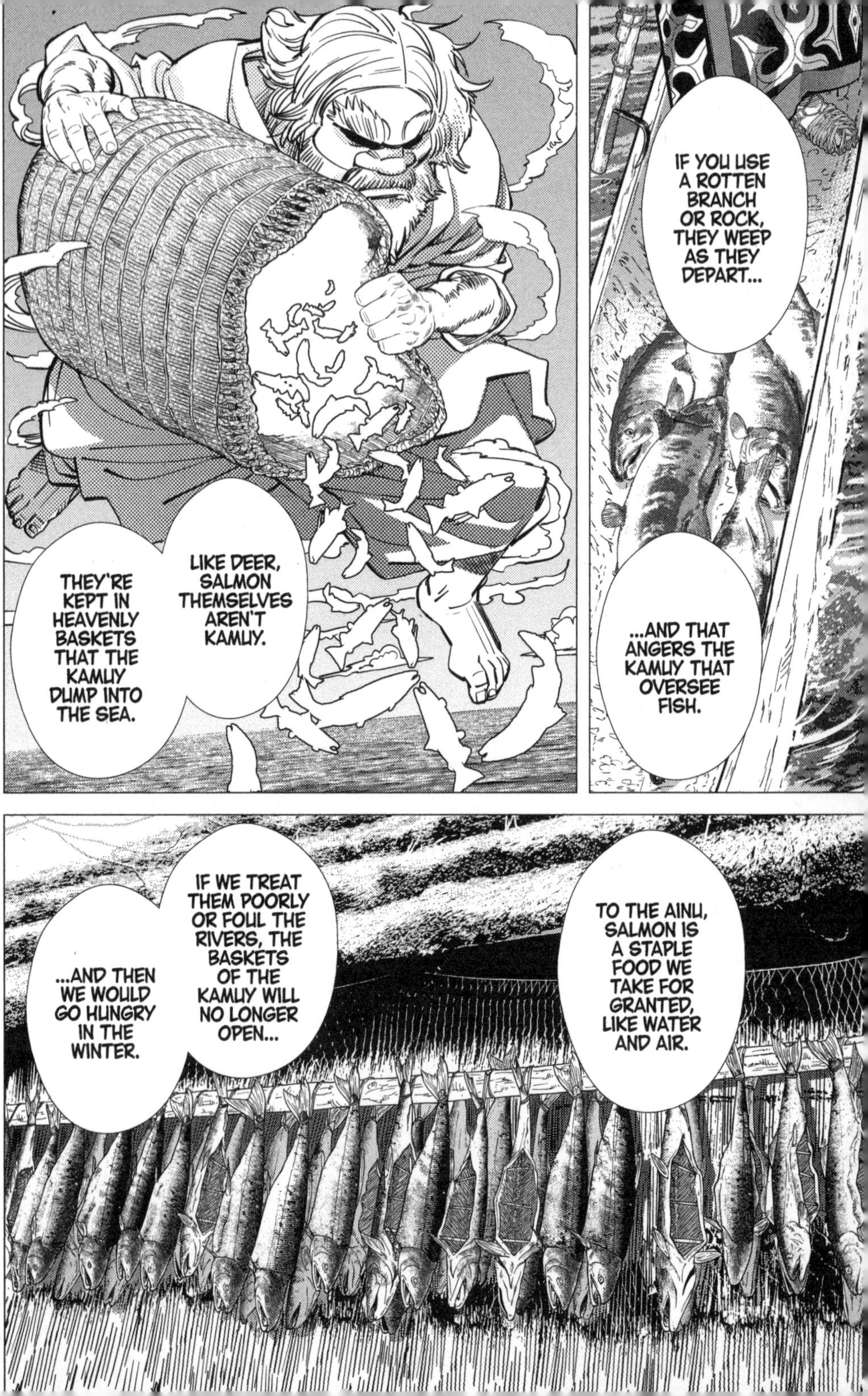
IF YOU USE A ROTTEN BRANCH OR ROCK, THEY WEEP AS THEY DEPART...
...AND THAT ANGERS THE KAMUY THAT OVERSEE FISH.
LIKE DEER, SALMON THEMSELVES AREN'T KAMUY.
THEY'RE KEPT IN HEAVENLY BASKETS THAT THE KAMUY DUMP INTO THE SEA.
TO THE AINU, SALMON IS A STAPLE FOOD WE TAKE FOR GRANTED, LIKE WATER AND AIR.
IF WE TREAT THEM POORLY OR FOUL THE RIVERS, THE BASKETS OF THE KAMUY WILL NO LONGER OPEN...
...AND THEN WE WOULD GO HUNGRY IN THE WINTER.

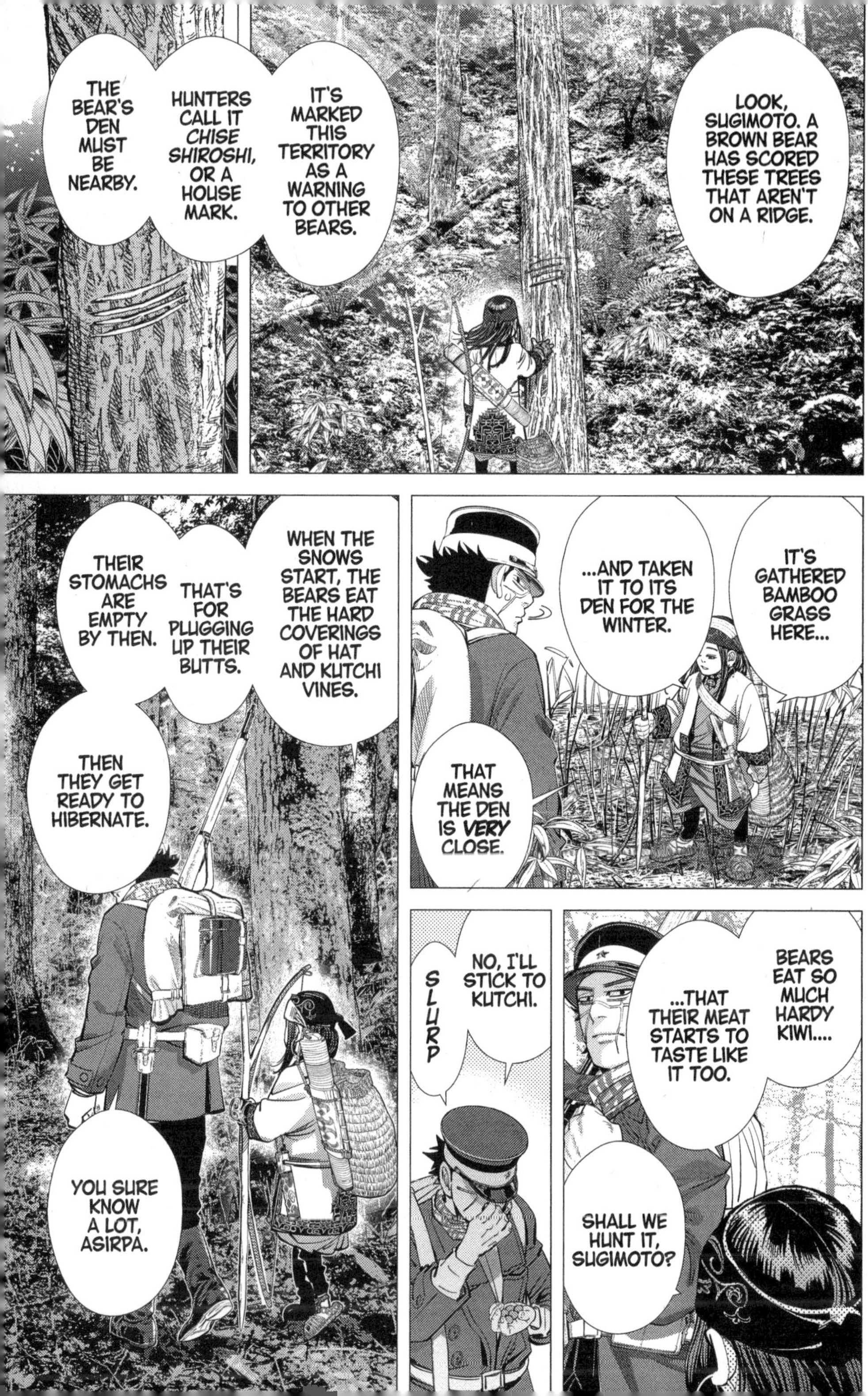
LOOK, SUGIMOTO. A BROWN BEAR HAS SCORED THESE TREES THAT AREN'T ON A RIDGE.
IT'S MARKED THIS TERRITORY AS A WARNING TO OTHER BEARS.
HUNTERS CALL IT CHISE SHIROSHI, OR A HOUSE MARK.
THE BEAR'S DEN MUST BE NEARBY.
IT'S GATHERED BAMBOO GRASS HERE...
...AND TAKEN IT TO ITS DEN FOR THE WINTER.
THAT MEANS THE DEN IS *VERY* CLOSE.
BEARS EAT SO MUCH HARDY KIWI....
...THAT THEIR MEAT STARTS TO TASTE LIKE IT TOO.
SHALL WE HUNT IT, SUGIMOTO?
NO, I'LL STICK TO KUTCHI.
SLURP
WHEN THE SNOWS START, THE BEARS EAT THE HARD COVERINGS OF HAT AND KUTCHI VINES.
THAT'S FOR PLUGGING UP THEIR BUTTS.
THEIR STOMACHS ARE EMPTY BY THEN.
THEN THEY GET READY TO HIBERNATE.
YOU SURE KNOW A LOT, ASIRPA.

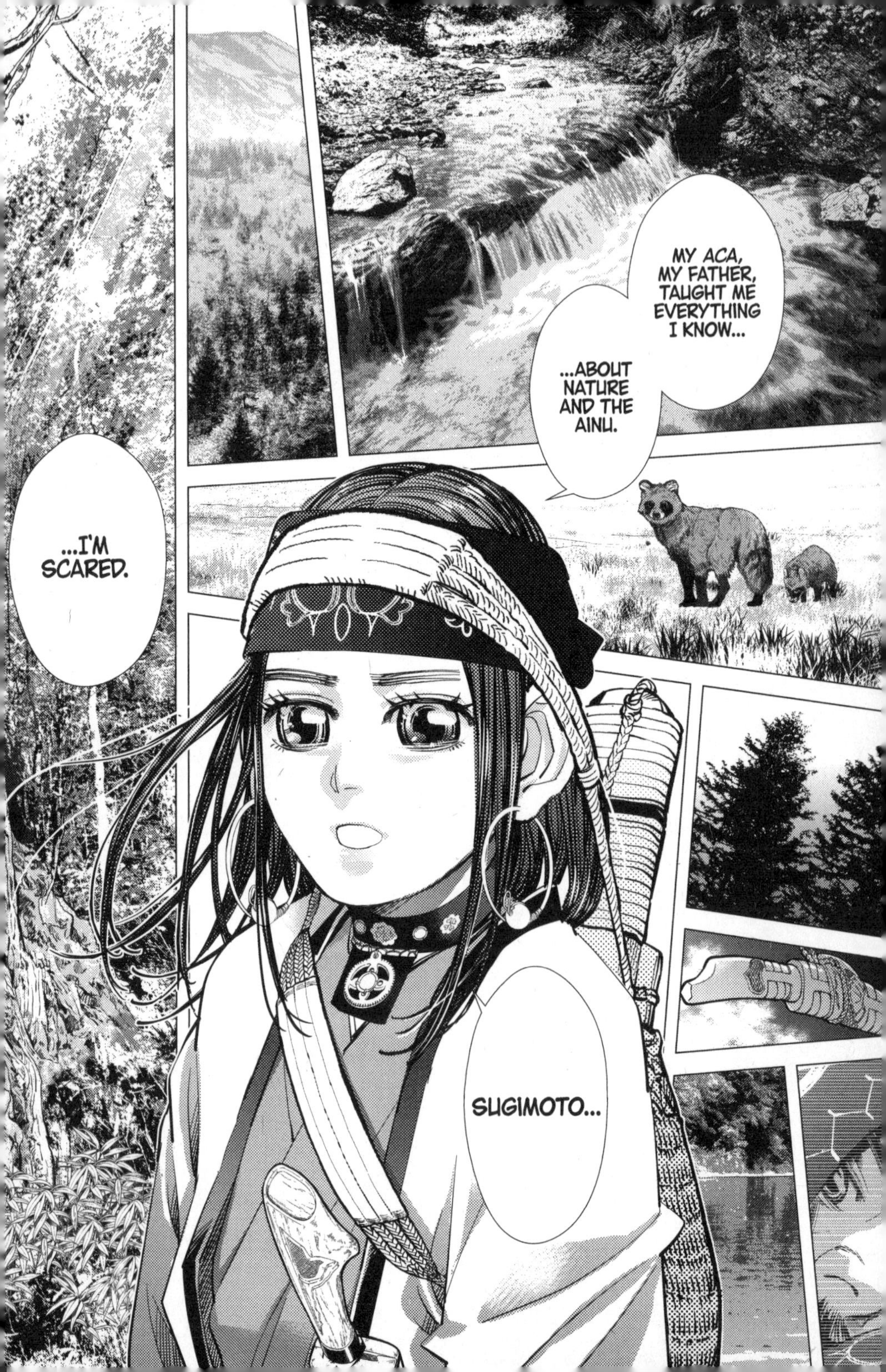
MY ACA, MY FATHER, TAUGHT ME EVERYTHING I KNOW...
...ABOUT NATURE AND THE AINU.
SUGIMOTO...
...I'M SCARED.

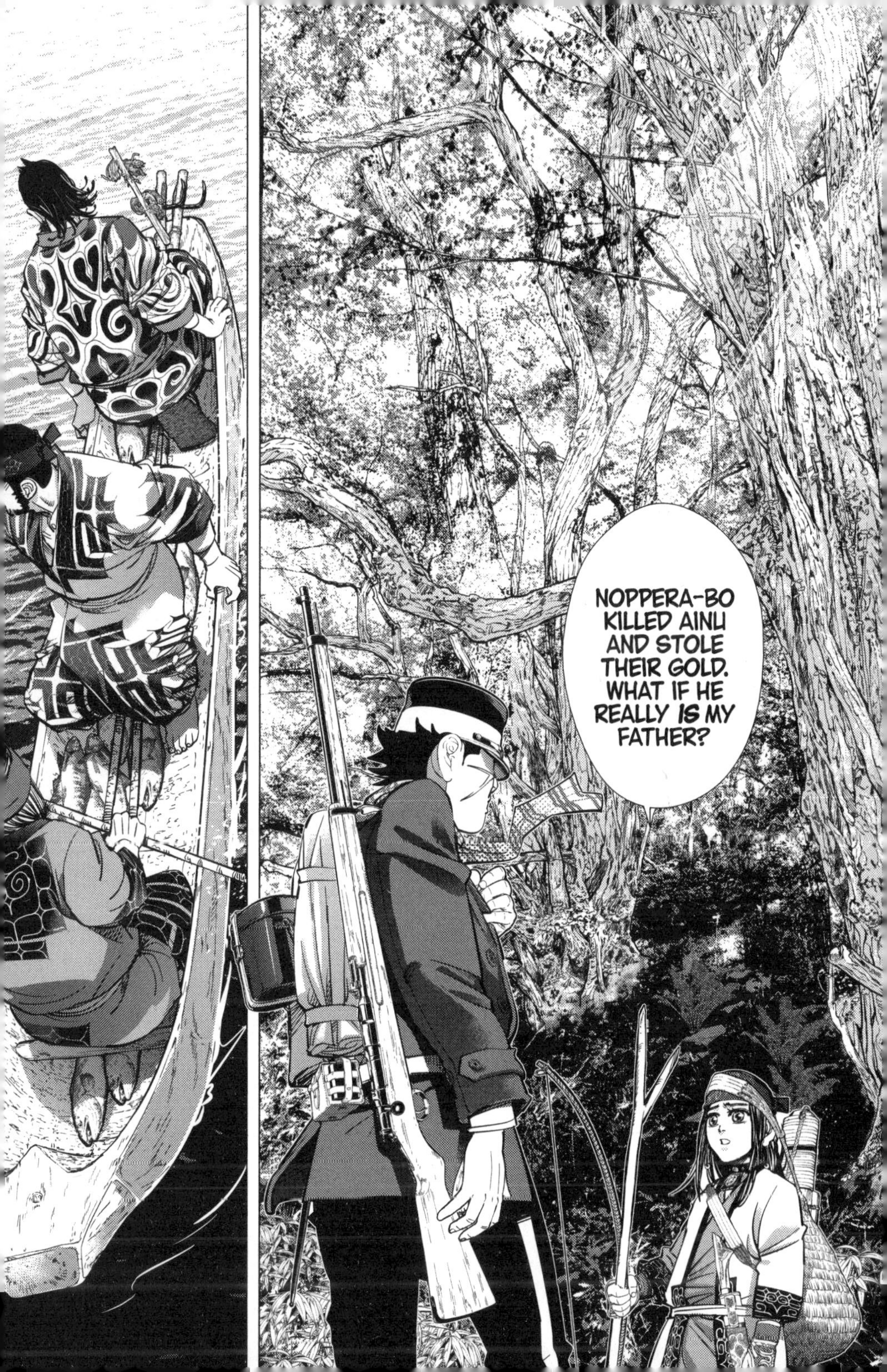
NOPPERA-BO KILLED AINU AND STOLE THEIR GOLD. WHAT IF HE REALLY IS MY FATHER?

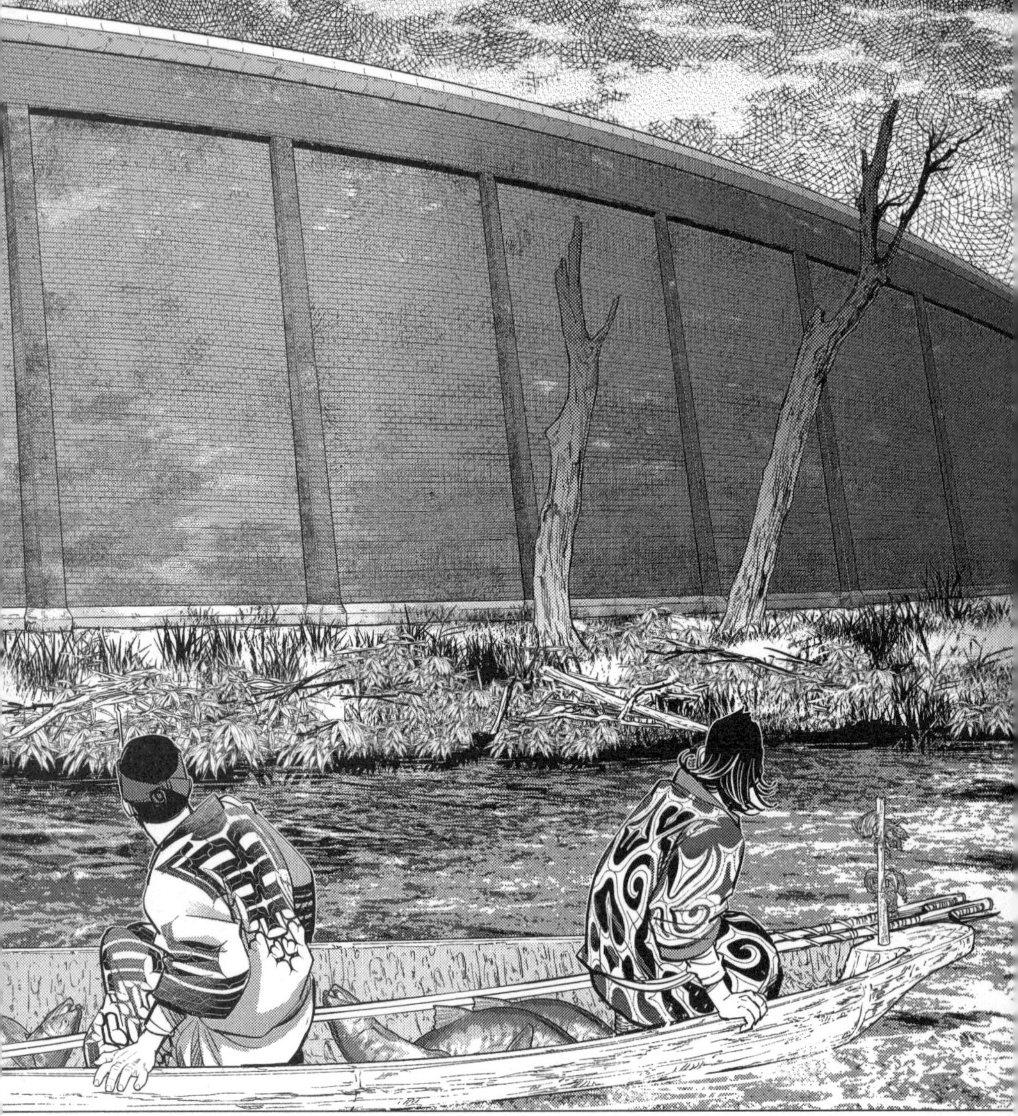
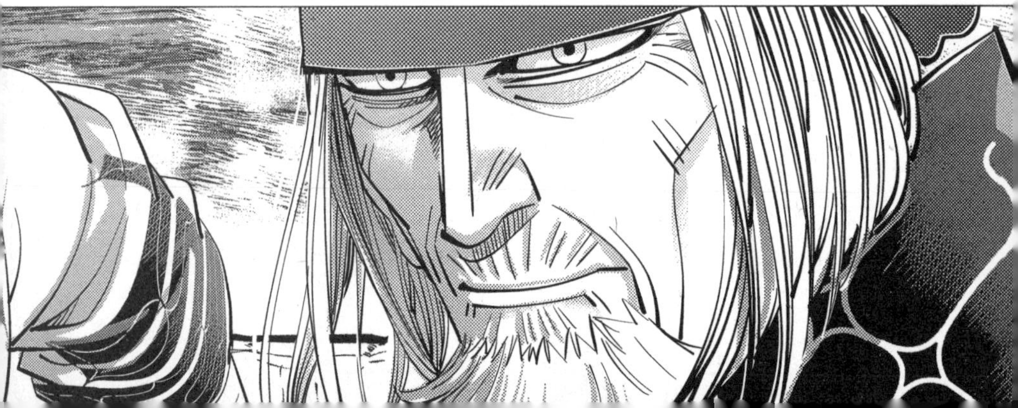

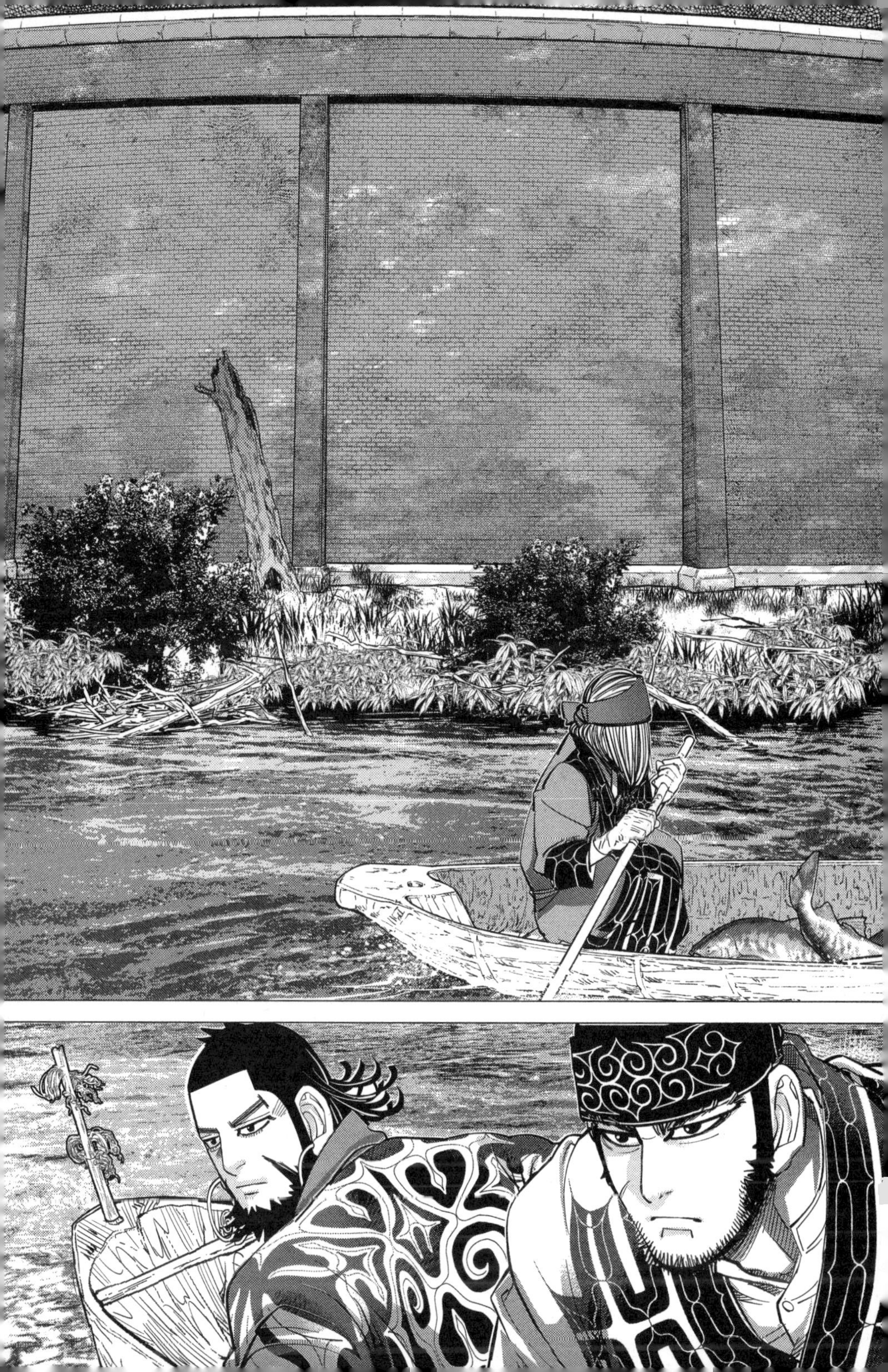

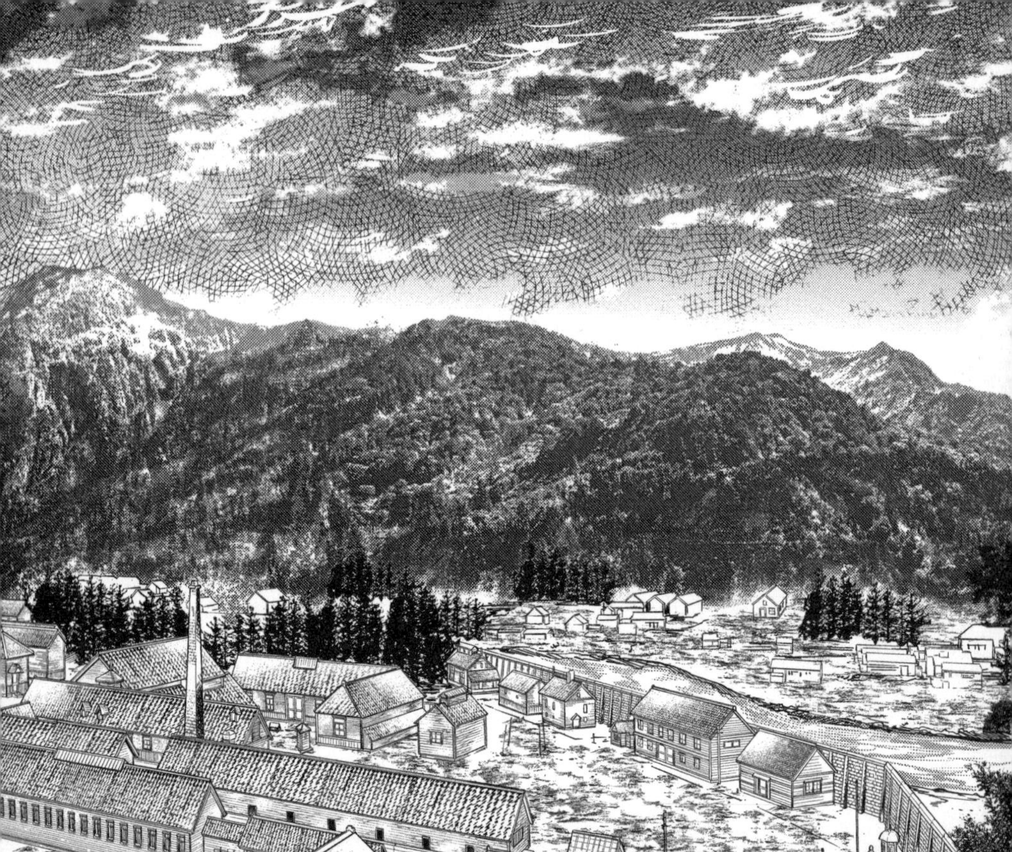
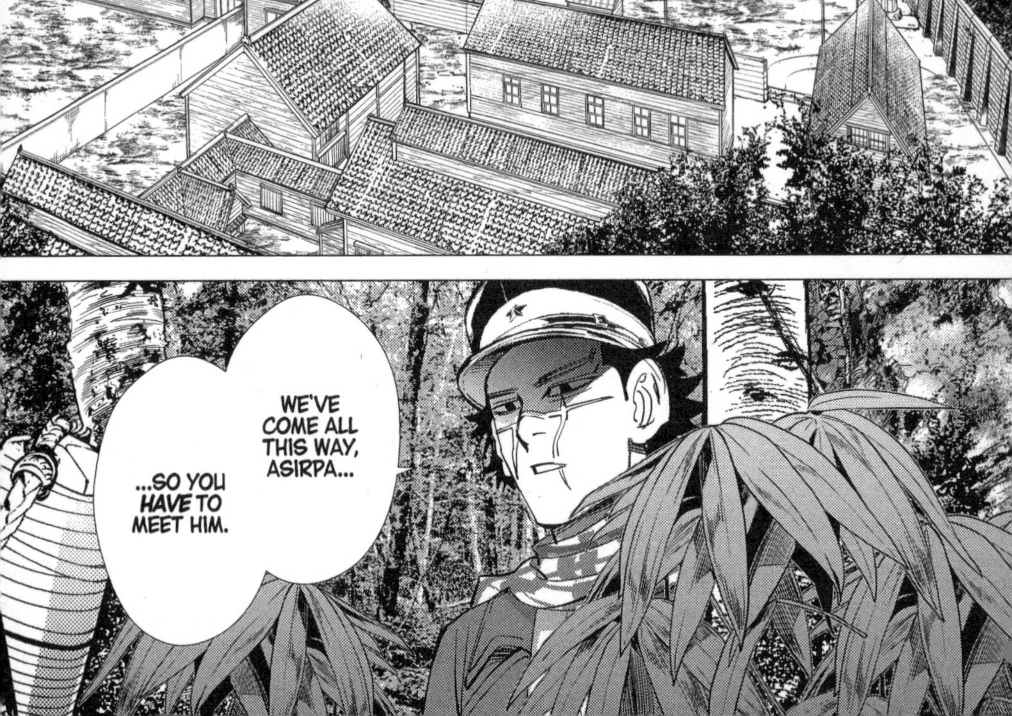
WE'VE COME ALL THIS WAY, ASIRPA...
...SO YOU HAVE TO MEET HIM.

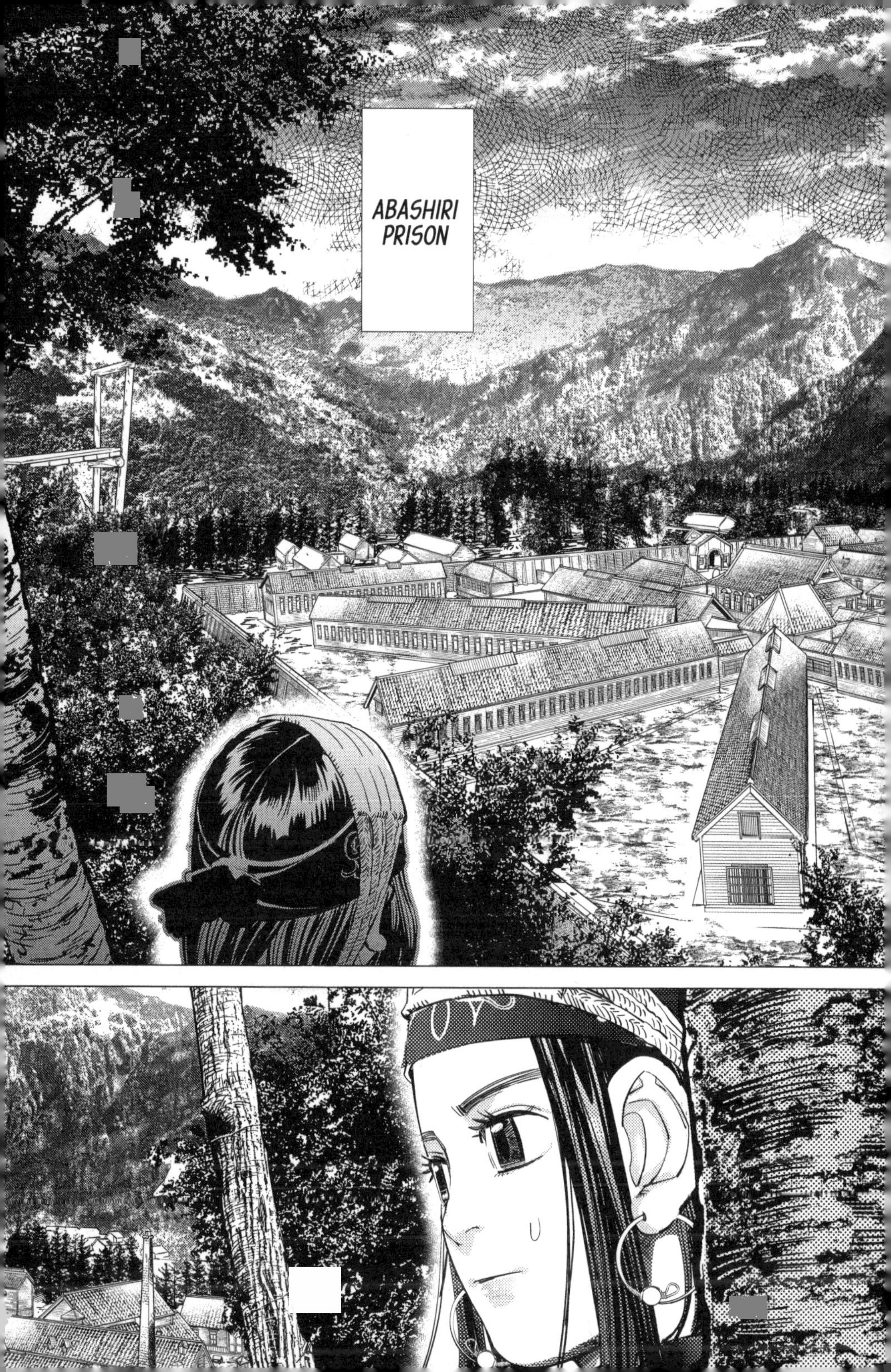
ABASHIRI PRISON

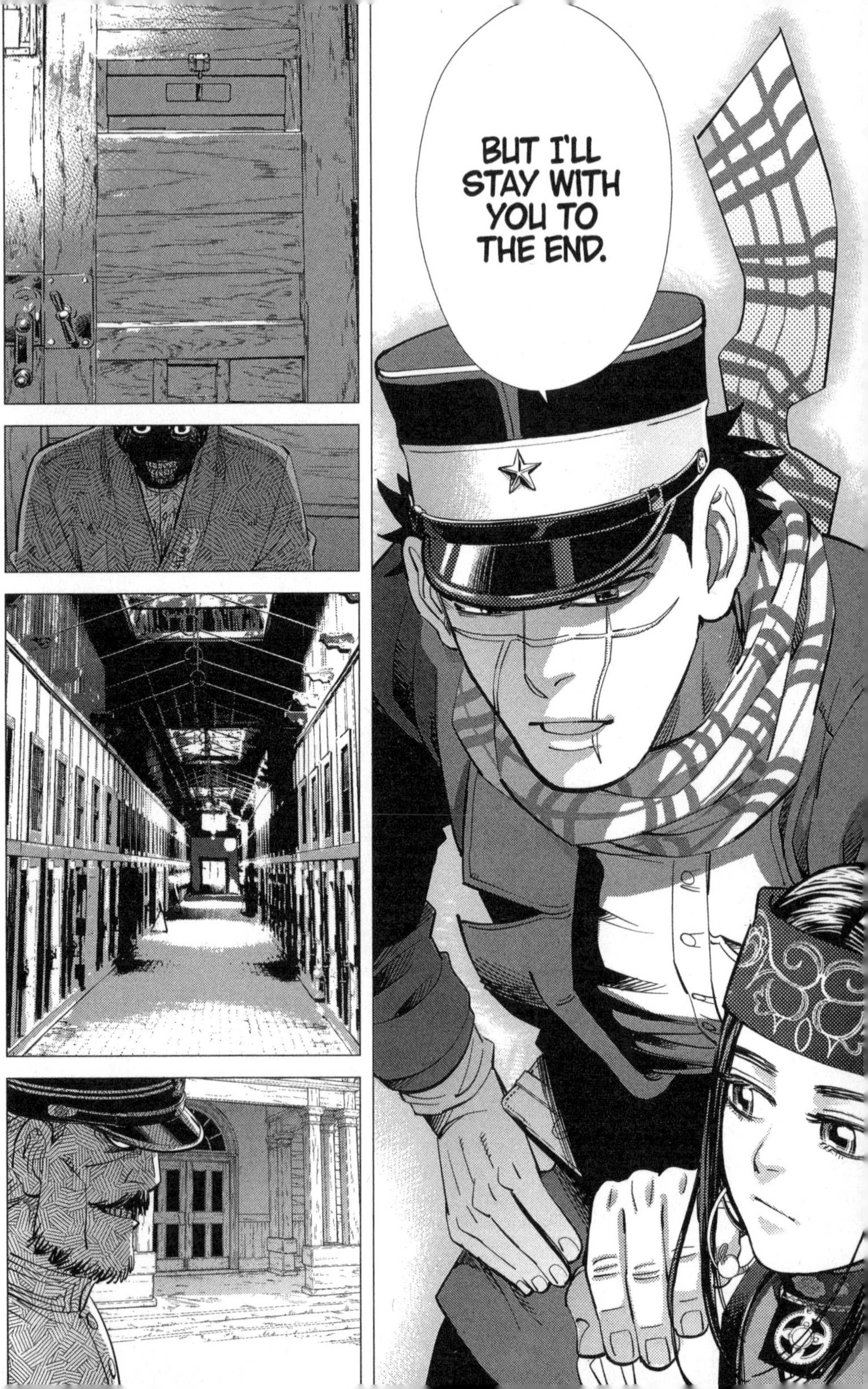
BUT I'LL STAY WITH YOU TO THE END.

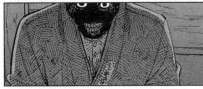

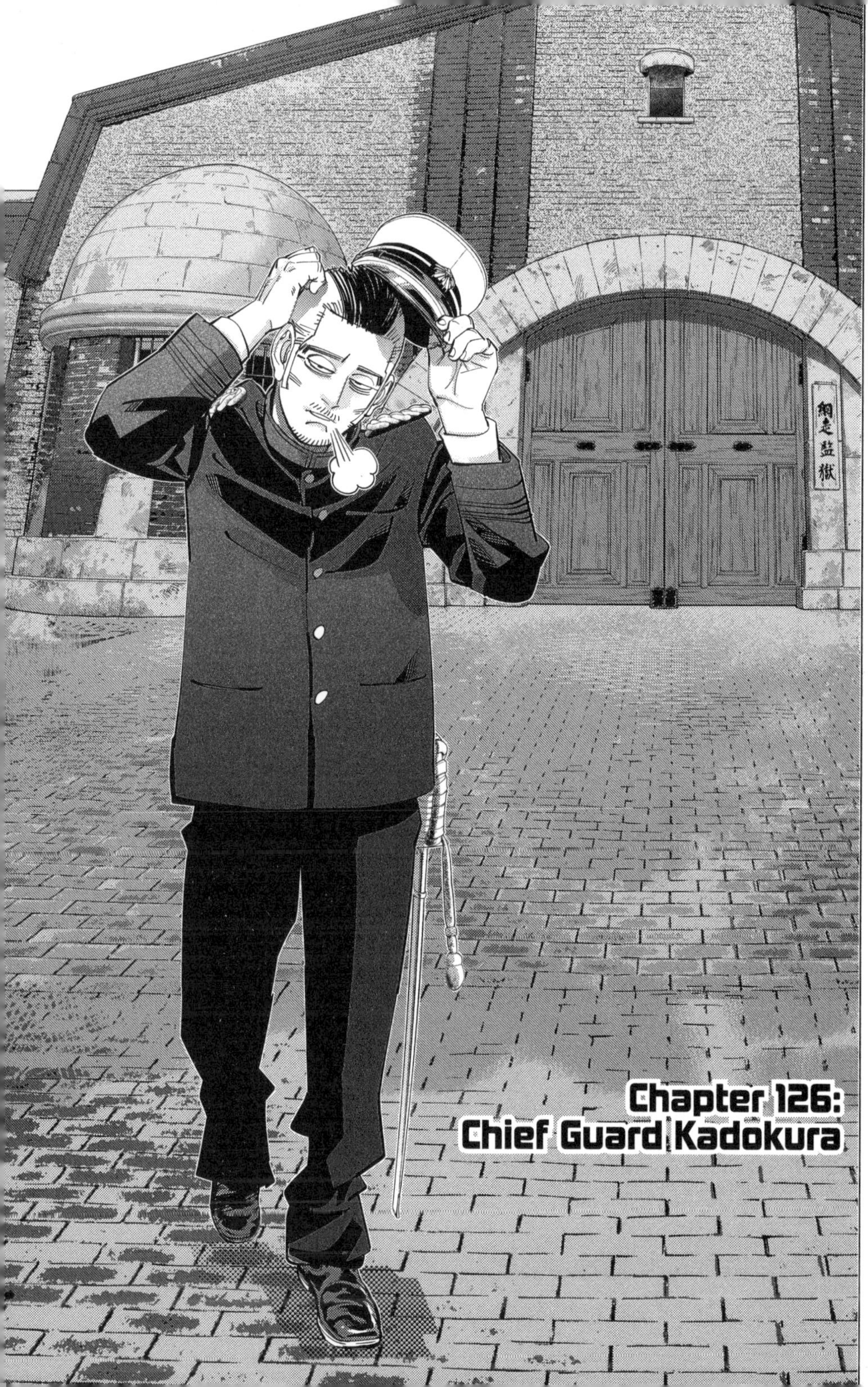
網走監獄
Chapter 126:
Chief Guard Kadokura

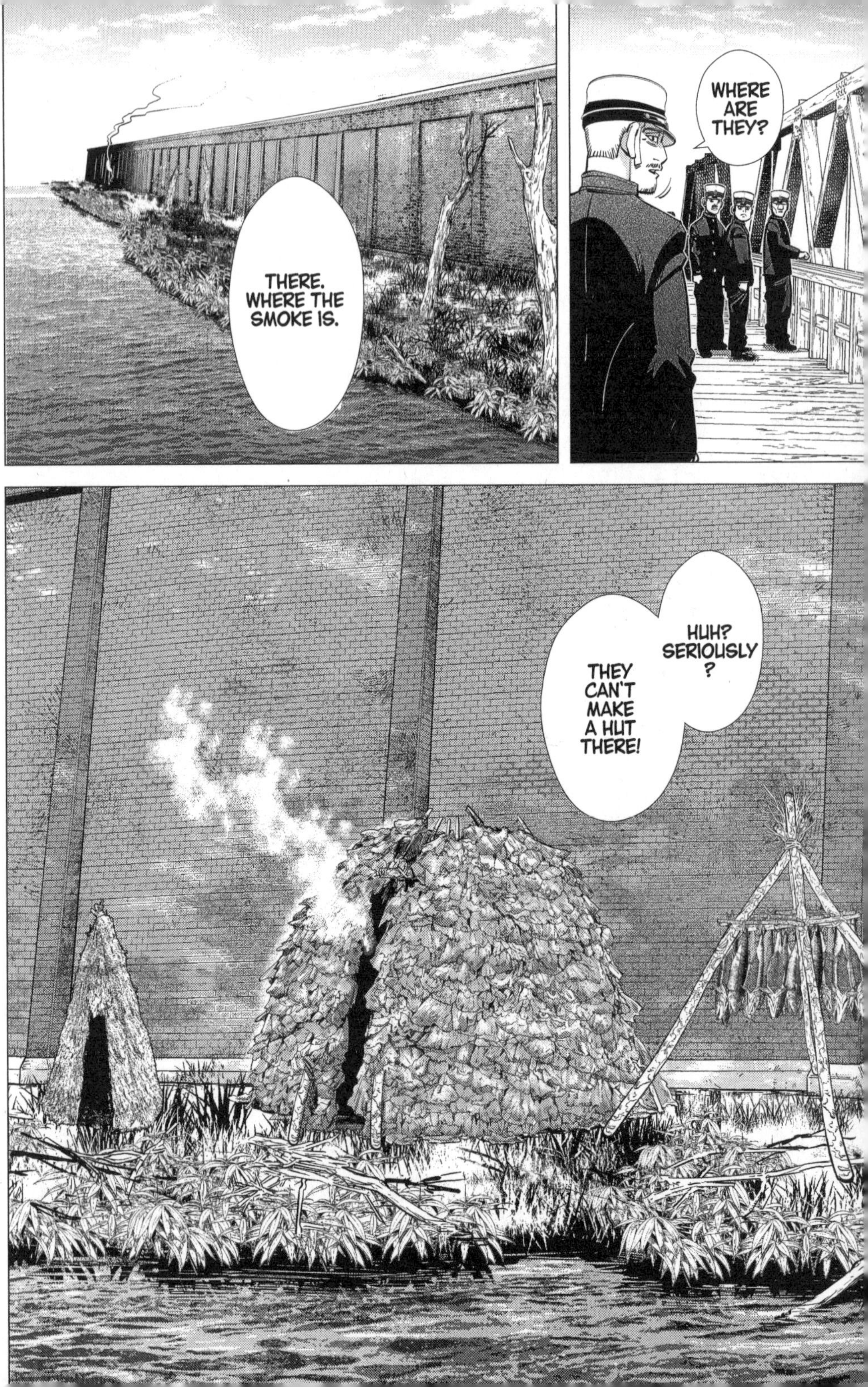
WHERE ARE THEY?
THERE. WHERE THE SMOKE IS.
HUH? SERIOUSLY?
THEY CAN'T MAKE A HUT THERE!

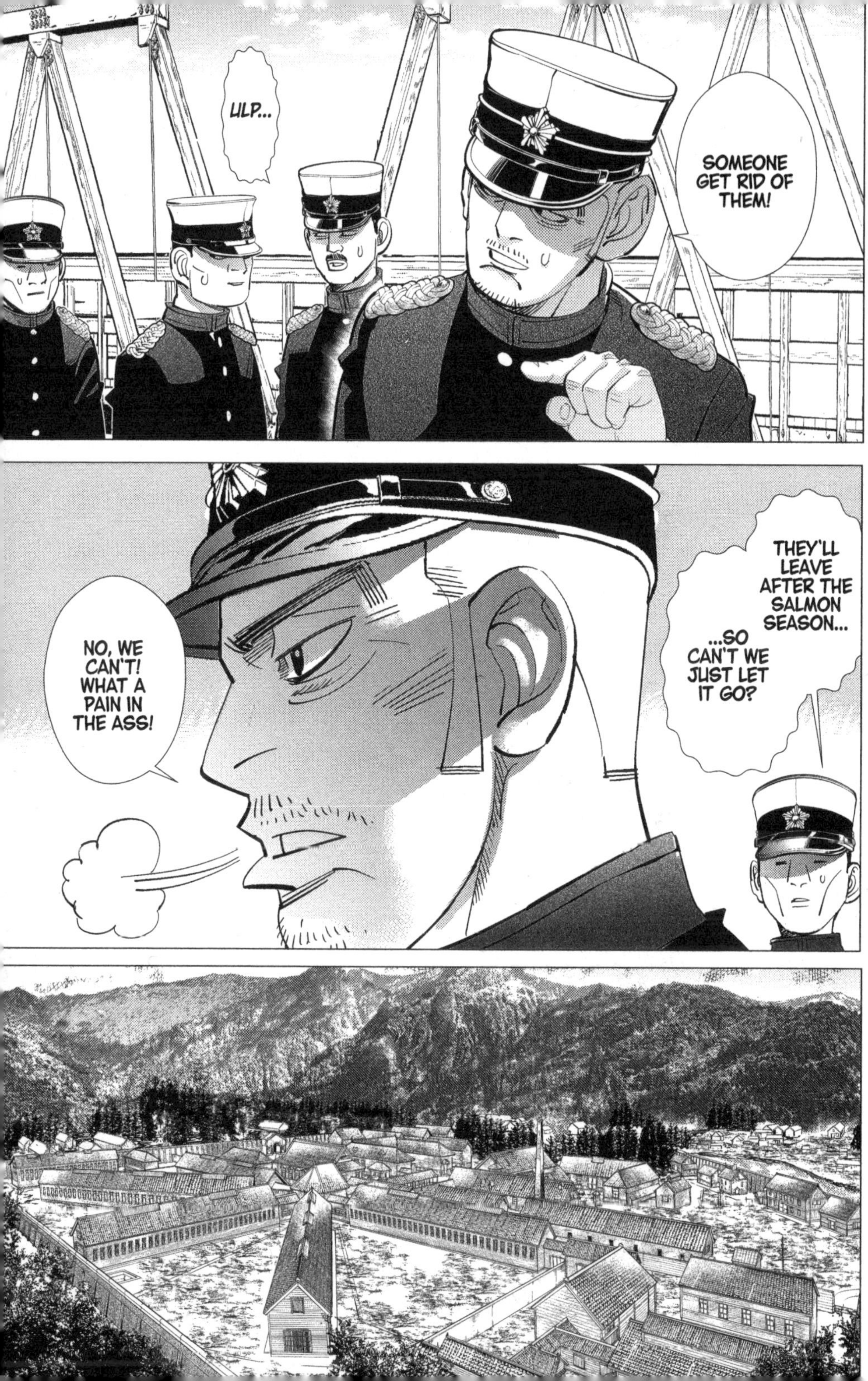
SOMEONE GET RID OF THEM!
ULP...
THEY'LL LEAVE AFTER THE SALMON SEASON...
...SO CAN'T WE JUST LET IT GO?
NO, WE CAN'T! WHAT A PAIN IN THE ASS!

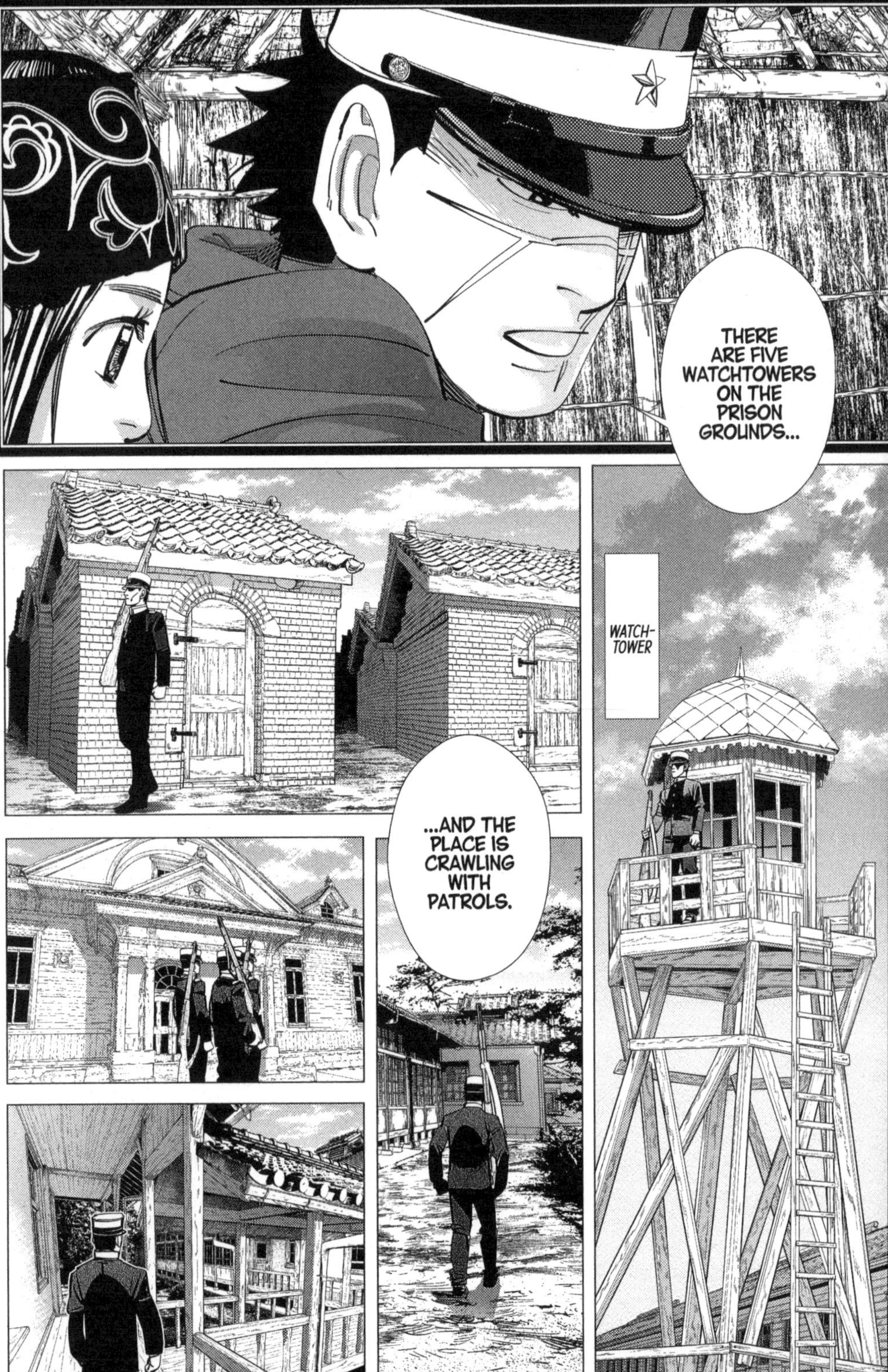
THERE ARE FIVE WATCHTOWERS ON THE PRISON GROUNDS...
WATCH-TOWER
...AND THE PLACE IS CRAWLING WITH PATROLS.

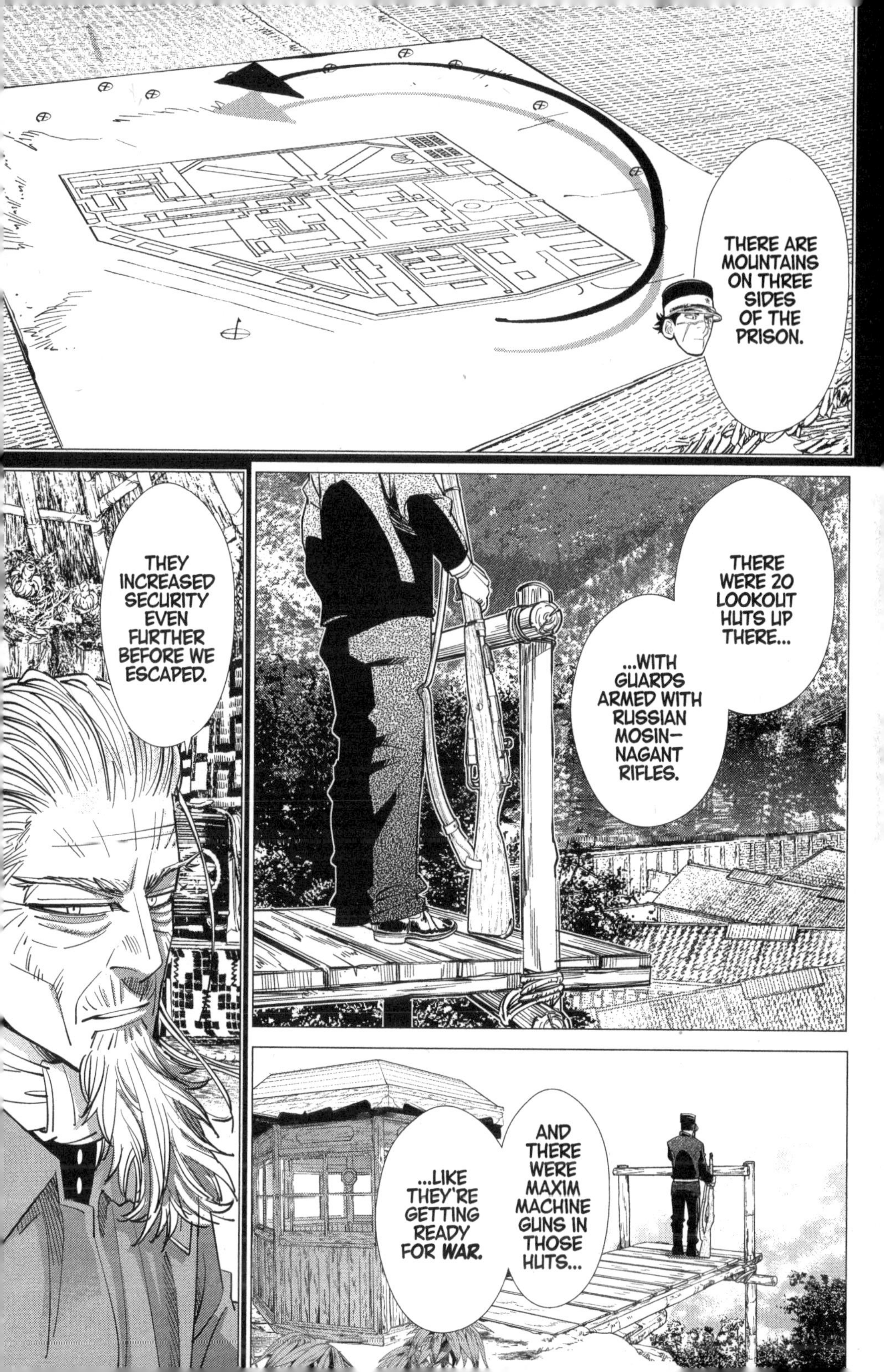
THERE ARE MOUNTAINS ON THREE SIDES OF THE PRISON.
THERE WERE 20 LOOKOUT HUTS UP THERE...
...WITH GUARDS ARMED WITH RUSSIAN MOSIN-NAGANT RIFLES.
AND THERE WERE MAXIM MACHINE GUNS IN THOSE HUTS...
...LIKE THEY'RE GETTING READY FOR WAR.
THEY INCREASED SECURITY EVEN FURTHER BEFORE WE ESCAPED.

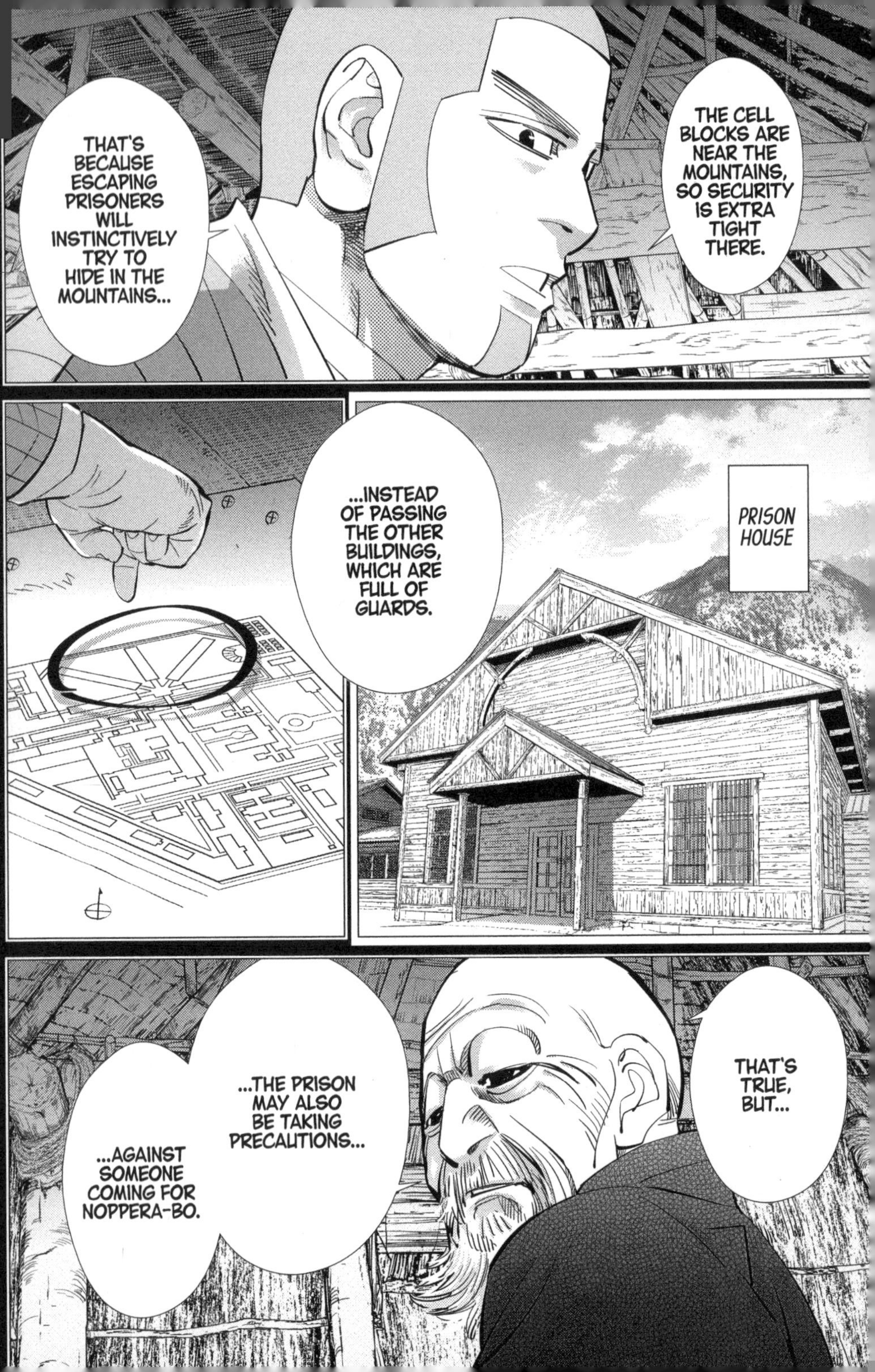
THE CELL BLOCKS ARE NEAR THE MOUNTAINS, SO SECURITY IS EXTRA TIGHT THERE.
THAT'S BECAUSE ESCAPING PRISONERS WILL INSTINCTIVELY TRY TO HIDE IN THE MOUNTAINS...
...INSTEAD OF PASSING THE OTHER BUILDINGS, WHICH ARE FULL OF GUARDS.
PRISON HOUSE
THAT'S TRUE, BUT...
...THE PRISON MAY ALSO BE TAKING PRECAUTIONS...
...AGAINST SOMEONE COMING FOR NOPPERA-BO.

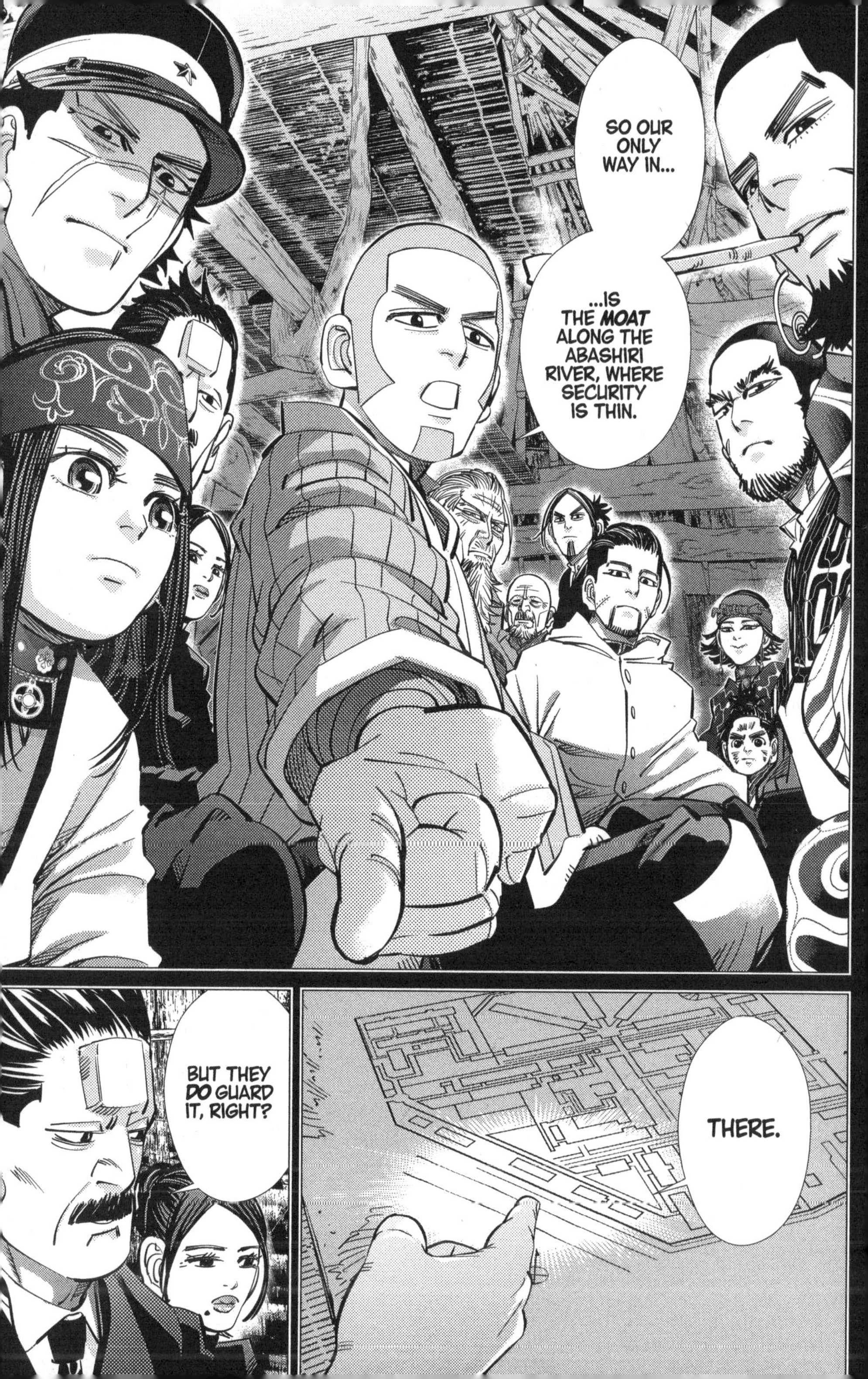
SO OUR ONLY WAY IN...
...IS THE *MOAT* ALONG THE ABASHIRI RIVER, WHERE SECURITY IS THIN.
THERE.
BUT THEY *DO* GUARD IT, RIGHT?

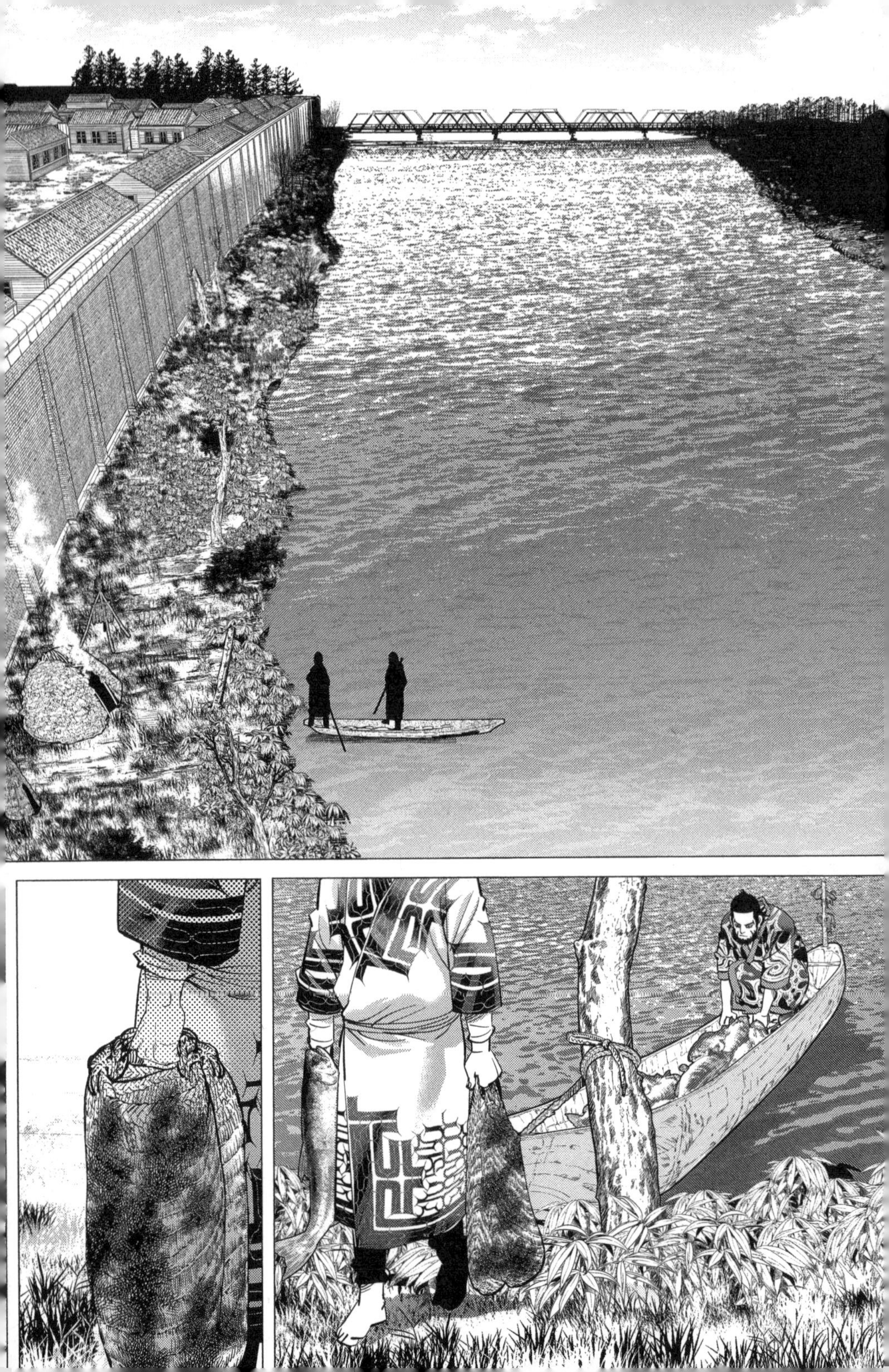

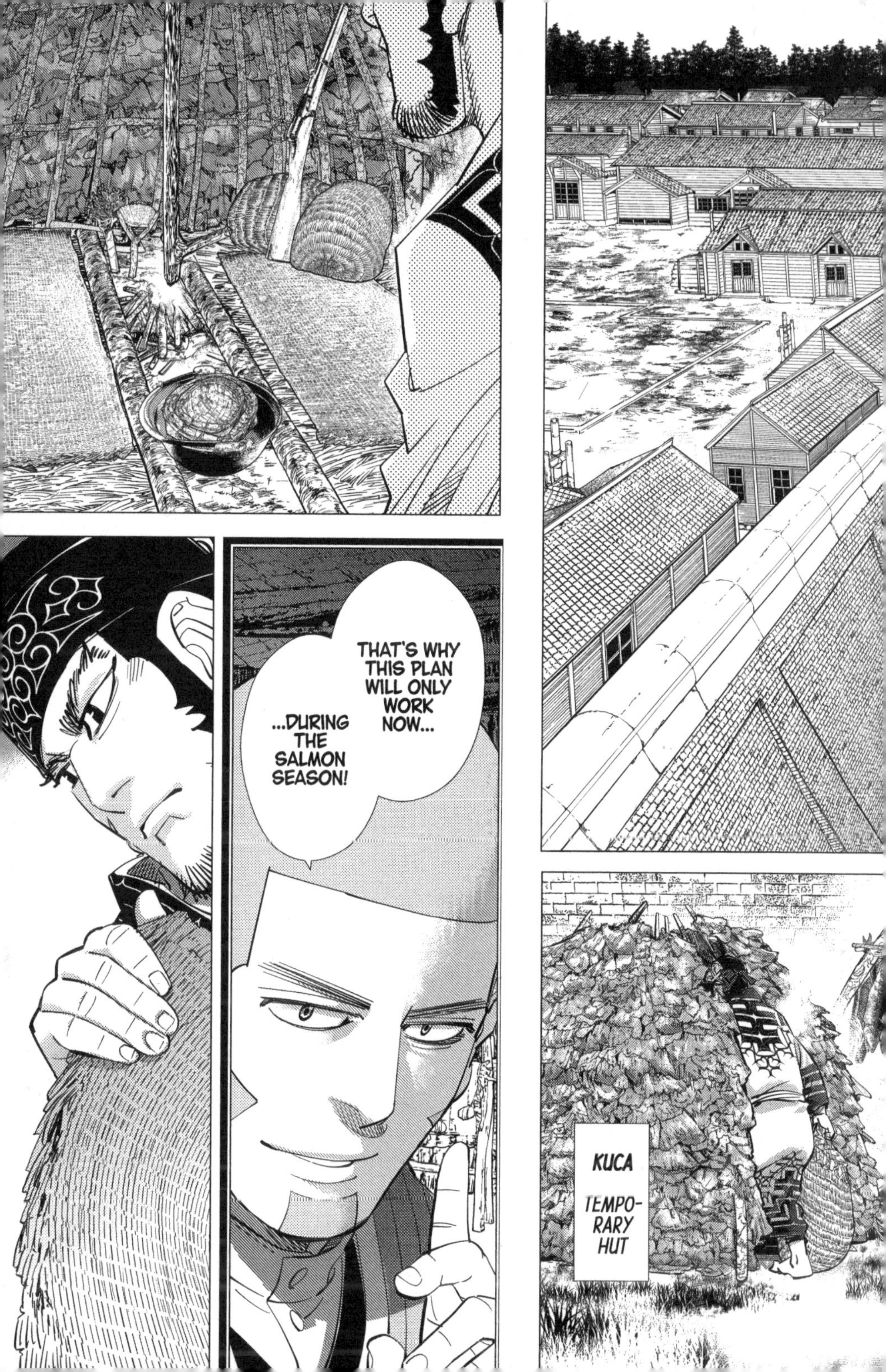
KUCA
TEMPORARY HUT
THAT'S WHY THIS PLAN WILL ONLY WORK NOW...
...DURING THE SALMON SEASON!

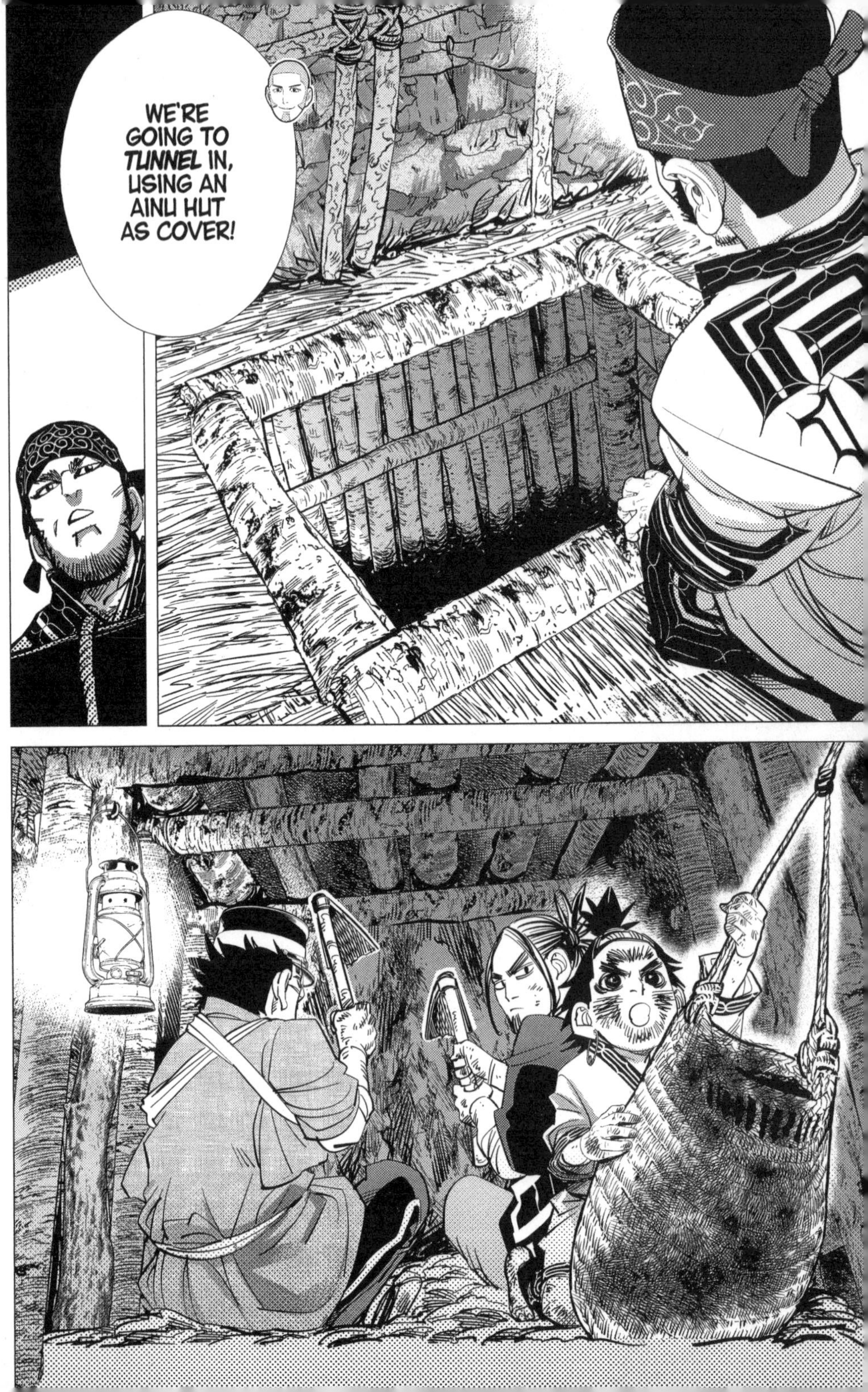
WE'RE GOING TO TUNNEL IN, USING AN AINU HUT AS COVER!

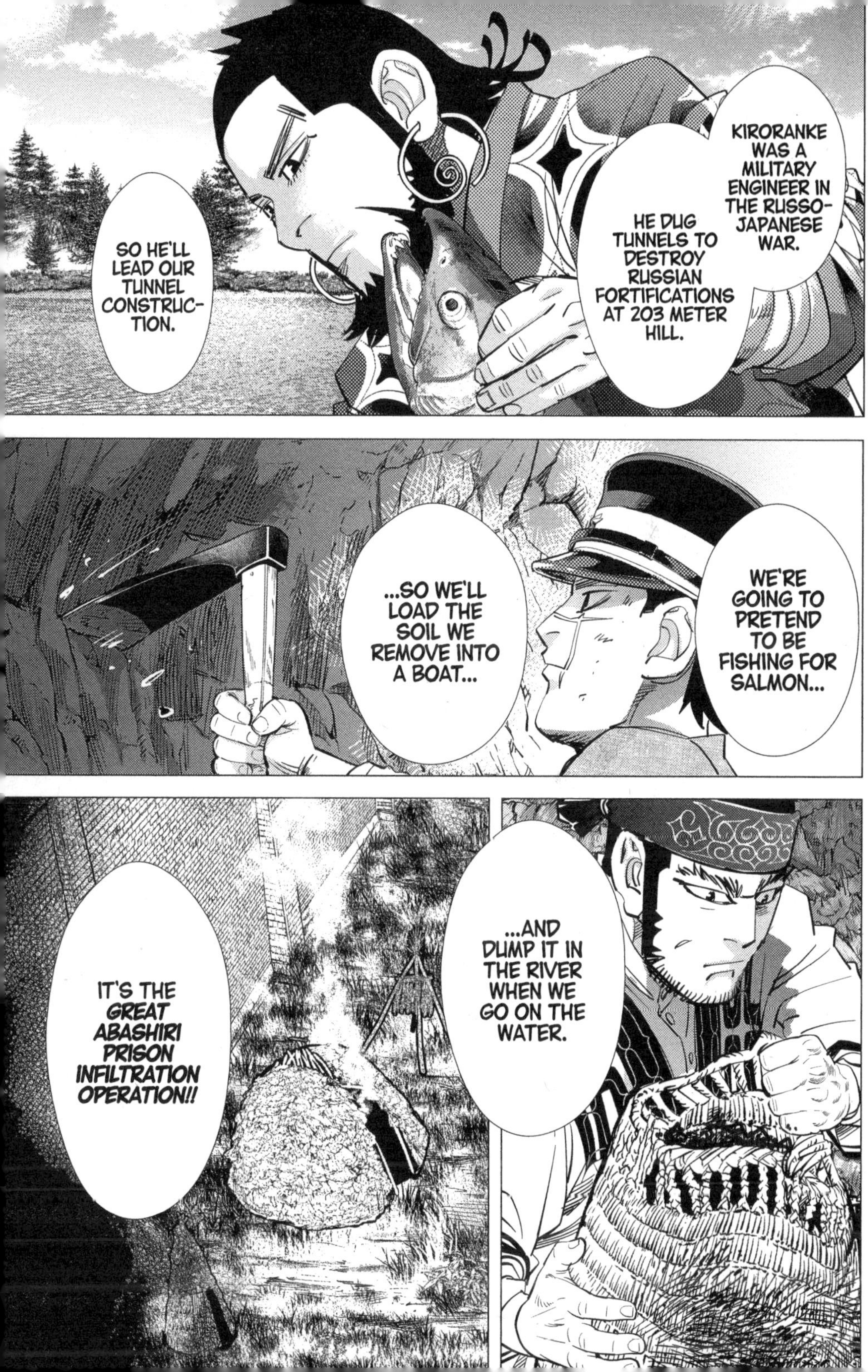
KIRORANKE WAS A MILITARY ENGINEER IN THE RUSSO-JAPANESE WAR.
HE DUG TUNNELS TO DESTROY RUSSIAN FORTIFICATIONS AT 203 METER HILL.
SO HE'LL LEAD OUR TUNNEL CONSTRUCTION.
WE'RE GOING TO PRETEND TO BE FISHING FOR SALMON...
...SO WE'LL LOAD THE SOIL WE REMOVE INTO A BOAT...
...AND DUMP IT IN THE RIVER WHEN WE GO ON THE WATER.
IT'S THE GREAT ABASHIRI PRISON INFILTRATION OPERATION!!

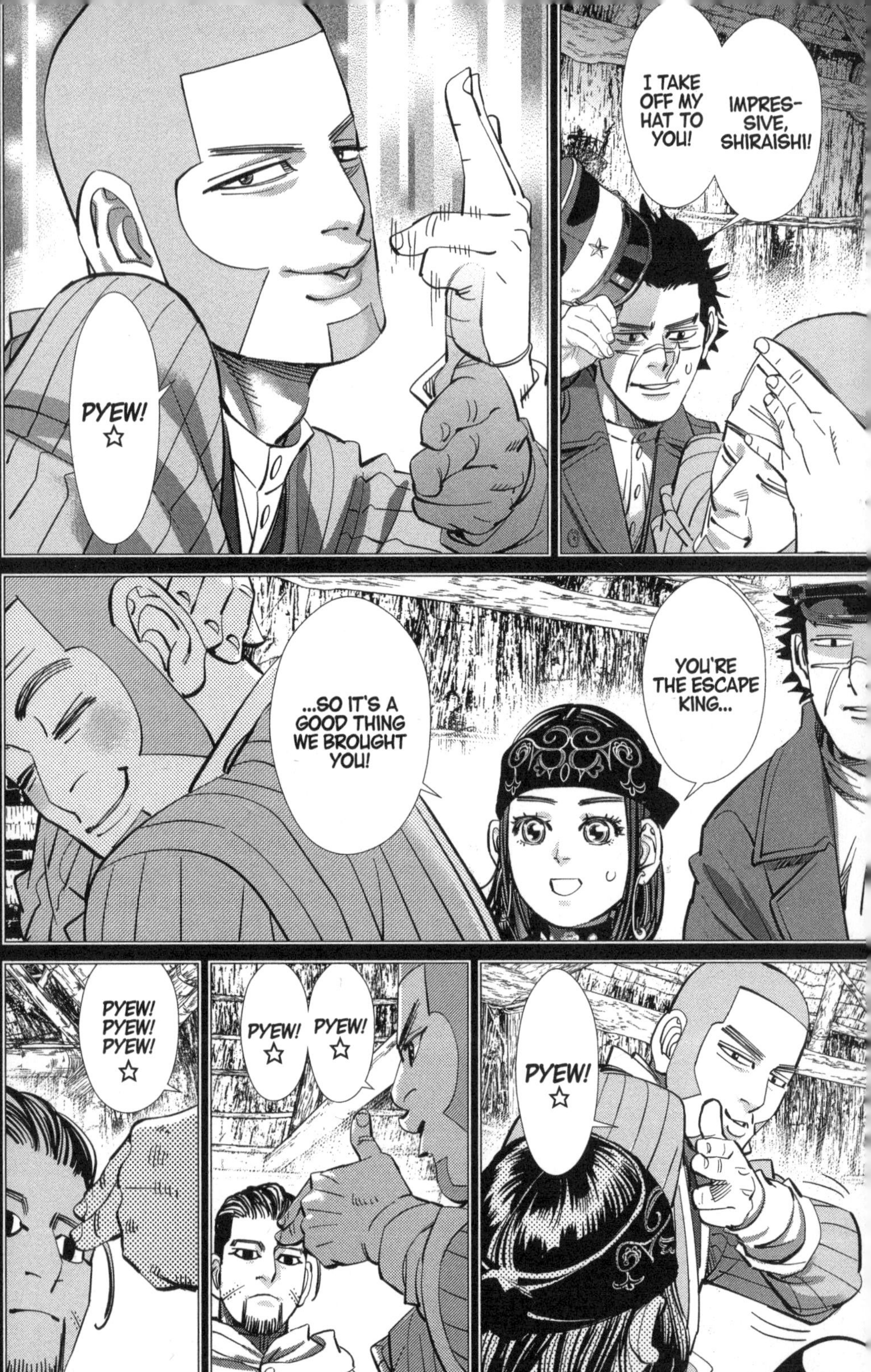
IMPRESSIVE, SHIRAISHI!
I TAKE OFF MY HAT TO YOU!
PYEW! ☆
YOU'RE THE ESCAPE KING...
...SO IT'S A GOOD THING WE BROUGHT YOU!
PYEW! ☆
PYEW! ☆
PYEW! ☆
PYEW! PYEW! PYEW! ☆

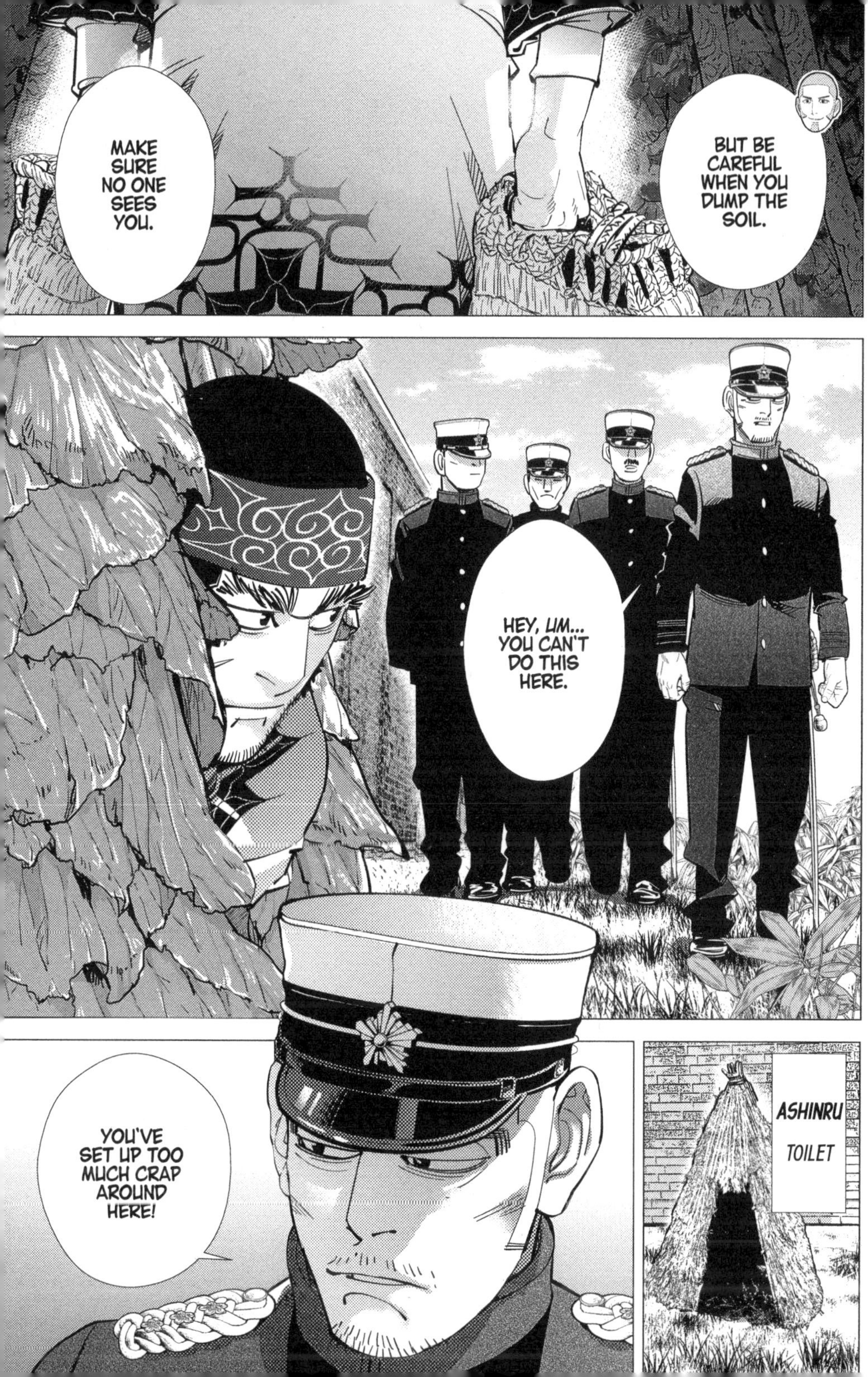
BUT BE CAREFUL WHEN YOU DUMP THE SOIL.
MAKE SURE NO ONE SEES YOU.
HEY, UM... YOU CAN'T DO THIS HERE.
ASHINRU
TOILET
YOU'VE SET UP TOO MUCH CRAP AROUND HERE!

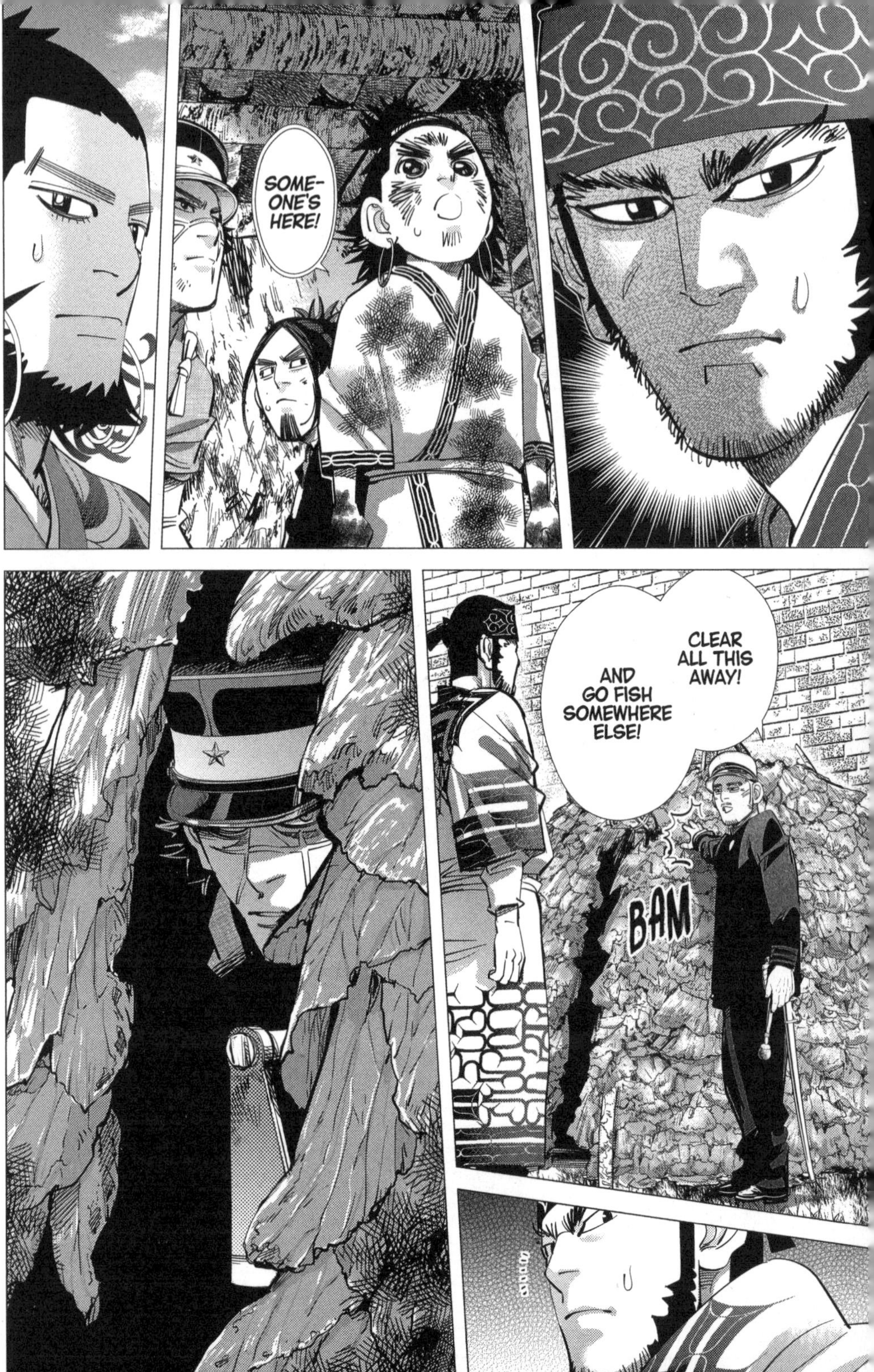
SOME-ONE'S HERE!
CLEAR ALL THIS AWAY!
AND GO FISH SOMEWHERE ELSE!
BAM

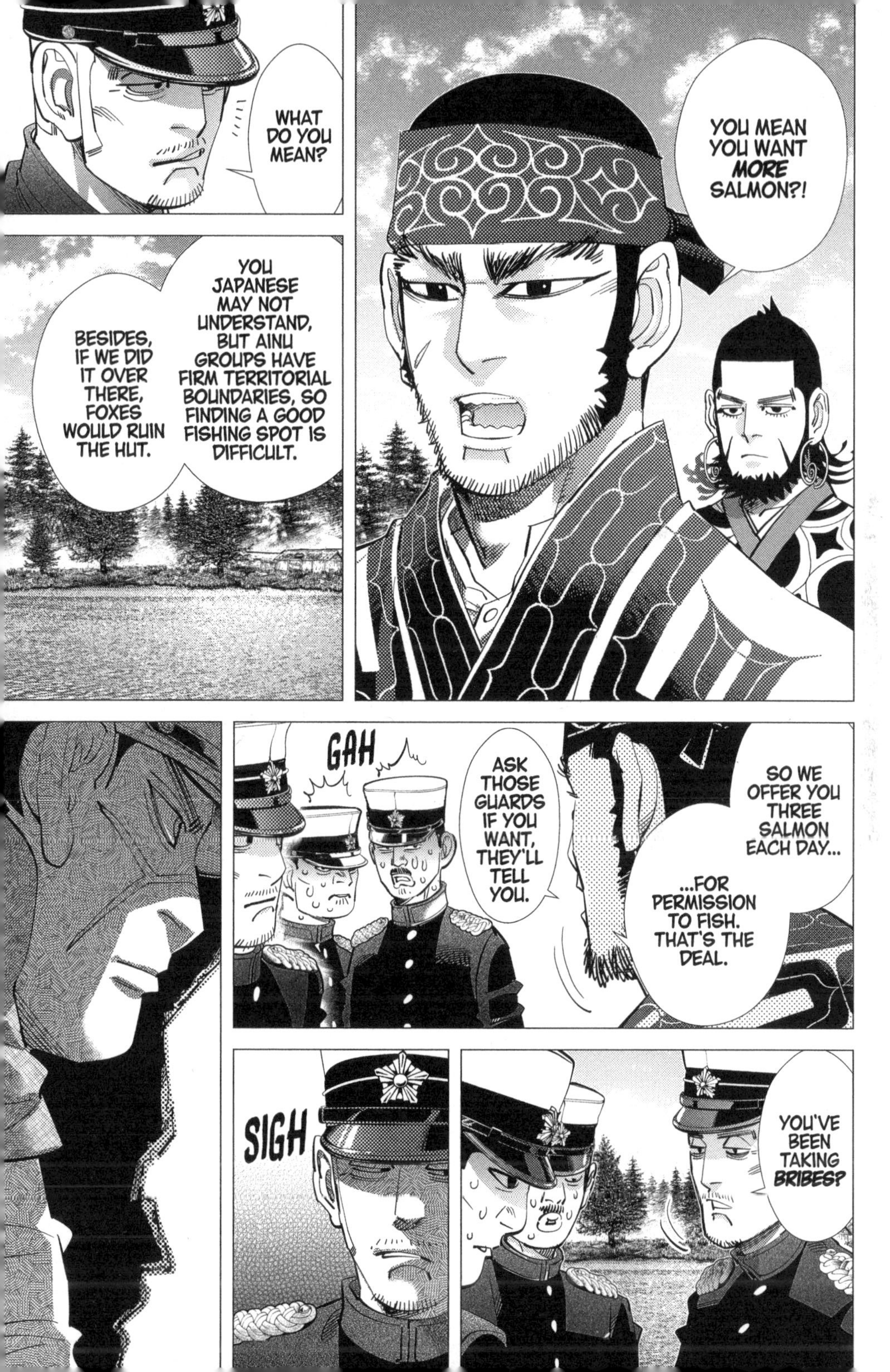
YOU MEAN YOU WANT MORE SALMON?!
WHAT DO YOU MEAN?
YOU JAPANESE MAY NOT UNDERSTAND, BUT AINU GROUPS HAVE FIRM TERRITORIAL BOUNDARIES, SO FINDING A GOOD FISHING SPOT IS DIFFICULT.
BESIDES, IF WE DID IT OVER THERE, FOXES WOULD RUIN THE HUT.
SO WE OFFER YOU THREE SALMON EACH DAY...
...FOR PERMISSION TO FISH. THAT'S THE DEAL.
ASK THOSE GUARDS IF YOU WANT, THEY'LL TELL YOU.
GAH
YOU'VE BEEN TAKING BRIBES?
SIGH

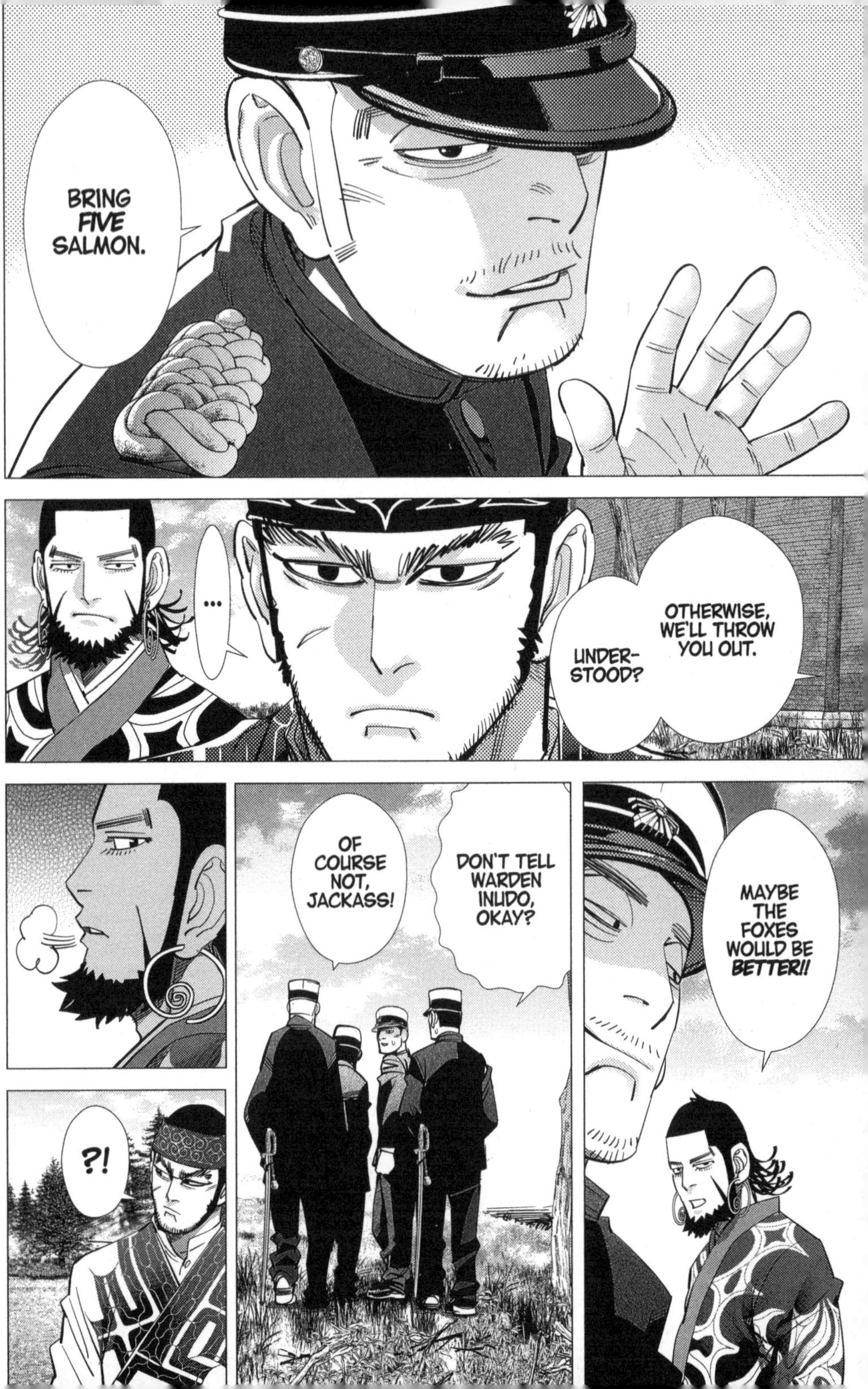
BRING FIVE SALMON.
OTHERWISE, WE'LL THROW YOU OUT.
UNDER-STOOD?
...
MAYBE THE FOXES WOULD BE BETTER!!
DON'T TELL WARDEN INUDO, OKAY?
OF COURSE NOT, JACKASS!
?!

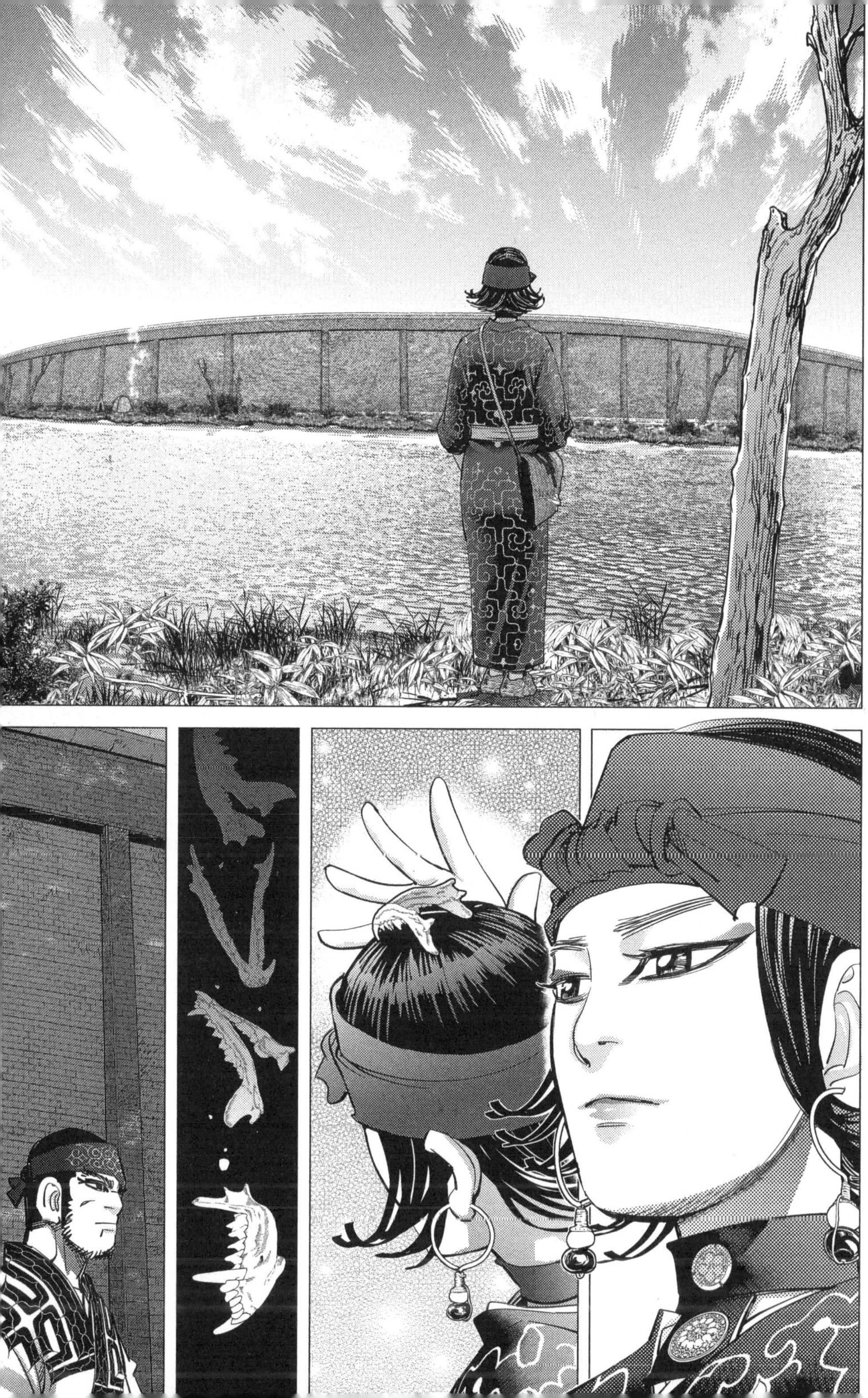

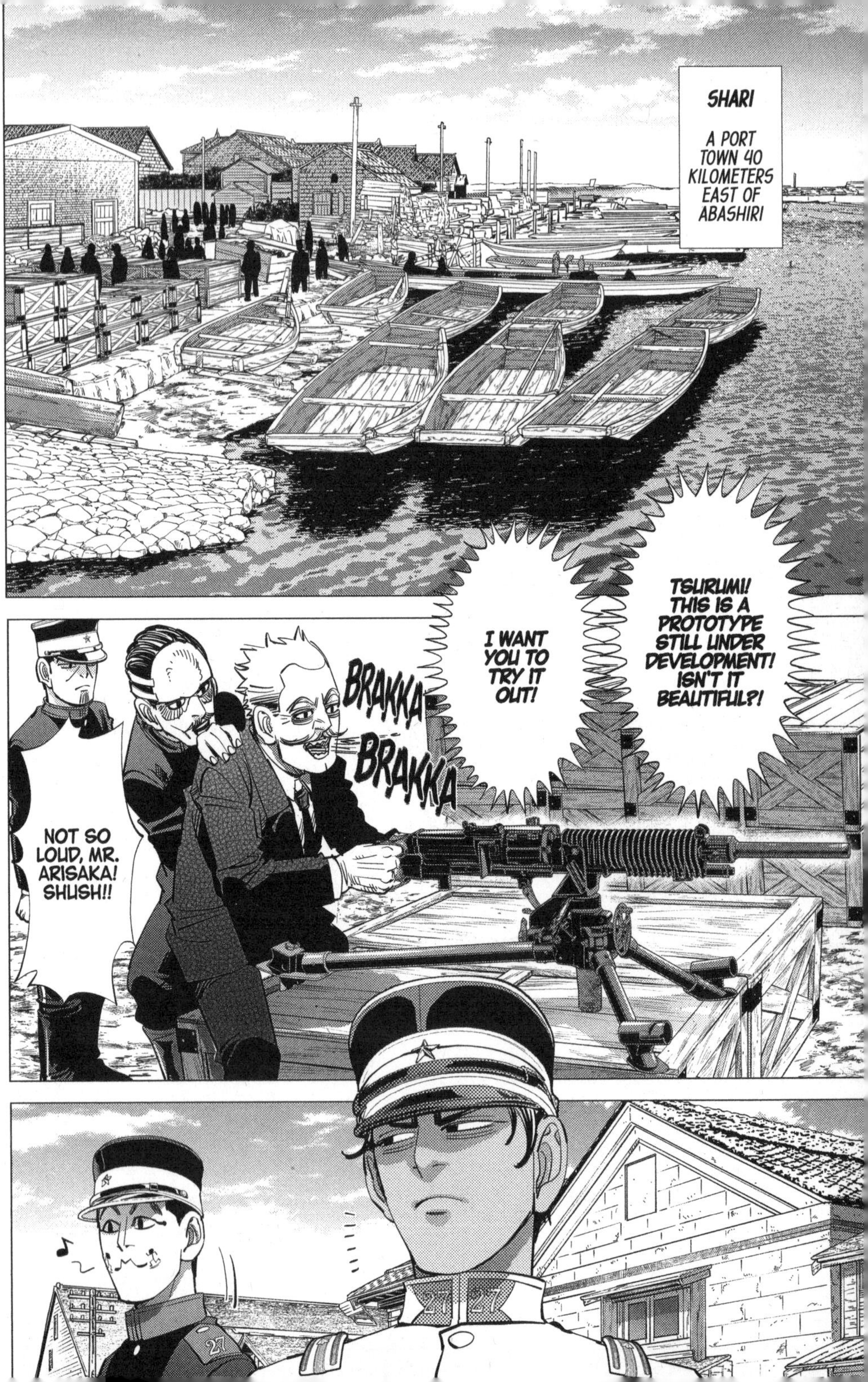
SHARI
A PORT TOWN 40 KILOMETERS EAST OF ABASHIRI
TSURUMI! THIS IS A PROTOTYPE STILL UNDER DEVELOPMENT! ISN'T IT BEAUTIFUL?!
I WANT YOU TO TRY IT OUT!
BRAKKA BRAKKA
NOT SO LOUD, MR. ARISAKA! SHUSH!!

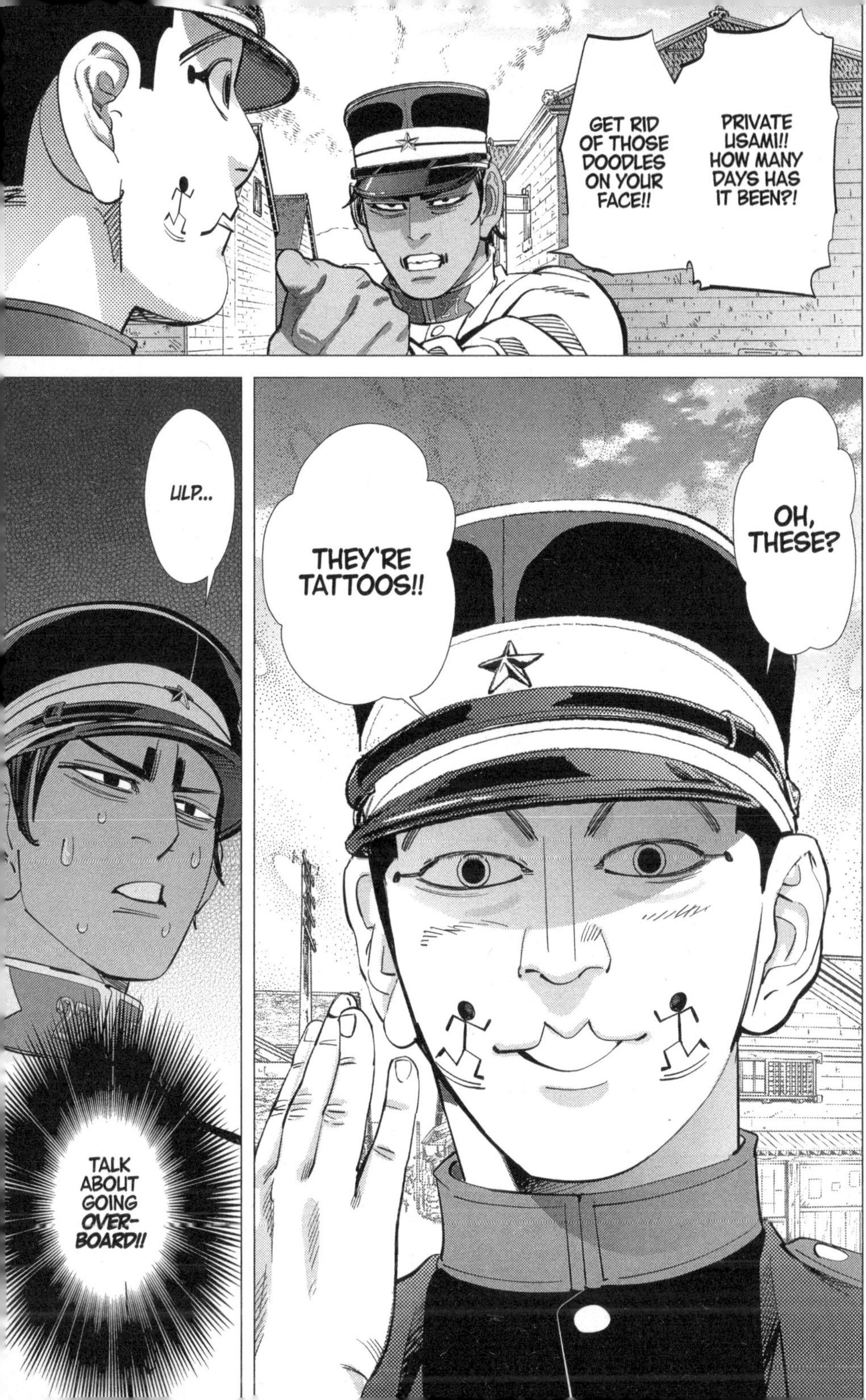
PRIVATE USAMI!! HOW MANY DAYS HAS IT BEEN?!
GET RID OF THOSE DOODLES ON YOUR FACE!!
OH, THESE?
THEY'RE TATTOOS!!
ULP...
TALK ABOUT GOING OVER-BOARD!!

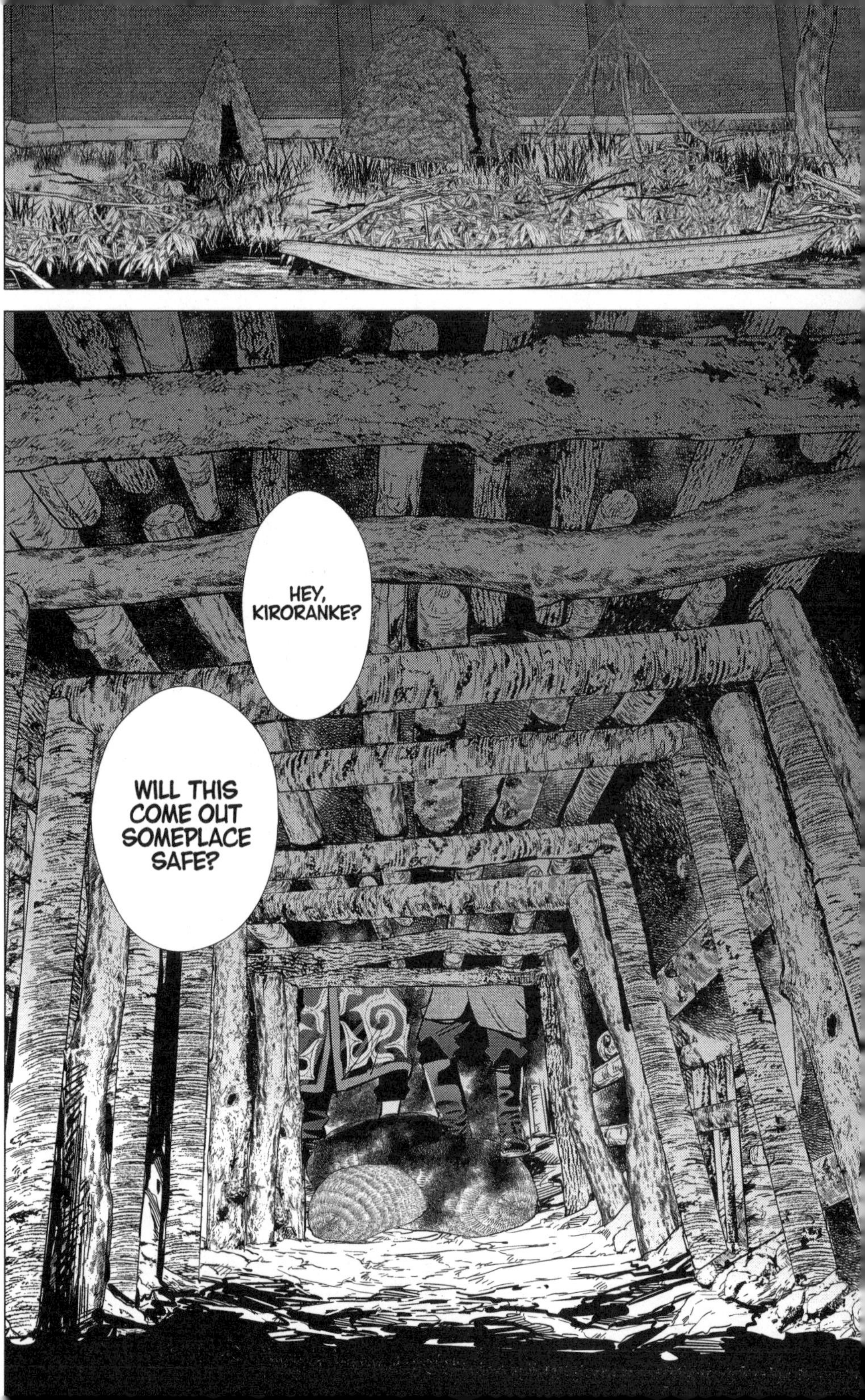
HEY, KIRORANKE?
WILL THIS COME OUT SOMEPLACE SAFE?

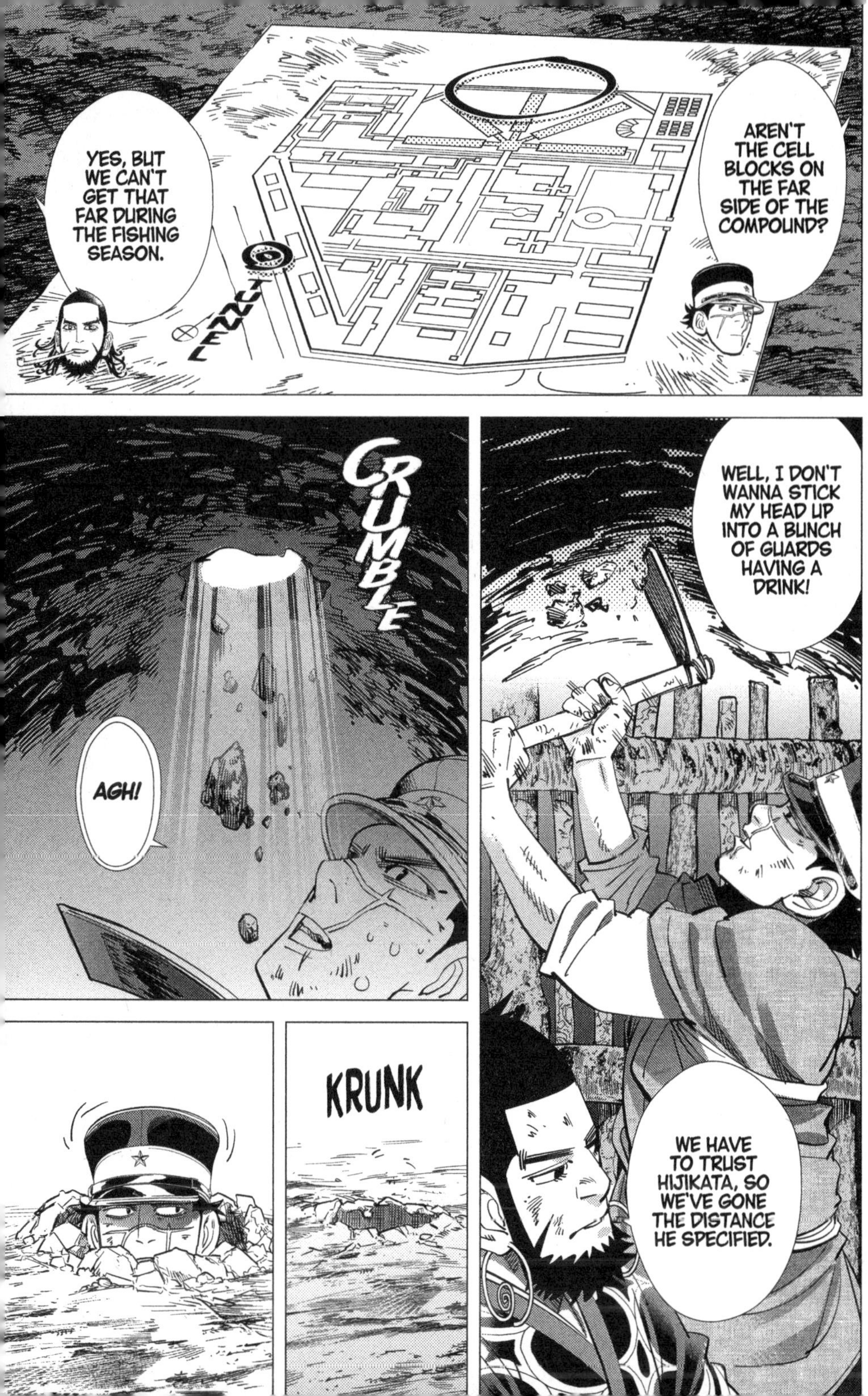
AREN'T THE CELL BLOCKS ON THE FAR SIDE OF THE COMPOUND?
YES, BUT WE CAN'T GET THAT FAR DURING THE FISHING SEASON.
TUNNEL
WELL, I DON'T WANNA STICK MY HEAD UP INTO A BUNCH OF GUARDS HAVING A DRINK!
WE HAVE TO TRUST HIJIKATA, SO WE'VE GONE THE DISTANCE HE SPECIFIED.
CRUMBLE
AGH!
KRUNK

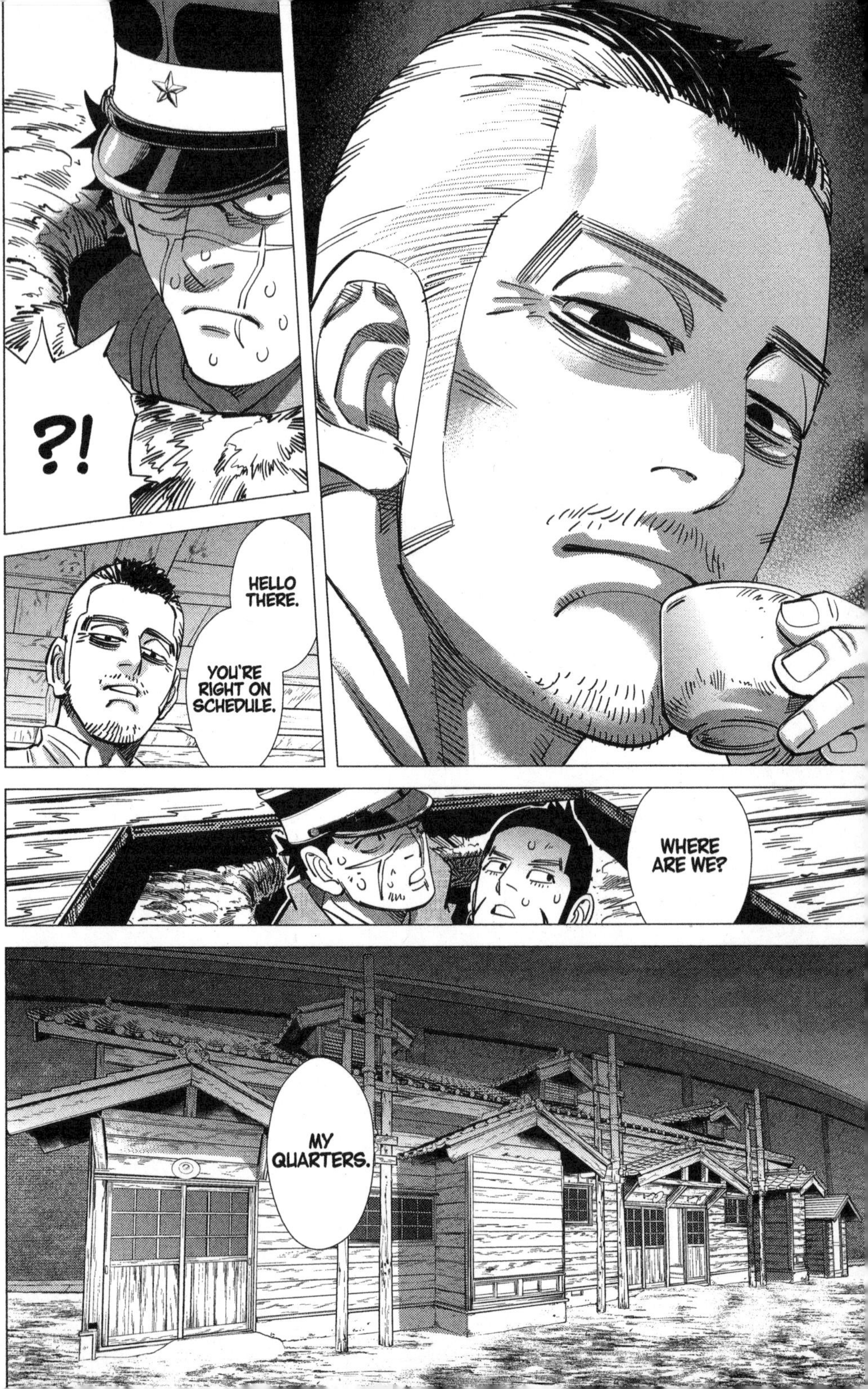
?!
HELLO THERE.
YOU'RE RIGHT ON SCHEDULE.
WHERE ARE WE?
MY QUARTERS.

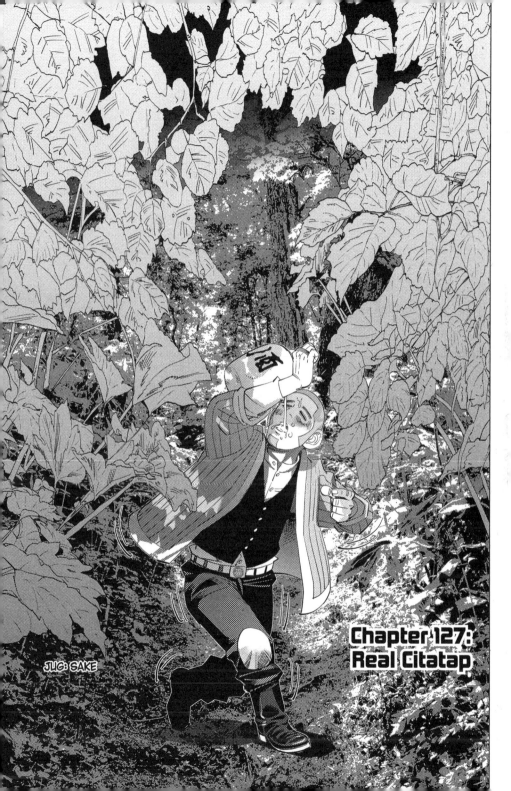

JUG: SAKE

Chapter 127:
Real Citatap

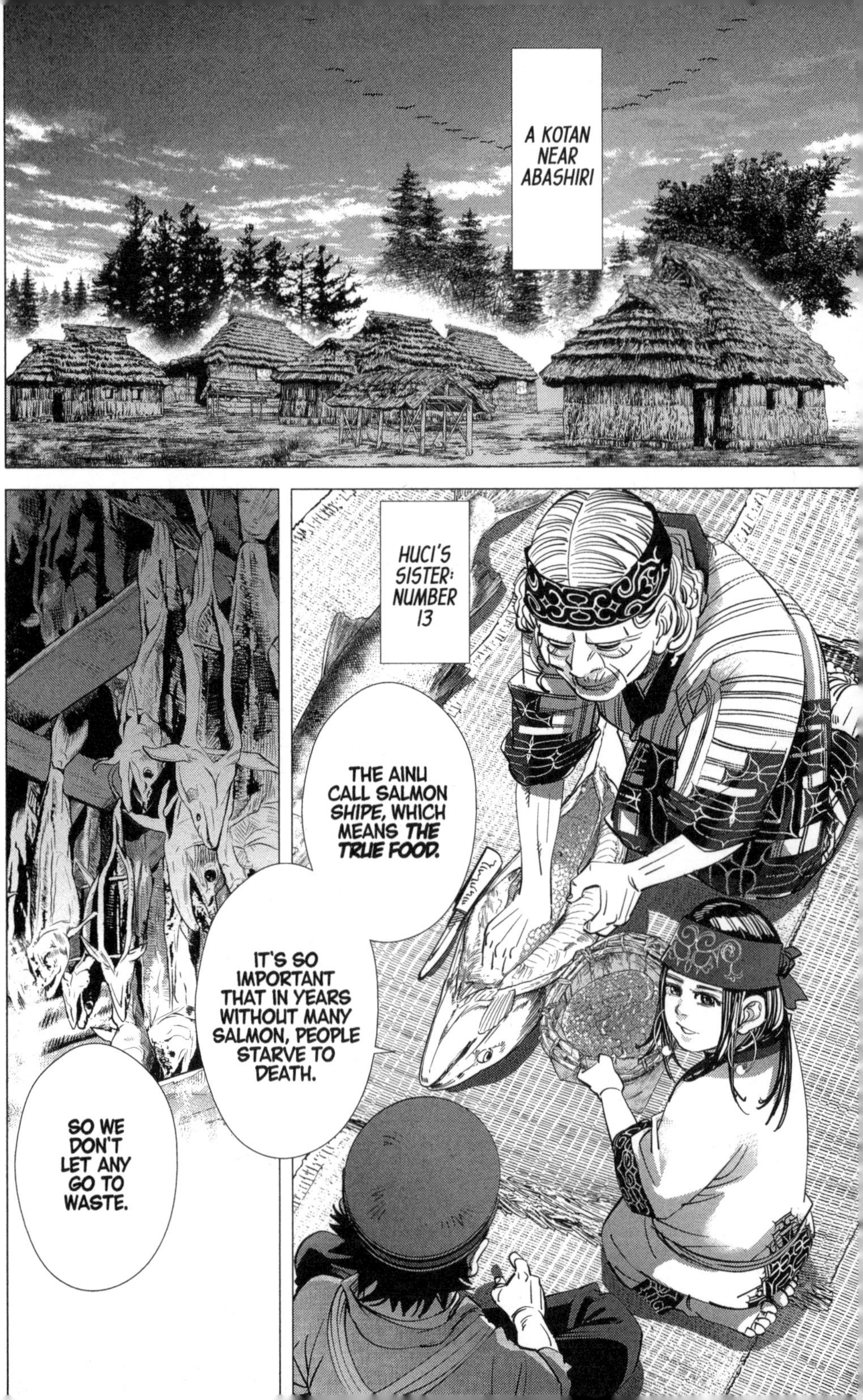
A KOTAN NEAR ABASHIRI
HUCI'S SISTER: NUMBER 13
THE AINU CALL SALMON SHIPE, WHICH MEANS THE TRUE FOOD.
IT'S SO IMPORTANT THAT IN YEARS WITHOUT MANY SALMON, PEOPLE STARVE TO DEATH.
SO WE DON'T LET ANY GO TO WASTE.

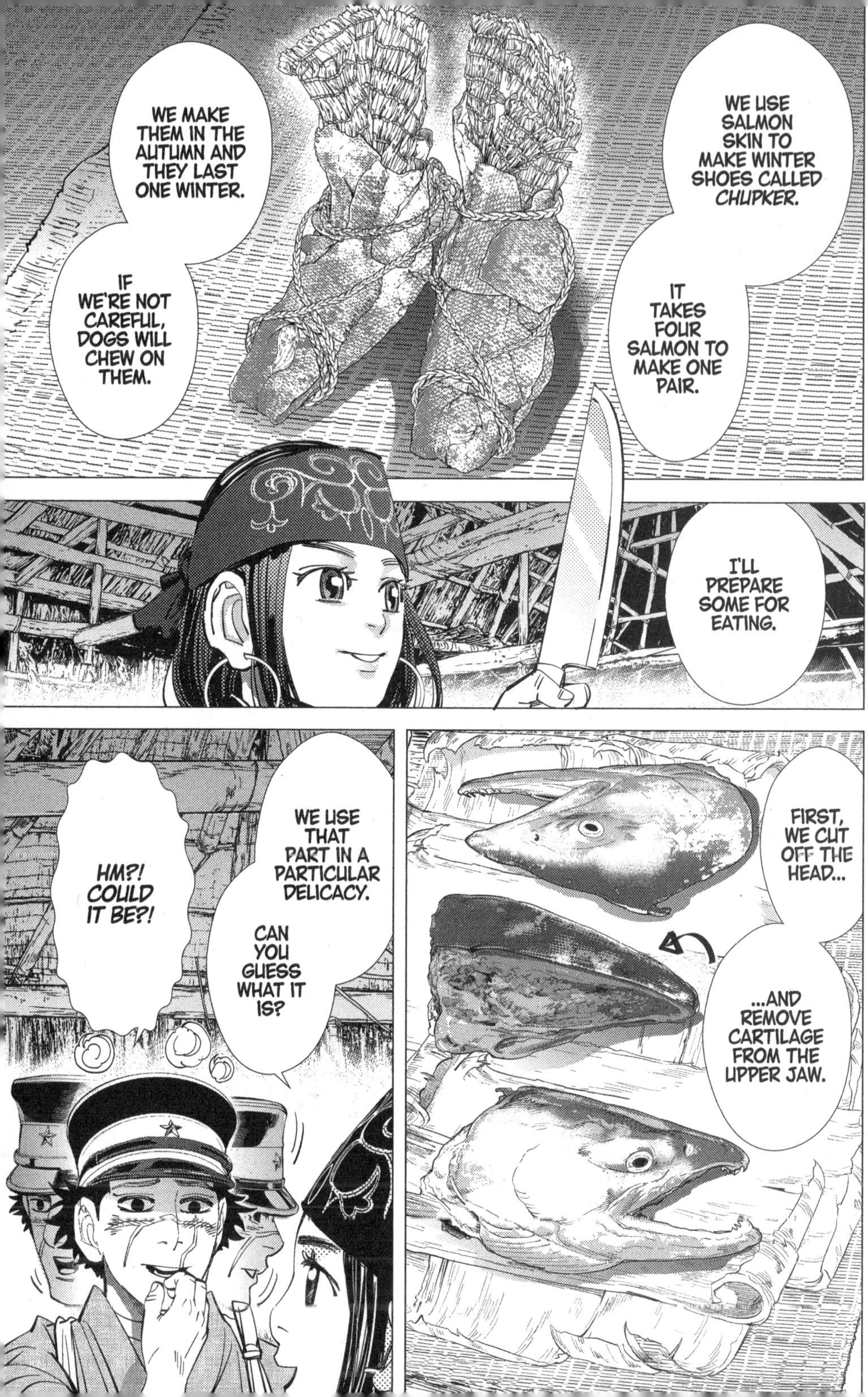
WE USE SALMON SKIN TO MAKE WINTER SHOES CALLED CHUPKER.
IT TAKES FOUR SALMON TO MAKE ONE PAIR.
WE MAKE THEM IN THE AUTUMN AND THEY LAST ONE WINTER.
IF WE'RE NOT CAREFUL, DOGS WILL CHEW ON THEM.
I'LL PREPARE SOME FOR EATING.
FIRST, WE CUT OFF THE HEAD...
...AND REMOVE CARTILAGE FROM THE UPPER JAW.
WE USE THAT PART IN A PARTICULAR DELICACY.
CAN YOU GUESS WHAT IT IS?
HM?! COULD IT BE?!

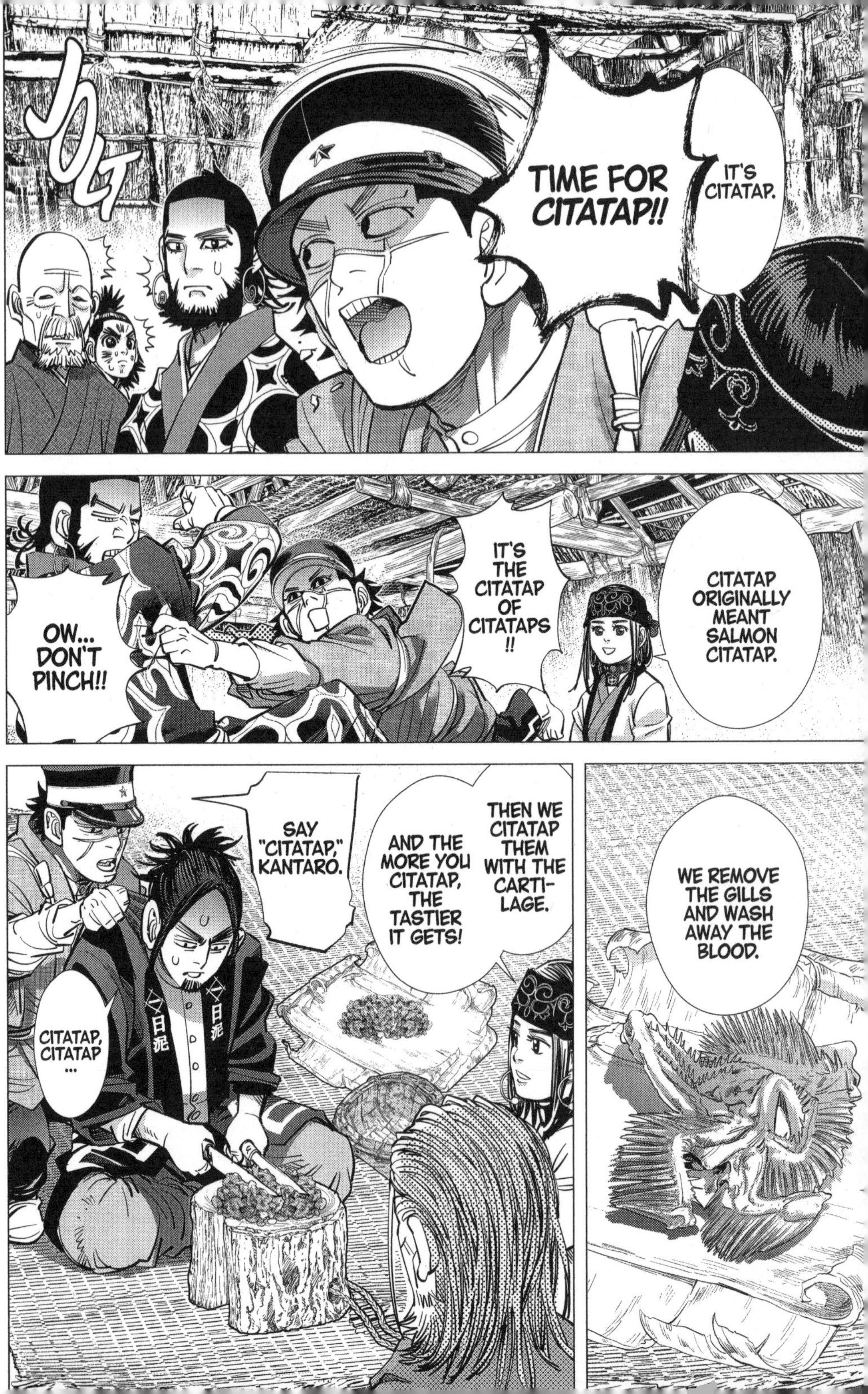
IT'S CITATAP.
TIME FOR CITATAP!!
JOLT
CITATAP ORIGINALLY MEANT SALMON CITATAP.
IT'S THE CITATAP OF CITATAPS!!
OW... DON'T PINCH!!
WE REMOVE THE GILLS AND WASH AWAY THE BLOOD.
THEN WE CITATAP THEM WITH THE CARTI-LAGE.
AND THE MORE YOU CITATAP, THE TASTIER IT GETS!
SAY "CITATAP," KANTARO.
CITATAP, CITATAP ...
日泥

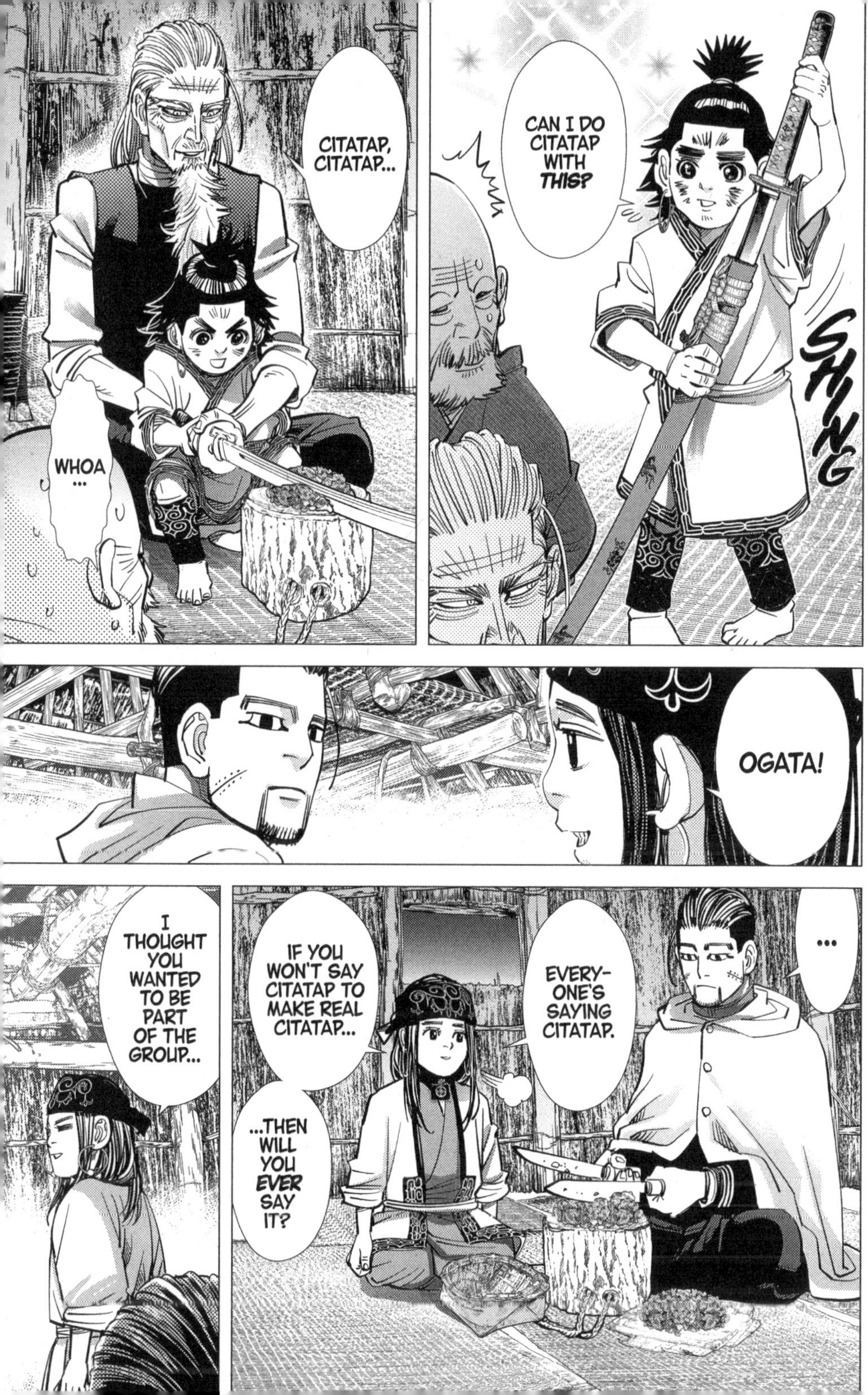
CAN I DO CITATAP WITH THIS?
SHING
CITATAP, CITATAP...
WHOA ...
OGATA!
...
EVERY-ONE'S SAYING CITATAP.
IF YOU WON'T SAY CITATAP TO MAKE REAL CITATAP...
...THEN WILL YOU EVER SAY IT?
I THOUGHT YOU WANTED TO BE PART OF THE GROUP...

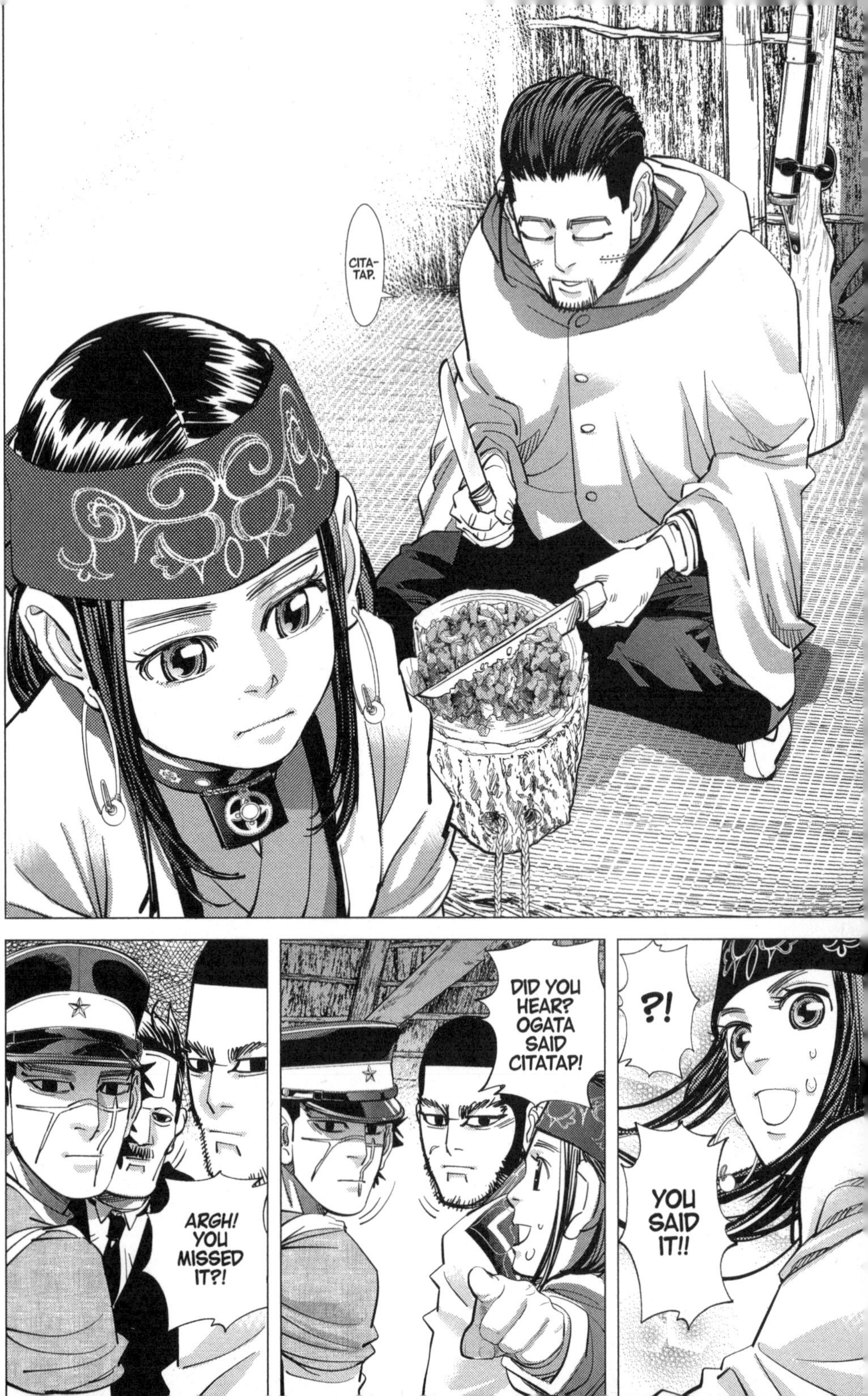
CITA-TAP.
?!
YOU SAID IT!!
DID YOU HEAR? OGATA SAID CITATAP!
ARGH! YOU MISSED IT?!

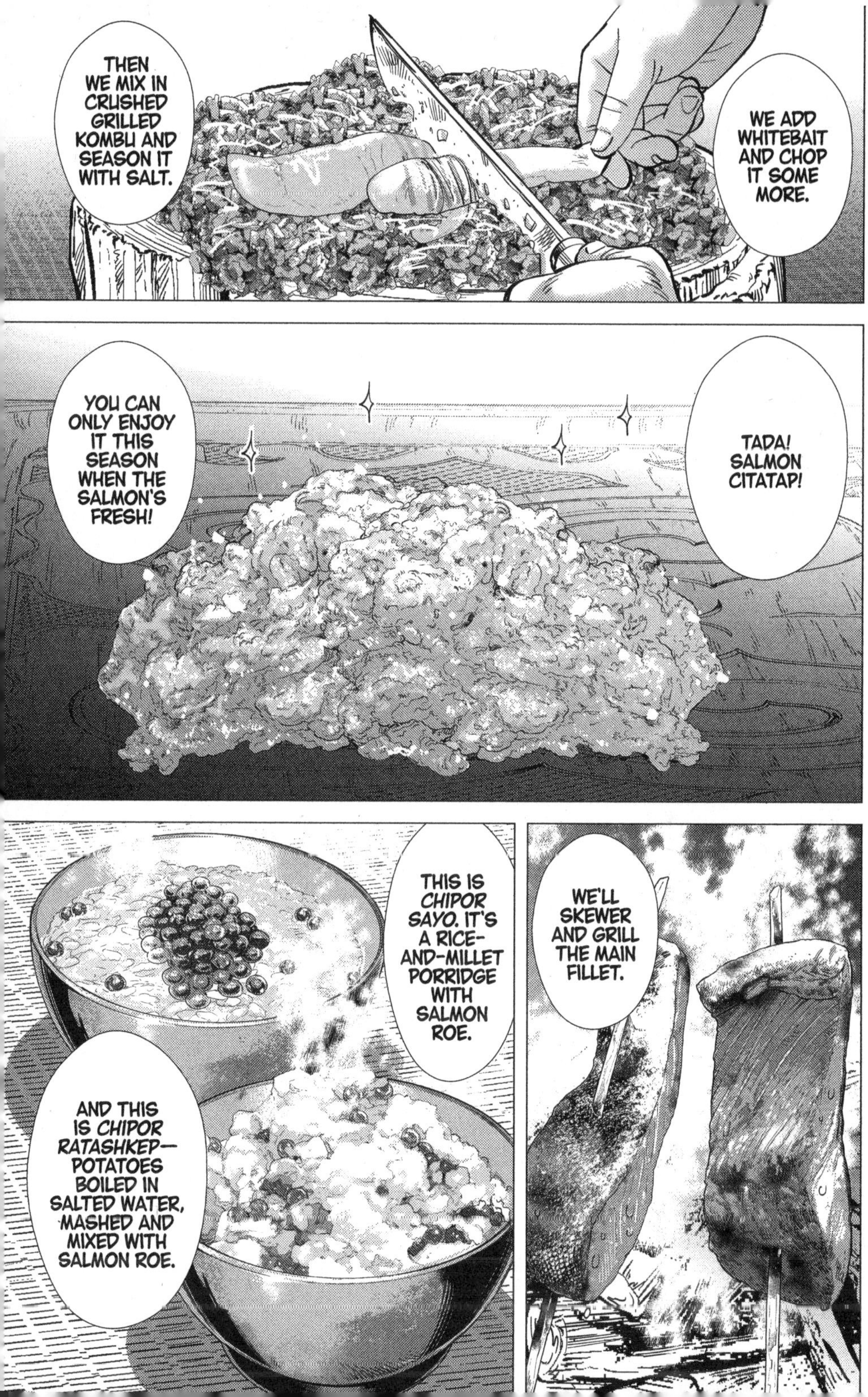
WE ADD WHITEBAIT AND CHOP IT SOME MORE.
THEN WE MIX IN CRUSHED GRILLED KOMBU AND SEASON IT WITH SALT.
TADA! SALMON CITATAP!
YOU CAN ONLY ENJOY IT THIS SEASON WHEN THE SALMON'S FRESH!
WE'LL SKEWER AND GRILL THE MAIN FILLET.
THIS IS *CHIPOR SAYO*. IT'S A RICE-AND-MILLET PORRIDGE WITH SALMON ROE.
AND THIS IS *CHIPOR RATASHKEP*—POTATOES BOILED IN SALTED WATER, MASHED AND MIXED WITH SALMON ROE.

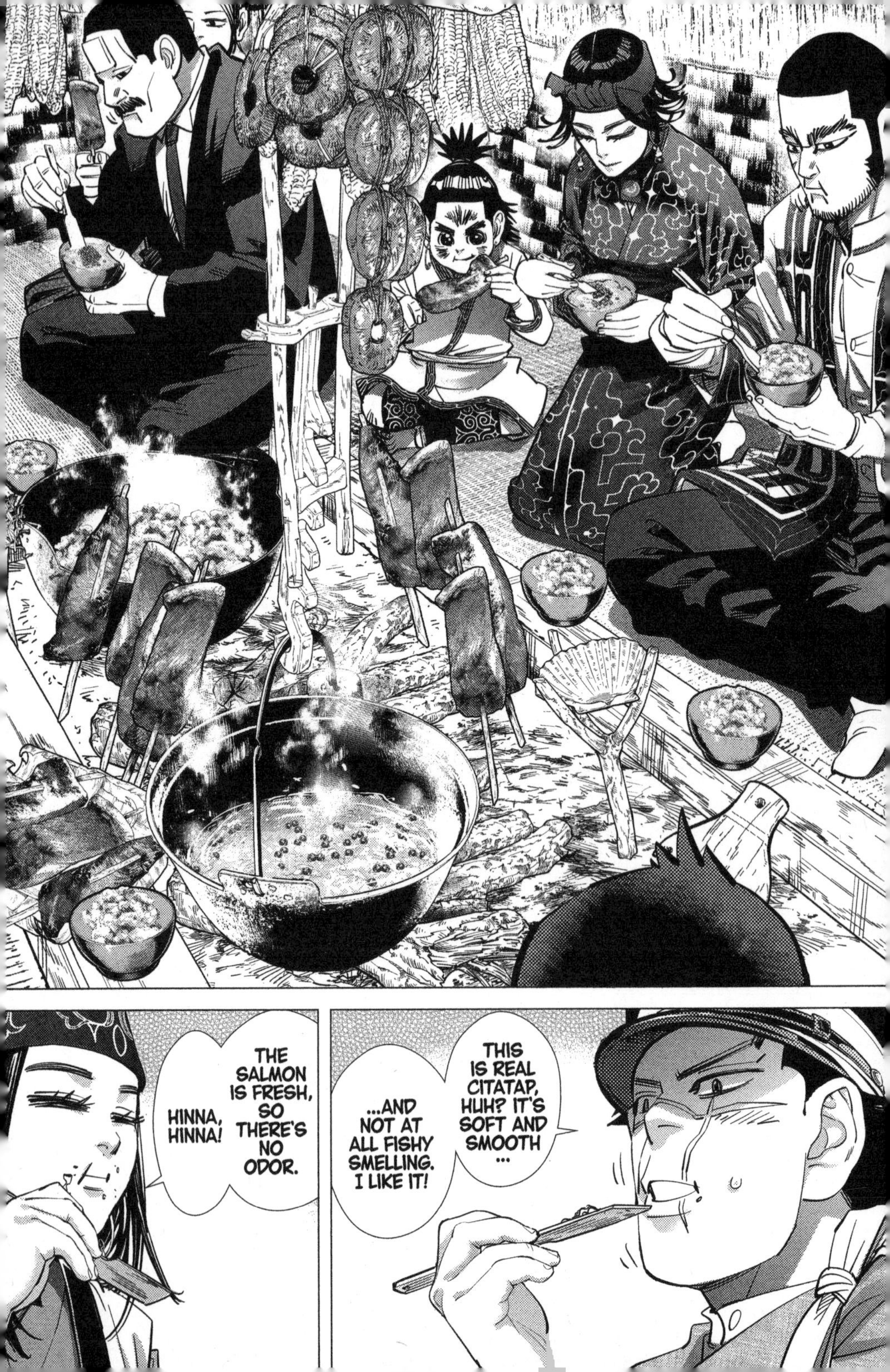
THIS IS REAL CITATAP, HUH? IT'S SOFT AND SMOOTH ...
...AND NOT AT ALL FISHY SMELLING. I LIKE IT!
THE SALMON IS FRESH, SO THERE'S NO ODOR.
HINNA, HINNA!

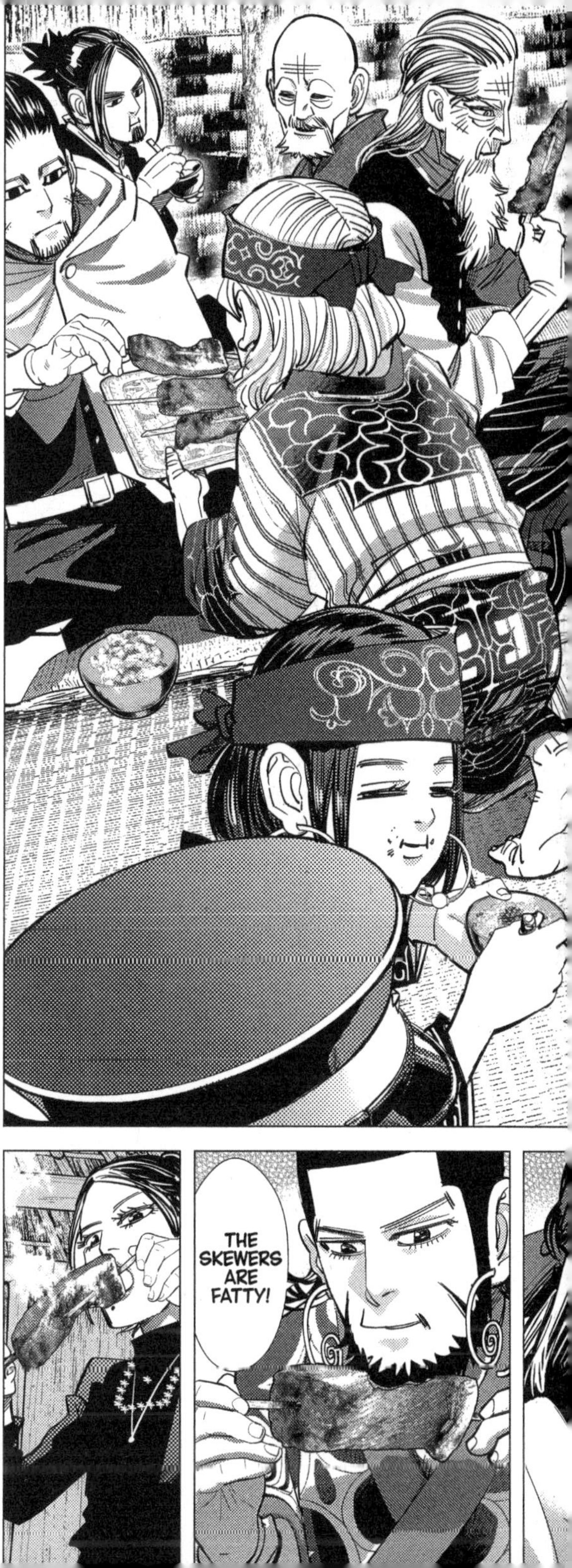
THE SKEWERS ARE FATTY!

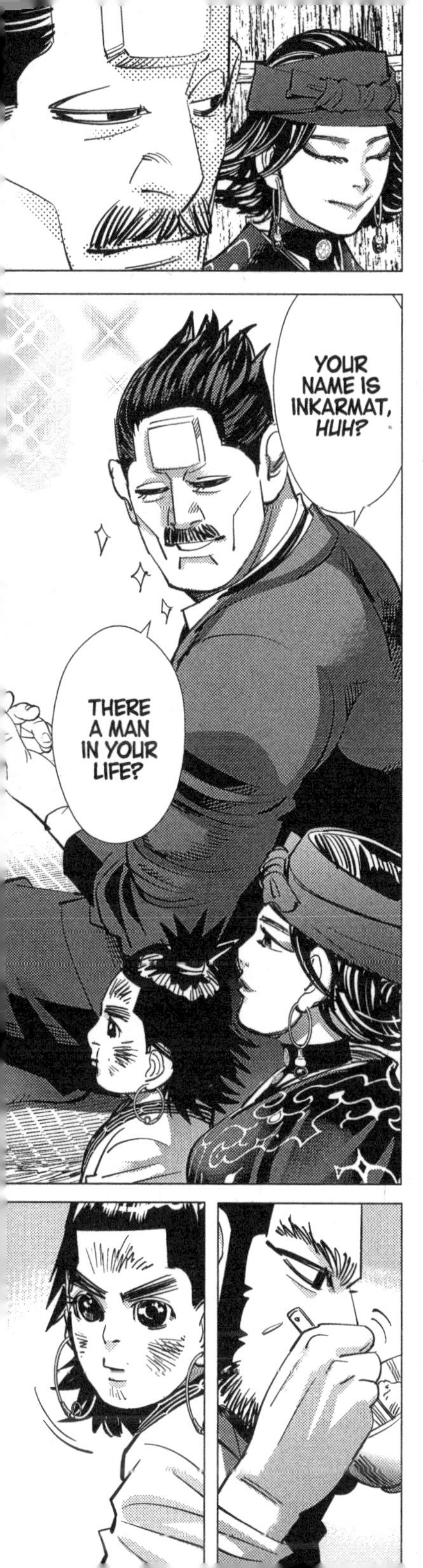
YOUR NAME IS INKARMAT, HUH?
THERE A MAN IN YOUR LIFE?

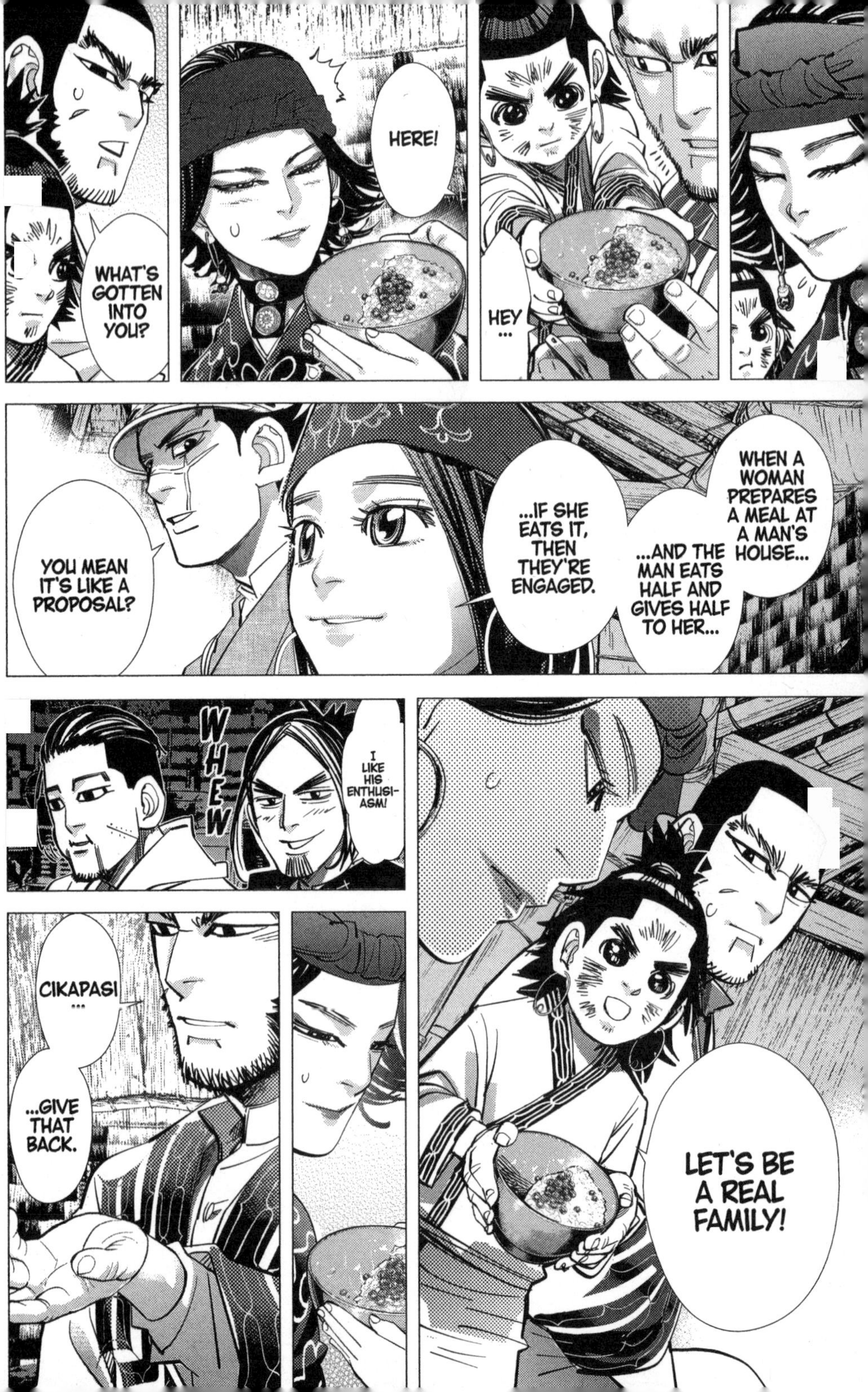
HEY ...
HERE!
WHAT'S GOTTEN INTO YOU?
WHEN A WOMAN PREPARES A MEAL AT A MAN'S HOUSE...
...AND THE MAN EATS HALF AND GIVES HALF TO HER...
...IF SHE EATS IT, THEN THEY'RE ENGAGED.
YOU MEAN IT'S LIKE A PROPOSAL?
LET'S BE A REAL FAMILY!
WHEW
I LIKE HIS ENTHUSI-ASM!
CIKAPASI ...
...GIVE THAT BACK.

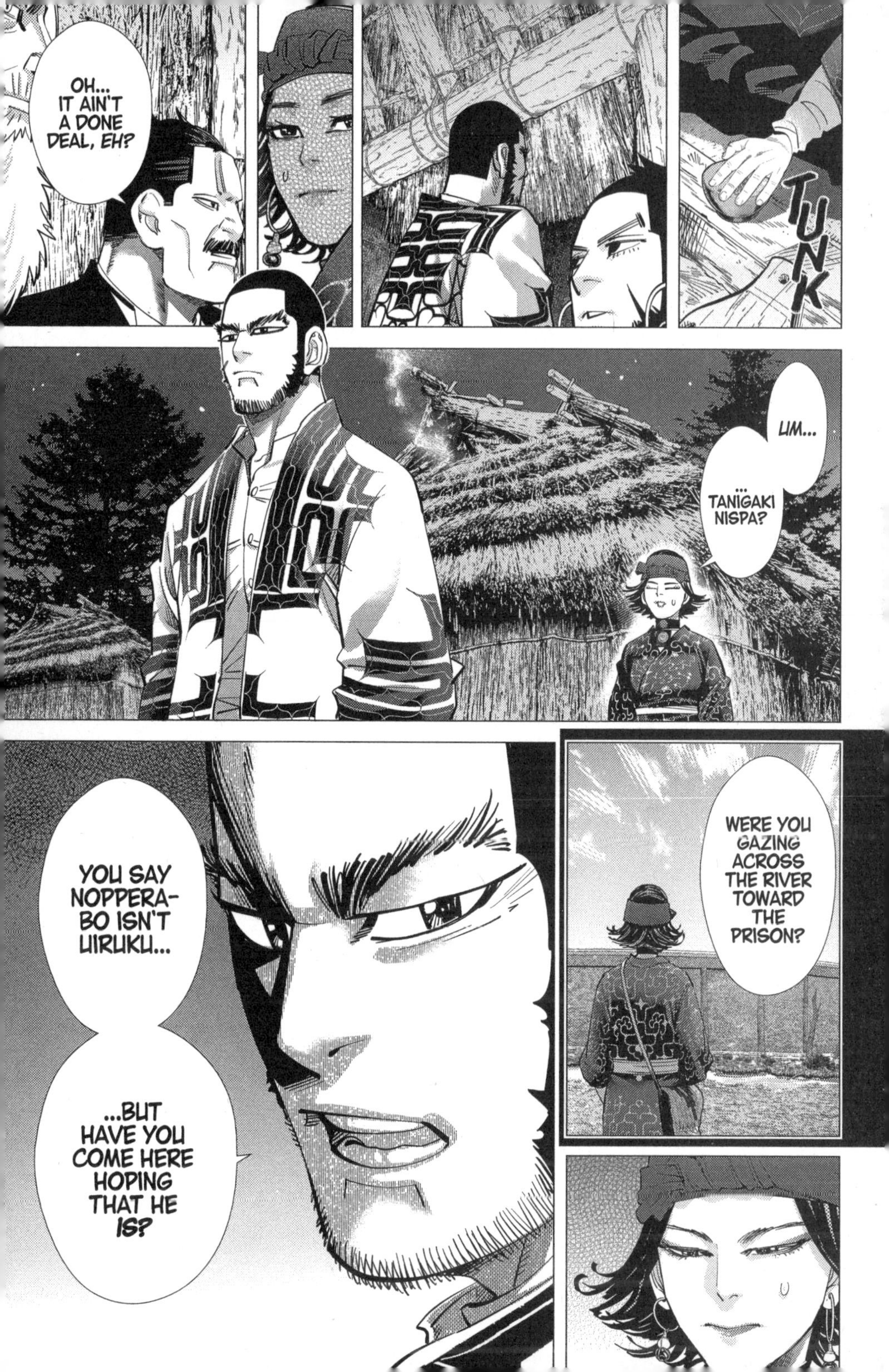
TUNK
OH... IT AIN'T A DONE DEAL, EH?
UM...
...TANIGAKI NISPA?
WERE YOU GAZING ACROSS THE RIVER TOWARD THE PRISON?
YOU SAY NOPPERA-BO ISN'T UIRUKU...
...BUT HAVE YOU COME HERE HOPING THAT HE IS?

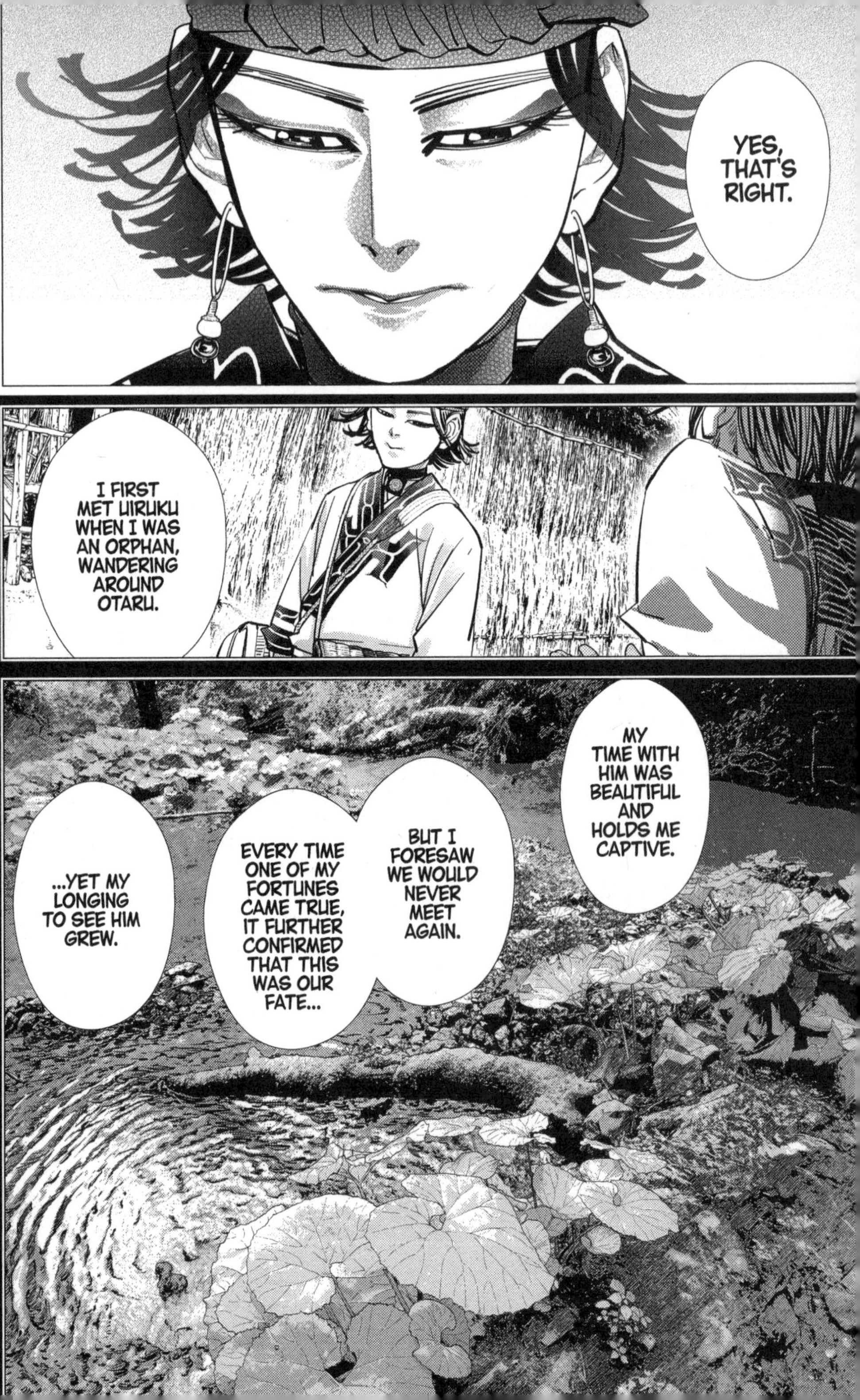
YES, THAT'S RIGHT.
I FIRST MET WIRUKU WHEN I WAS AN ORPHAN, WANDERING AROUND OTARU.
MY TIME WITH HIM WAS BEAUTIFUL AND HOLDS ME CAPTIVE.
BUT I FORESAW WE WOULD NEVER MEET AGAIN.
EVERY TIME ONE OF MY FORTUNES CAME TRUE, IT FURTHER CONFIRMED THAT THIS WAS OUR FATE...
...YET MY LONGING TO SEE HIM GREW.

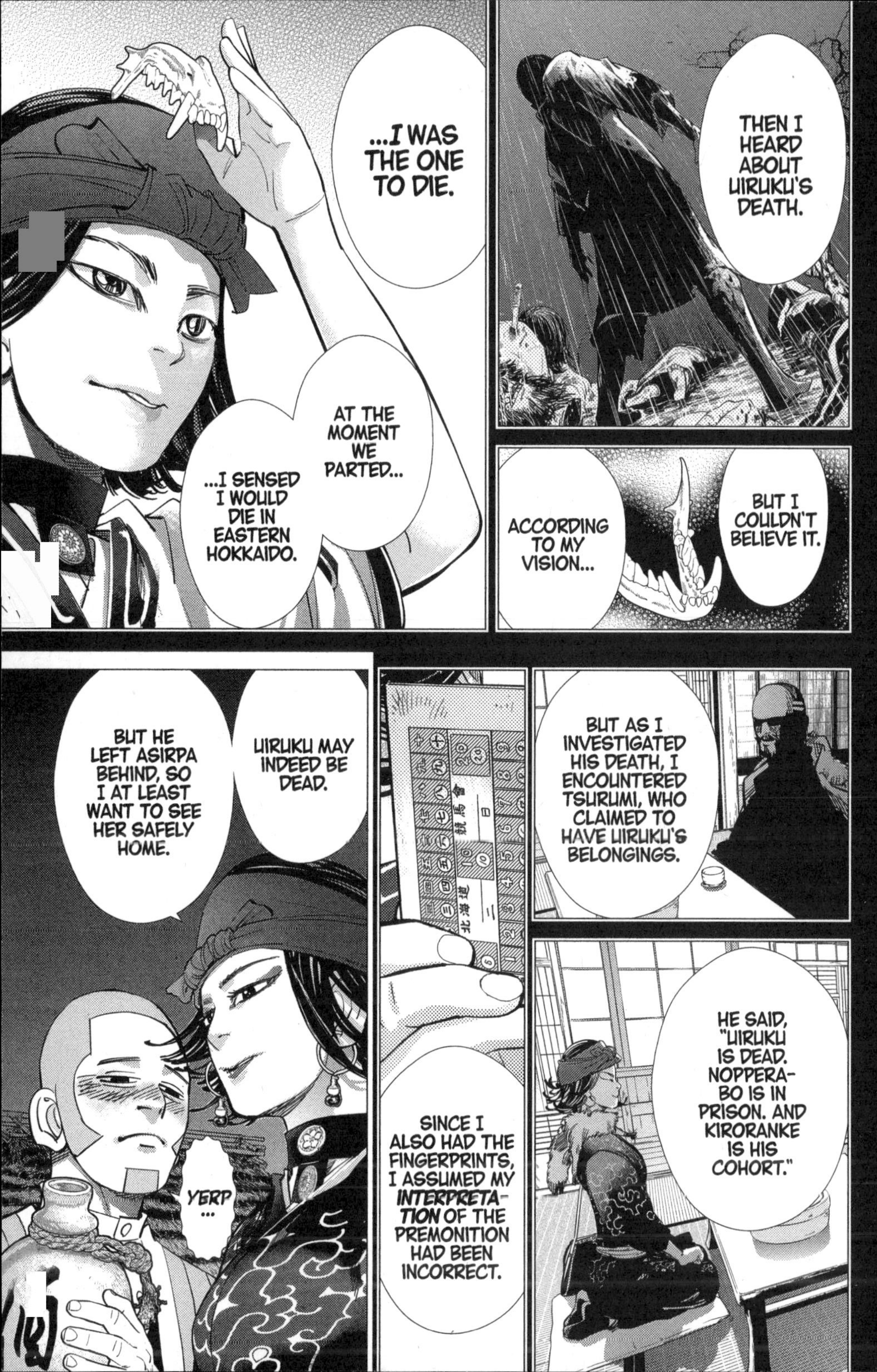
THEN I HEARD ABOUT UIRUKU'S DEATH.
BUT I COULDN'T BELIEVE IT.
ACCORDING TO MY VISION...
...I WAS THE ONE TO DIE.
AT THE MOMENT WE PARTED...
...I SENSED I WOULD DIE IN EASTERN HOKKAIDO.
BUT AS I INVESTIGATED HIS DEATH, I ENCOUNTERED TSURUMI, WHO CLAIMED TO HAVE UIRUKU'S BELONGINGS.
HE SAID, "UIRUKU IS DEAD. NOPPERA-BO IS IN PRISON. AND KIRORANKE IS HIS COHORT."
SINCE I ALSO HAD THE FINGERPRINTS, I ASSUMED MY *INTERPRETATION* OF THE PREMONITION HAD BEEN INCORRECT.
UIRUKU MAY INDEED BE DEAD.
BUT HE LEFT ASIRPA BEHIND, SO I AT LEAST WANT TO SEE HER SAFELY HOME.
YERP...

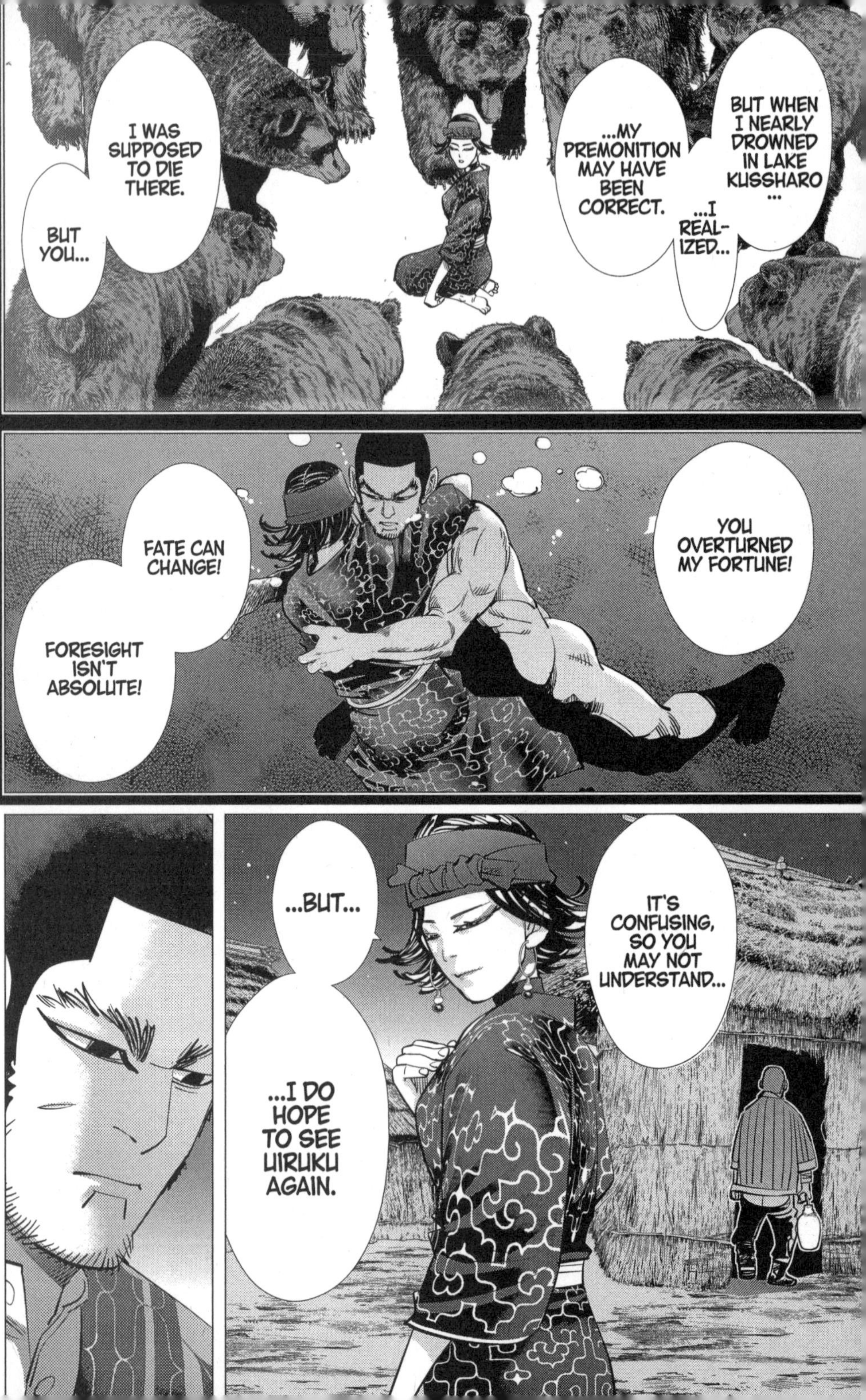
BUT WHEN I NEARLY DROWNED IN LAKE KUSSHARO...
...I REALIZED...
...MY PREMONITION MAY HAVE BEEN CORRECT.
I WAS SUPPOSED TO DIE THERE.
BUT YOU...
YOU OVERTURNED MY FORTUNE!
FATE CAN CHANGE!
FORESIGHT ISN'T ABSOLUTE!
IT'S CONFUSING, SO YOU MAY NOT UNDERSTAND...
...BUT...
...I DO HOPE TO SEE UIRUKU AGAIN.

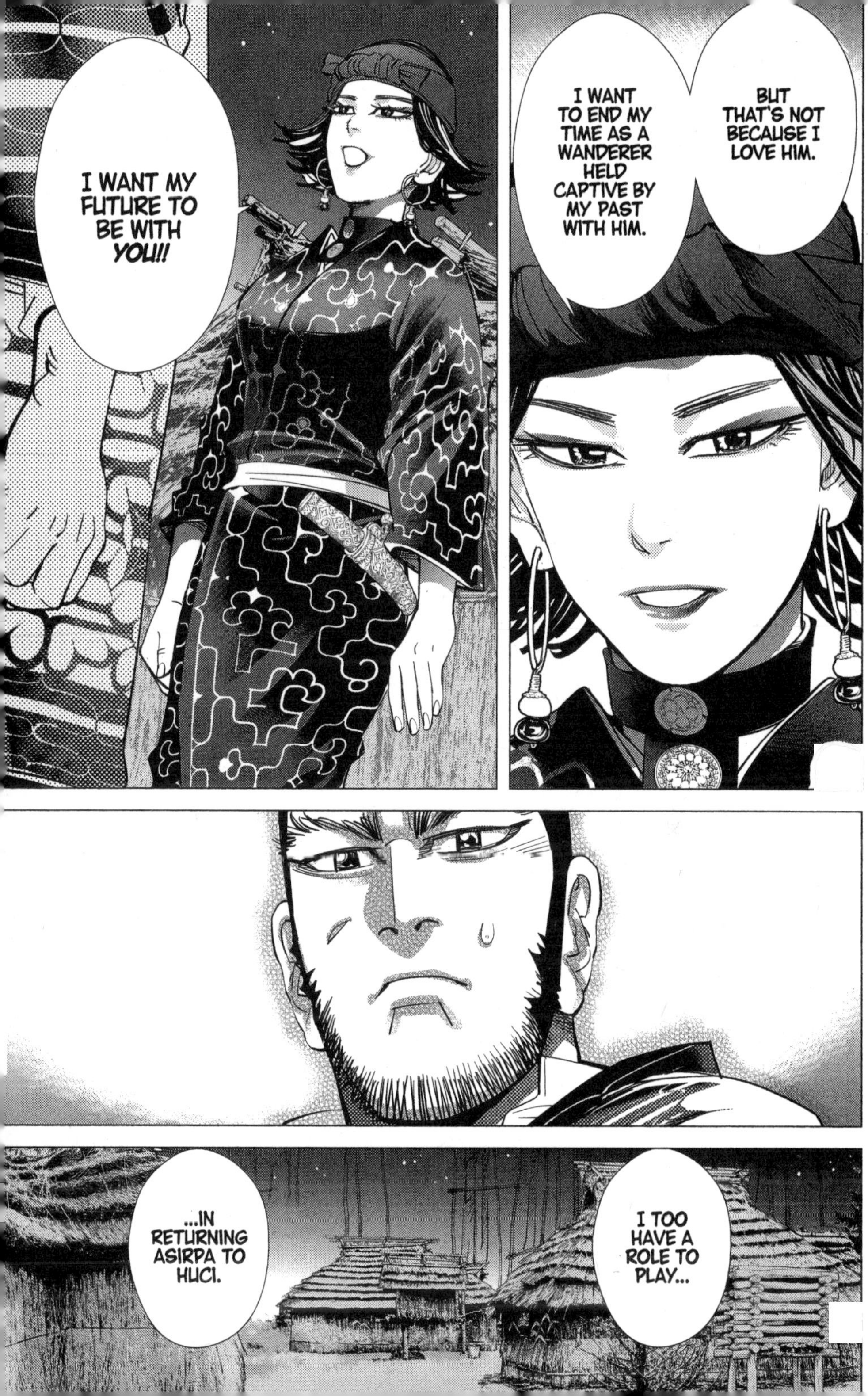
BUT THAT'S NOT BECAUSE I LOVE HIM.
I WANT TO END MY TIME AS A WANDERER HELD CAPTIVE BY MY PAST WITH HIM.
I WANT MY FUTURE TO BE WITH *YOU!!*
I TOO HAVE A ROLE TO PLAY...
...IN RETURNING ASIRPA TO HUCI.

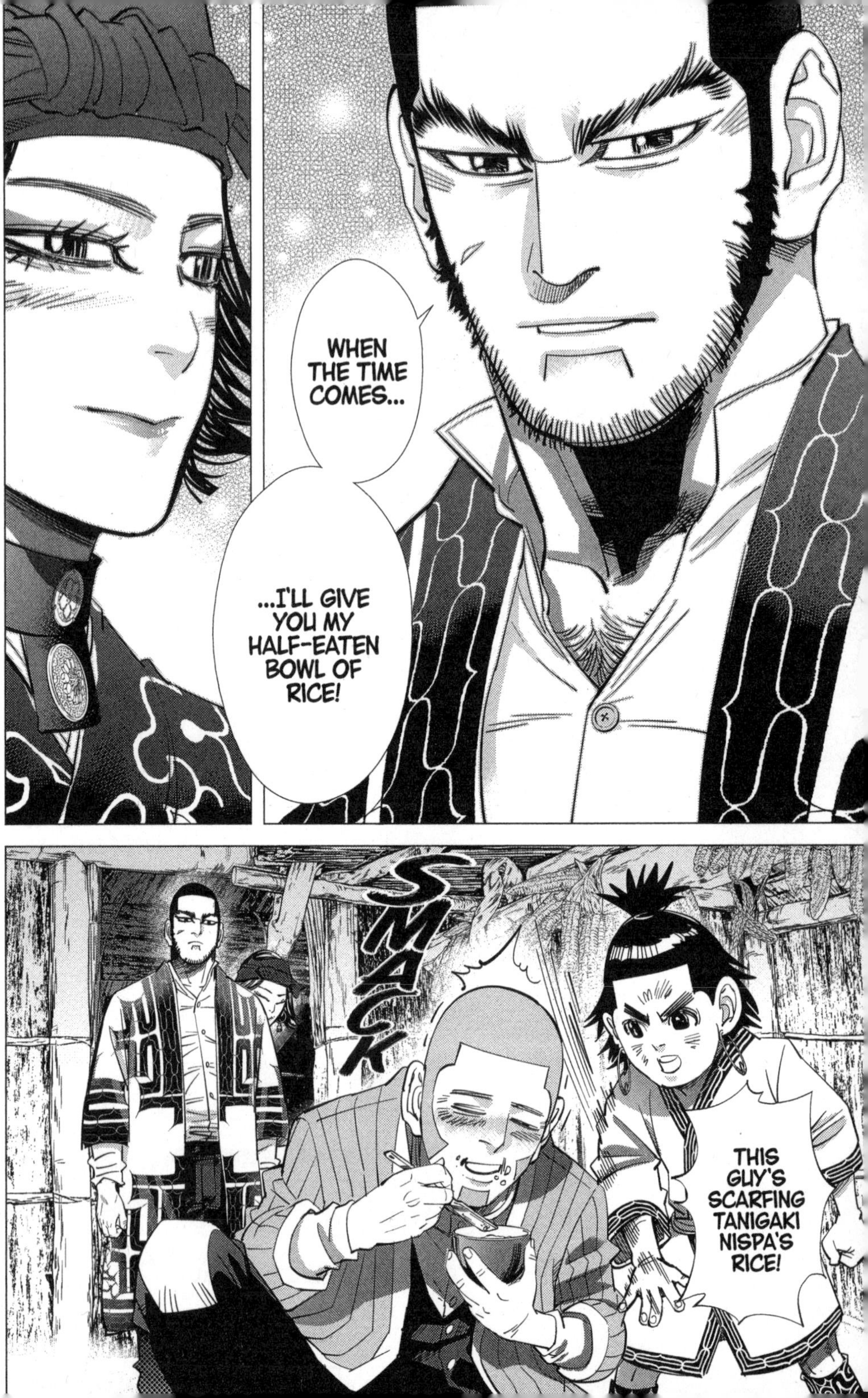
WHEN THE TIME COMES...
...I'LL GIVE YOU MY HALF-EATEN BOWL OF RICE!
SMACK
THIS GUY'S SCARFING TANIGAKI NISPA'S RICE!

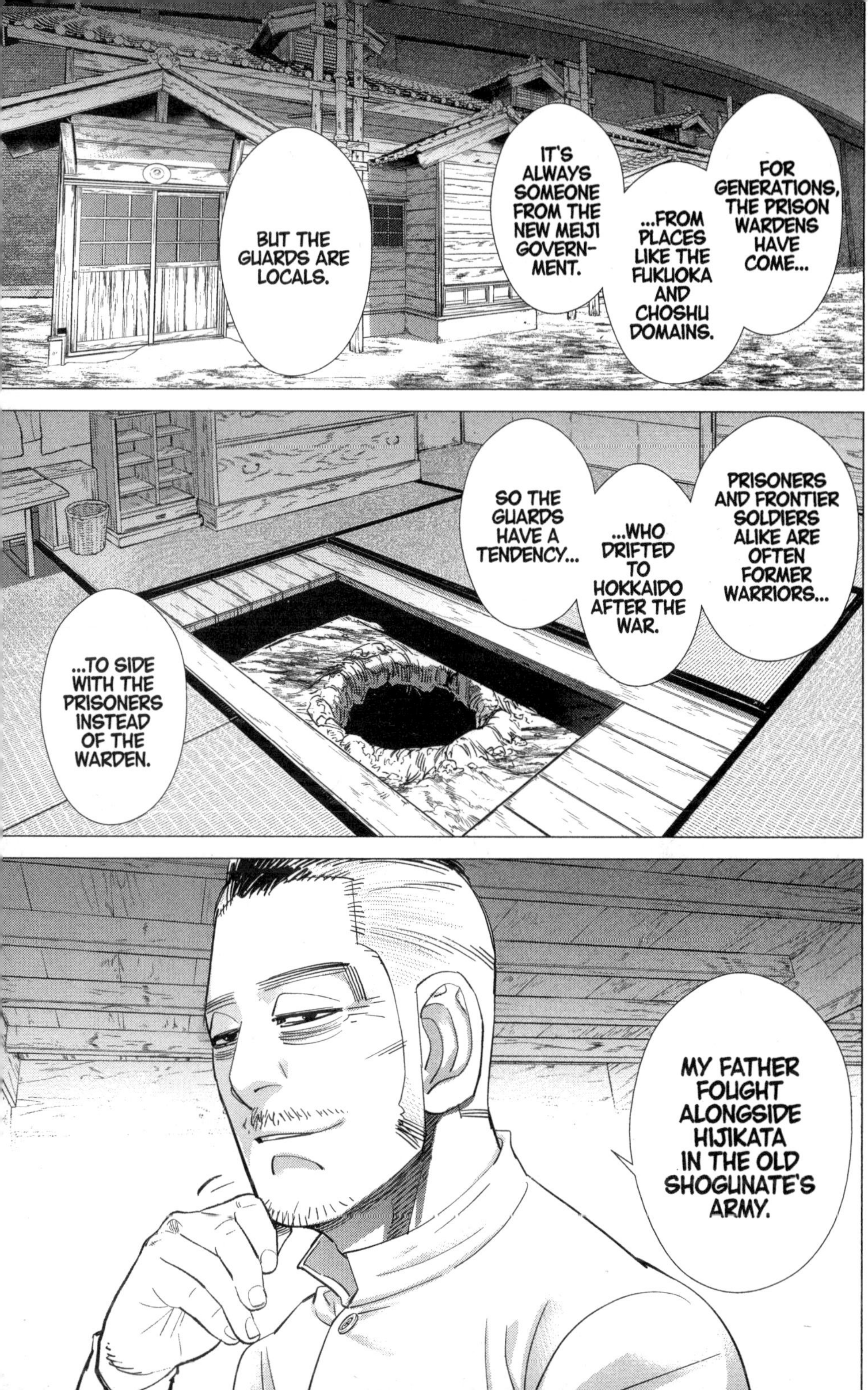
FOR GENERATIONS, THE PRISON WARDENS HAVE COME...
...FROM PLACES LIKE THE FUKUOKA AND CHOSHU DOMAINS.
IT'S ALWAYS SOMEONE FROM THE NEW MEIJI GOVERNMENT.
BUT THE GUARDS ARE LOCALS.
PRISONERS AND FRONTIER SOLDIERS ALIKE ARE OFTEN FORMER WARRIORS...
...WHO DRIFTED TO HOKKAIDO AFTER THE WAR.
SO THE GUARDS HAVE A TENDENCY...
...TO SIDE WITH THE PRISONERS INSTEAD OF THE WARDEN.
MY FATHER FOUGHT ALONGSIDE HIJIKATA IN THE OLD SHOGUNATE'S ARMY.

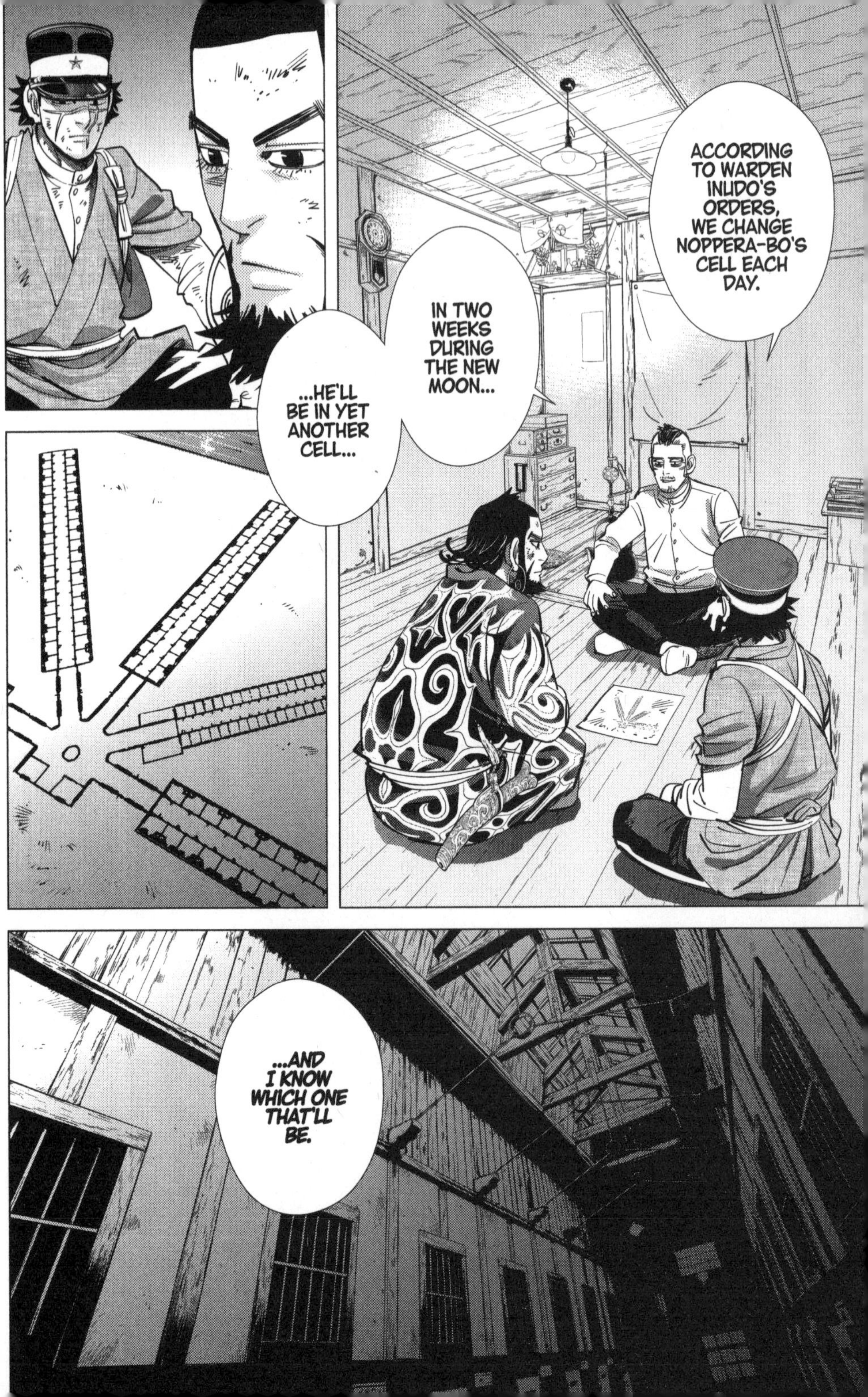
ACCORDING TO WARDEN INUDO'S ORDERS, WE CHANGE NOPPERA-BO'S CELL EACH DAY.
IN TWO WEEKS DURING THE NEW MOON...
...HE'LL BE IN YET ANOTHER CELL...
...AND I KNOW WHICH ONE THAT'LL BE.

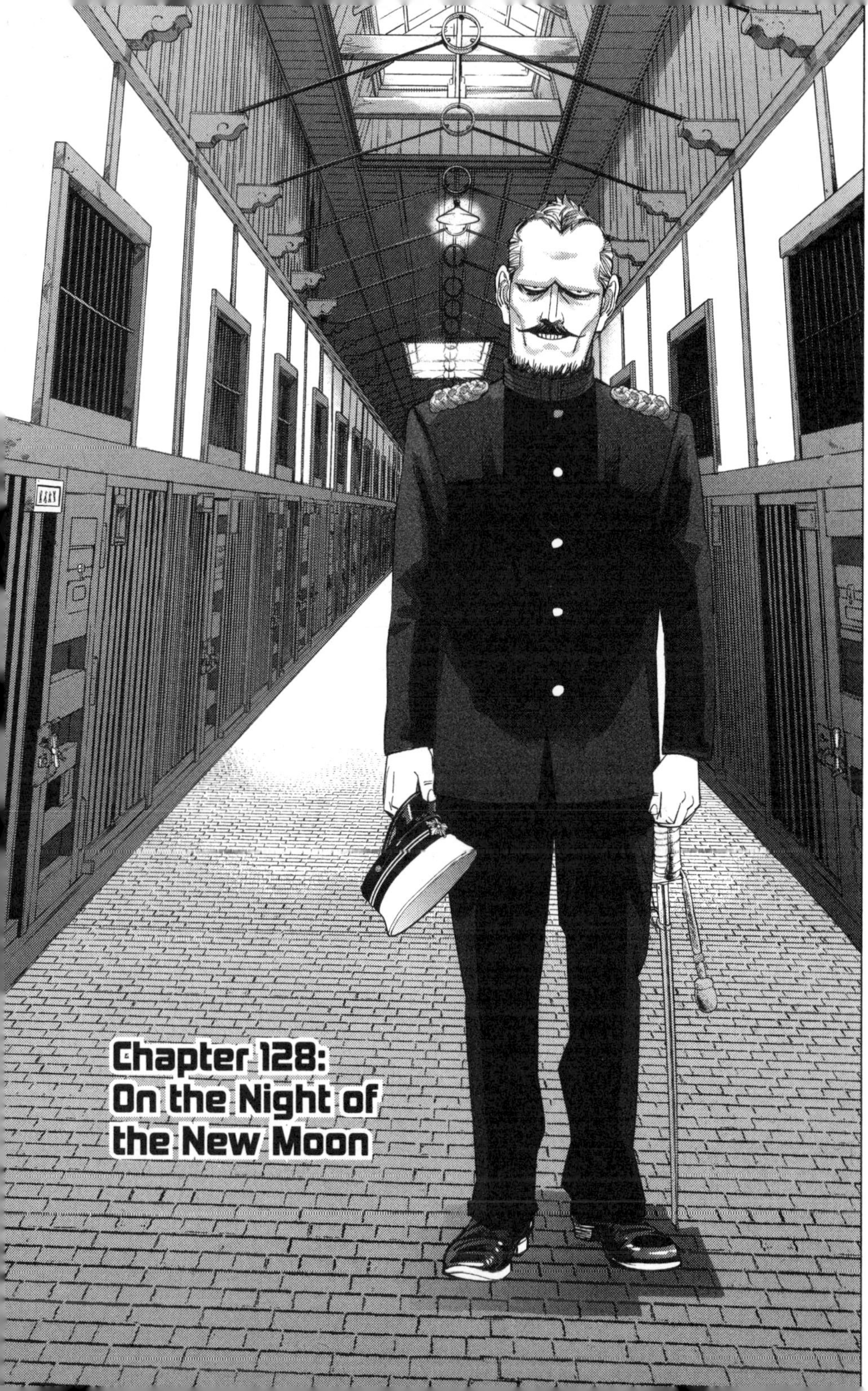
Chapter 128:
On the Night of
the New Moon

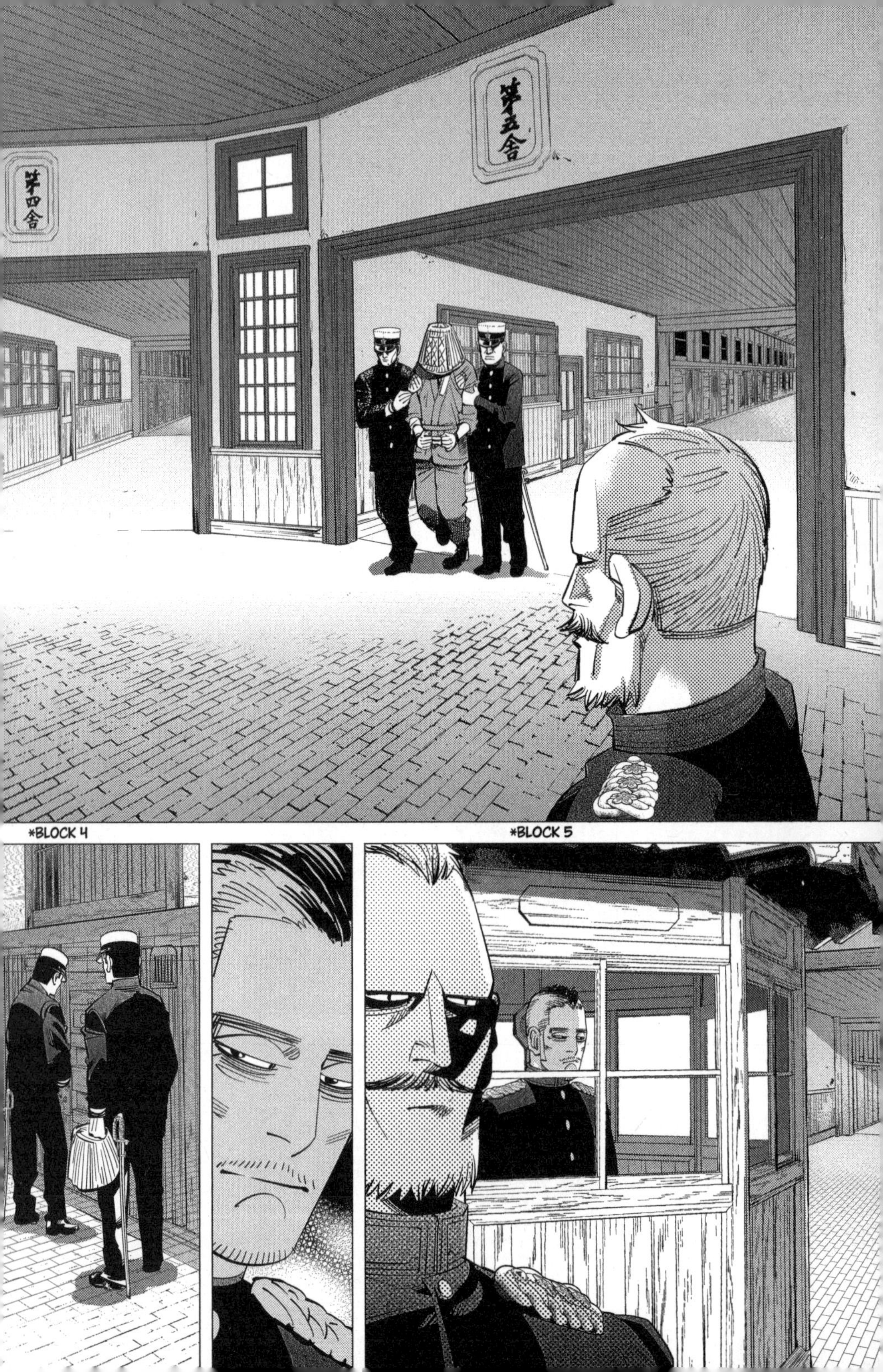
第五舎
第四舎
*BLOCK 5
*BLOCK 4

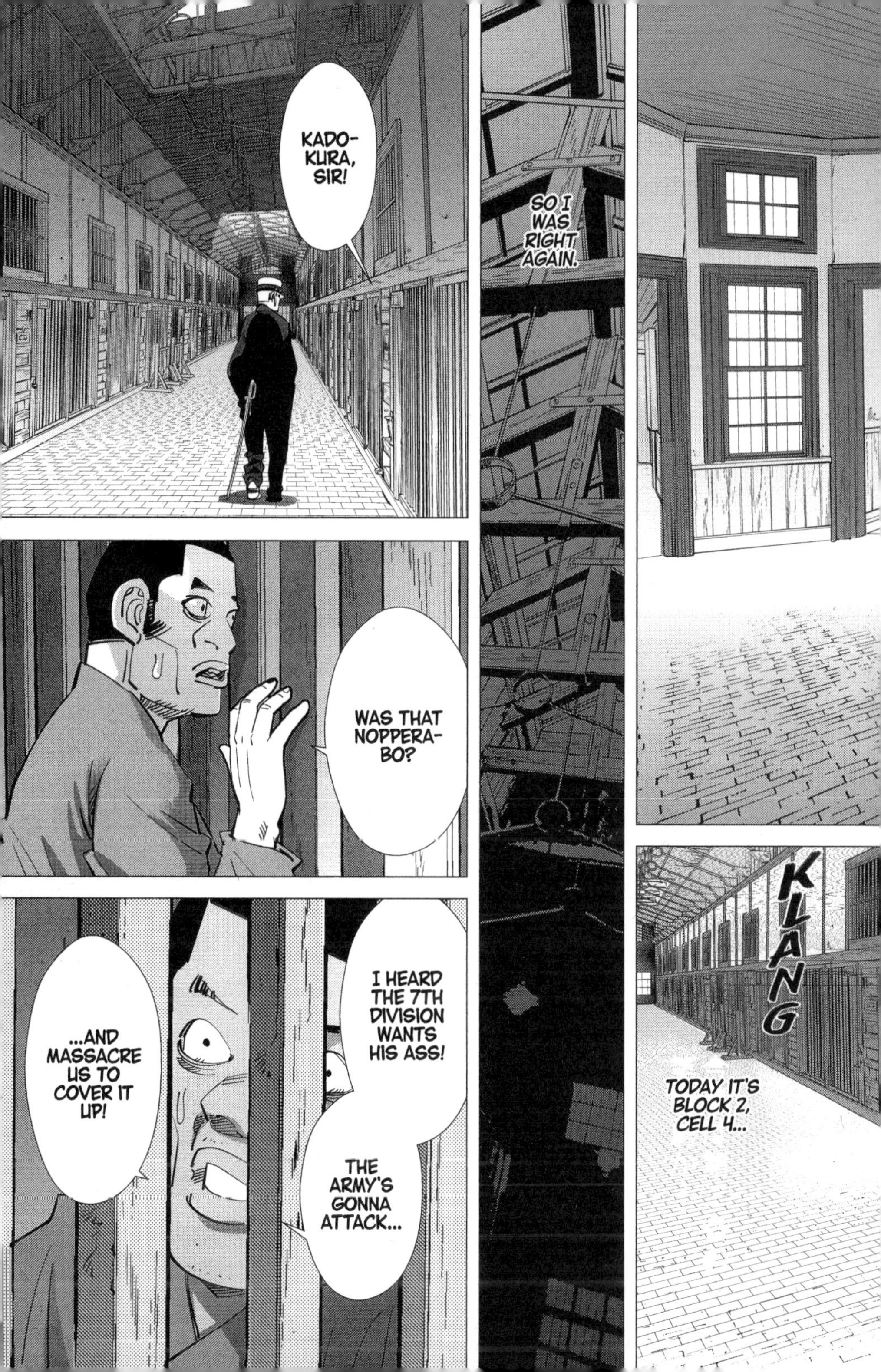
KLANG
TODAY IT'S BLOCK 2, CELL 4...
SO I WAS RIGHT AGAIN.
KADO-KURA, SIR!
WAS THAT NOPPERA-BO?
I HEARD THE 7TH DIVISION WANTS HIS ASS!
THE ARMY'S GONNA ATTACK...
...AND MASSACRE US TO COVER IT UP!

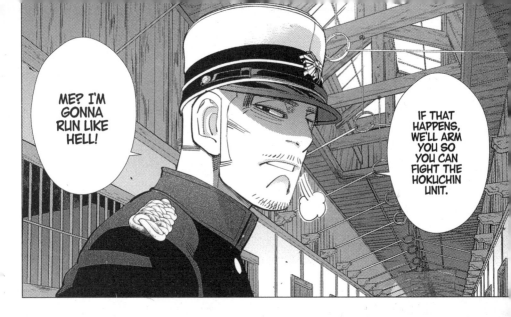

IF THAT HAPPENS, WE'LL ARM YOU SO YOU CAN FIGHT THE HOKUCHIN UNIT.
ME? I'M GONNA RUN LIKE HELL!
NOPPERA-BO'S CELL ON THE NIGHT OF THE NEW MOON...
...WILL BE CELL 66, BLOCK 4.

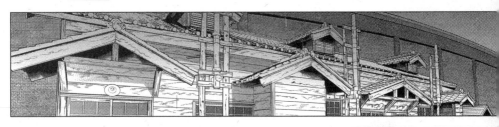

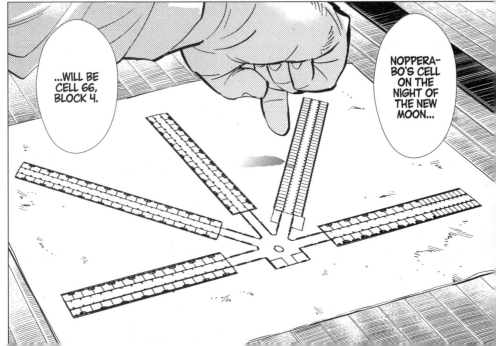

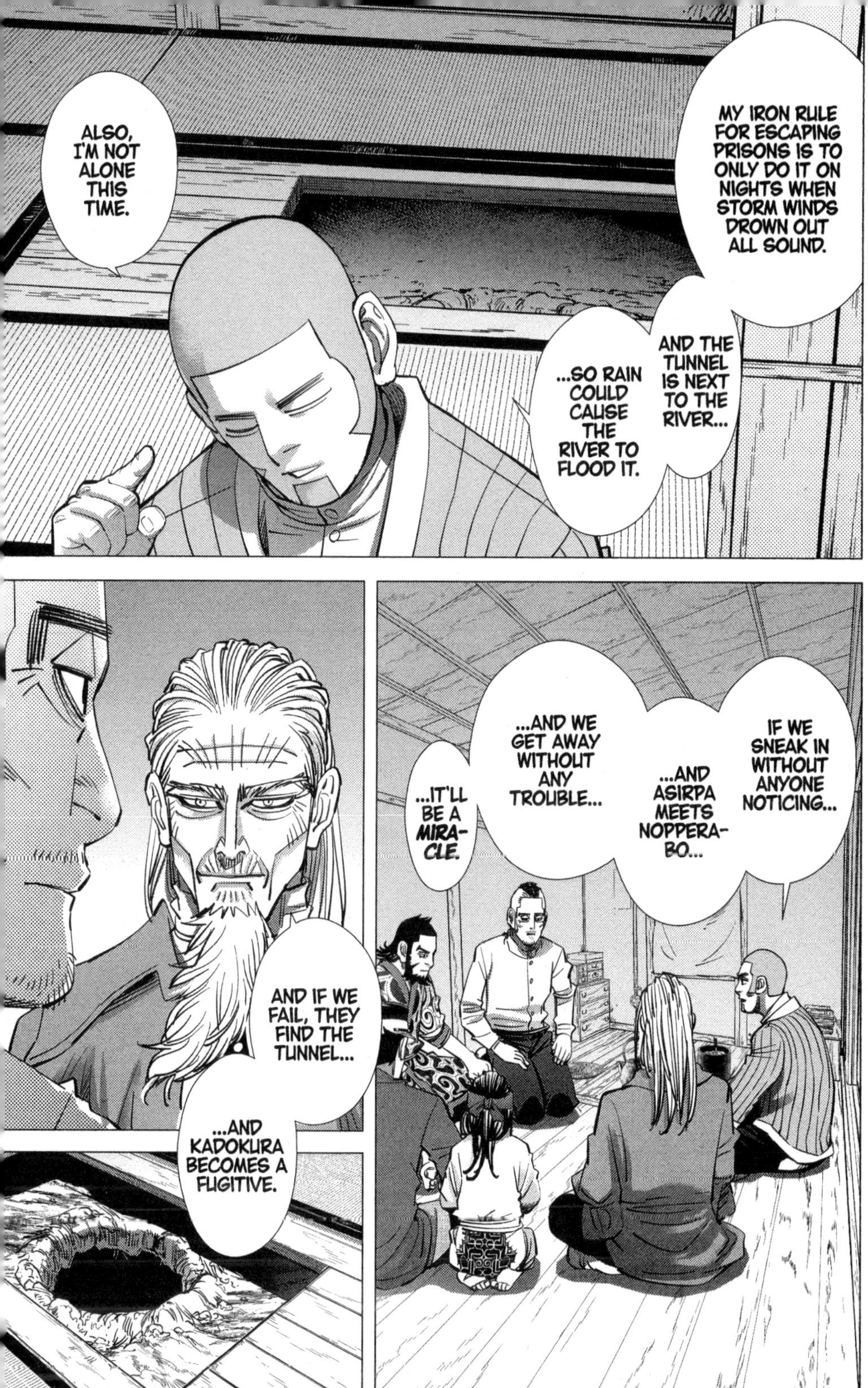
MY IRON RULE FOR ESCAPING PRISONS IS TO ONLY DO IT ON NIGHTS WHEN STORM WINDS DROWN OUT ALL SOUND.
AND THE TUNNEL IS NEXT TO THE RIVER...
...SO RAIN COULD CAUSE THE RIVER TO FLOOD IT.
ALSO, I'M NOT ALONE THIS TIME.
IF WE SNEAK IN WITHOUT ANYONE NOTICING...
...AND ASIRPA MEETS NOPPERA-BO...
...AND WE GET AWAY WITHOUT ANY TROUBLE...
...IT'LL BE A MIRACLE.
AND IF WE FAIL, THEY FIND THE TUNNEL...
...AND KADOKURA BECOMES A FUGITIVE.

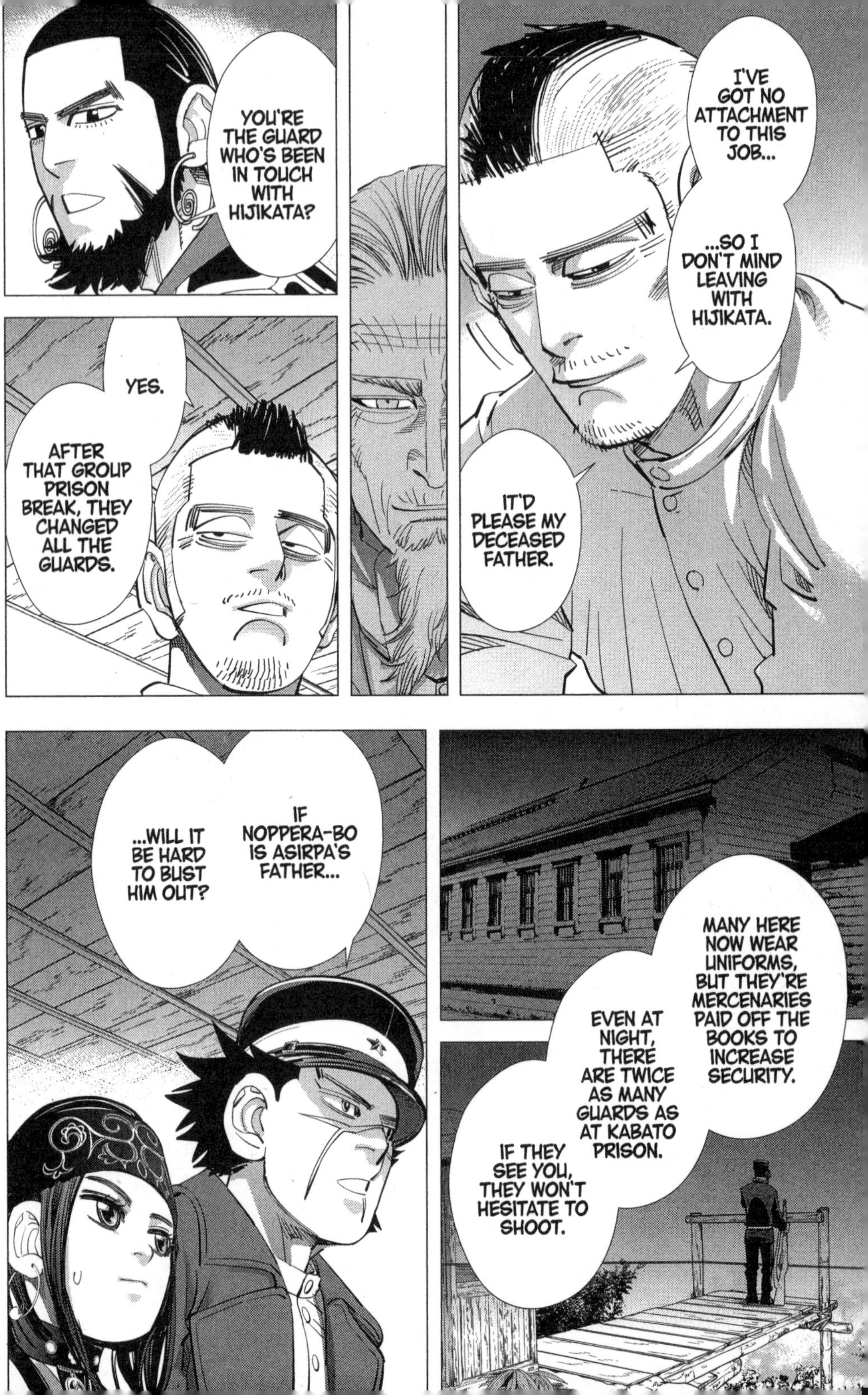
I'VE GOT NO ATTACHMENT TO THIS JOB...
...SO I DON'T MIND LEAVING WITH HIJIKATA.
IT'D PLEASE MY DECEASED FATHER.
YOU'RE THE GUARD WHO'S BEEN IN TOUCH WITH HIJIKATA?
YES.
AFTER THAT GROUP PRISON BREAK, THEY CHANGED ALL THE GUARDS.
MANY HERE NOW WEAR UNIFORMS, BUT THEY'RE MERCENARIES PAID OFF THE BOOKS TO INCREASE SECURITY.
EVEN AT NIGHT, THERE ARE TWICE AS MANY GUARDS AS AT KABATO PRISON.
IF THEY SEE YOU, THEY WON'T HESITATE TO SHOOT.
IF NOPPERA-BO IS ASIRPA'S FATHER...
...WILL IT BE HARD TO BUST HIM OUT?

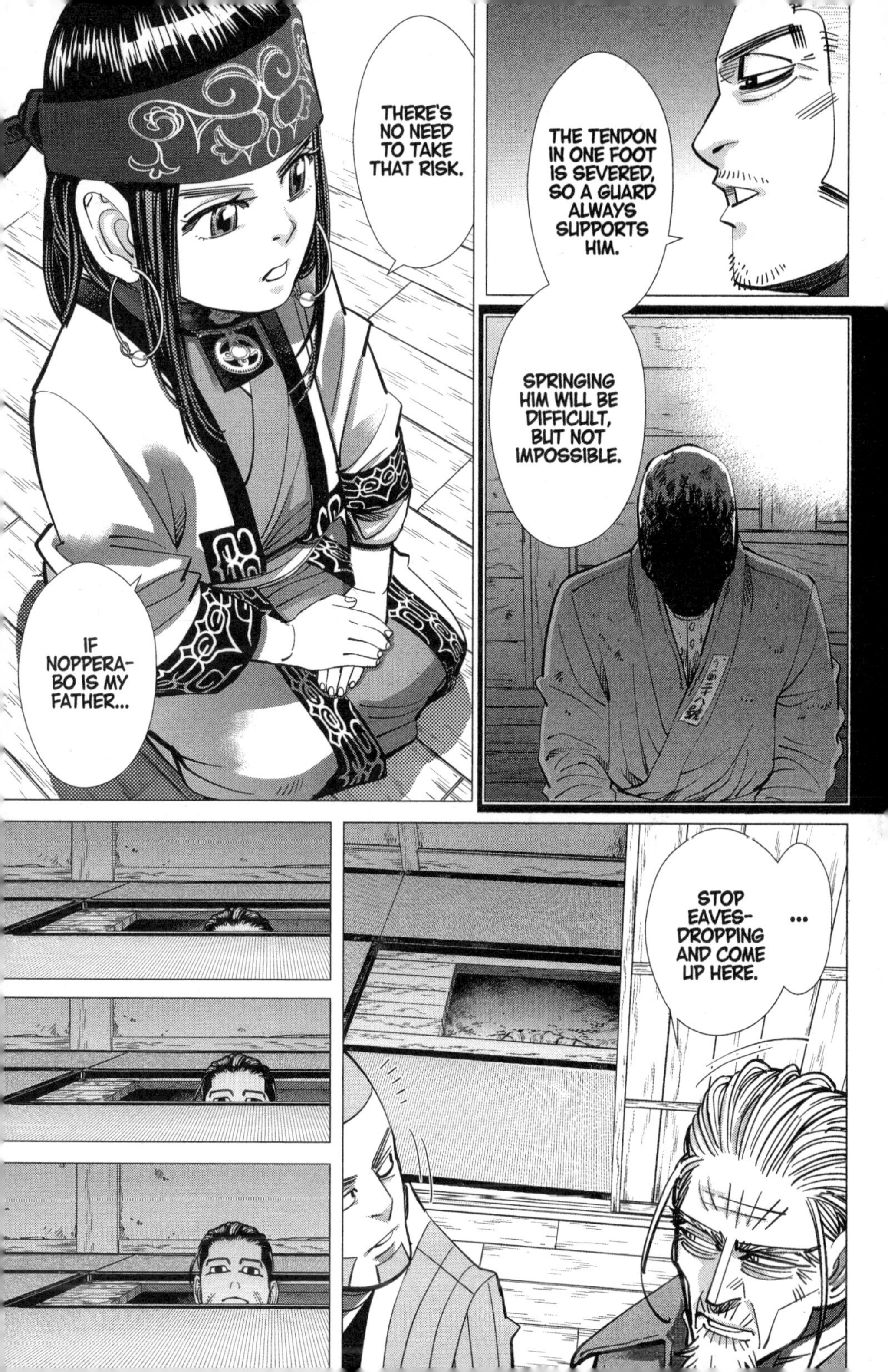
THE TENDON IN ONE FOOT IS SEVERED, SO A GUARD ALWAYS SUPPORTS HIM.
SPRINGING HIM WILL BE DIFFICULT, BUT NOT IMPOSSIBLE.
...
THERE'S NO NEED TO TAKE THAT RISK.
IF NOPPERA-BO IS MY FATHER...
...
STOP EAVES-DROPPING AND COME UP HERE.

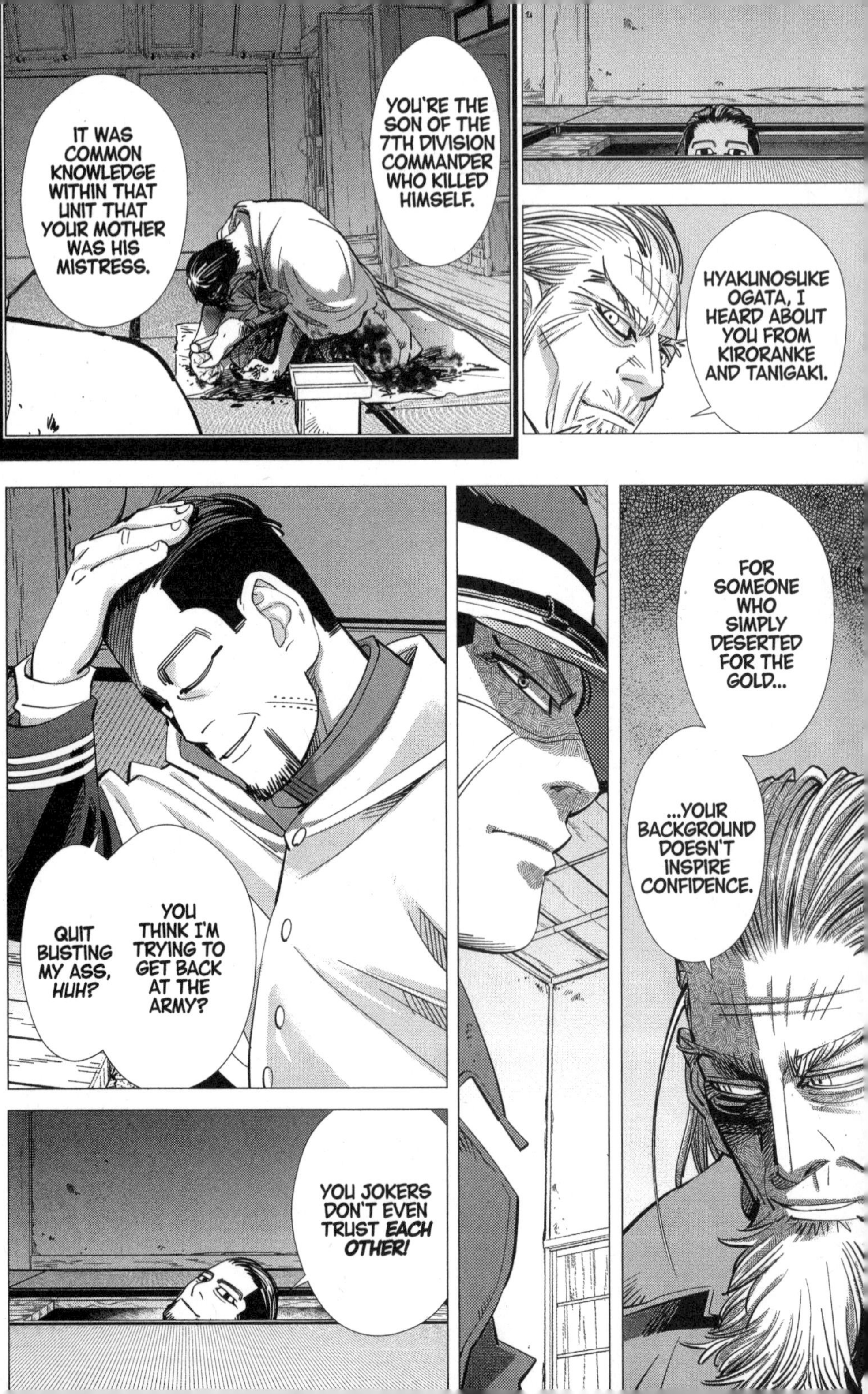
HYAKUNOSUKE OGATA, I HEARD ABOUT YOU FROM KIRORANKE AND TANIGAKI.
YOU'RE THE SON OF THE 7TH DIVISION COMMANDER WHO KILLED HIMSELF.
IT WAS COMMON KNOWLEDGE WITHIN THAT UNIT THAT YOUR MOTHER WAS HIS MISTRESS.
FOR SOMEONE WHO SIMPLY DESERTED FOR THE GOLD...
...YOUR BACKGROUND DOESN'T INSPIRE CONFIDENCE.
YOU THINK I'M TRYING TO GET BACK AT THE ARMY?
QUIT BUSTING MY ASS, HUH?
YOU JOKERS DON'T EVEN TRUST *EACH OTHER!*

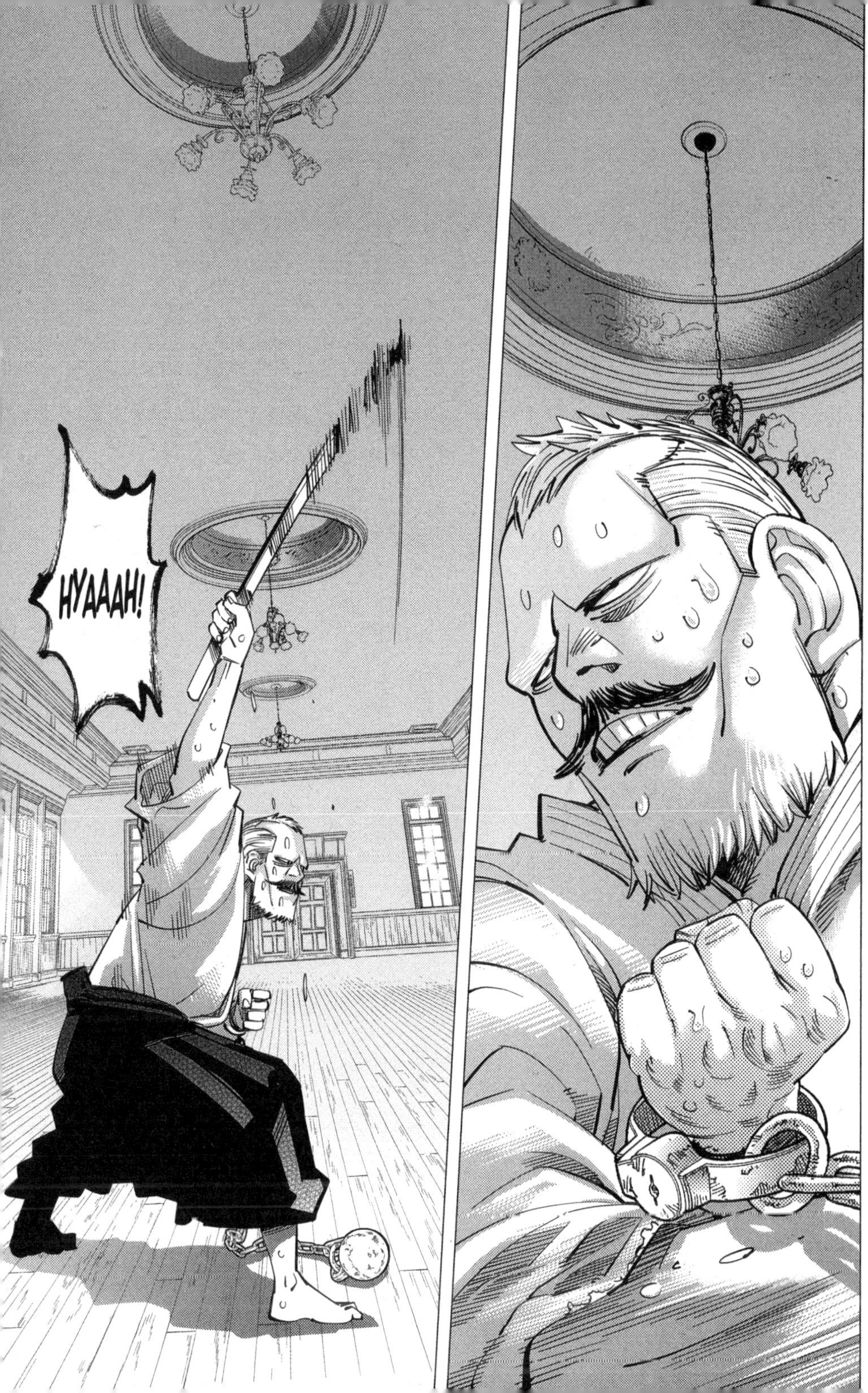
HYAAAH!

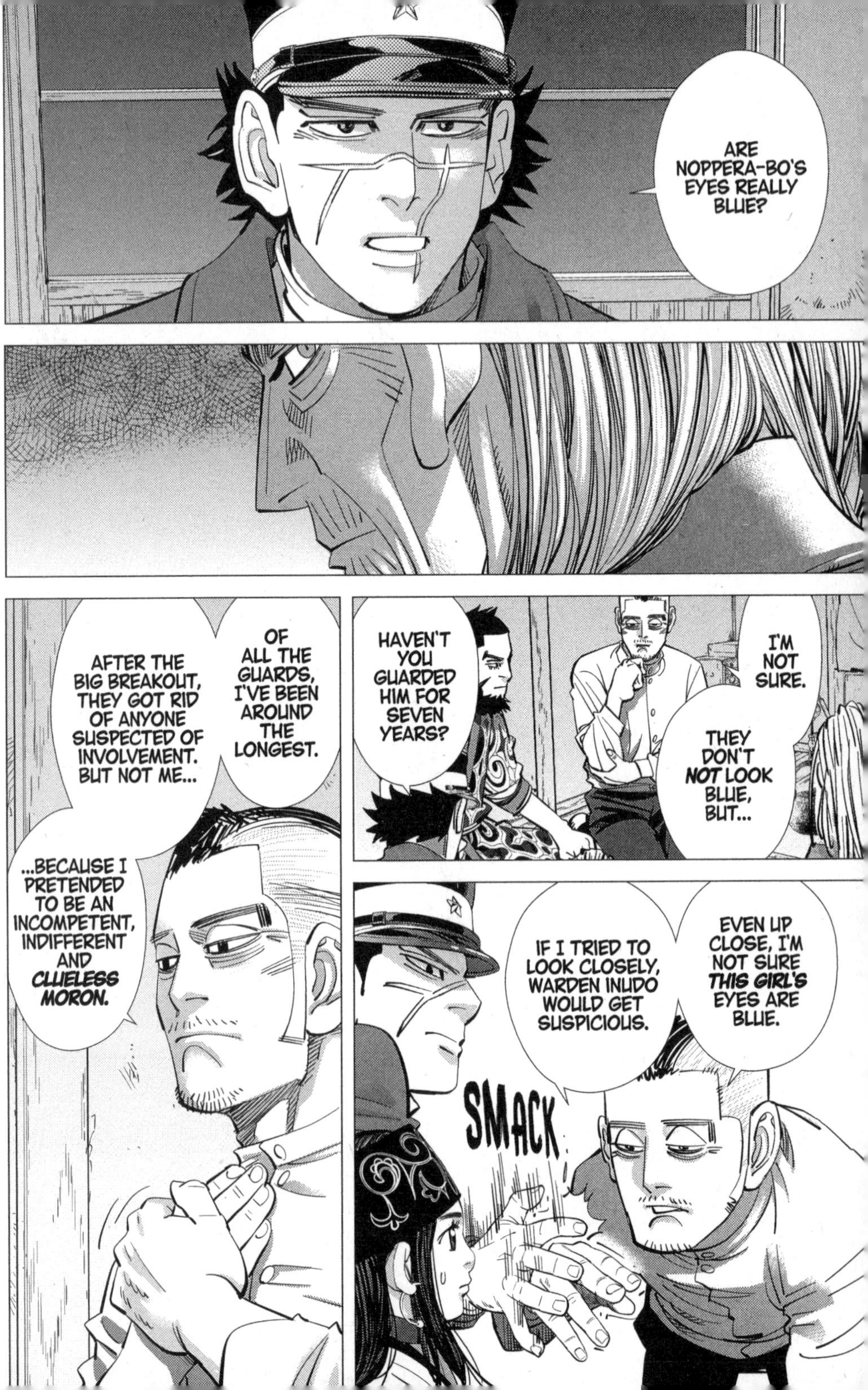
ARE NOPPERA-BO'S EYES REALLY BLUE?
HAVEN'T YOU GUARDED HIM FOR SEVEN YEARS?
I'M NOT SURE.
THEY DON'T *NOT* LOOK BLUE, BUT...
EVEN UP CLOSE, I'M NOT SURE *THIS GIRL'S* EYES ARE BLUE.
IF I TRIED TO LOOK CLOSELY, WARDEN INUDO WOULD GET SUSPICIOUS.
SMACK
OF ALL THE GUARDS, I'VE BEEN AROUND THE LONGEST.
AFTER THE BIG BREAKOUT, THEY GOT RID OF ANYONE SUSPECTED OF INVOLVEMENT. BUT NOT ME...
...BECAUSE I PRETENDED TO BE AN INCOMPETENT, INDIFFERENT AND *CLUELESS MORON.*

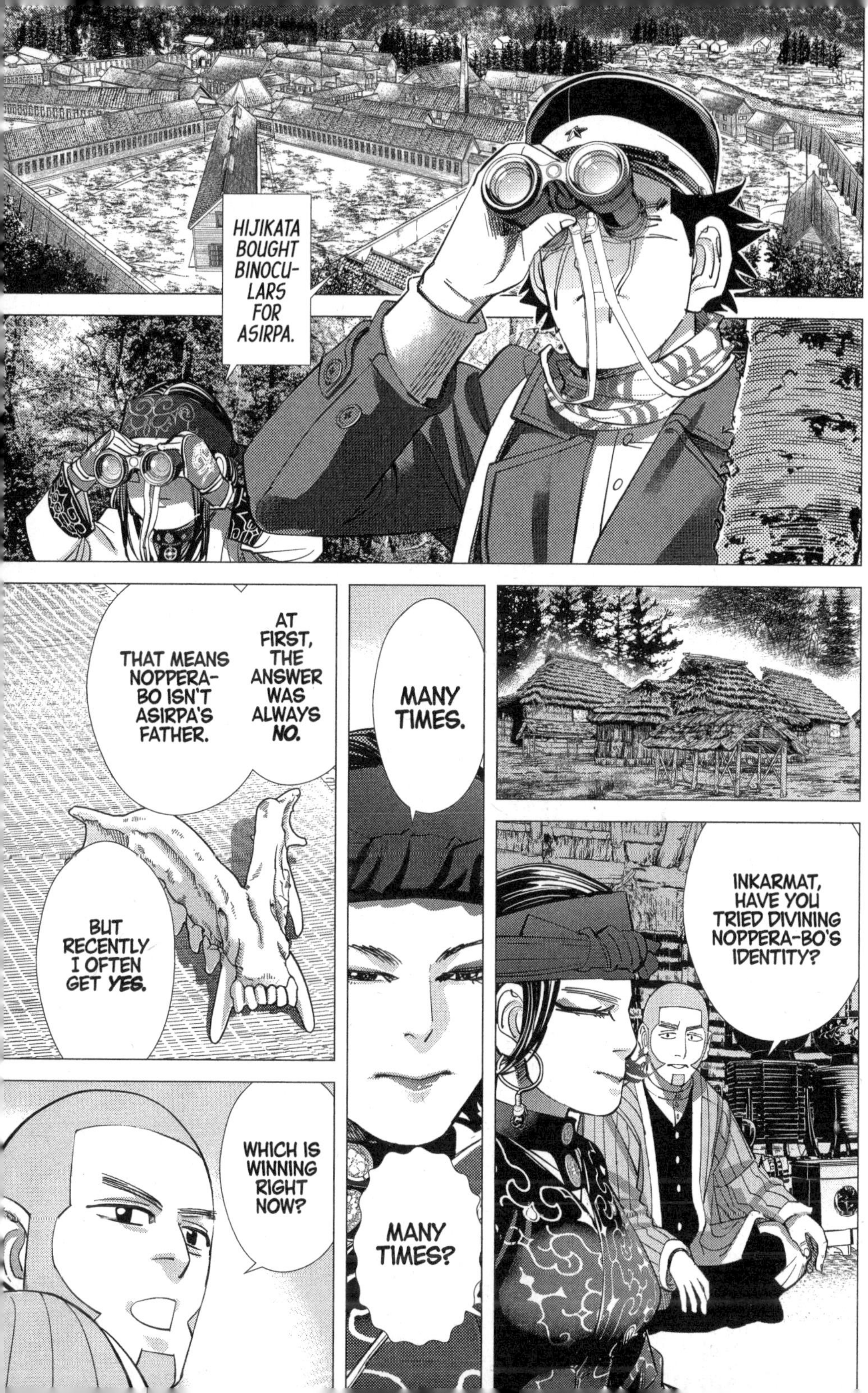
HIJIKATA BOUGHT BINOCULARS FOR ASIRPA.
INKARMAT, HAVE YOU TRIED DIVINING NOPPERA-BO'S IDENTITY?
MANY TIMES.
MANY TIMES?
AT FIRST, THE ANSWER WAS ALWAYS NO.
THAT MEANS NOPPERA-BO ISN'T ASIRPA'S FATHER.
BUT RECENTLY I OFTEN GET YES.
WHICH IS WINNING RIGHT NOW?

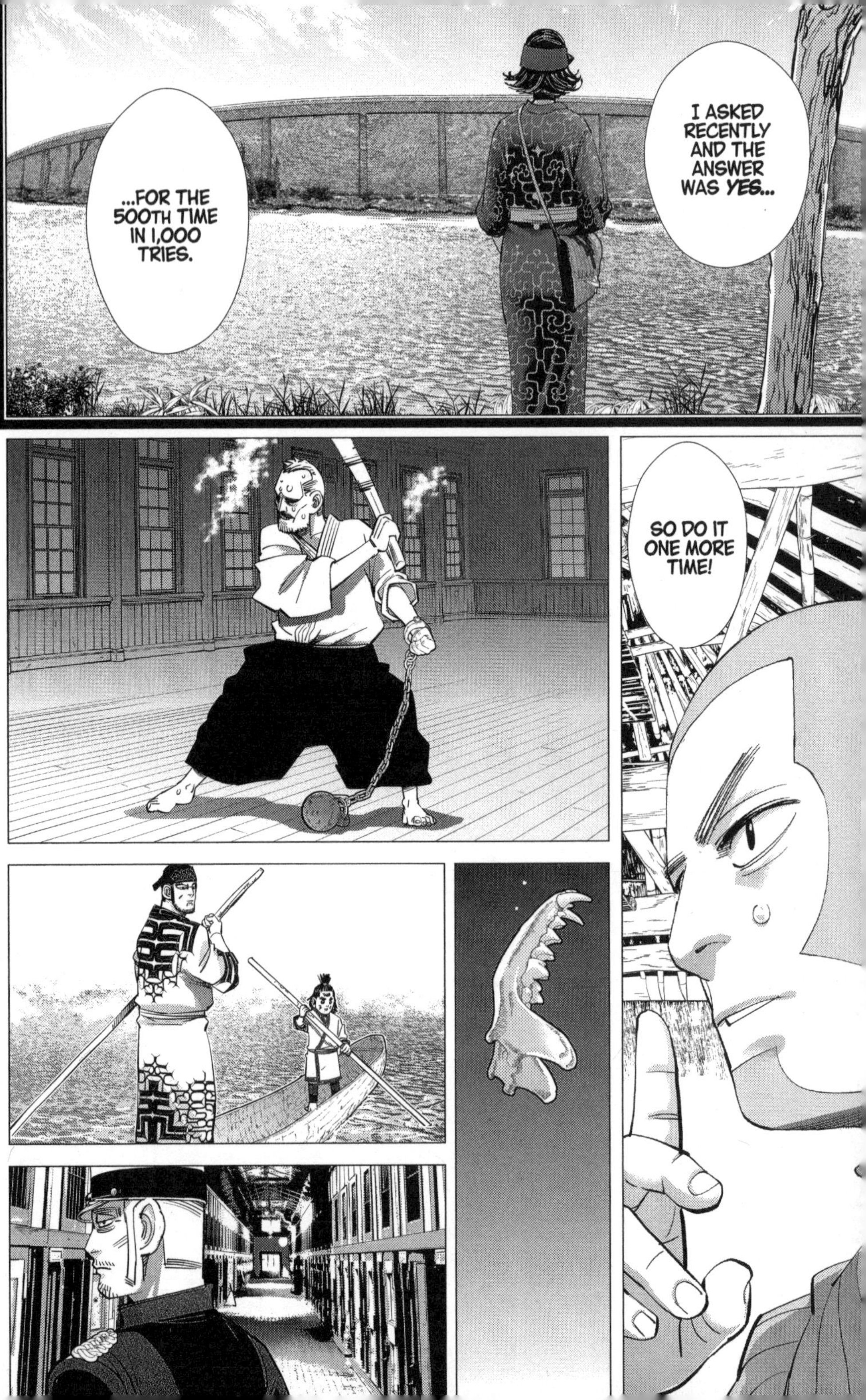
I ASKED RECENTLY AND THE ANSWER WAS *YES*...
...FOR THE 500TH TIME IN 1,000 TRIES.
SO DO IT ONE MORE TIME!

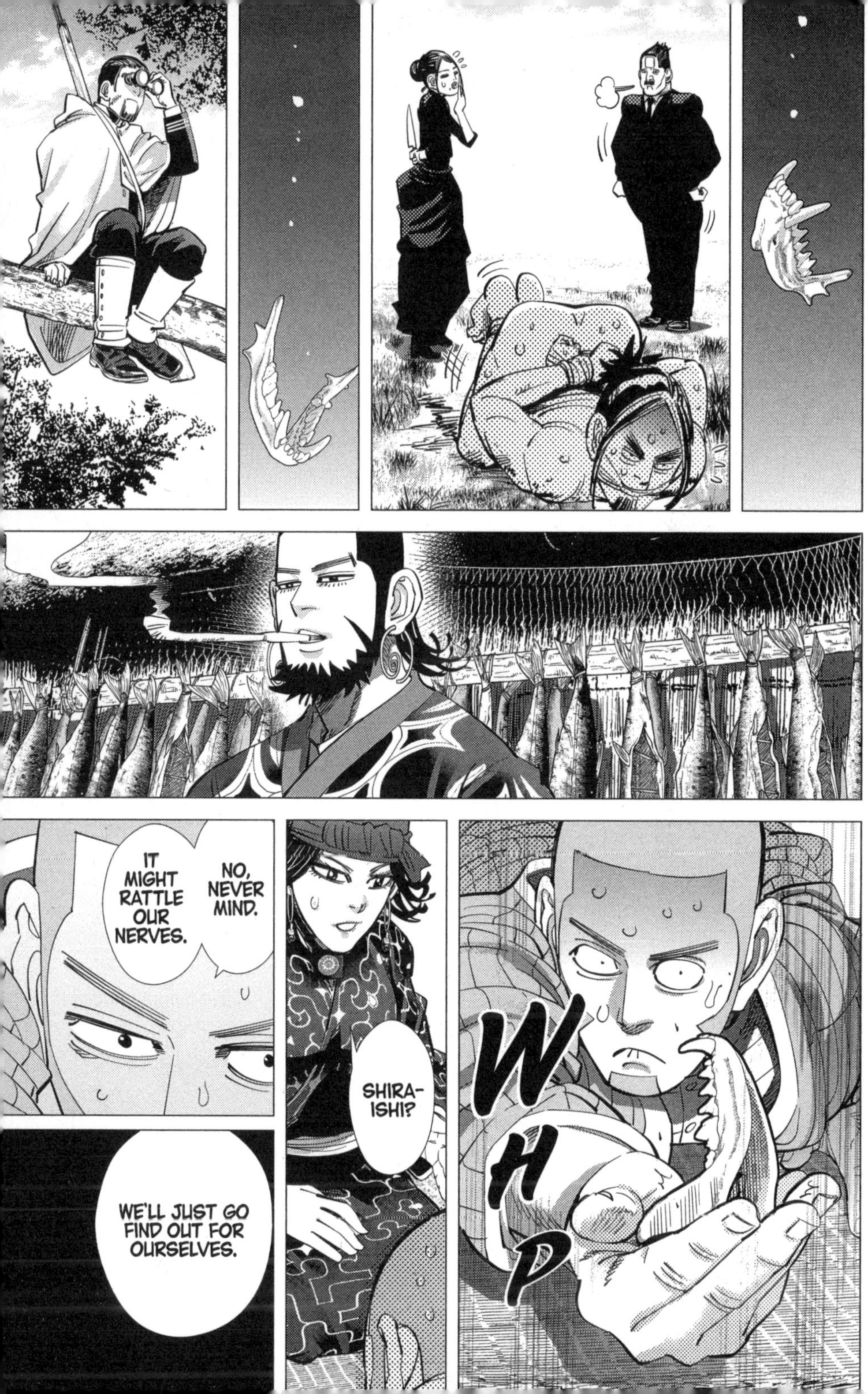
WHP
SHIRA-ISHI?
NO, NEVER MIND.
IT MIGHT RATTLE OUR NERVES.
WE'LL JUST GO FIND OUT FOR OURSELVES.

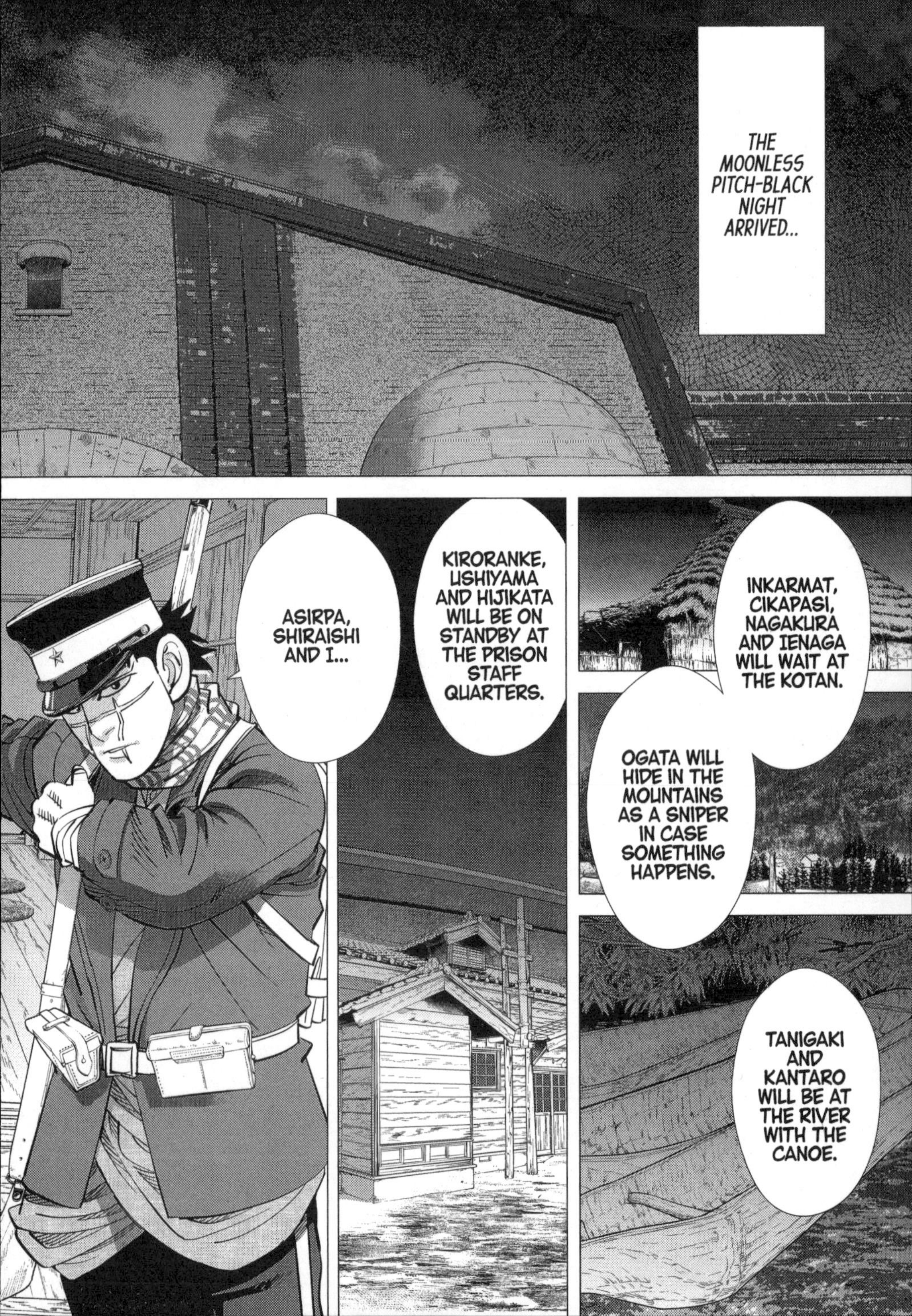
THE MOONLESS PITCH-BLACK NIGHT ARRIVED...
INKARMAT, CIKAPASI, NAGAKURA AND IENAGA WILL WAIT AT THE KOTAN.
OGATA WILL HIDE IN THE MOUNTAINS AS A SNIPER IN CASE SOMETHING HAPPENS.
TANIGAKI AND KANTARO WILL BE AT THE RIVER WITH THE CANOE.
KIRORANKE, USHIYAMA AND HIJIKATA WILL BE ON STANDBY AT THE PRISON STAFF QUARTERS.
ASIRPA, SHIRAISHI AND I...

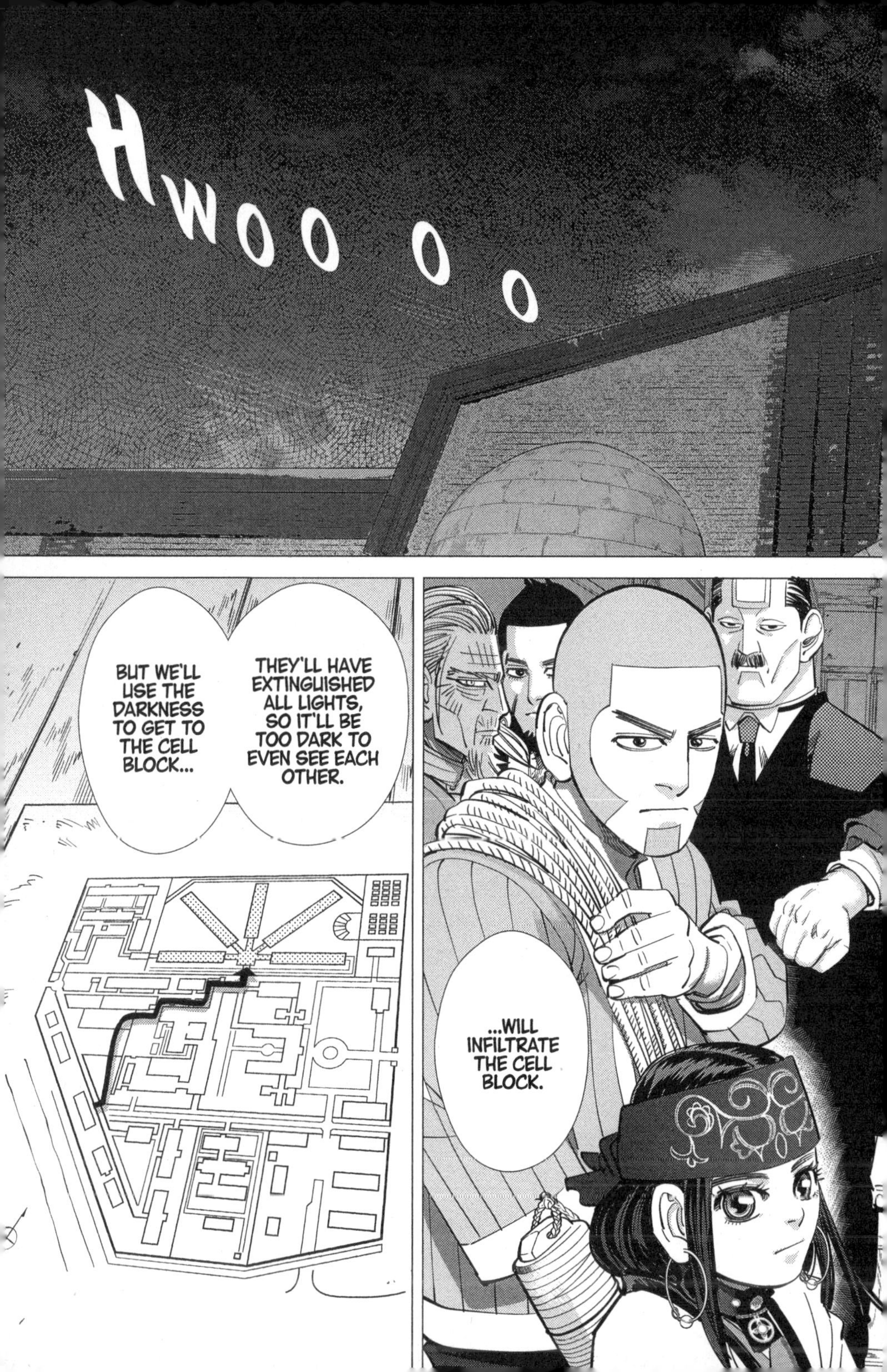
HWOO O O
...WILL INFILTRATE THE CELL BLOCK.
THEY'LL HAVE EXTINGUISHED ALL LIGHTS, SO IT'LL BE TOO DARK TO EVEN SEE EACH OTHER.
BUT WE'LL USE THE DARKNESS TO GET TO THE CELL BLOCK...

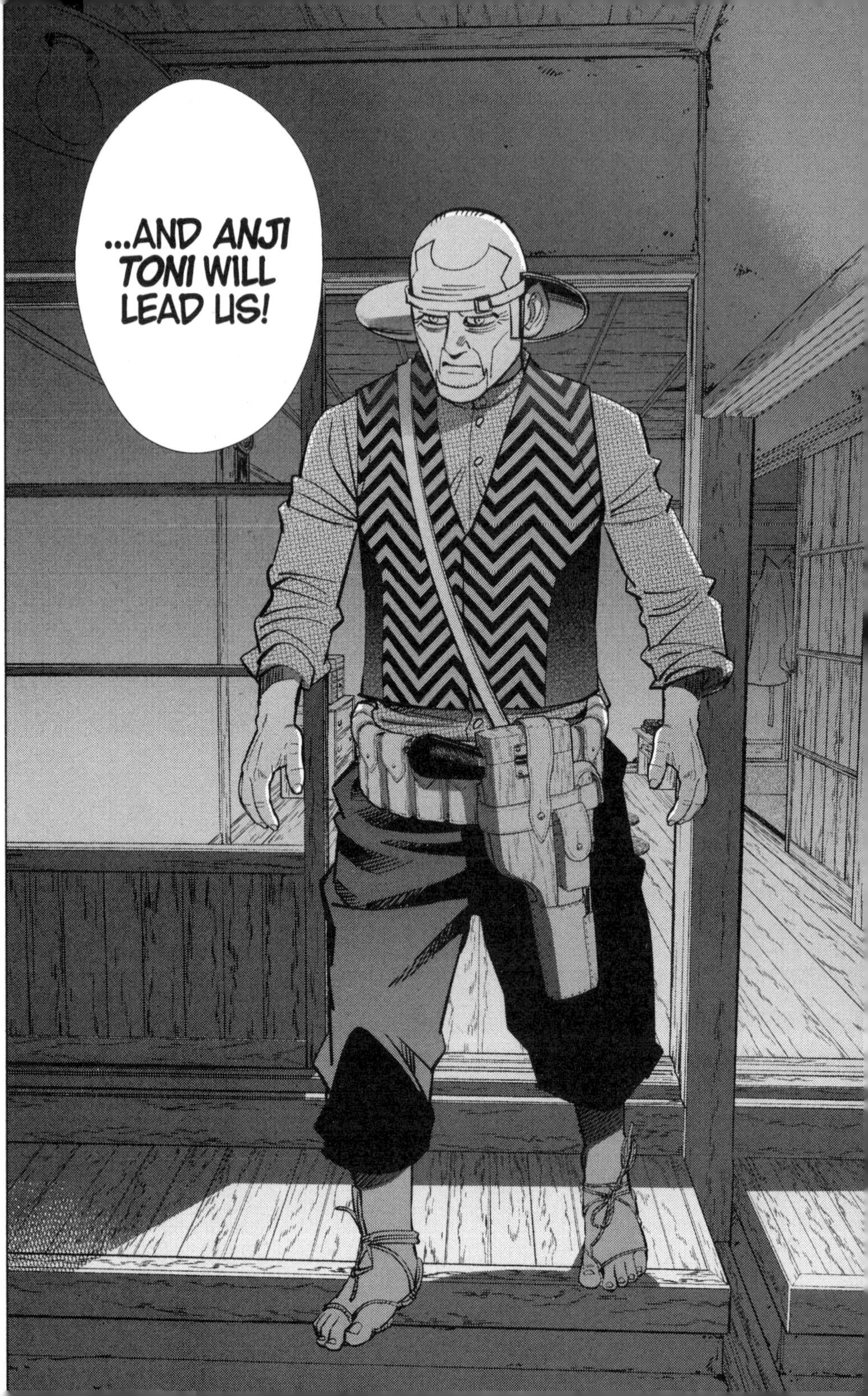
...AND ANJI TONI WILL LEAD US!

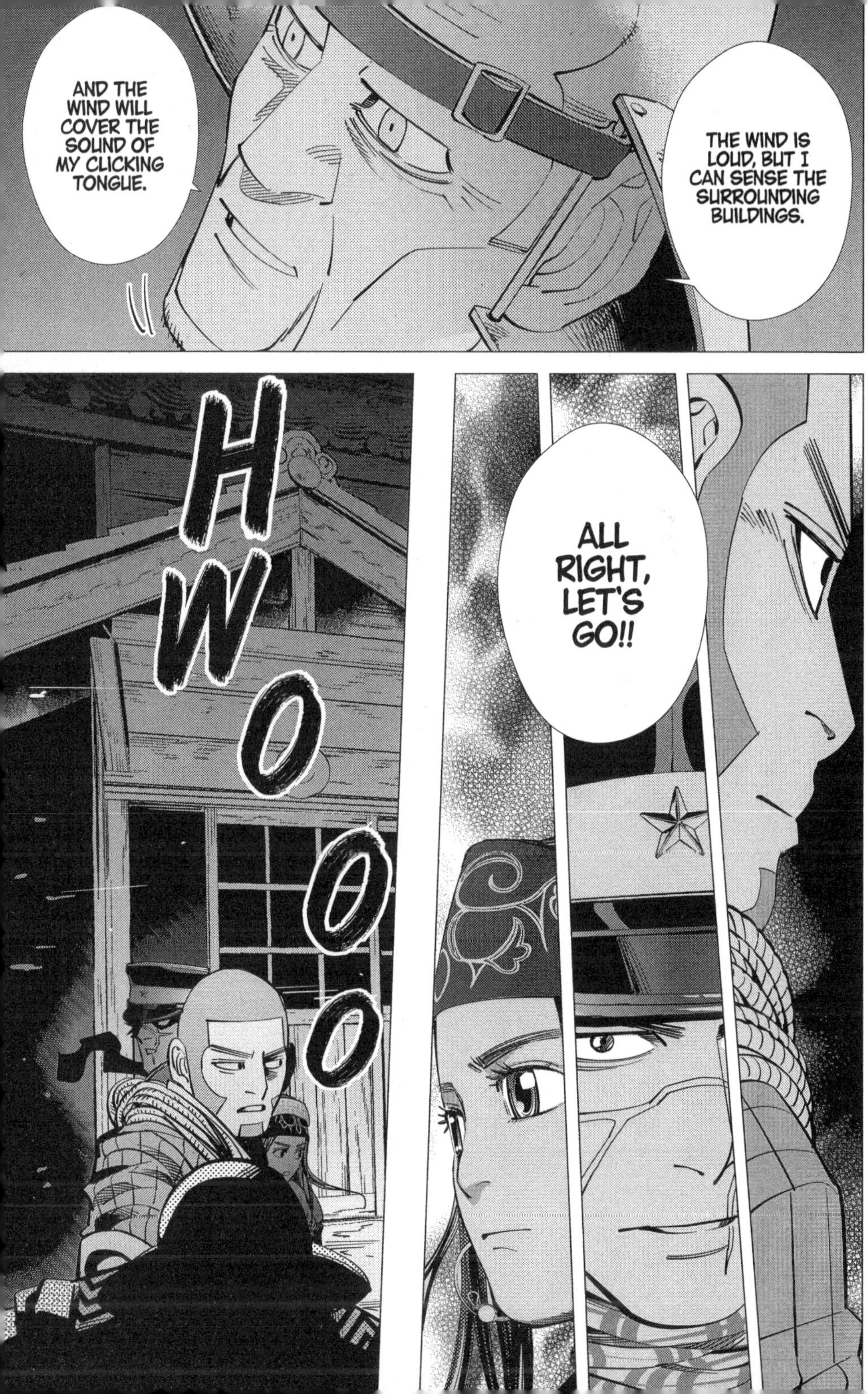
THE WIND IS LOUD, BUT I CAN SENSE THE SURROUNDING BUILDINGS.
AND THE WIND WILL COVER THE SOUND OF MY CLICKING TONGUE.
ALL RIGHT, LET'S GO!!
HWOOOO

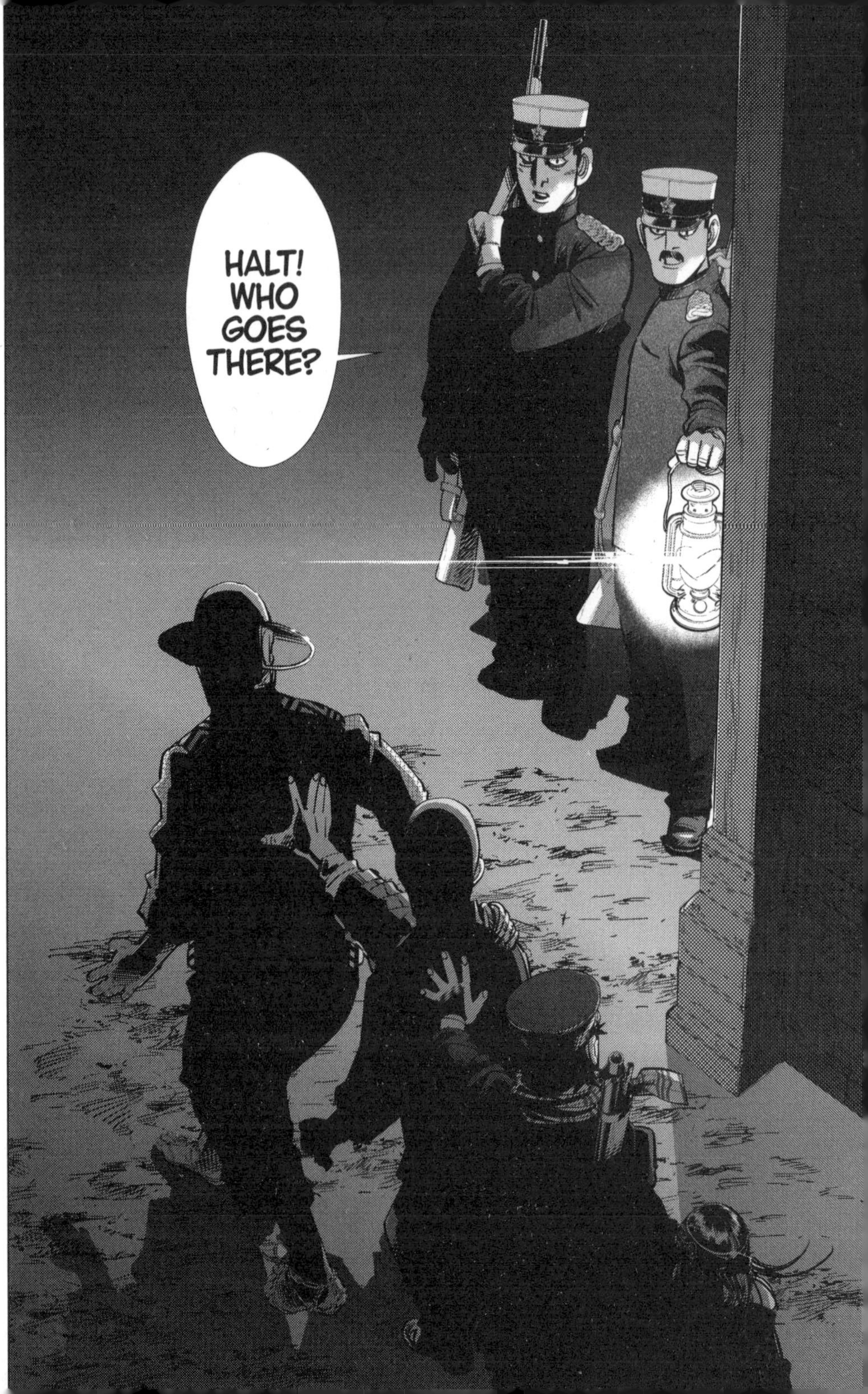
HALT! WHO GOES THERE?

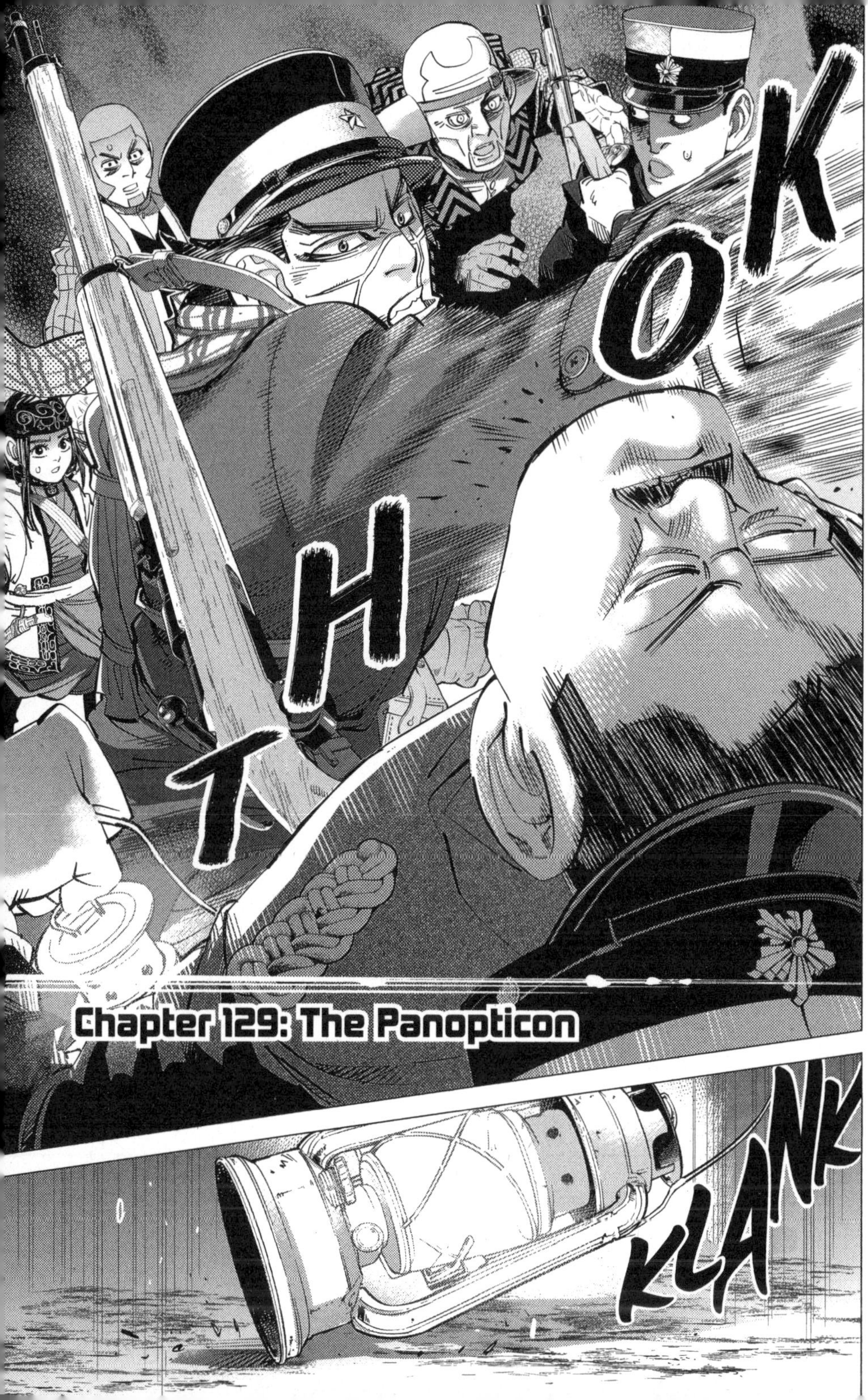
THOK
Chapter 129: The Panopticon
KLANK

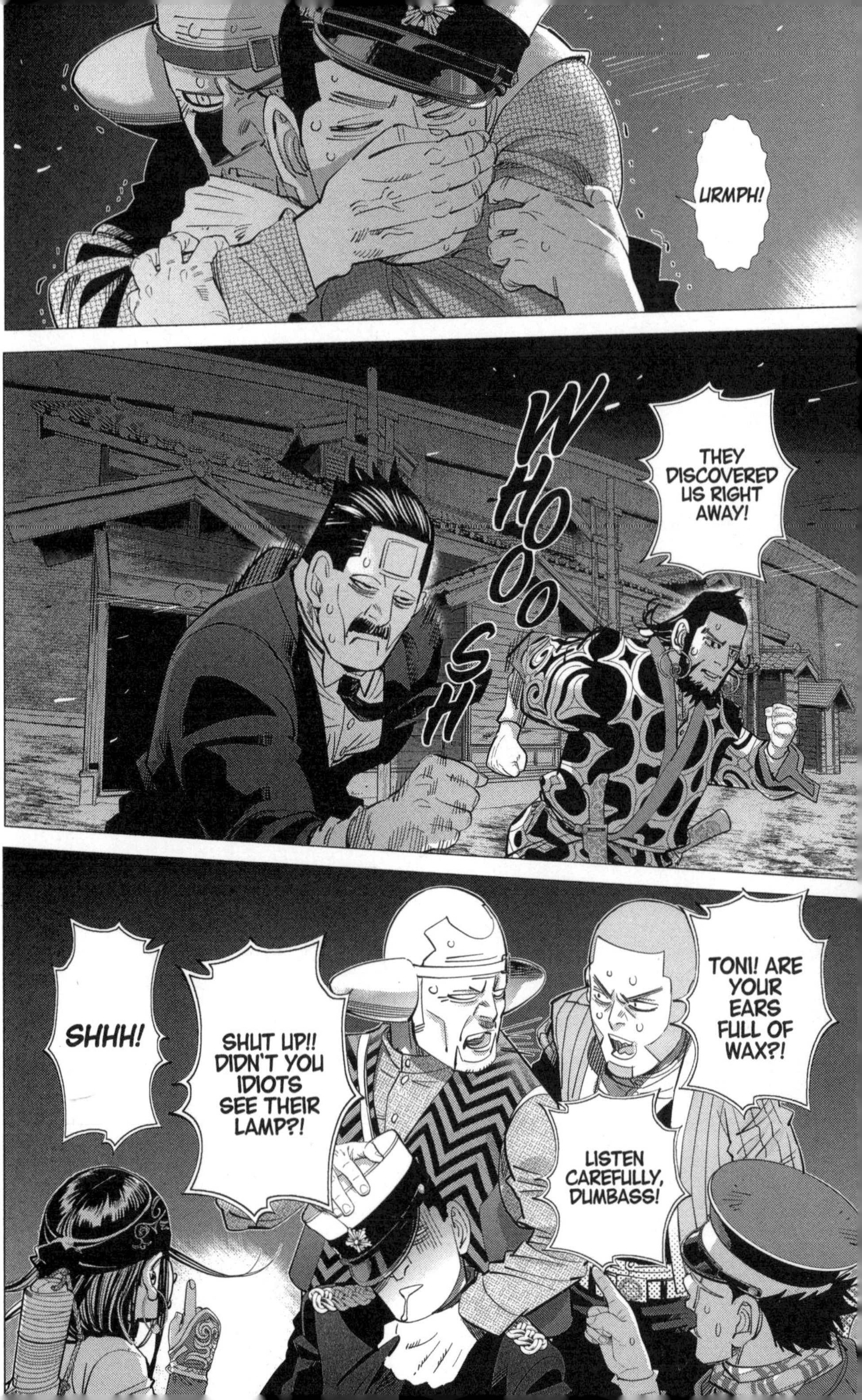
URMPH!
THEY DISCOVERED US RIGHT AWAY!
WHOOOOSH
TONI! ARE YOUR EARS FULL OF WAX?!
LISTEN CAREFULLY, DUMBASS!
SHUT UP!! DIDN'T YOU IDIOTS SEE THEIR LAMP?!
SHHH!

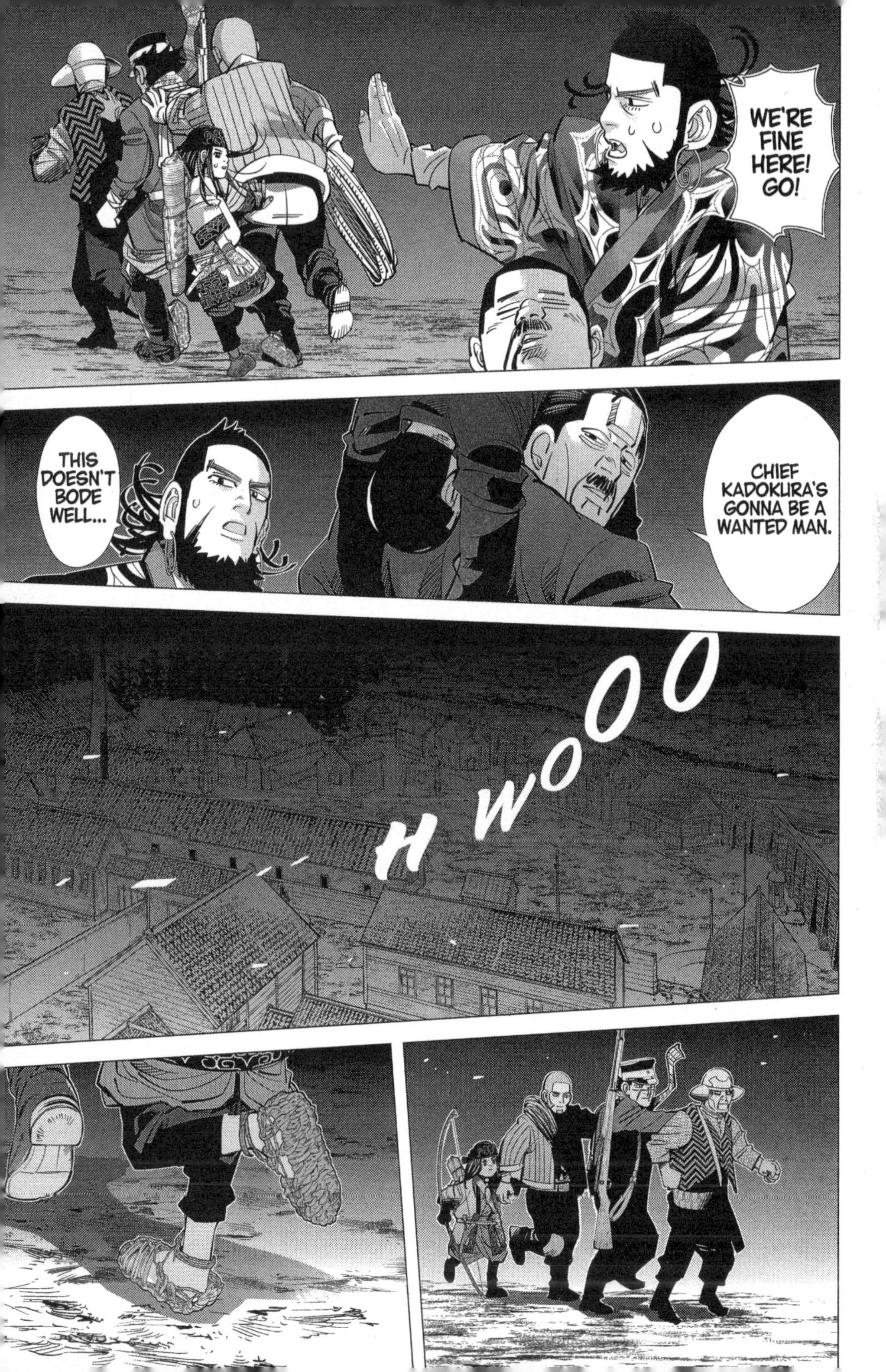
WE'RE FINE HERE! GO!
CHIEF KADOKURA'S GONNA BE A WANTED MAN.
THIS DOESN'T BODE WELL...
HWOOOO

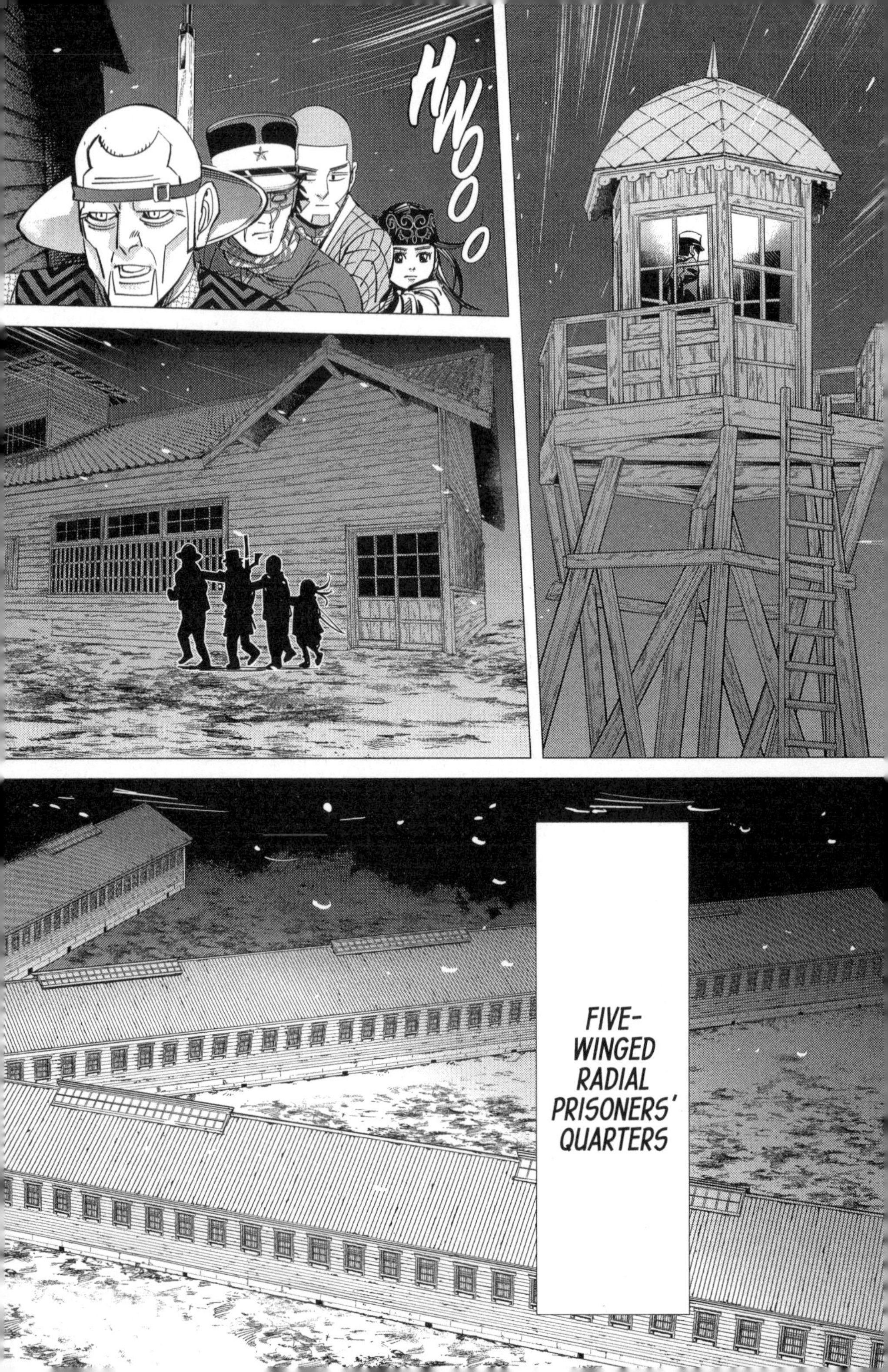
HWOOOO
FIVE-WINGED RADIAL PRISONERS' QUARTERS

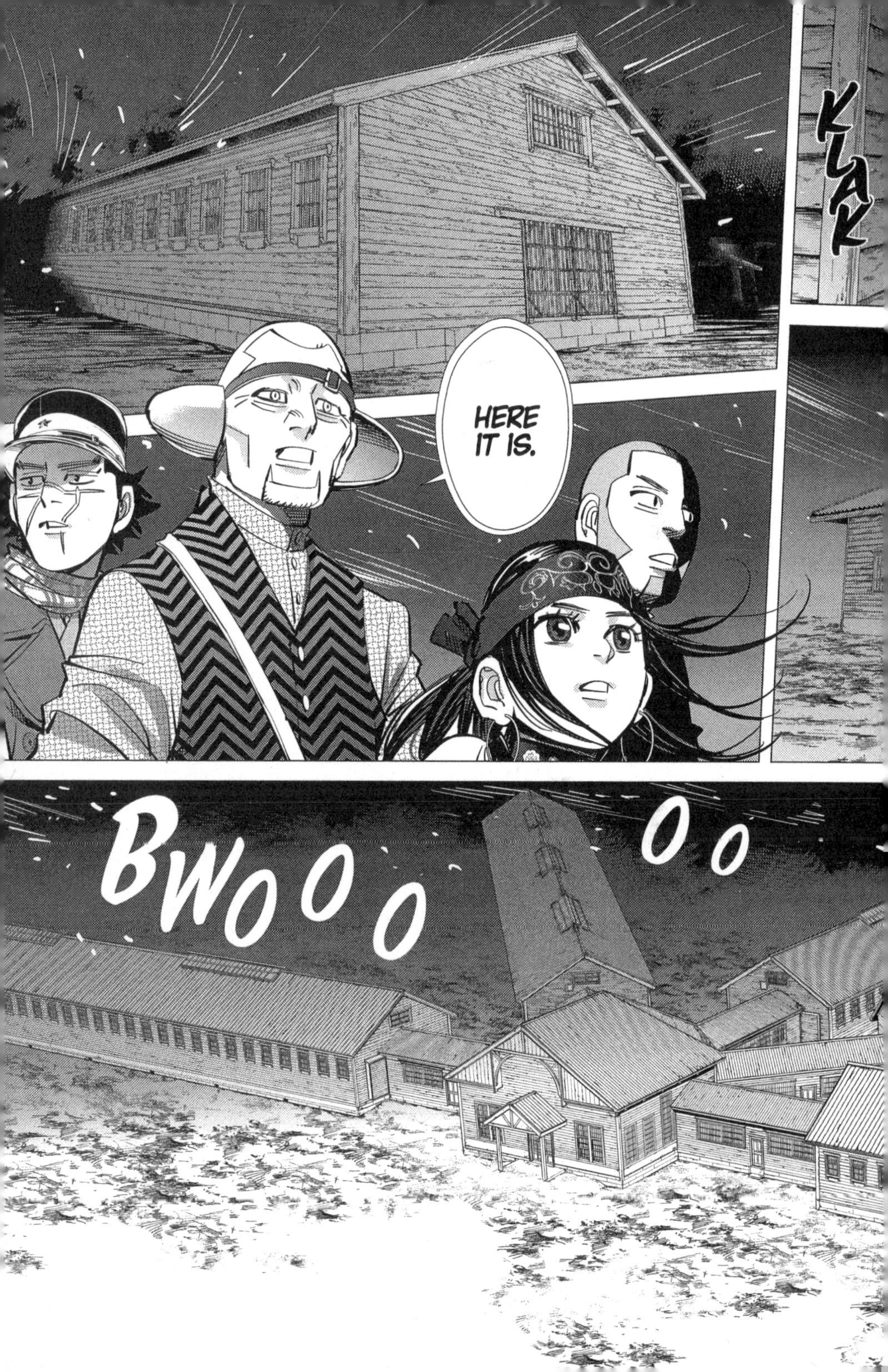
KLAK
HERE IT IS.
BWOOOO OO

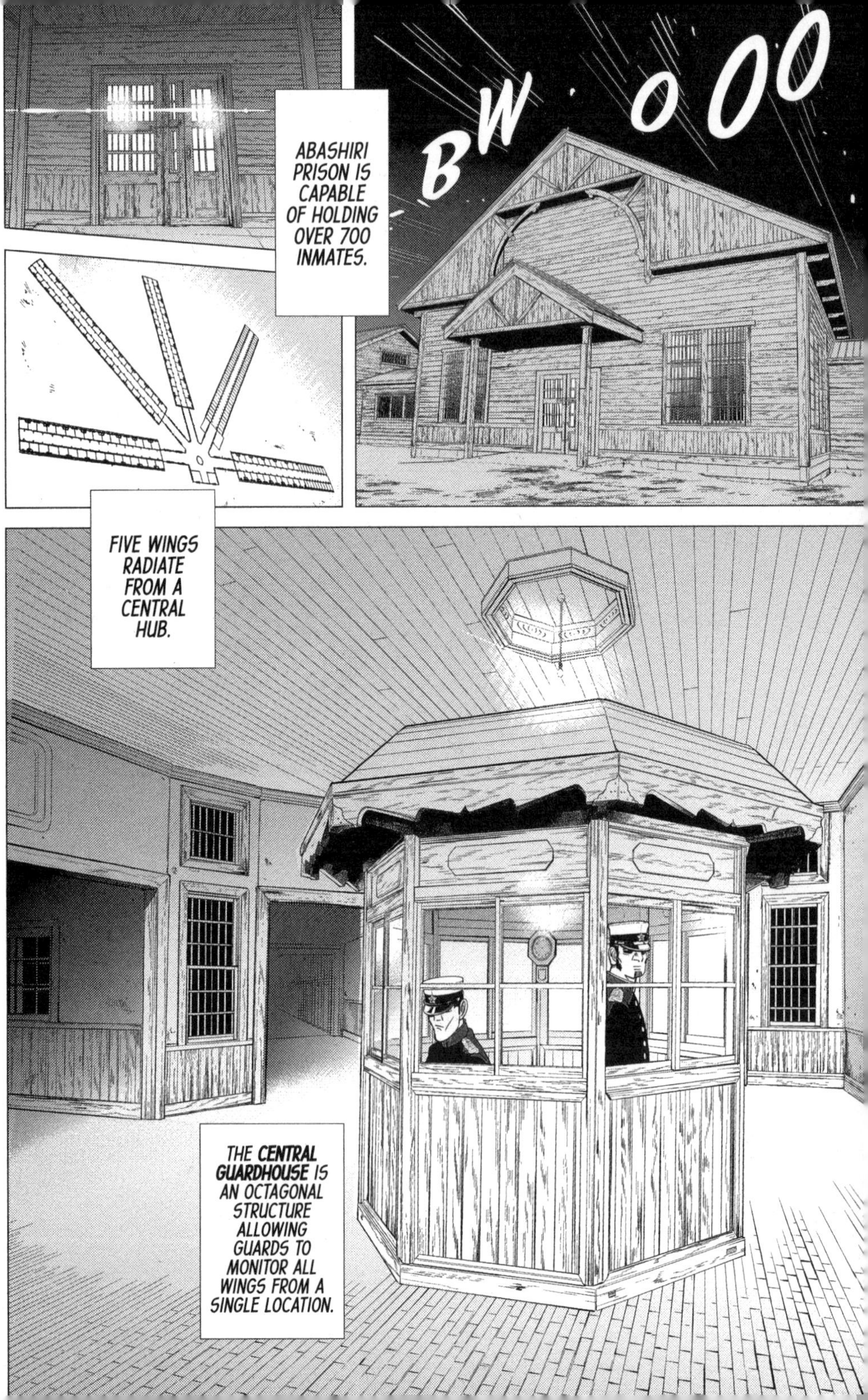
BWOOO
ABASHIRI PRISON IS CAPABLE OF HOLDING OVER 700 INMATES.
FIVE WINGS RADIATE FROM A CENTRAL HUB.
THE **CENTRAL GUARDHOUSE** IS AN OCTAGONAL STRUCTURE ALLOWING GUARDS TO MONITOR ALL WINGS FROM A SINGLE LOCATION.

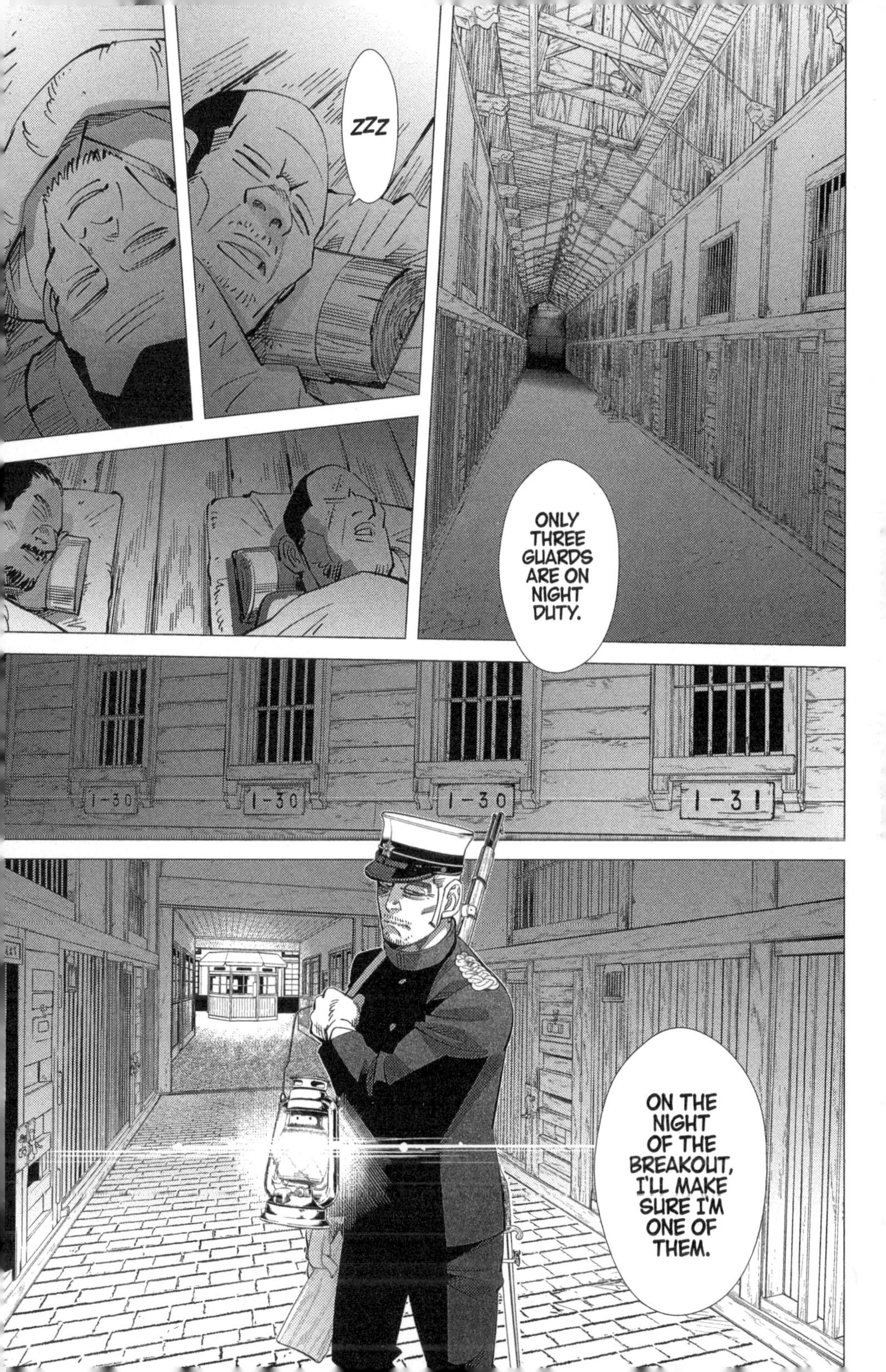

ONLY THREE GUARDS ARE ON NIGHT DUTY.
ZZZ
1-31
1-30
1-30
1-30
ON THE NIGHT OF THE BREAKOUT, I'LL MAKE SURE I'M ONE OF THEM.

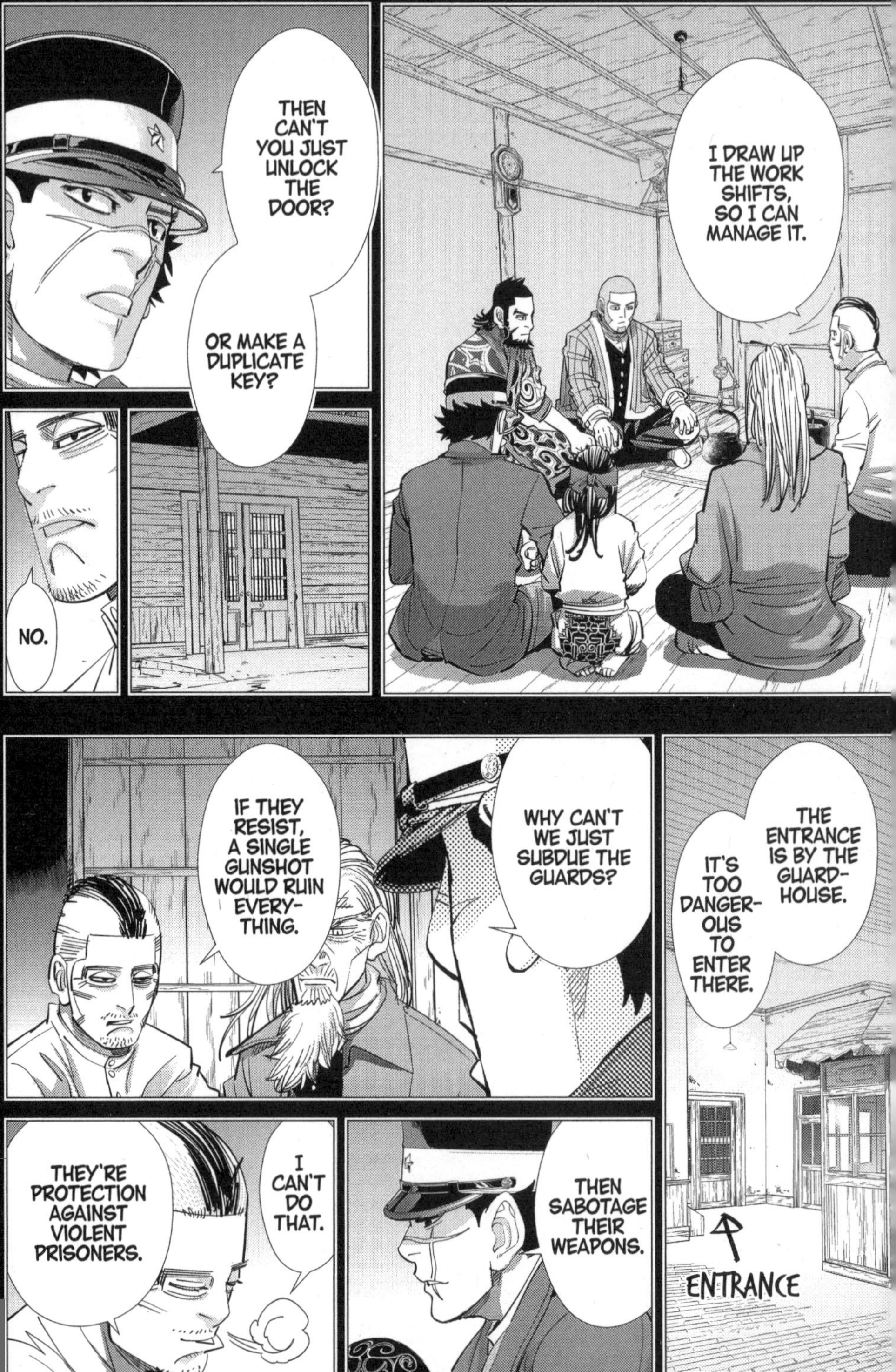
I DRAW UP THE WORK SHIFTS, SO I CAN MANAGE IT.
THEN CAN'T YOU JUST UNLOCK THE DOOR?
OR MAKE A DUPLICATE KEY?
NO.
THE ENTRANCE IS BY THE GUARD-HOUSE.
IT'S TOO DANGER-OUS TO ENTER THERE.
ENTRANCE
WHY CAN'T WE JUST SUBDUE THE GUARDS?
IF THEY RESIST, A SINGLE GUNSHOT WOULD RUIN EVERY-THING.
THEN SABOTAGE THEIR WEAPONS.
I CAN'T DO THAT.
THEY'RE PROTECTION AGAINST VIOLENT PRISONERS.

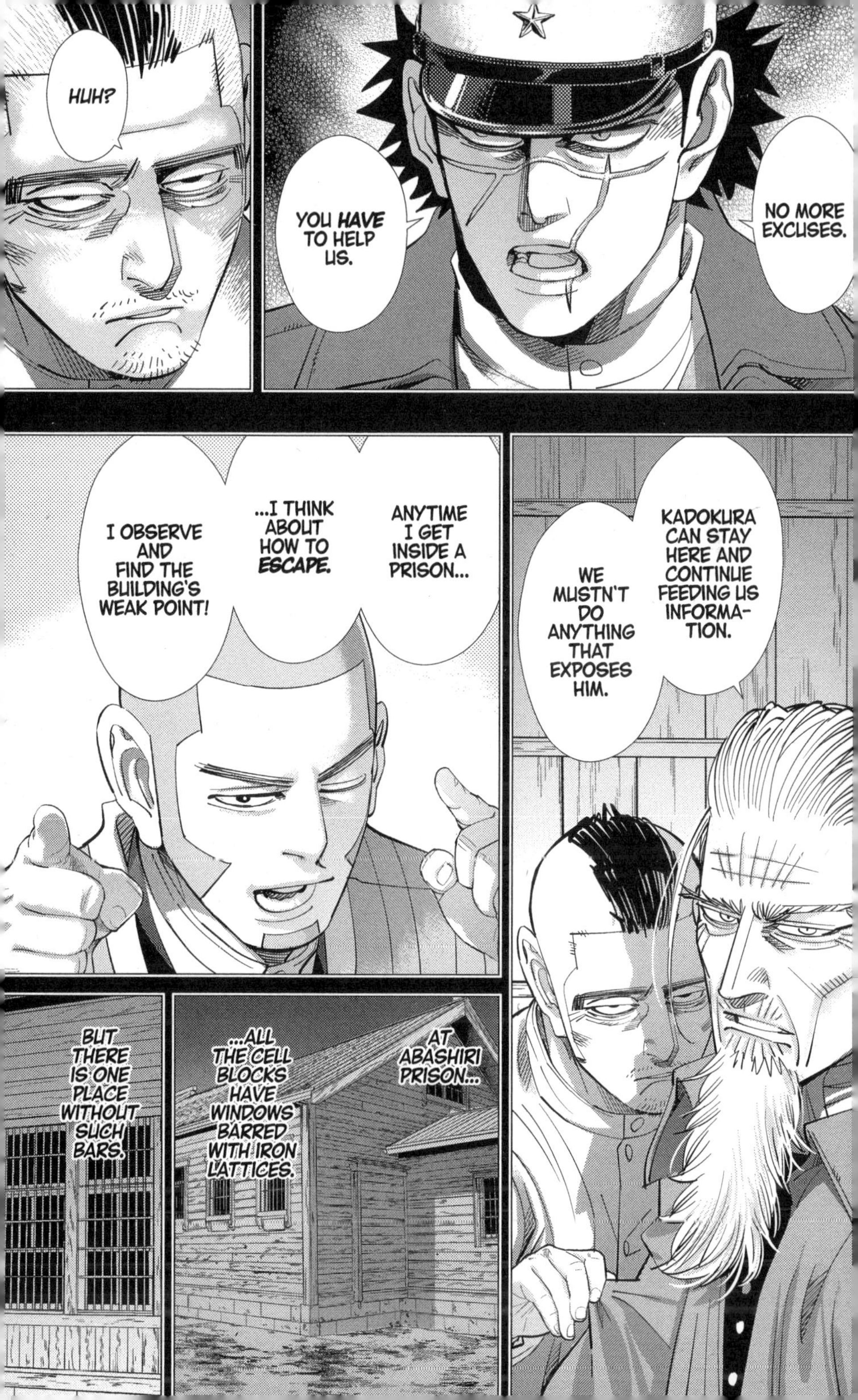
NO MORE EXCUSES.
YOU HAVE TO HELP US.
HUH?
KADOKURA CAN STAY HERE AND CONTINUE FEEDING US INFORMATION.
WE MUSTN'T DO ANYTHING THAT EXPOSES HIM.
ANYTIME I GET INSIDE A PRISON...
...I THINK ABOUT HOW TO ESCAPE.
I OBSERVE AND FIND THE BUILDING'S WEAK POINT!
AT ABASHIRI PRISON...
...ALL THE CELL BLOCKS HAVE WINDOWS BARRED WITH IRON LATTICES.
BUT THERE IS ONE PLACE WITHOUT SUCH BARS.

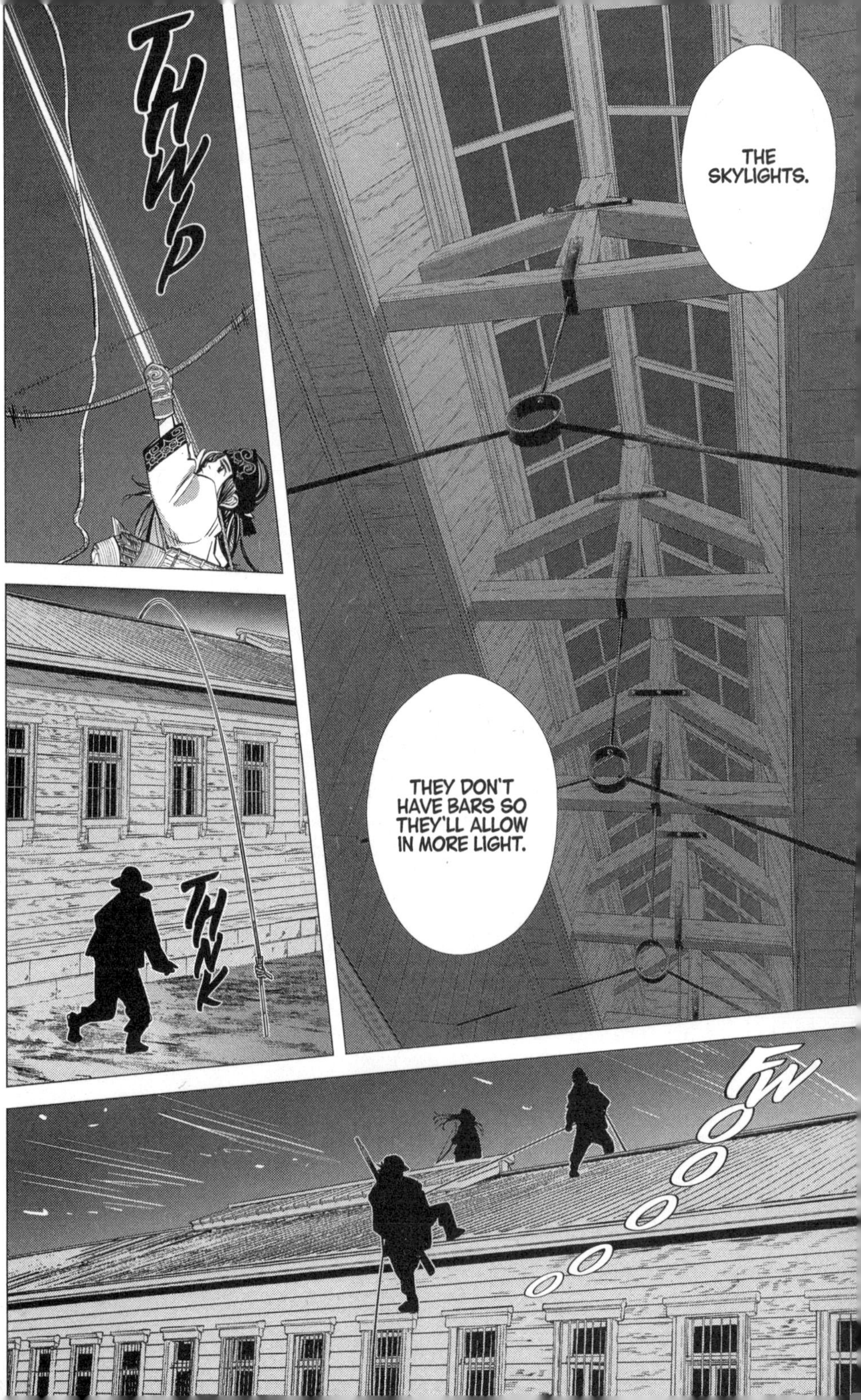
THE SKYLIGHTS.
THEY DON'T HAVE BARS SO THEY'LL ALLOW IN MORE LIGHT.
THWIP
THNK
FWOOOOOOOO

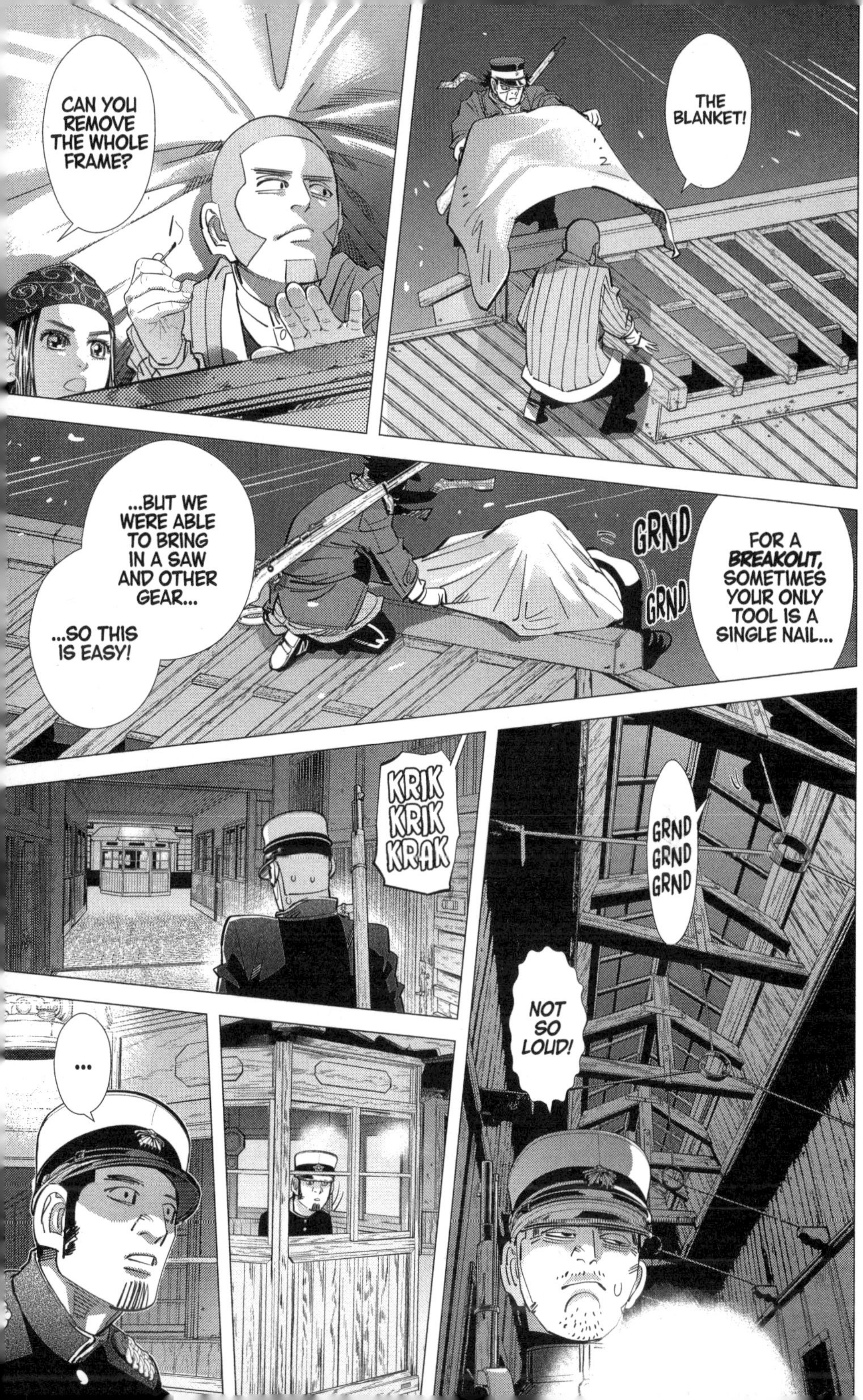
THE BLANKET!
CAN YOU REMOVE THE WHOLE FRAME?
FOR A BREAKOUT, SOMETIMES YOUR ONLY TOOL IS A SINGLE NAIL...
GRND
GRND
...BUT WE WERE ABLE TO BRING IN A SAW AND OTHER GEAR...
...SO THIS IS EASY!
GRND GRND GRND
NOT SO LOUD!
KRIK KRIK KRAK
...

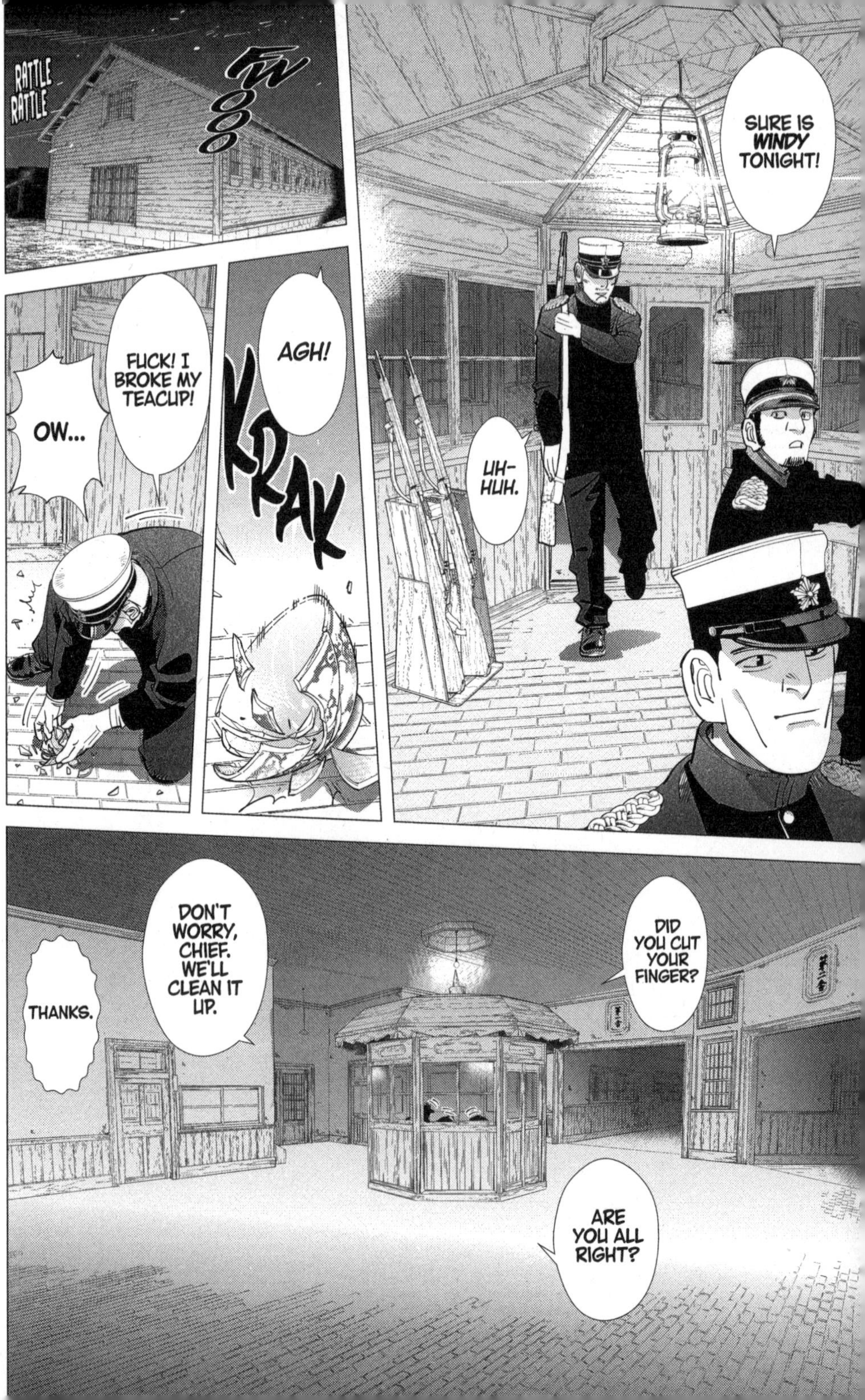
SURE IS WINDY TONIGHT!
UH-HUH.
FWOOO
RATTLE RATTLE
AGH!
KRAK
FUCK! I BROKE MY TEACUP!
OW...
DID YOU CUT YOUR FINGER?
ARE YOU ALL RIGHT?
DON'T WORRY, CHIEF. WE'LL CLEAN IT UP.
THANKS.

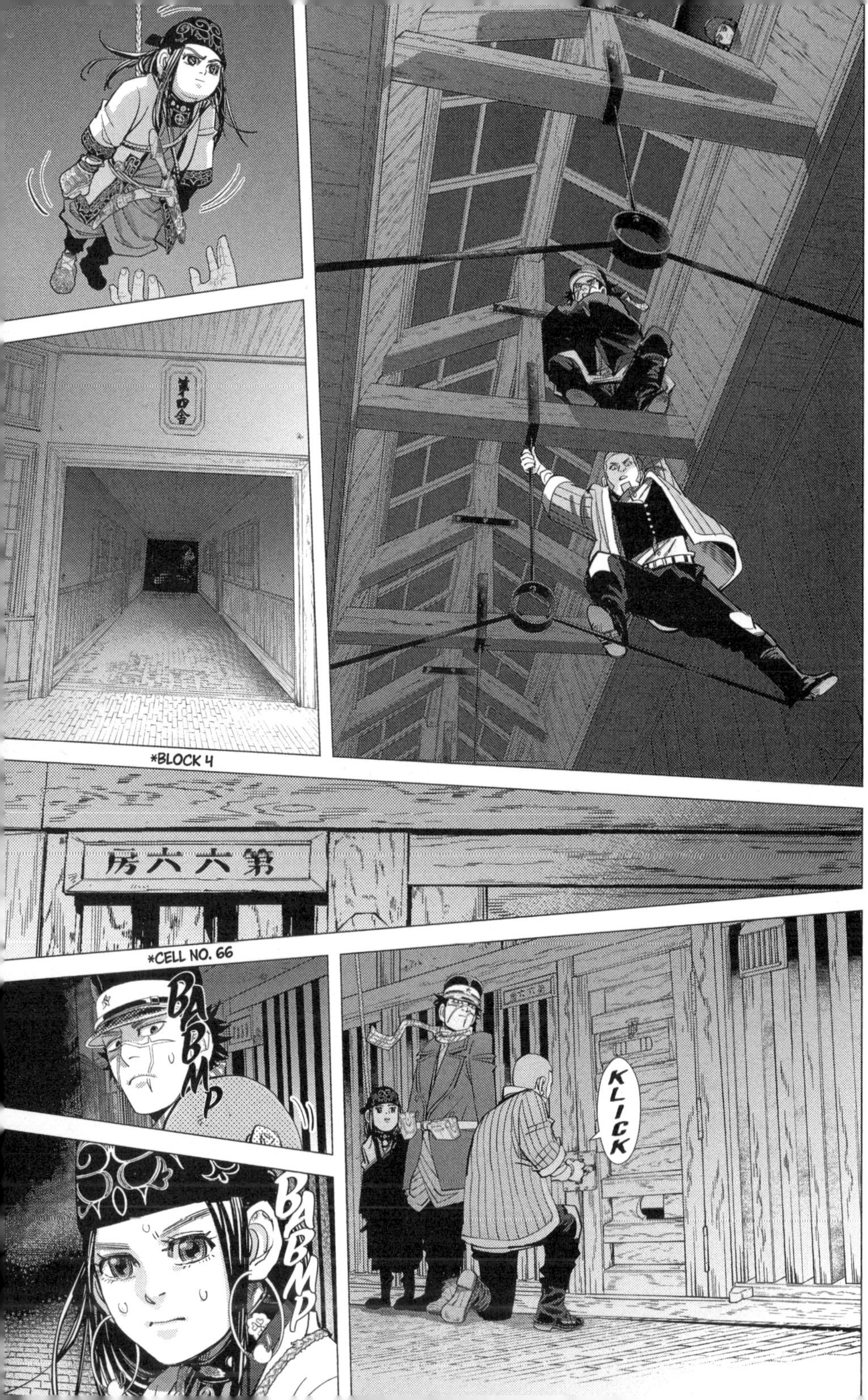
第四舎
*BLOCK 4
第六六房
*CELL NO. 66
KLICK
BABMP
BABMP

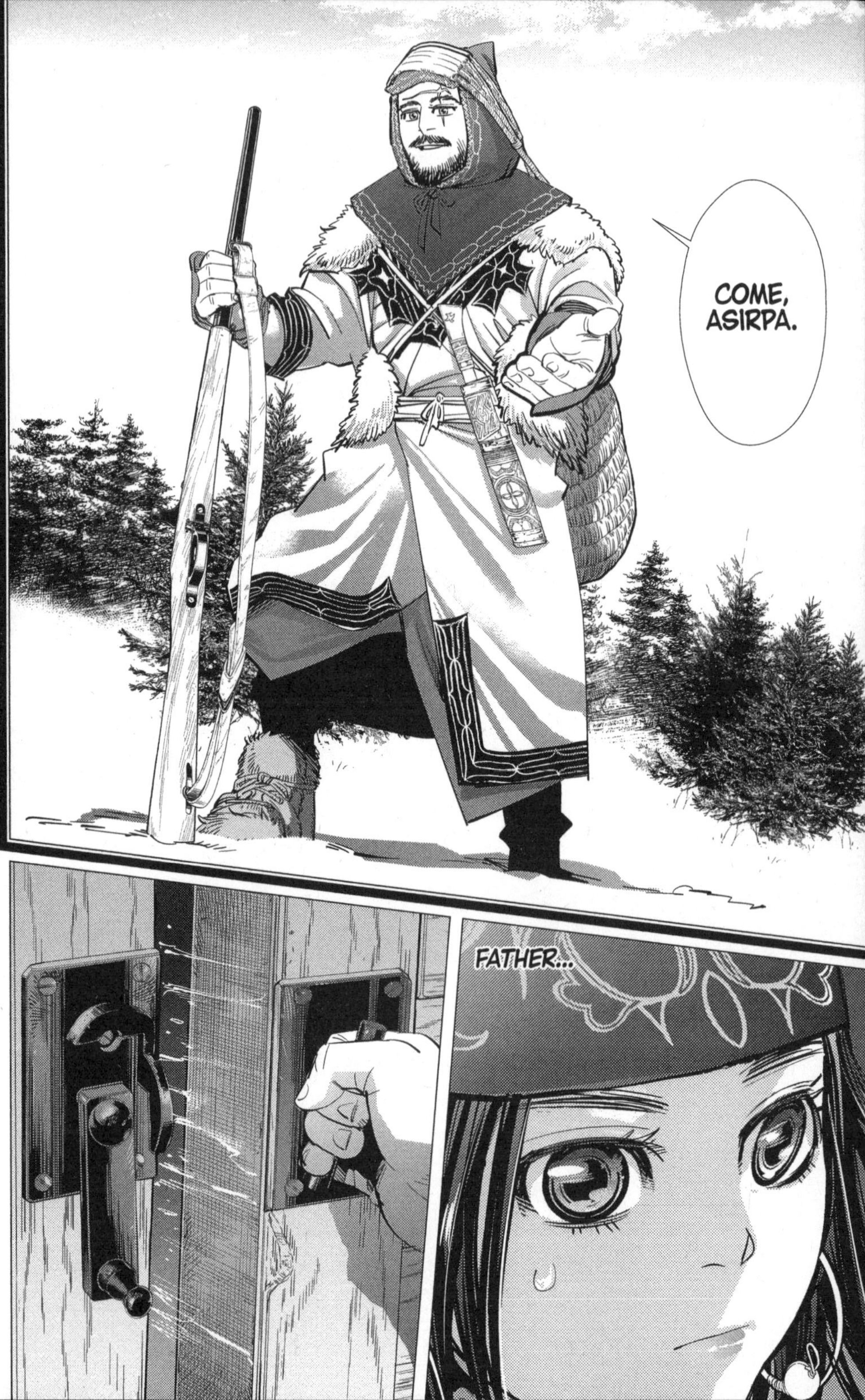
COME, ASIRPA.
FATHER...

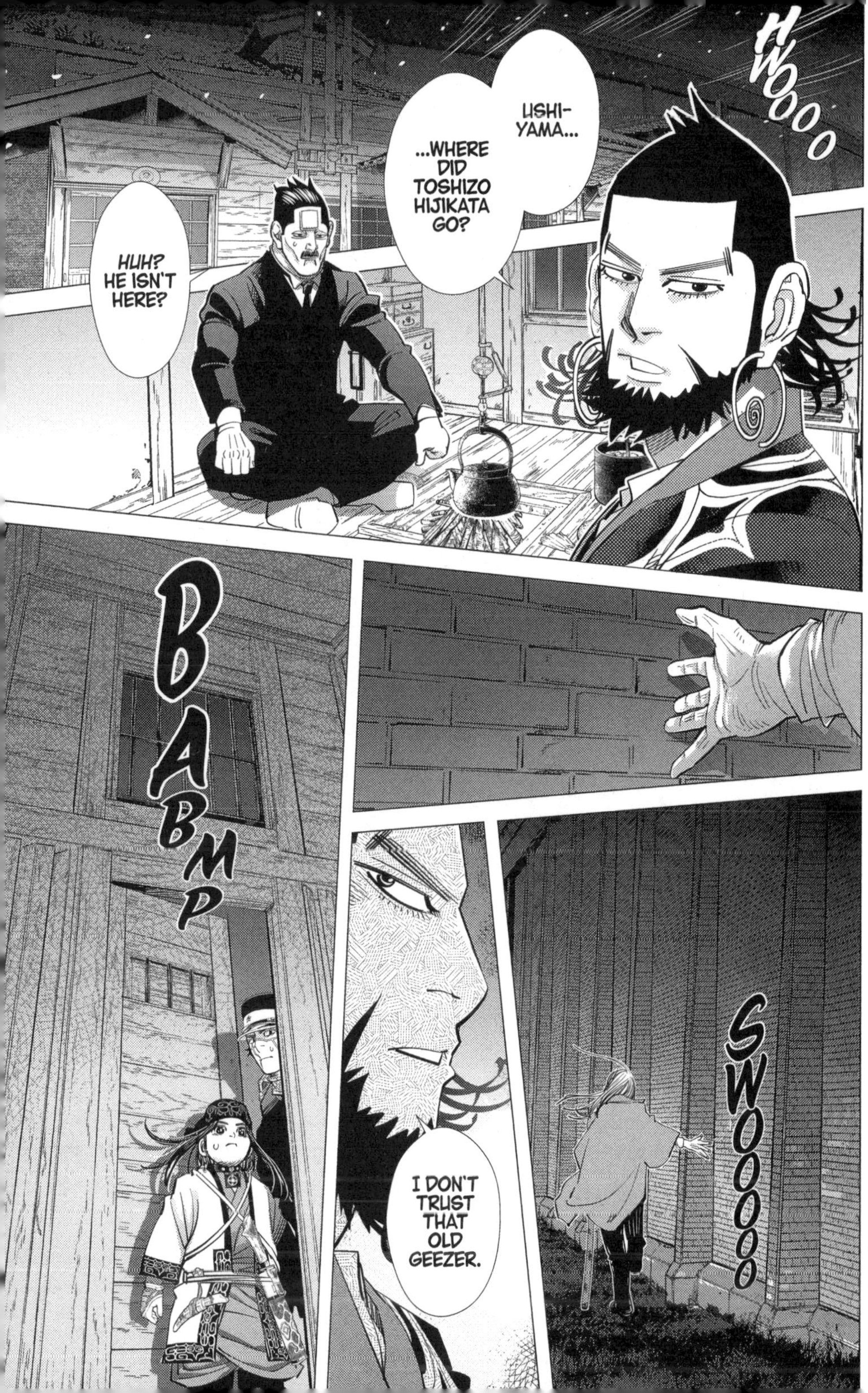
HWOOOO
USHI-YAMA...
...WHERE DID TOSHIZO HIJIKATA GO?
HUH? HE ISN'T HERE?
SWOOOOOO
I DON'T TRUST THAT OLD GEEZER.
BABMP

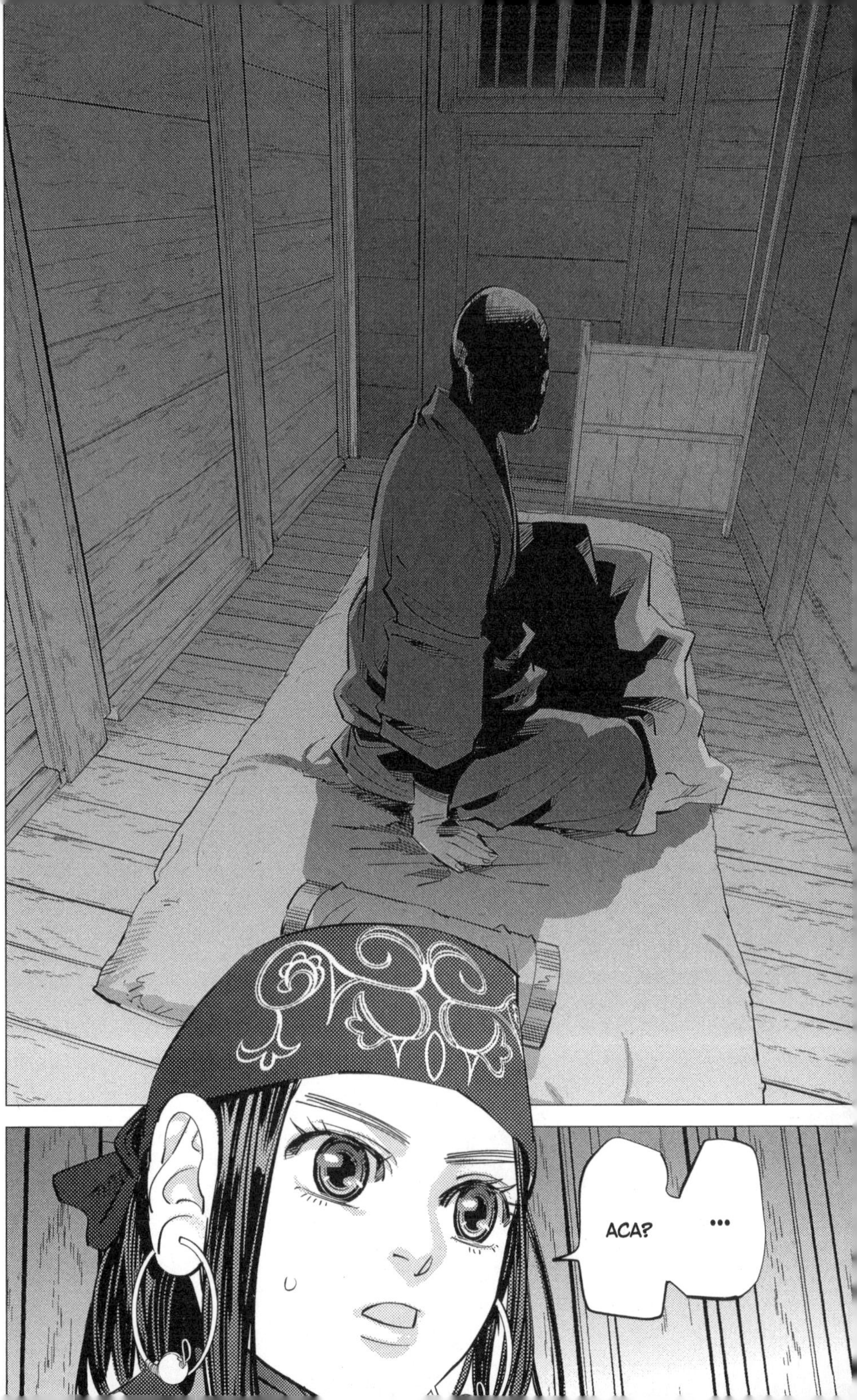
...
ACA?

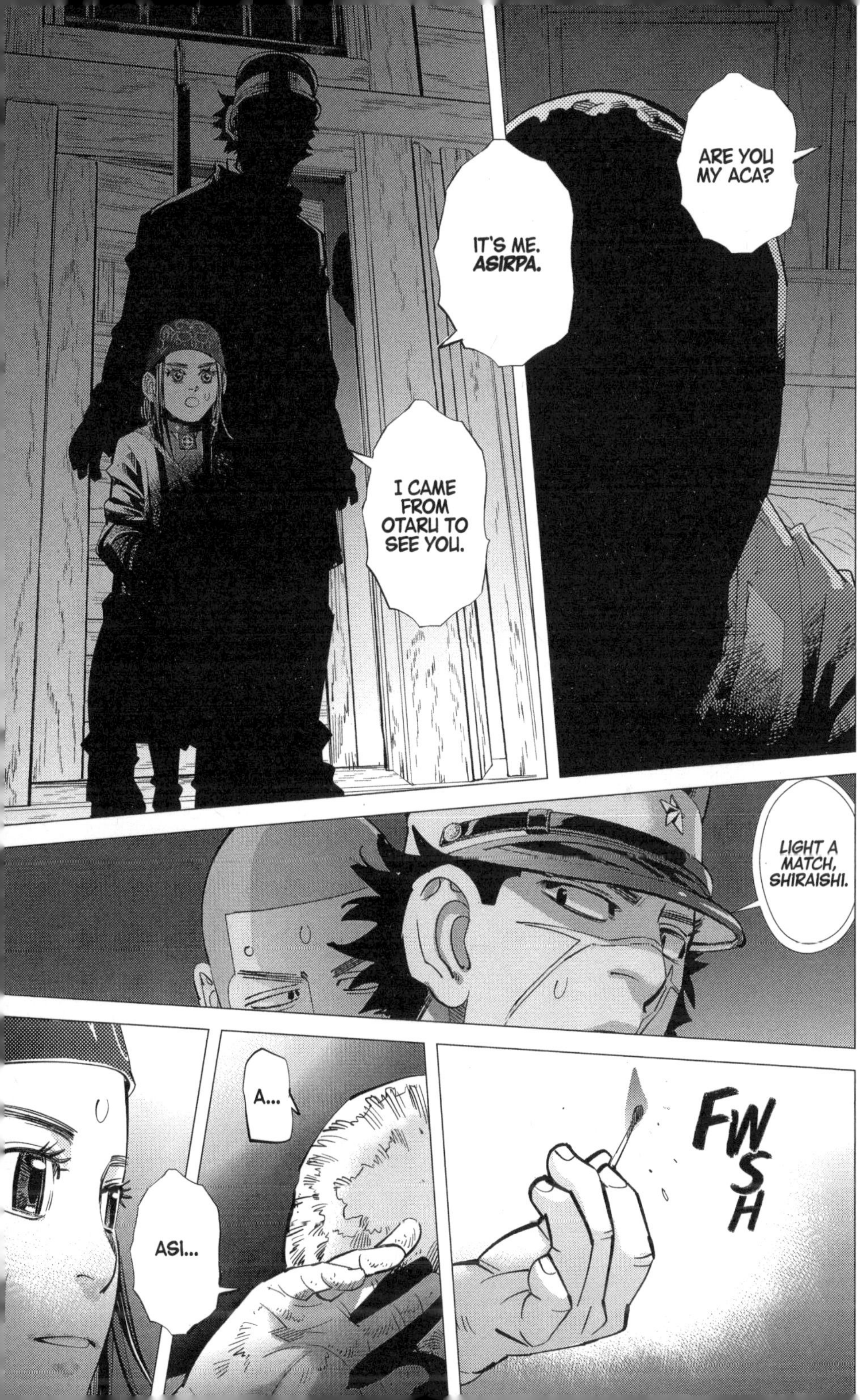
ARE YOU MY ACA?
IT'S ME. ASIRPA.
I CAME FROM OTARU TO SEE YOU.
LIGHT A MATCH, SHIRAISHI.
FWSH
A...
ASI...

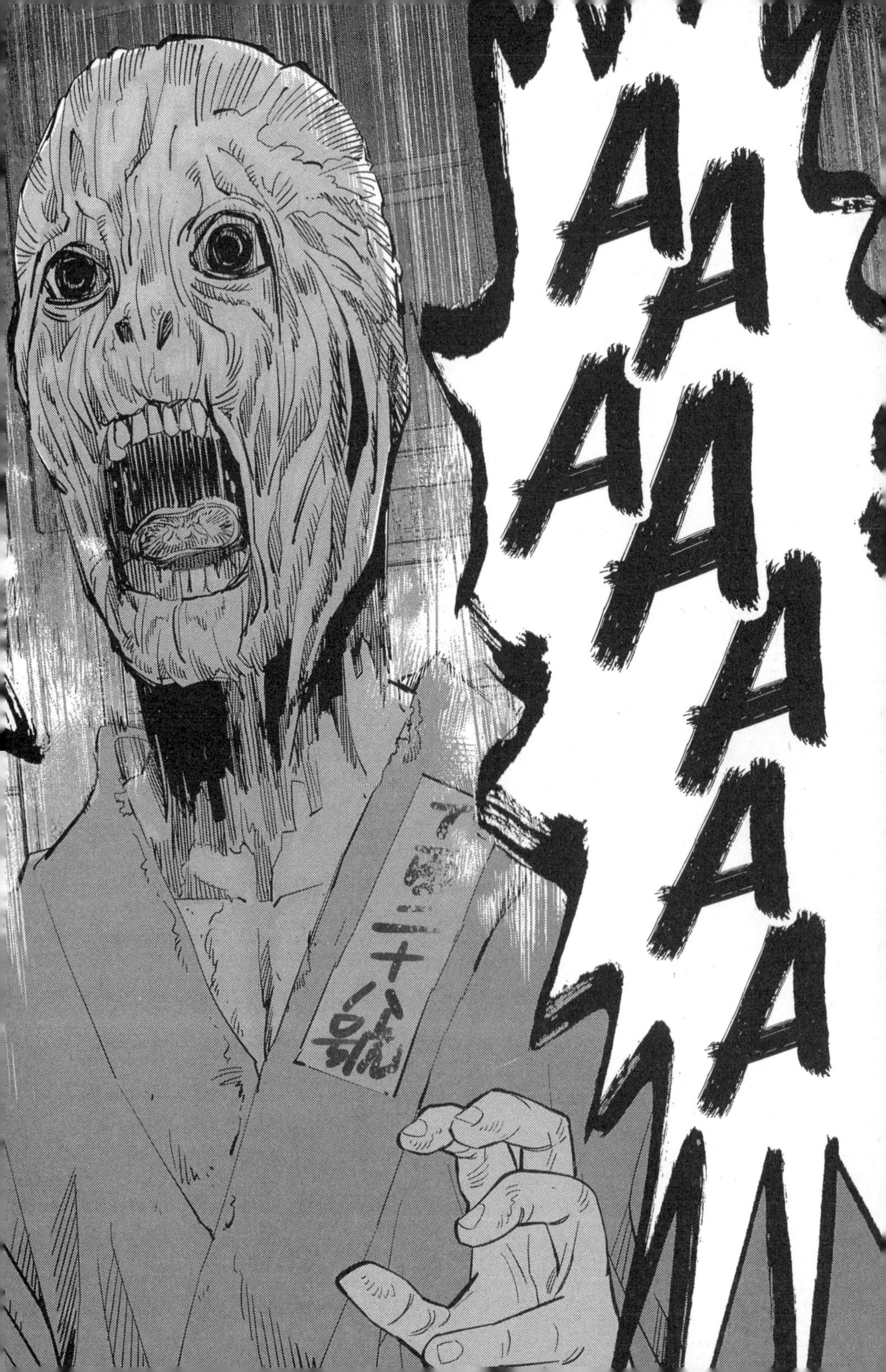

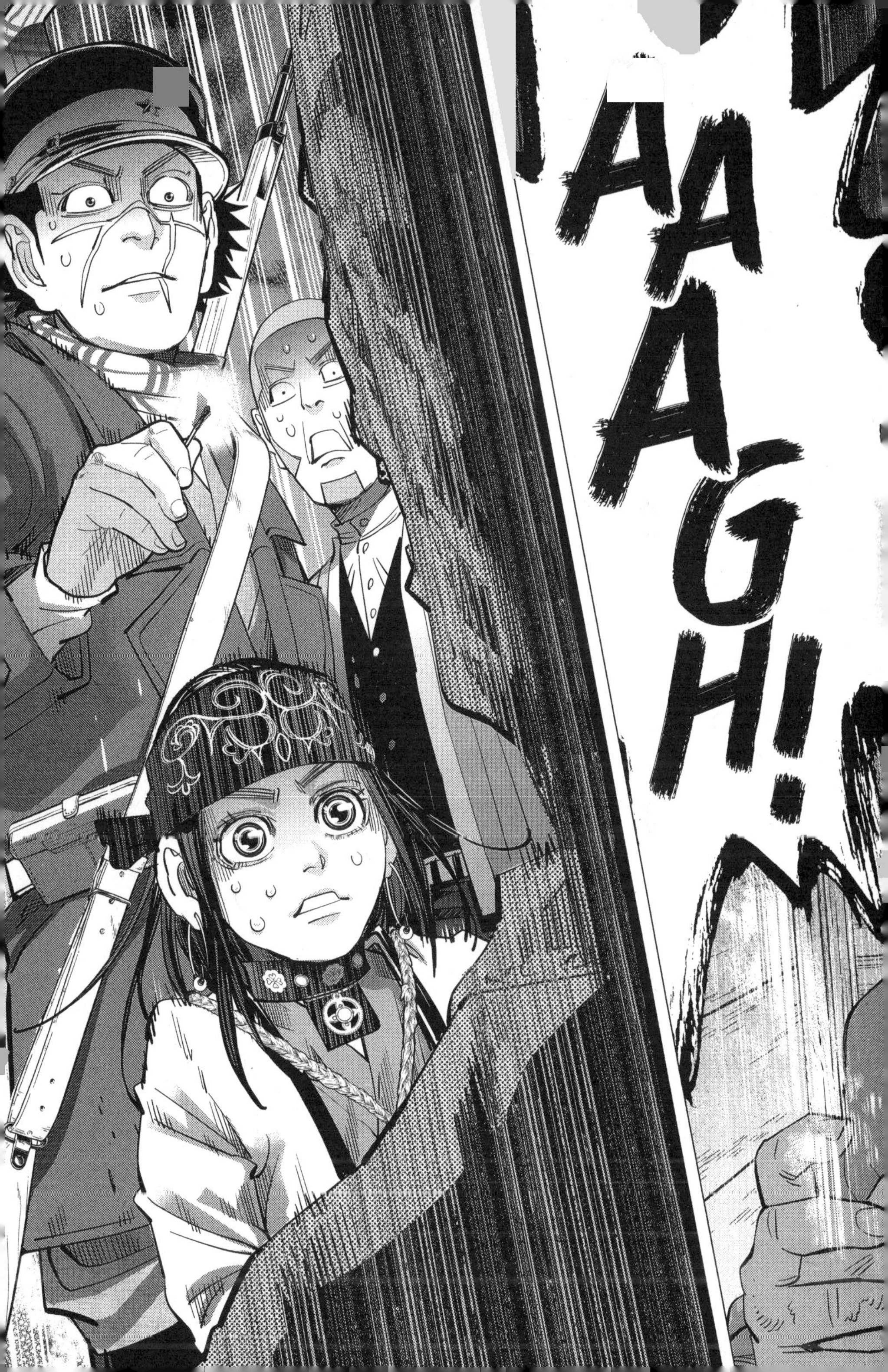
AAAGH!!

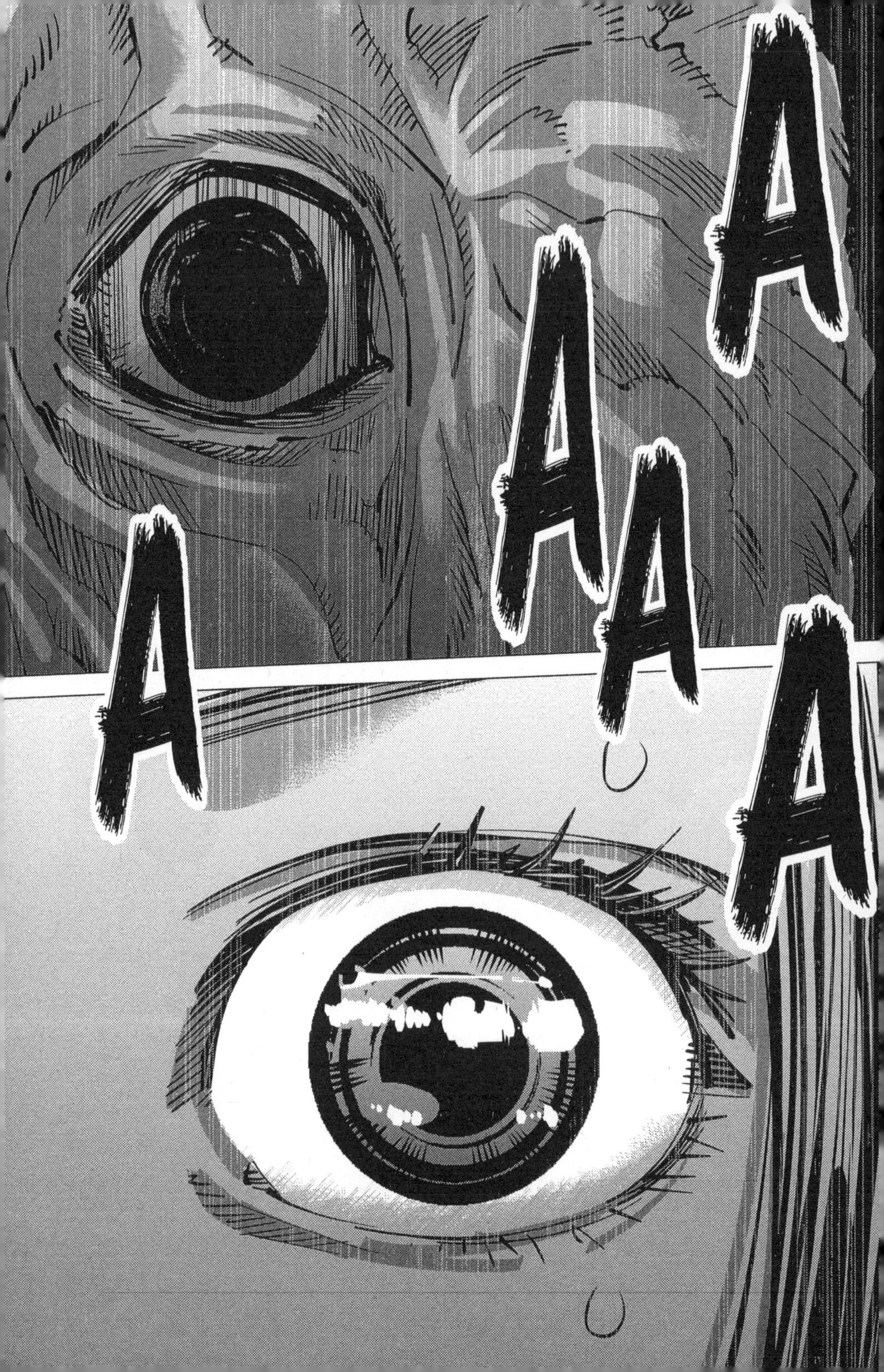
AAAAA

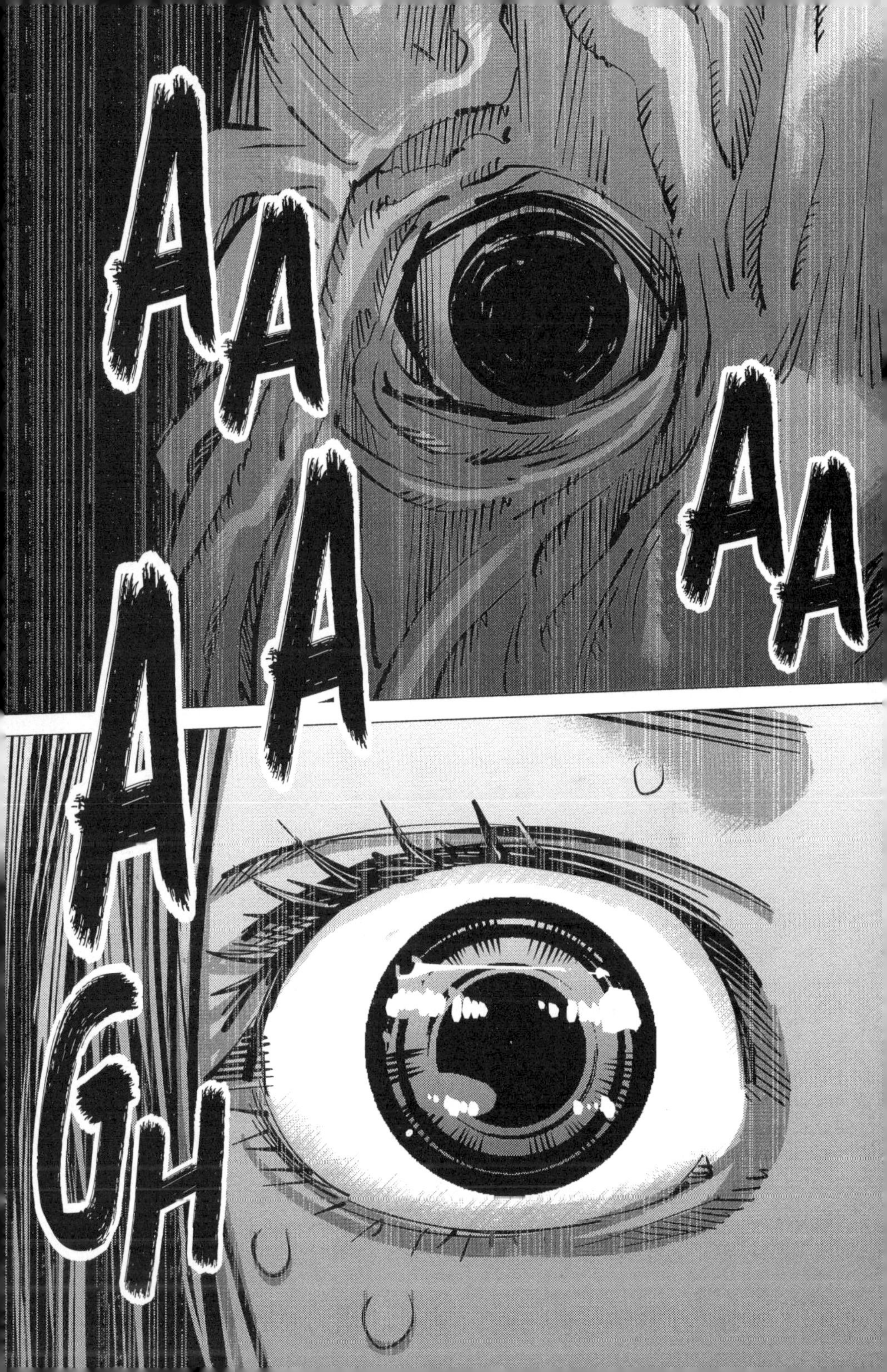
AAAAAAGH

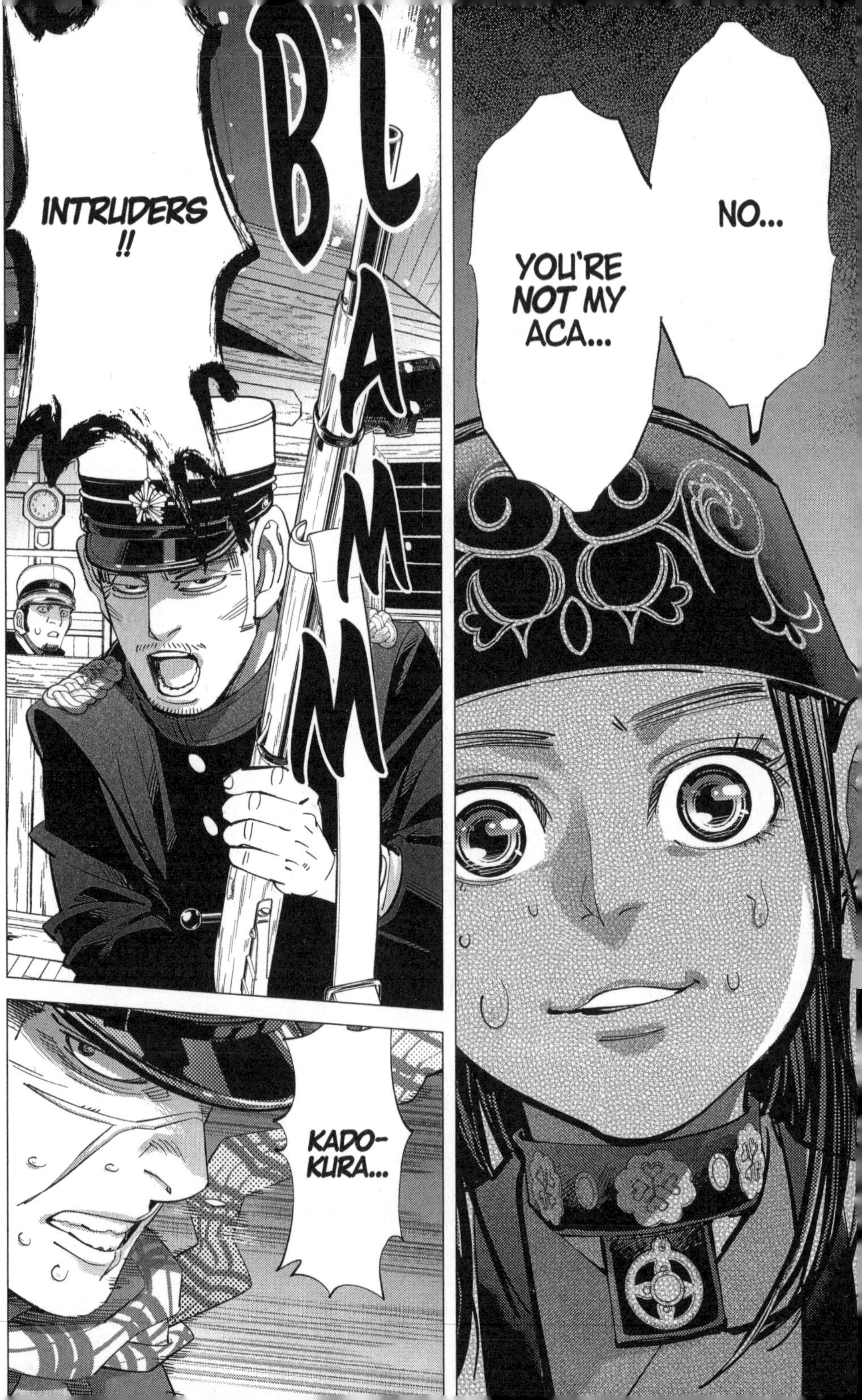
NO...
YOU'RE NOT MY ACA...
BLAMM
INTRUDERS !!
KADO-KURA...

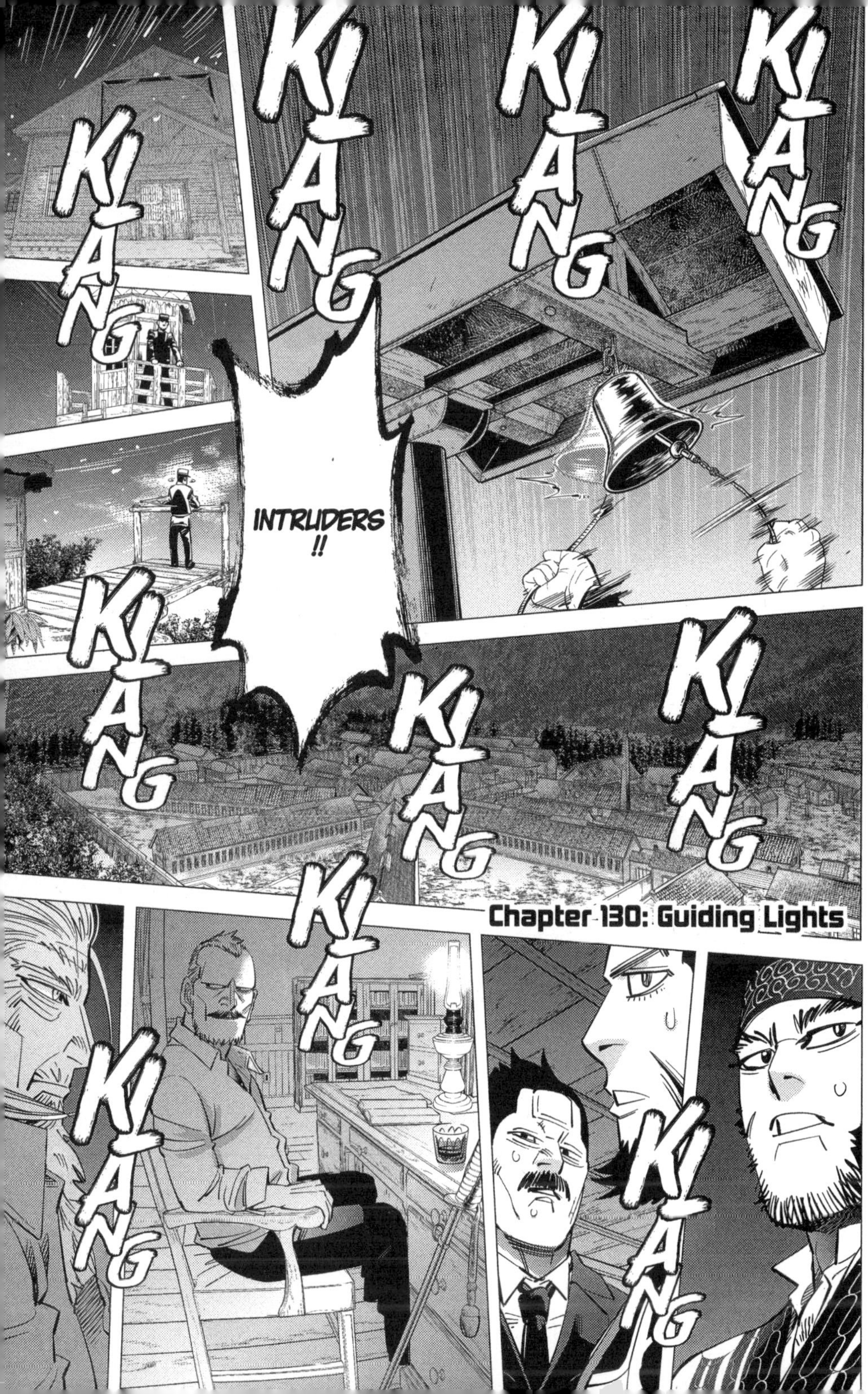
KLANG
KLANG
KLANG
INTRUDERS !!
KLANG
KLANG
KLANG
KLANG
Chapter 130: Guiding Lights
KLANG
KLANG
KLANG

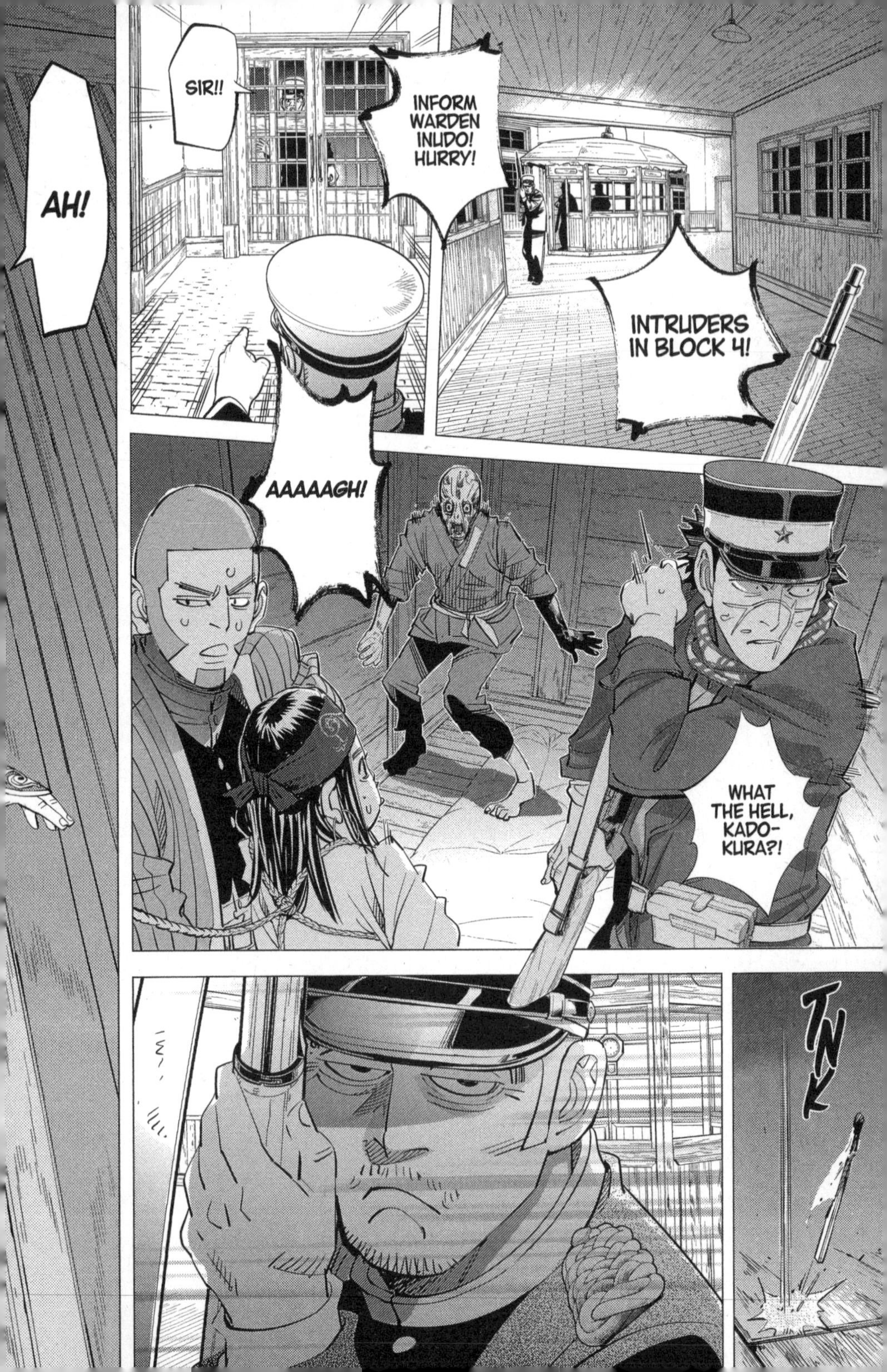
INTRUDERS IN BLOCK 4!
INFORM WARDEN INUDO! HURRY!
SIR!!
AAAAAGH!
WHAT THE HELL, KADO-KURA?!
TNK
AH!

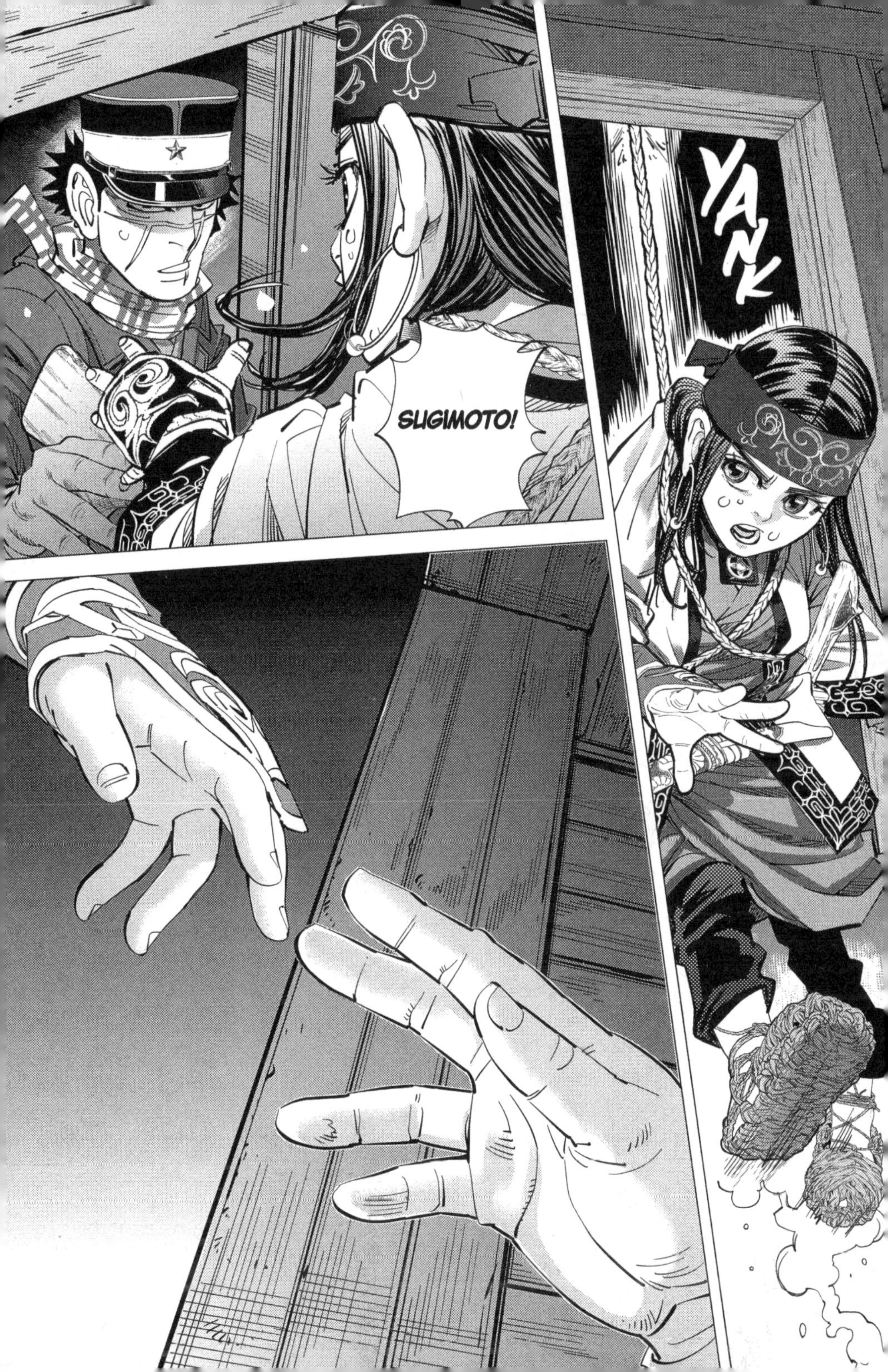
YANK
SUGIMOTO!

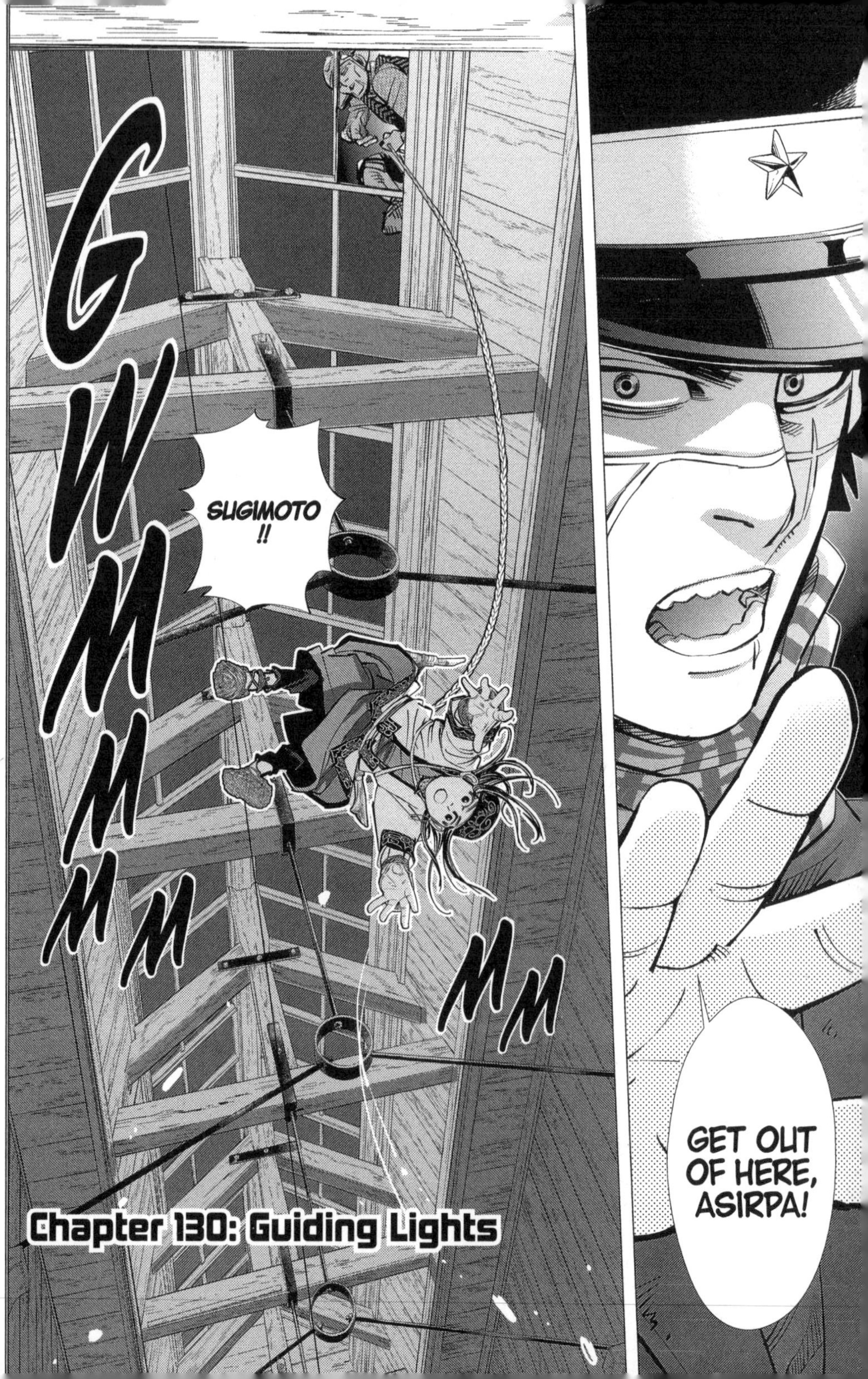
GET OUT OF HERE, ASIRPA!
SUGIMOTO !!
GWMMMMMM
MM
Chapter 130: Guiding Lights

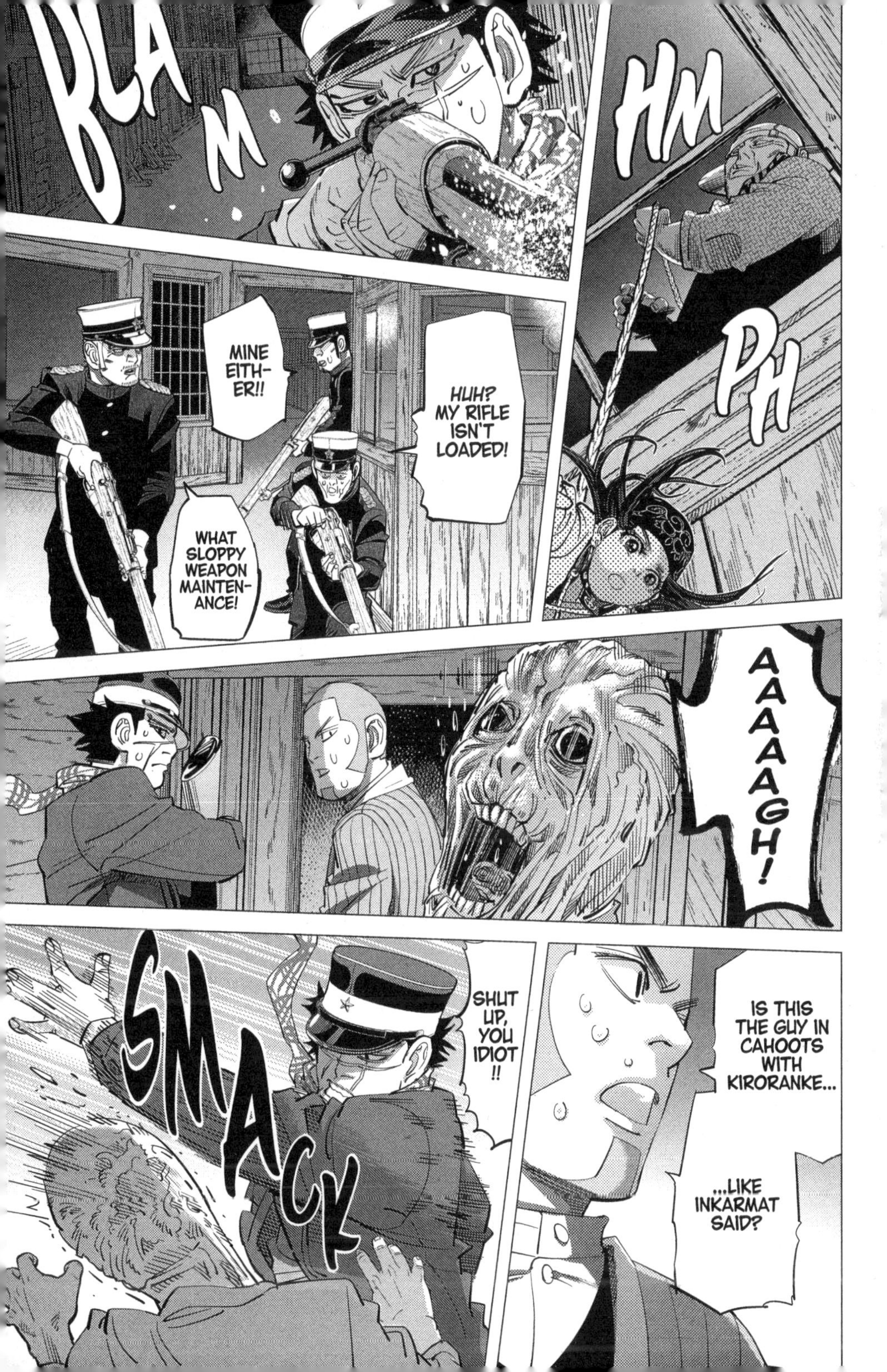

HM
PH
BLAM
HUH? MY RIFLE ISN'T LOADED!
MINE EITHER!!
WHAT SLOPPY WEAPON MAINTENANCE!
AAAAAGH!
IS THIS THE GUY IN CAHOOTS WITH KIRORANKE...
...LIKE INKARMAT SAID?
SHUT UP, YOU IDIOT!!
SMACK

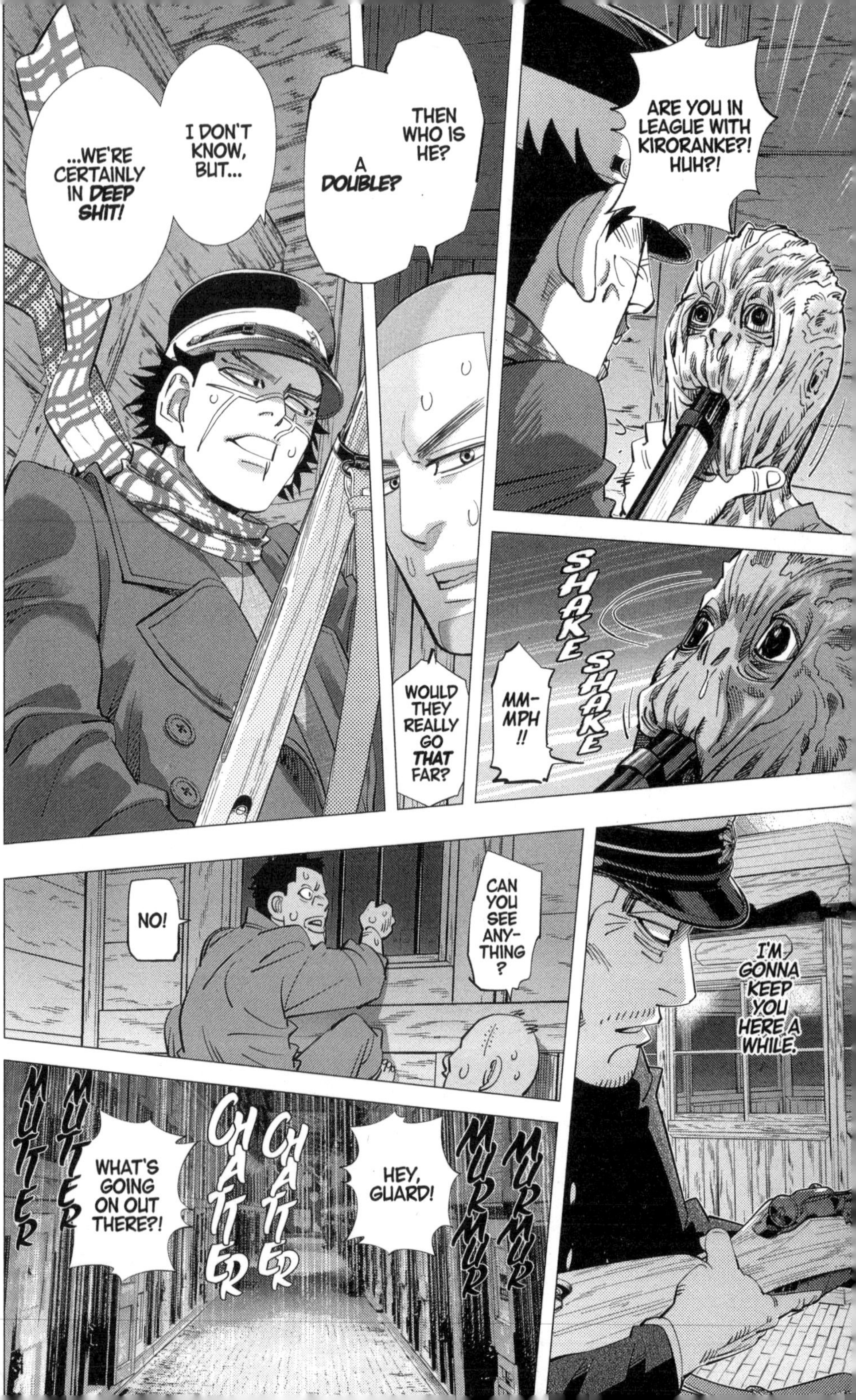
ARE YOU IN LEAGUE WITH KIRORANKE?! HUH?!
SHAKE SHAKE
MM-MPH!!
THEN WHO IS HE?
A DOUBLE?
I DON'T KNOW, BUT...
...WE'RE CERTAINLY IN DEEP SHIT!
WOULD THEY REALLY GO THAT FAR?
I'M GONNA KEEP YOU HERE A WHILE.
CAN YOU SEE ANY-THING?
NO!
MURMUR MURMUR
HEY, GUARD!
CHATTER CHATTER
WHAT'S GOING ON OUT THERE?!
MUTTER MUTTER

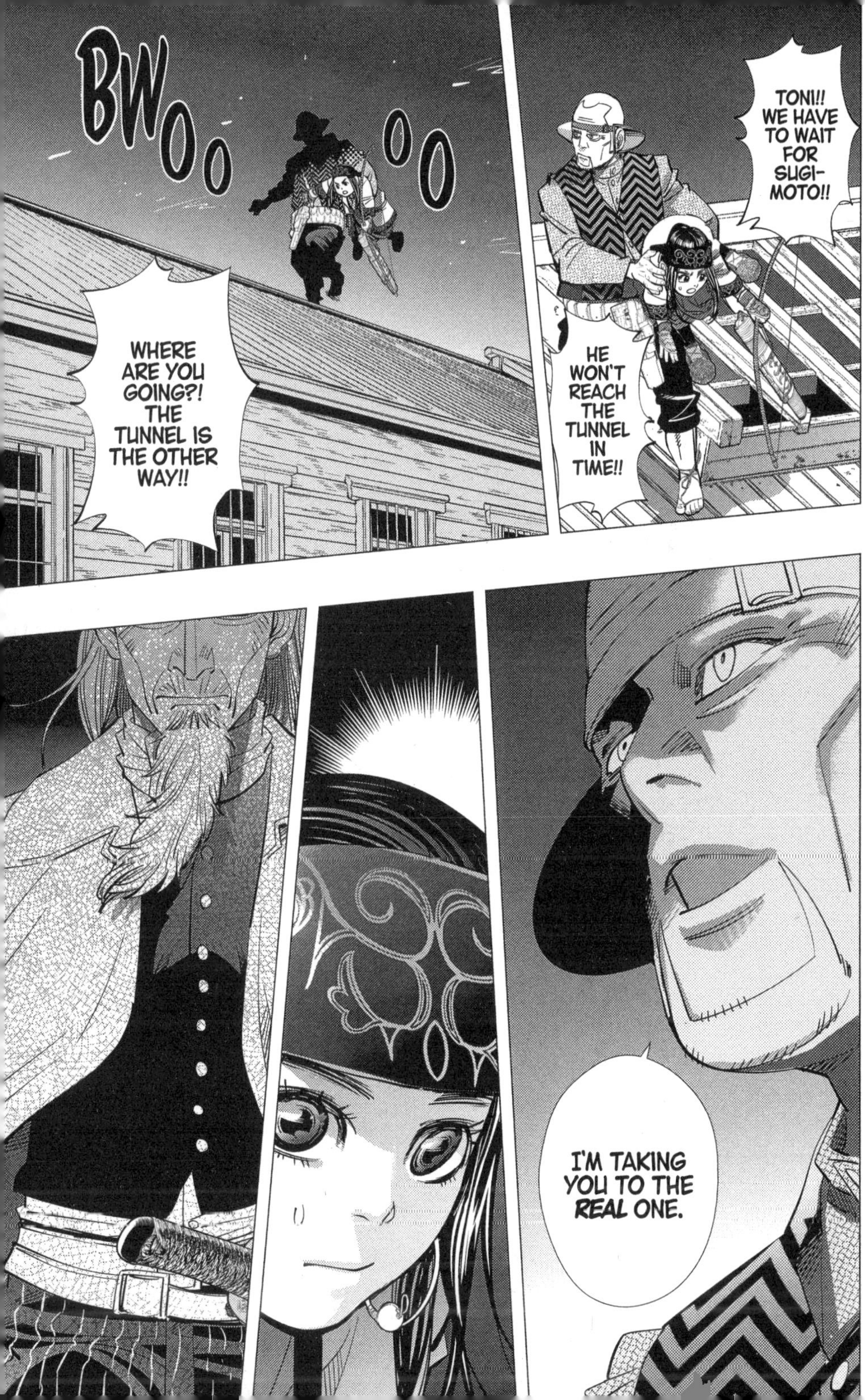
TONI!! WE HAVE TO WAIT FOR SUGI-MOTO!!
HE WON'T REACH THE TUNNEL IN TIME!!
BWOOOOO
WHERE ARE YOU GOING?! THE TUNNEL IS THE OTHER WAY!!
I'M TAKING YOU TO THE *REAL* ONE.

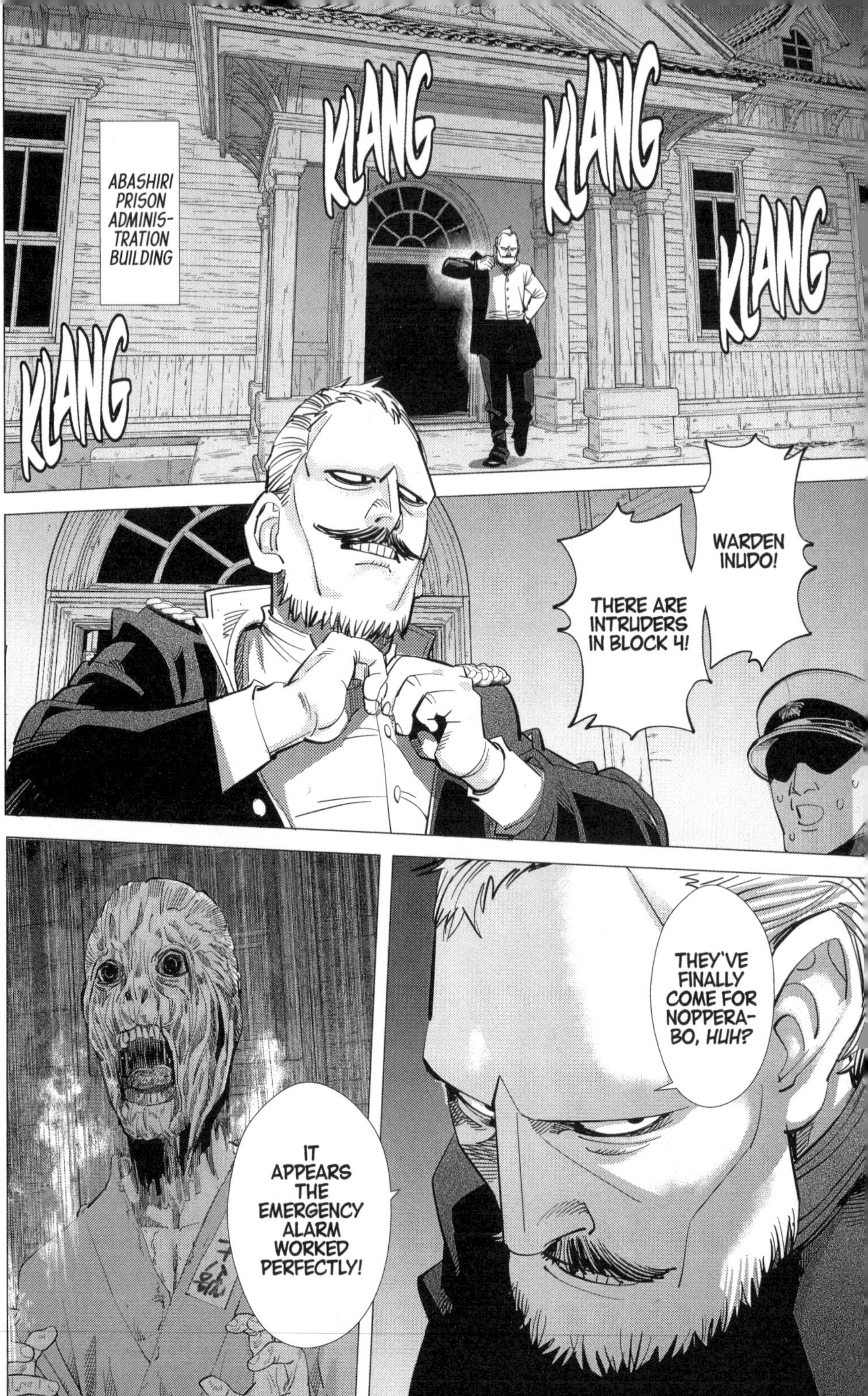
KLANG
KLANG
KLANG
KLANG
ABASHIRI PRISON ADMINISTRATION BUILDING
WARDEN INUDO!
THERE ARE INTRUDERS IN BLOCK 4!
THEY'VE FINALLY COME FOR NOPPERA-BO, HUH?
IT APPEARS THE EMERGENCY ALARM WORKED PERFECTLY!

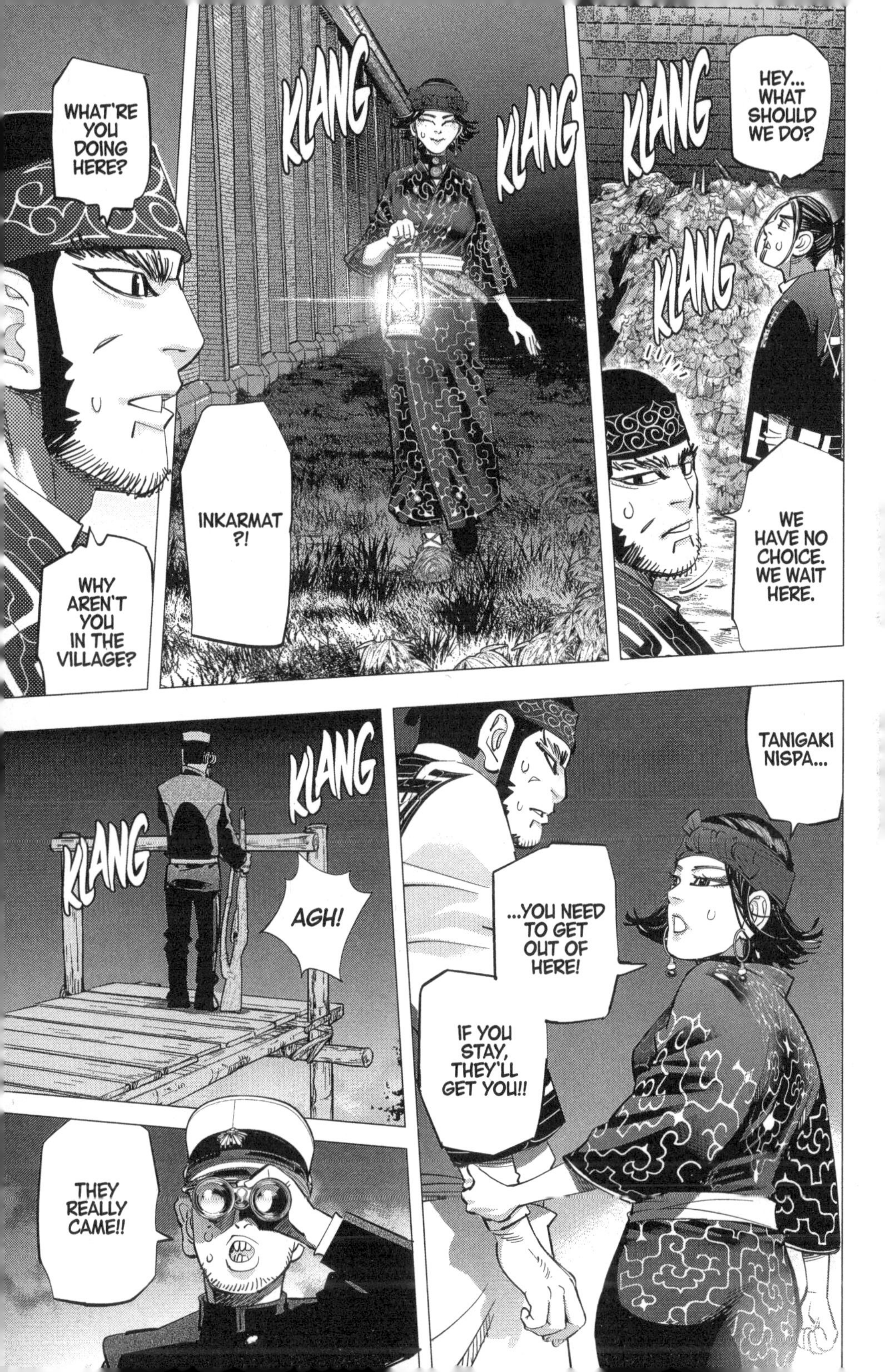
KLANG
HEY... WHAT SHOULD WE DO?
KLANG
WE HAVE NO CHOICE. WE WAIT HERE.
KLANG
KLANG
INKARMAT?!
WHAT'RE YOU DOING HERE?
WHY AREN'T YOU IN THE VILLAGE?
TANIGAKI NISPA...
...YOU NEED TO GET OUT OF HERE!
IF YOU STAY, THEY'LL GET YOU!!
KLANG
KLANG
AGH!
THEY REALLY CAME!!

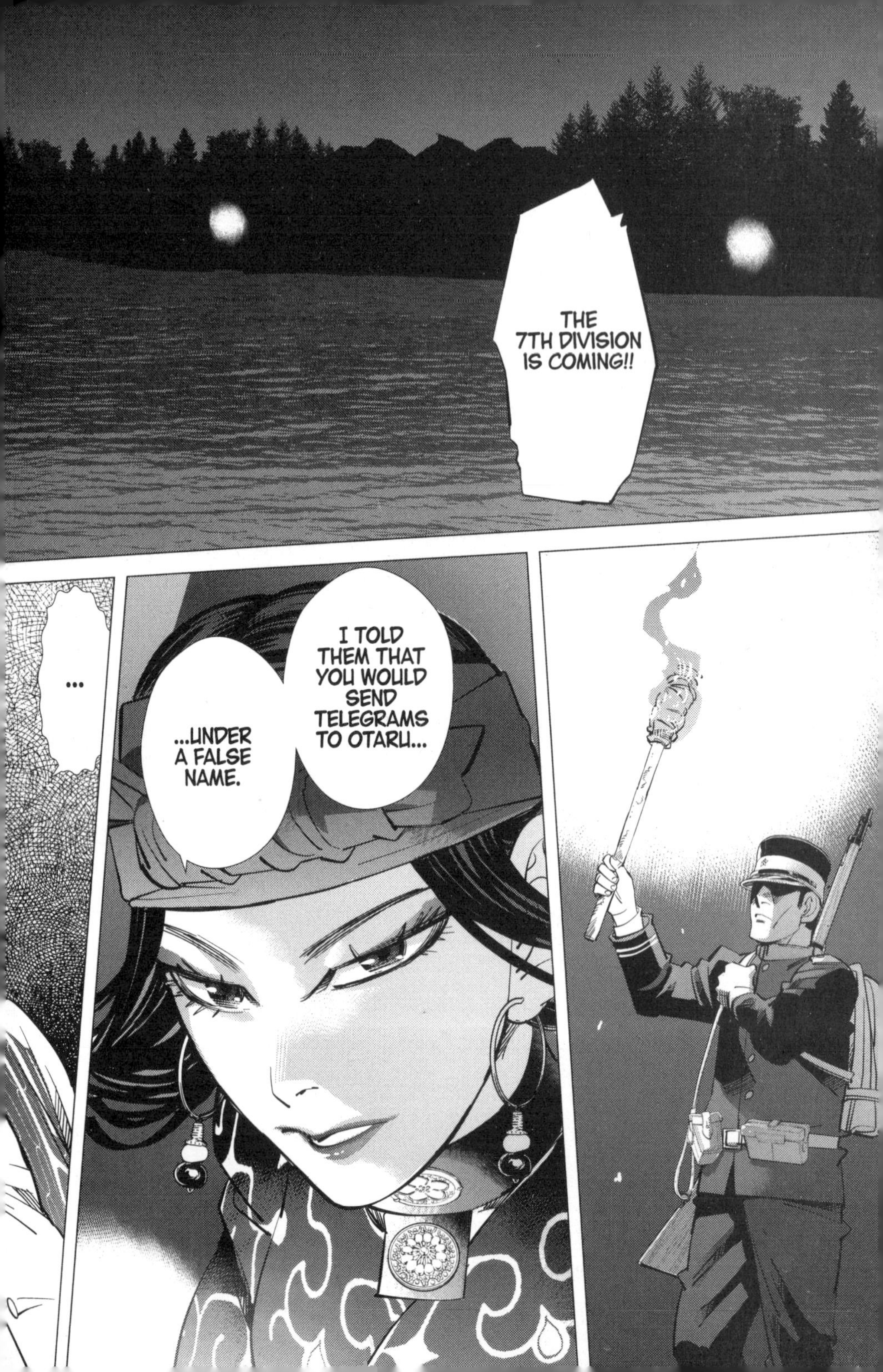
THE 7TH DIVISION IS COMING!!
I TOLD THEM THAT YOU WOULD SEND TELEGRAMS TO OTARU...
...UNDER A FALSE NAME.
...

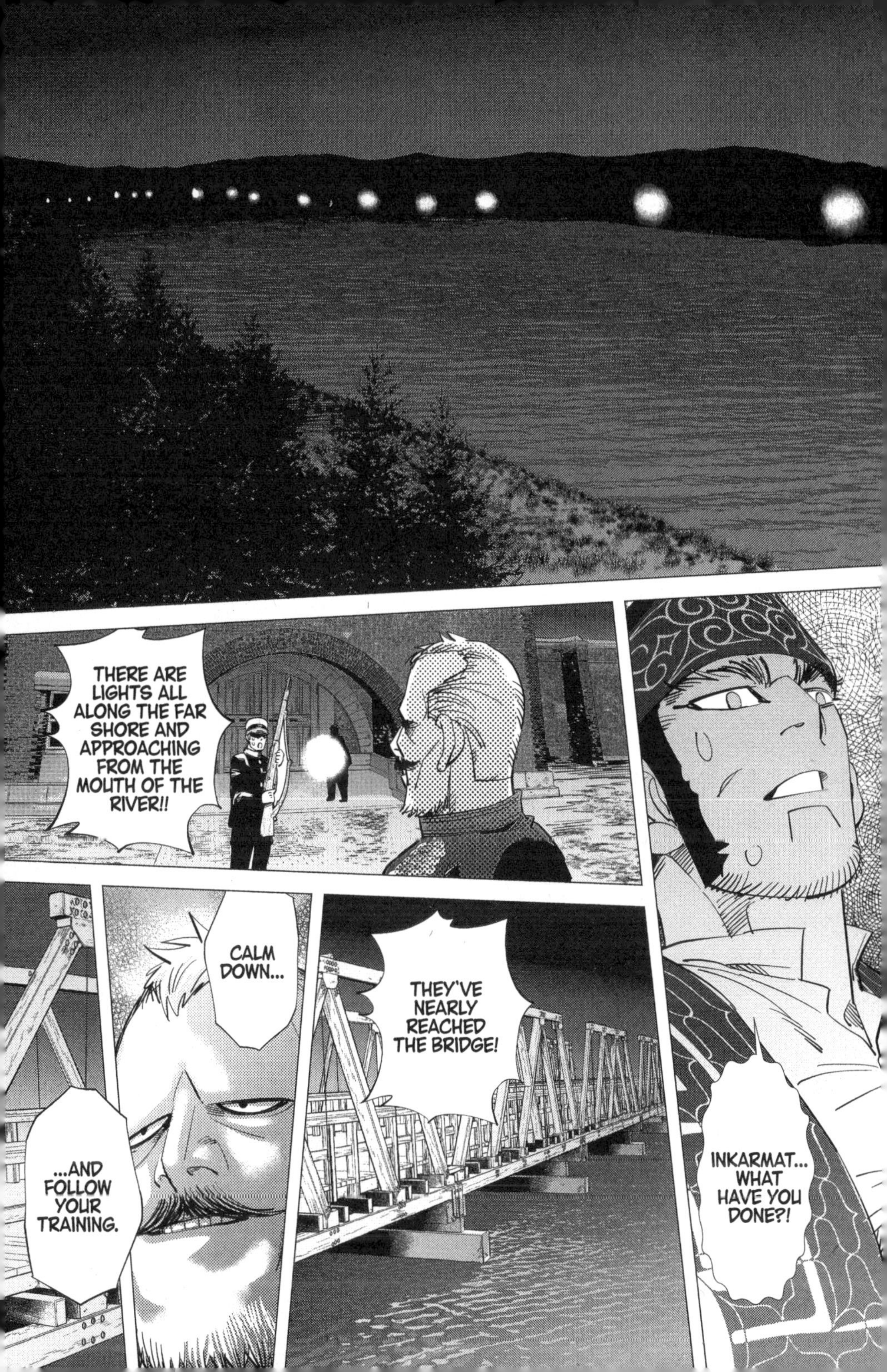
INKARMAT... WHAT HAVE YOU DONE?!
THERE ARE LIGHTS ALL ALONG THE FAR SHORE AND APPROACHING FROM THE MOUTH OF THE RIVER!!
THEY'VE NEARLY REACHED THE BRIDGE!
CALM DOWN...
...AND FOLLOW YOUR TRAINING.

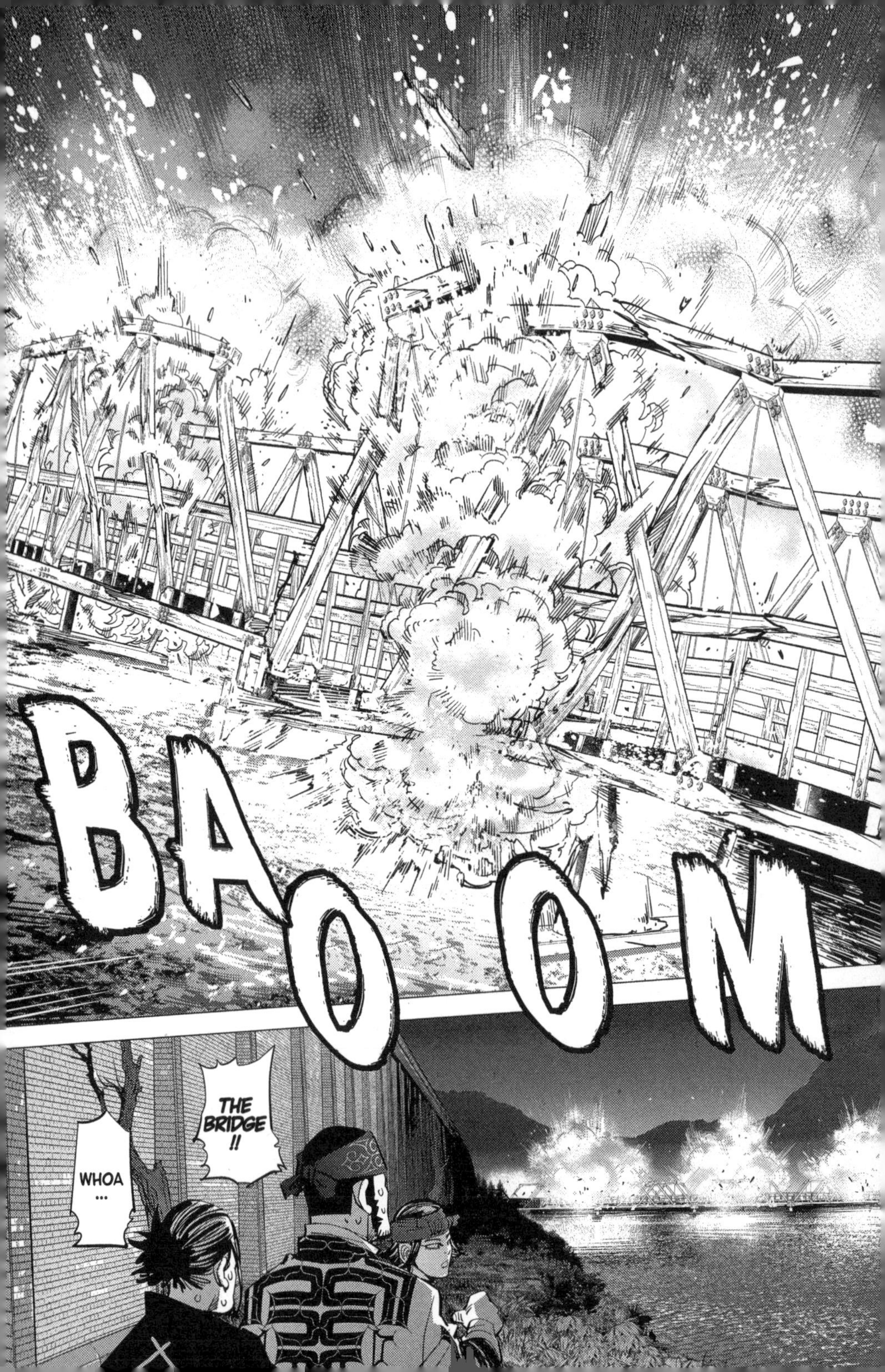
BAOOM
THE BRIDGE!!
WHOA...

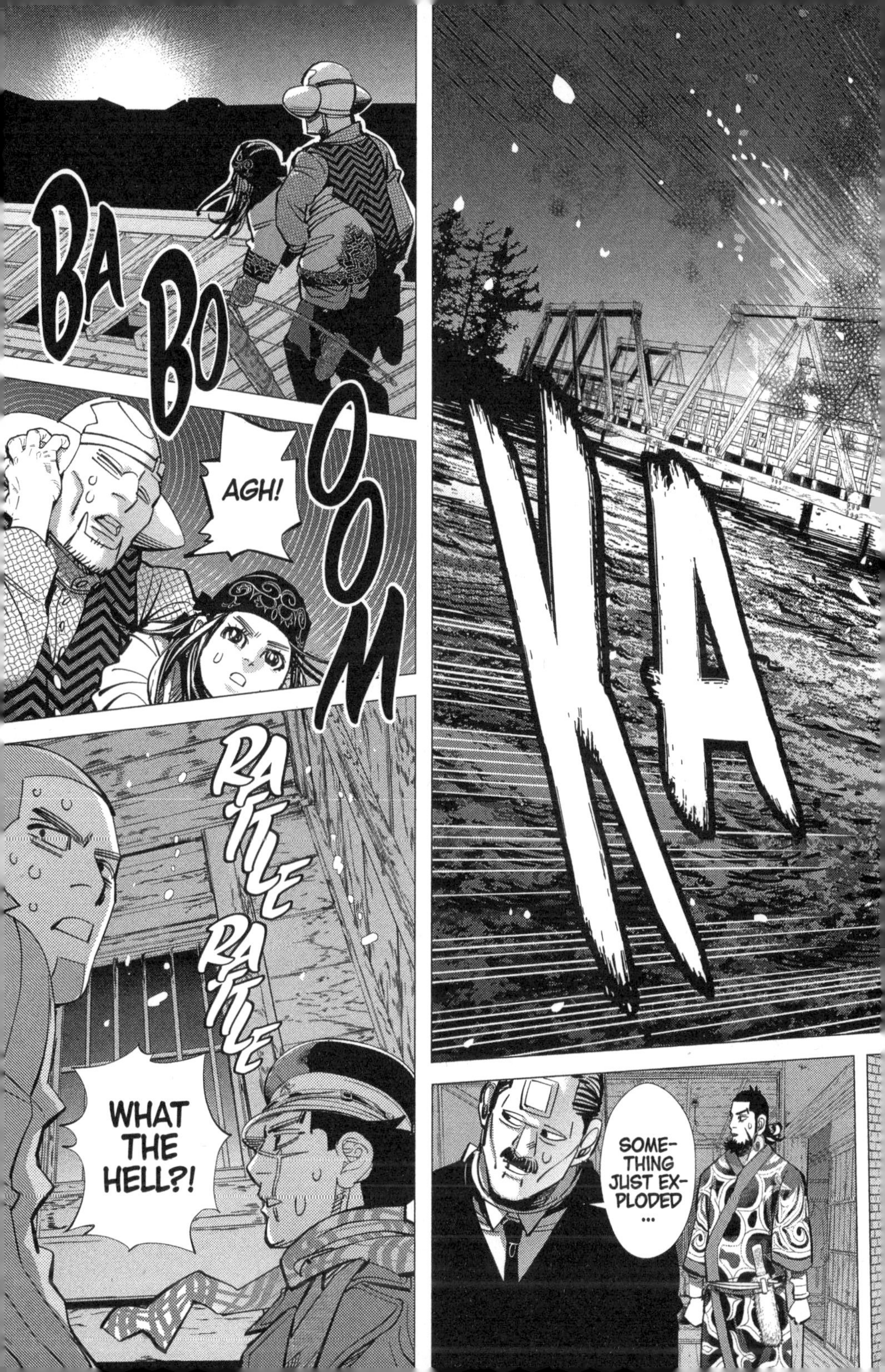
KA
SOME-THING JUST EX-PLODED ...
BABOOOM
AGH!
RATTLE RATTLE
WHAT THE HELL?!

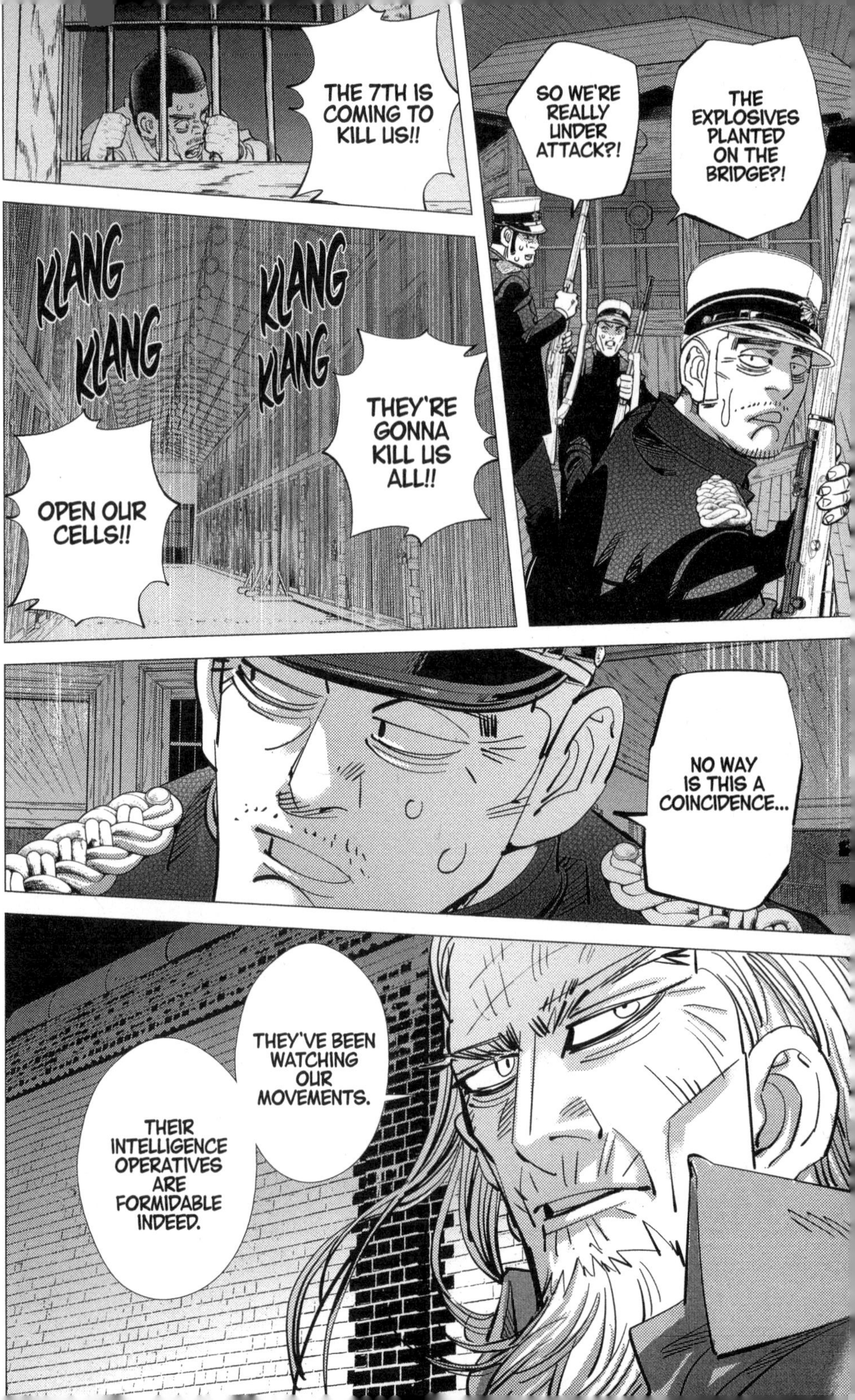
THE EXPLOSIVES PLANTED ON THE BRIDGE?!
SO WE'RE REALLY UNDER ATTACK?!
THE 7TH IS COMING TO KILL US!!
KLANG KLANG
KLANG KLANG
THEY'RE GONNA KILL US ALL!!
OPEN OUR CELLS!!
NO WAY IS THIS A COINCIDENCE...
THEY'VE BEEN WATCHING OUR MOVEMENTS.
THEIR INTELLIGENCE OPERATIVES ARE FORMIDABLE INDEED.

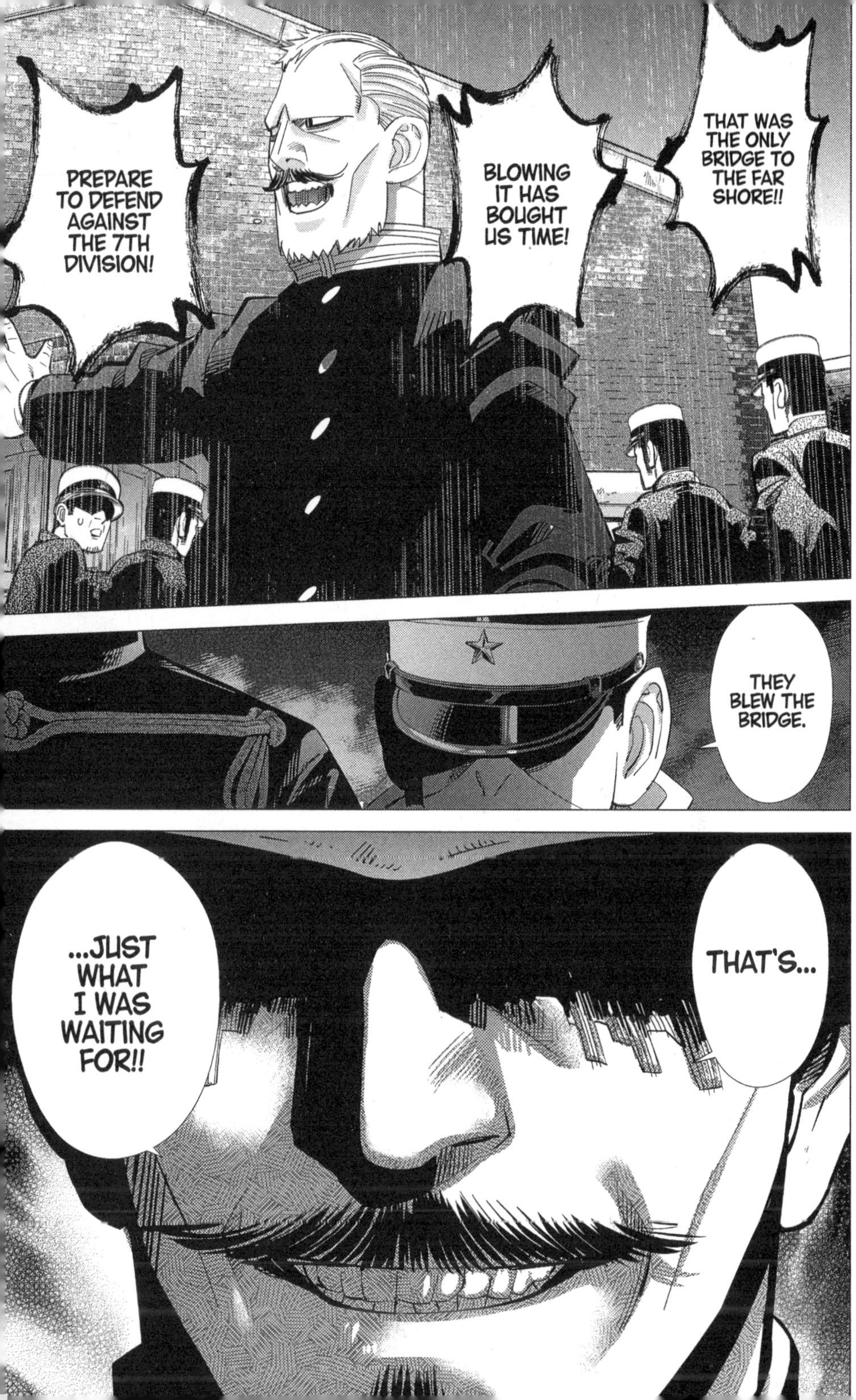
THAT WAS THE ONLY BRIDGE TO THE FAR SHORE!!
BLOWING IT HAS BOUGHT US TIME!
PREPARE TO DEFEND AGAINST THE 7TH DIVISION!
THEY BLEW THE BRIDGE.
THAT'S...
...JUST WHAT I WAS WAITING FOR!!

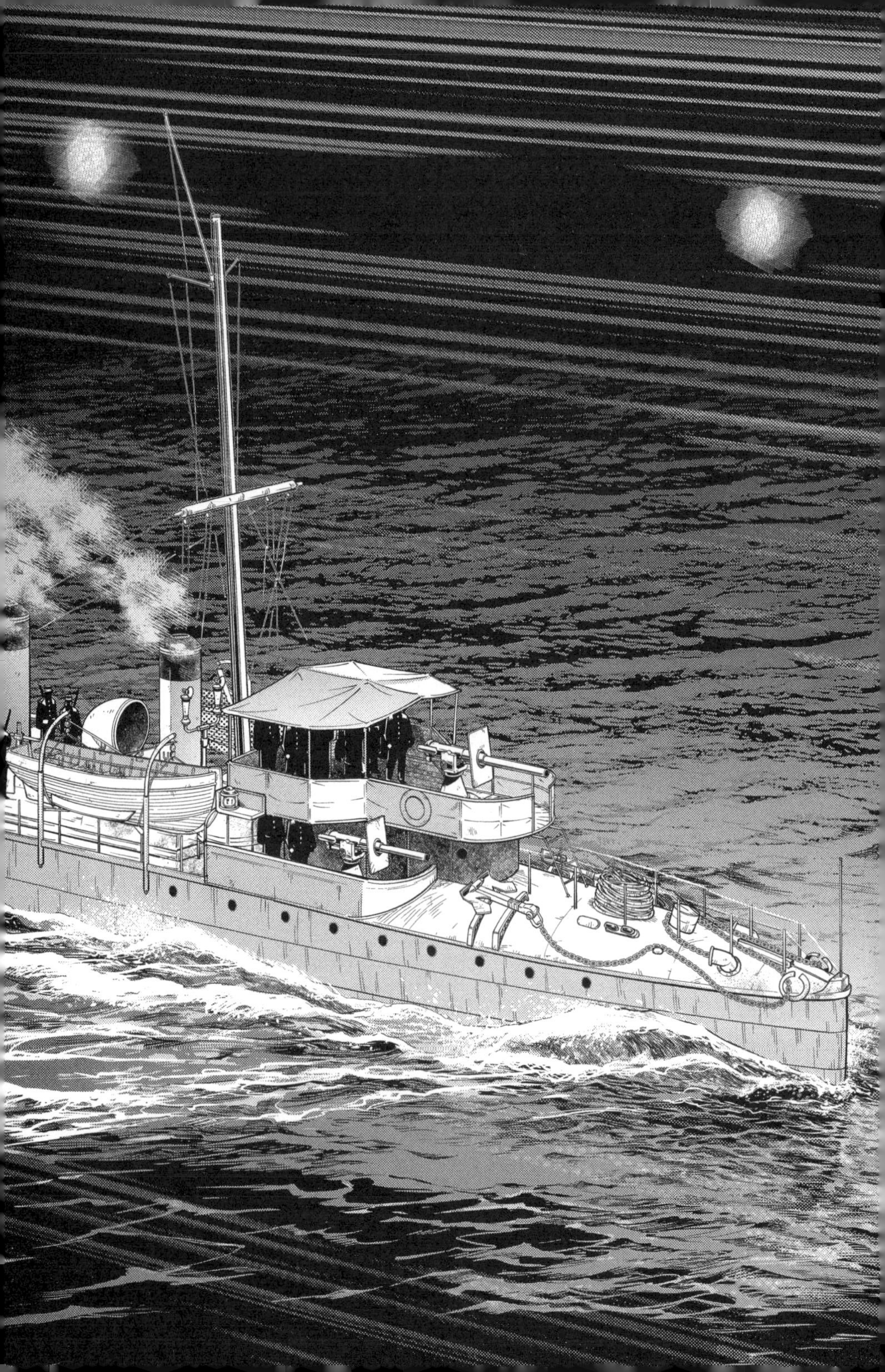

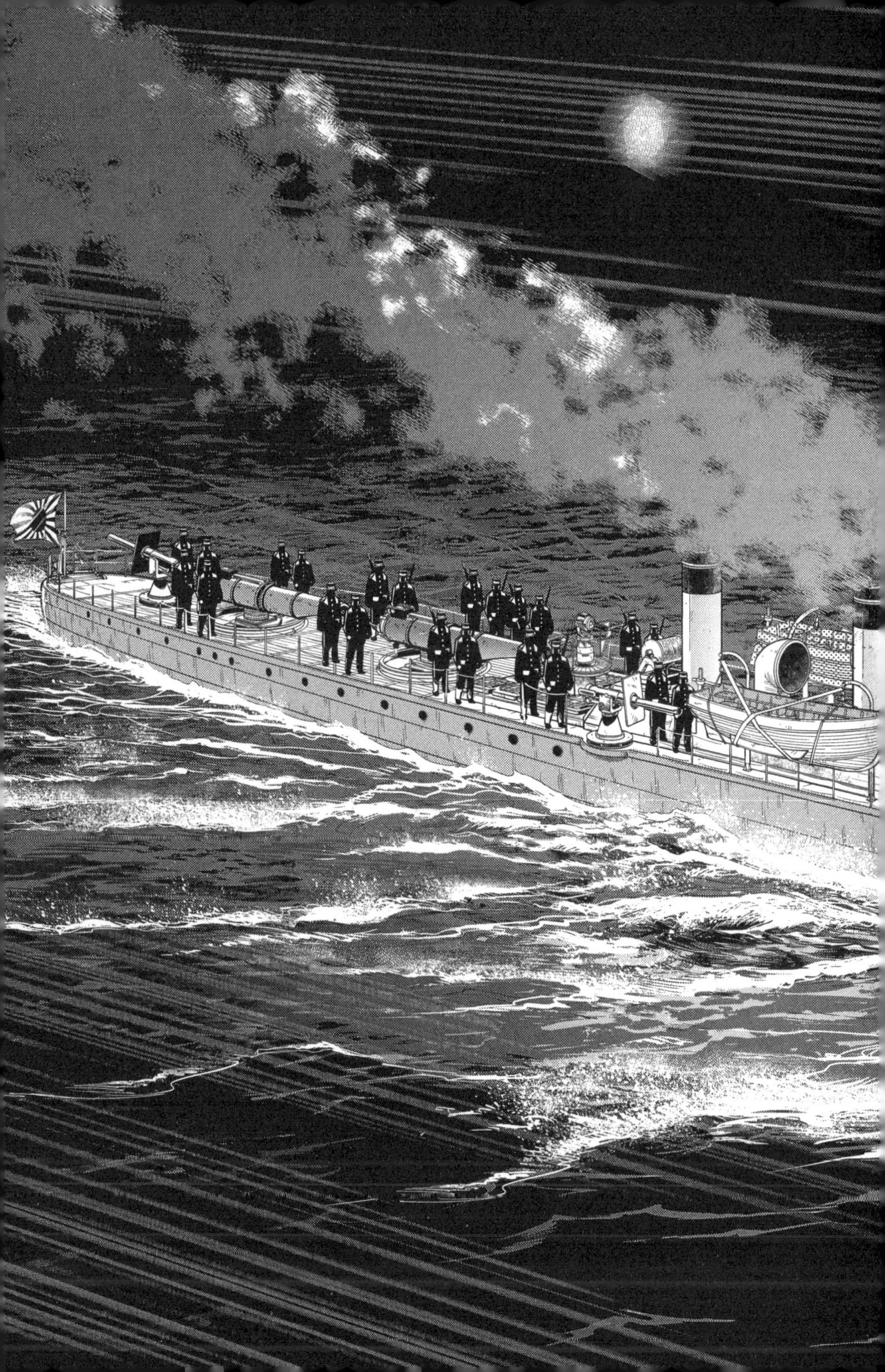

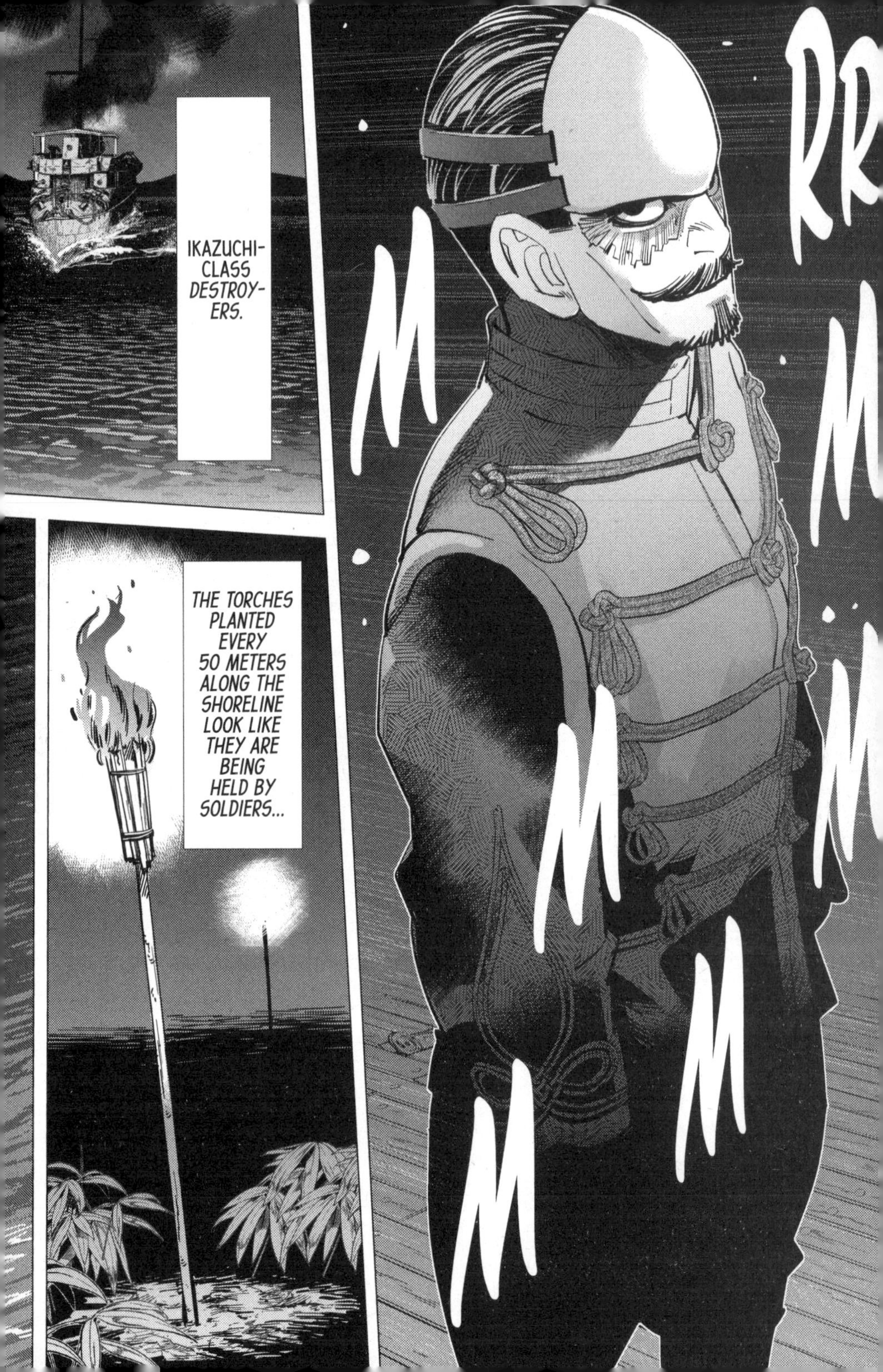
IKAZUCHI-CLASS DESTROY-ERS.
THE TORCHES PLANTED EVERY 50 METERS ALONG THE SHORELINE LOOK LIKE THEY ARE BEING HELD BY SOLDIERS...

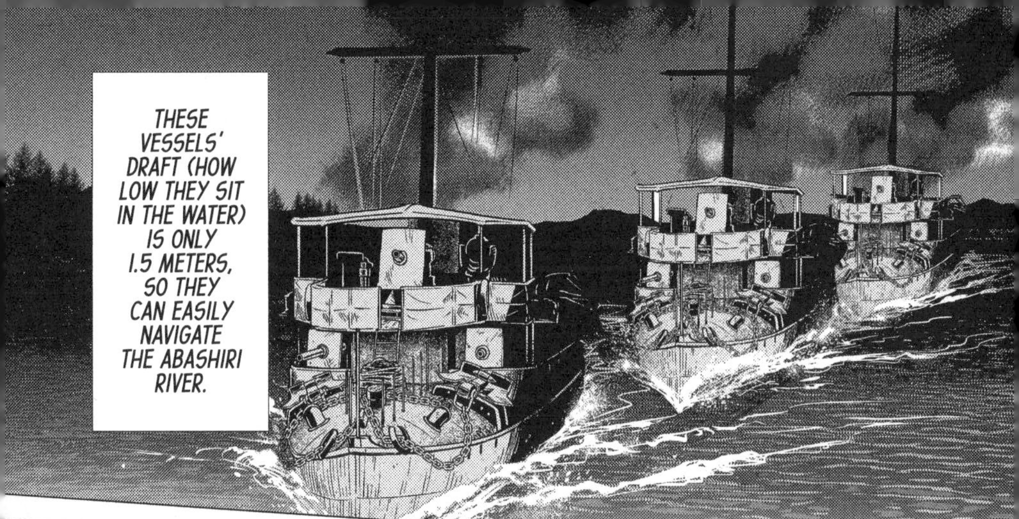
THESE VESSELS' DRAFT (HOW LOW THEY SIT IN THE WATER) IS ONLY 1.5 METERS, SO THEY CAN EASILY NAVIGATE THE ABASHIRI RIVER.
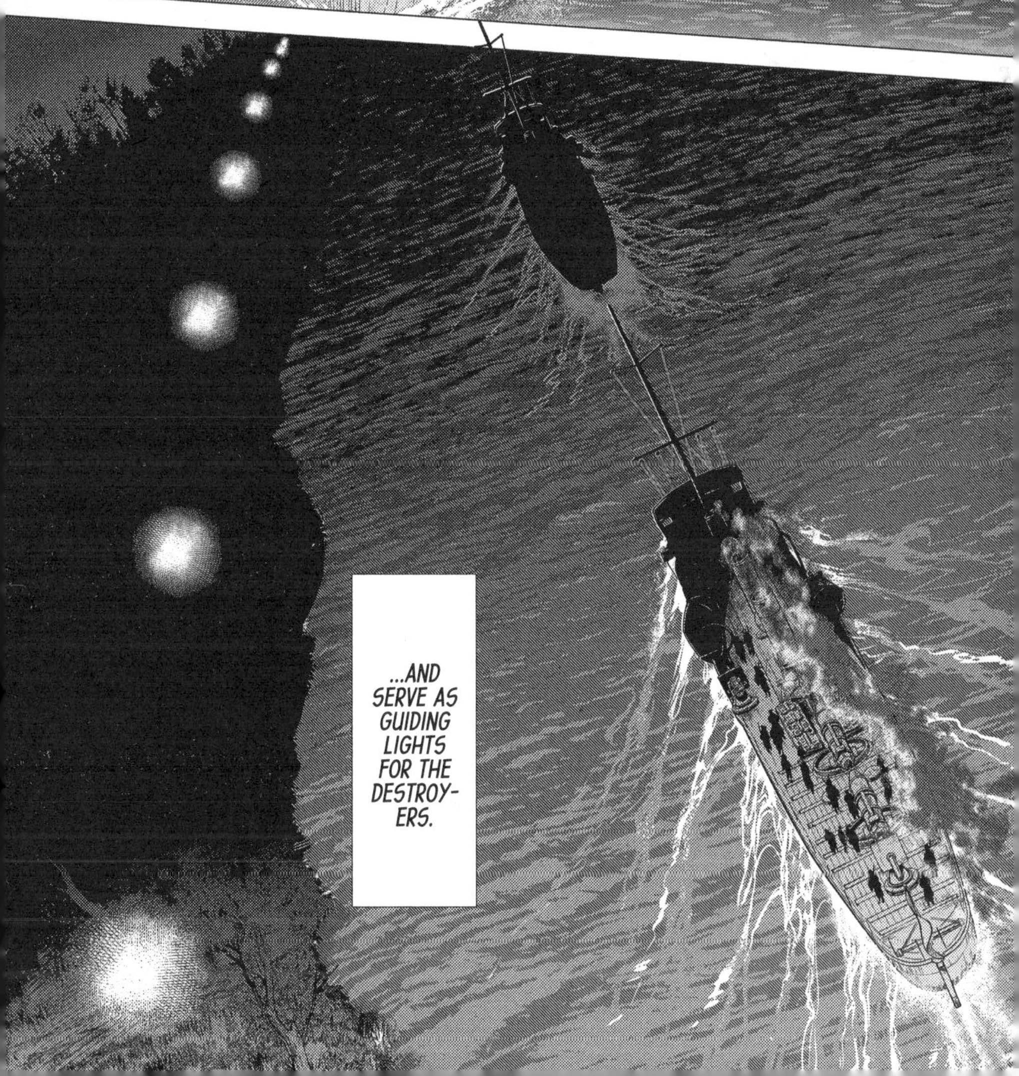
...AND SERVE AS GUIDING LIGHTS FOR THE DESTROY-ERS.

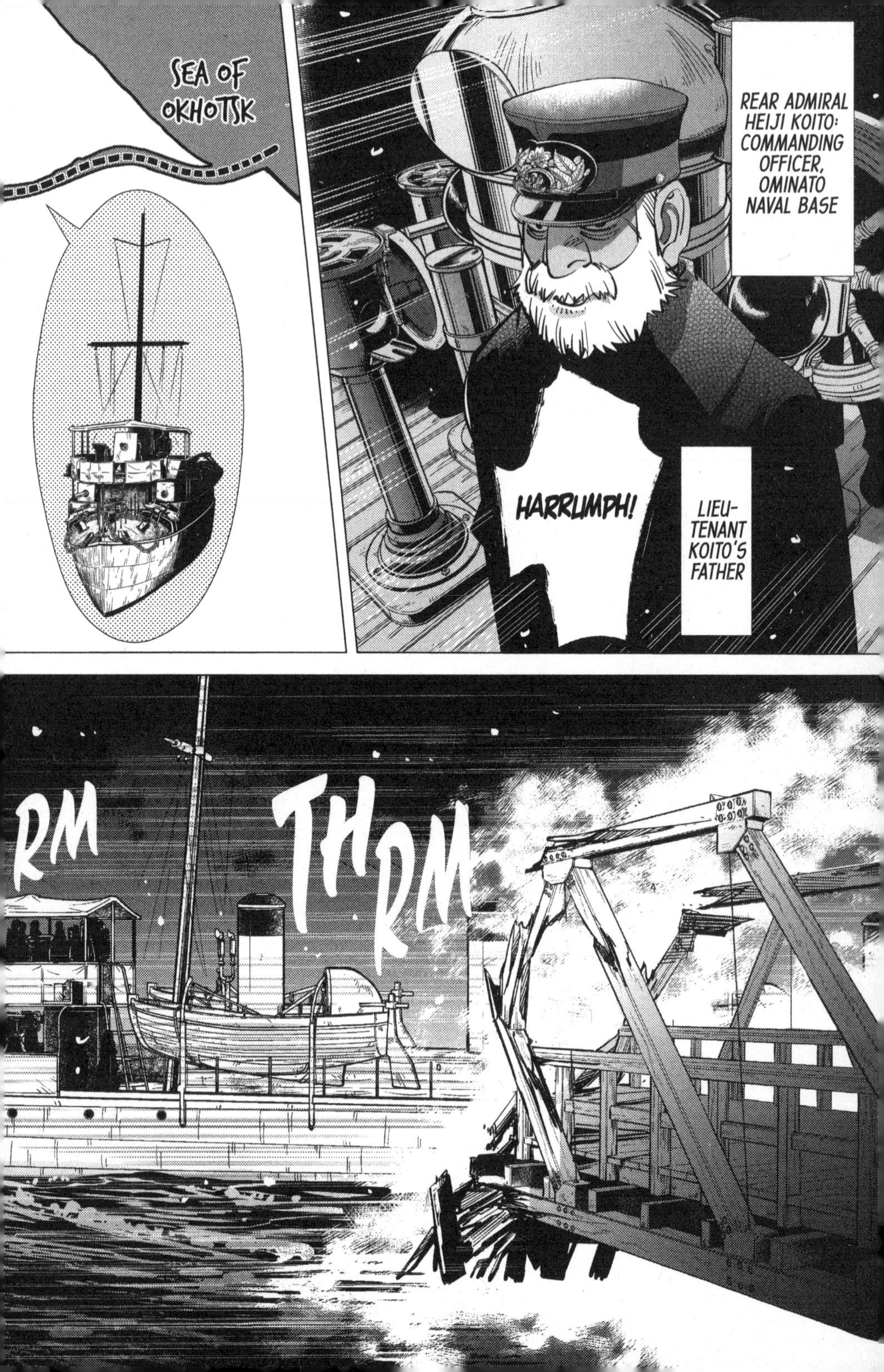
REAR ADMIRAL HEIJI KOITO: COMMANDING OFFICER, OMINATO NAVAL BASE
LIEU-TENANT KOITO'S FATHER
HARRUMPH!
SEA OF OKHOTSK
THRM
RM

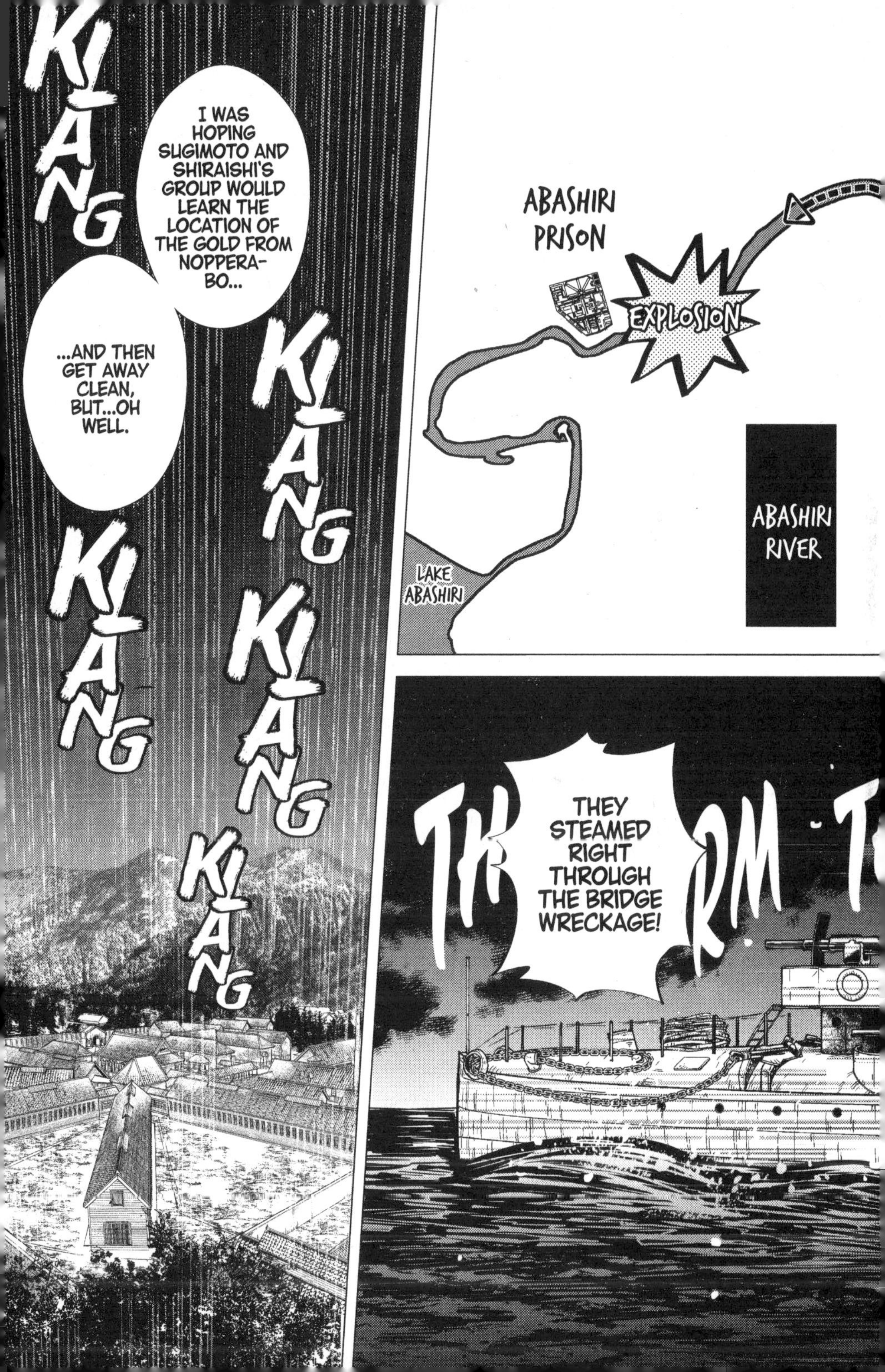
ABASHIRI PRISON
EXPLOSION
ABASHIRI RIVER
LAKE ABASHIRI
THEY STEAMED RIGHT THROUGH THE BRIDGE WRECKAGE!
KLANG
I WAS HOPING SUGIMOTO AND SHIRAISHI'S GROUP WOULD LEARN THE LOCATION OF THE GOLD FROM NOPPERA-BO...
...AND THEN GET AWAY CLEAN, BUT...OH WELL.
KLANG
KLANG
KLANG
KLANG

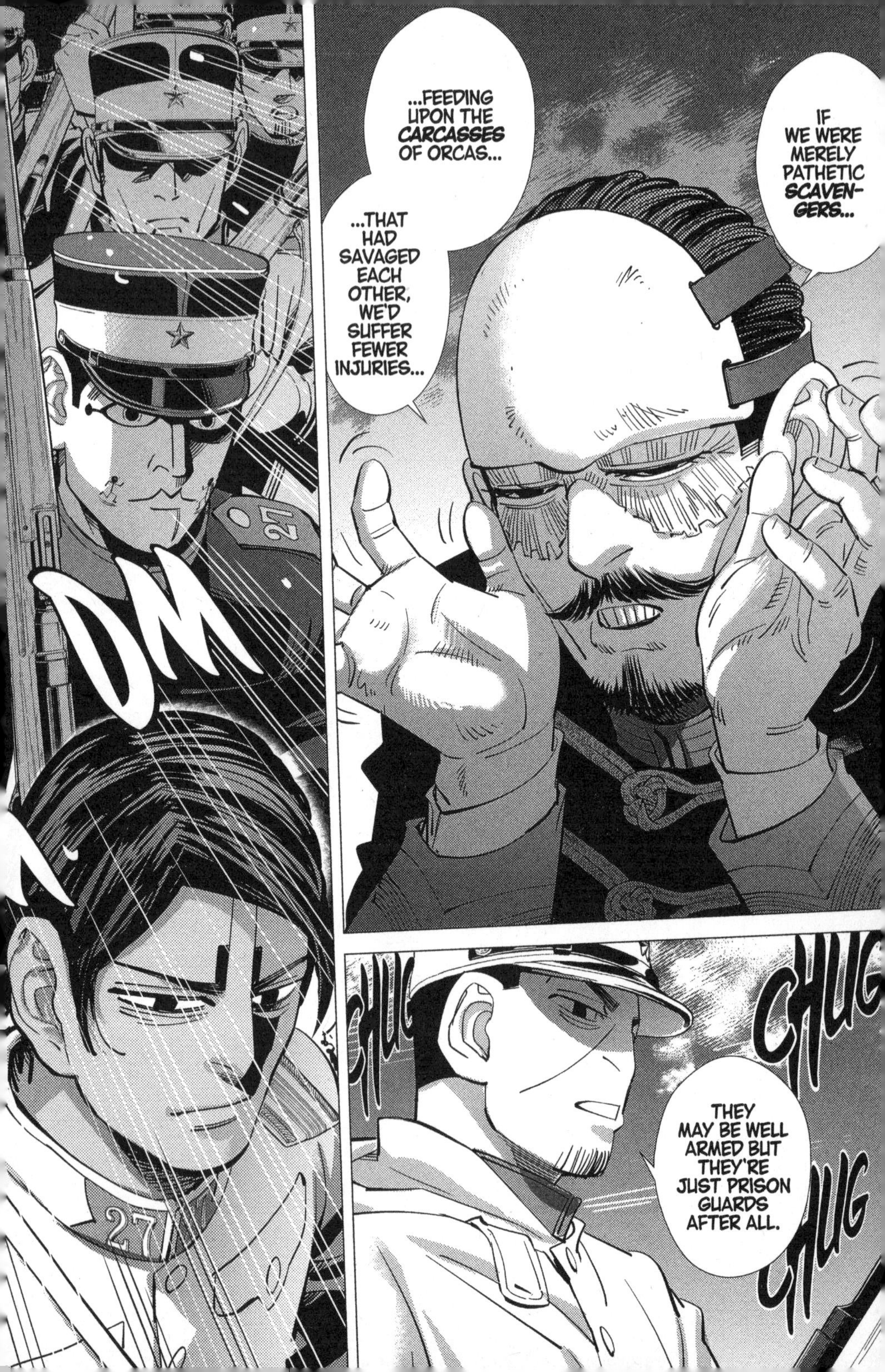
IF WE WERE MERELY PATHETIC SCAVENGERS...
...FEEDING UPON THE CARCASSES OF ORCAS...
...THAT HAD SAVAGED EACH OTHER, WE'D SUFFER FEWER INJURIES...
CHUG
CHUG
CHUG
THEY MAY BE WELL ARMED BUT THEY'RE JUST PRISON GUARDS AFTER ALL.
CHUG
DM

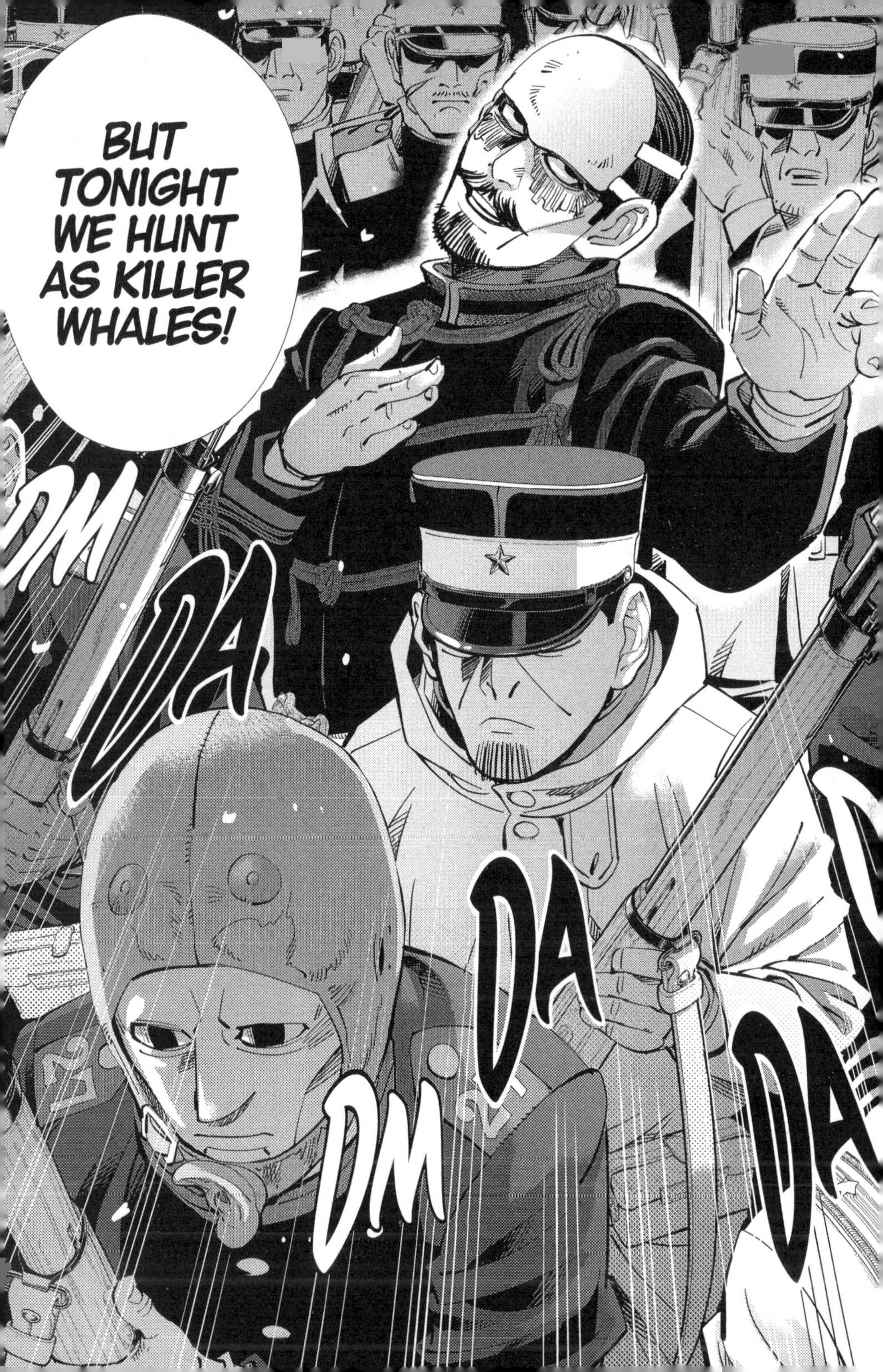
BUT TONIGHT WE HUNT AS KILLER WHALES!
DOM DA
DA
DOM DA
DA

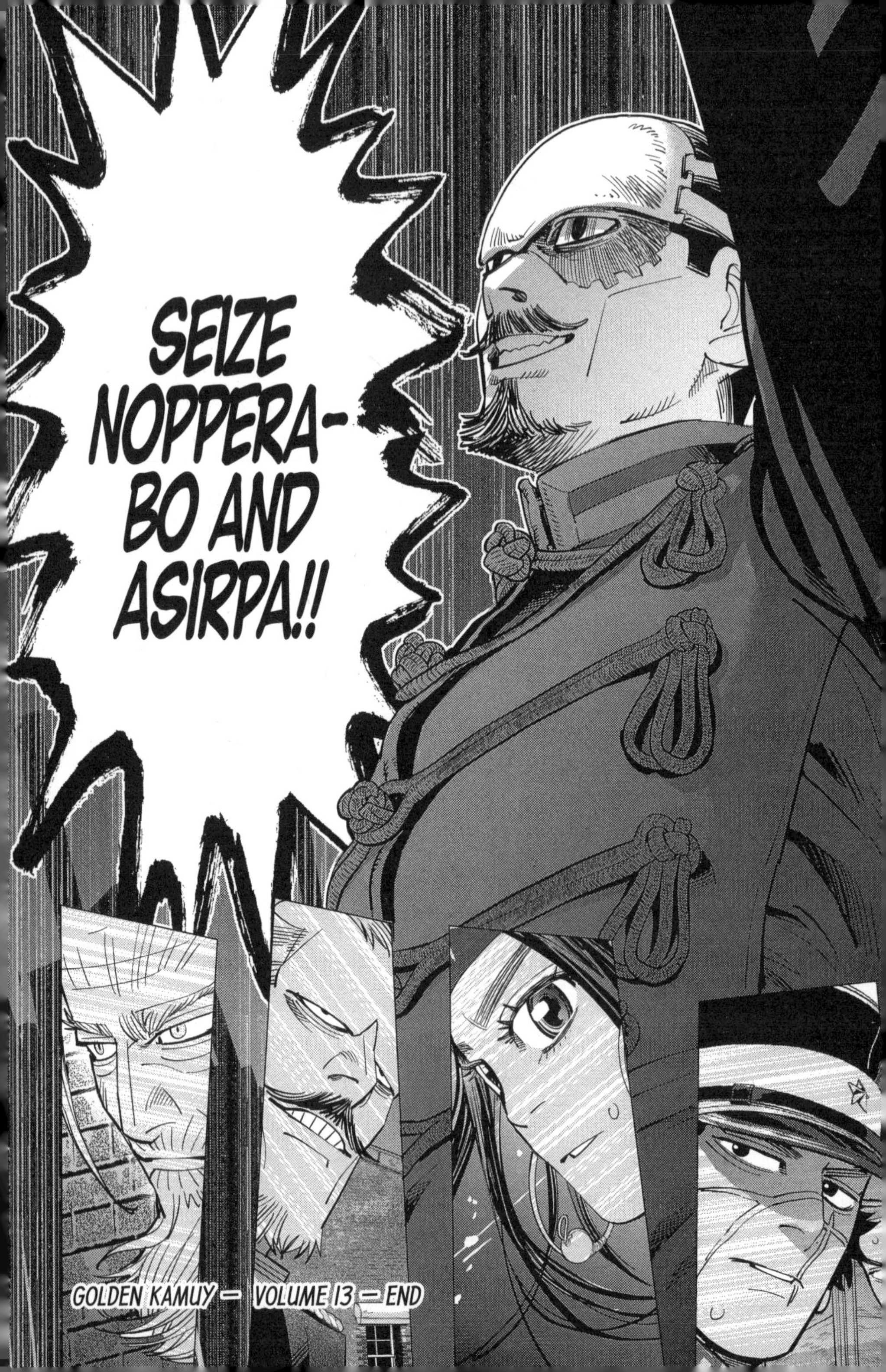
SEIZE NOPPERA-BO AND ASIRPA!!
GOLDEN KAMUY — VOLUME 13 — END

Ainu Language Supervision • Hiroshi Nakagawa

Cooperation from • Hokkaido Ainu Association and the Abashiri Prison Museum
Otaru City General Museum • Waseda University Aizu Museum • Goto, Kazunobu •
Botanic Garden and Museum, Hokkaido University • National Museum of Ethnology
Nibutani Ainu Culture Museum • The Ainu Museum • Moon Kabato Museum •
Kushiro City Museum • Atsuyo Hisai • Tatsuhiro Tokuda • Shigeharu Terui •
Torpedo boat destroyer consultant: Toshio Yamamoto

Photo Credits • Takayuki Monma Takanori Matsuda Kozo Ishikawa

Ainu Culture References

Chiri, Takanaka and Yokoyama, Takao. *Ainugo Eiri Jiten* (Ainu Language Illustrated Dictionary).
Tokyo: Kagyusha, 1994

Kayano, Shigeru. *Ainu no Mingu* (Ainu Folkcrafts). Kawagoe: Suzusawa Book Store, 1978

Kayano, Shigeru. *Kayano Shigeru no Ainugo Jiten* (Kayano Shigeru's Ainu Language Dictionary).
Tokyo: Sanseido, 1996

Musashino Art University – The Research Institute for Culture and Cultural History. *Ainu no Mingu Jissoku Zushu*
(Ainu Folkcrafts – Collection of Drawing and Figures). Biratori: Biratori-cho Council for Promoting Ainu Culture, 2014

Satouchi, Ai. *Ainu-shiki ekoroji-seikatsu: Haruzo Ekashi ni manabu shizen no chie* (Ainu Style Ecological Living:
Haruzo Ekashi Teaches the Wisdom of Nature). Tokyo: Kabushiki gaisha Shogakukan, 2008

Chiri, Yukie. *Ainu Shin'yoshu* (Chiri Yukie's Ainu Epic Tales). Tokyo: Iwanami Shoten, 1978

Namikawa, Kenji. *Ainu Minzoku no Kiseki* (The Path of the Ainu People).
Tokyo: Yamakawa Publishing, 2004

Mook. *Senjuumin Ainu Minzoku* (Bessatsu Taiyo) (The Ainu People (Extra Issue Taiyo).Tokyo: Heibonsha, 2004

Kinoshita, Seizo. *Shiraoikotan Kinoshita Seizo Isaku Shashin Shu* (Shiraoikotan: Kinoshita Seizo's Posthumous
Photography Collection). Hokkaido Shiraoi-gun Shiraoi-cho: Shiraoi Heritage Conservation Foundation, 1988

The Ainu Museum. *Ainu no Ifuku Bunka* (The Culture of Ainu Clothing). Hokkaido Shiraoi-gun Shiraoi-cho:
Shiraoi Ainu Museum, 1991.

Keira, Tomoko and Kaji, Sayaka. *Ainu no Shiki* (Ainu's Four Seasons). Tokyo: Akashi Shoten, 1995

Fukuoka, Itoko and Sato, Kazuko. *Ainu Shokubutsushi* (Ainu Botanical Journal). Chiba Urayasu-Shi: Sofukan, 1995

Hayakawa, Noboru. *Ainu no Minzoku* (Ainu Folklore). Iwasaki Bijutsusha, 1983

Sunazawa, Kura. *Ku Sukuppu Orushibe* (The Memories of My Generation). Hokkaido, Sapporo-shi:
Miyama Shobo, 1983

Haginaka, Miki et al., *Kikigaki Ainu no Shokuji* (Oral History of Ainu Diet).
Tokyo: Rural Culture Association Japan, 1992

Nakagawa, Hiroshi. *New Express Ainu Go*. Tokyo: Hakusuisha, 2013

Nakagawa, Hiroshi. *Ainugo Chitose Hogen Jiten* (The Ainu-Japanese dictionary). Chiba Urayasu-Shi: Sofukan, 1995

Nakagawa, Hiroshi and Nakamoto, Mutsuko. *Kamuy Yukara de Ainu Go wo Manabu*
Learning Ainu with Kamuy Yukar). Tokyo: Hakusuisha, 2007

Nakagawa, Hiroshi. *Katari au Kotoba no Chikara – Kamuy taohi to Ikiru Sekai*
(The Power of Spoken Words – Living in a World with Kamuy). Tokyo: Iwanami Shoten, 2010

Sarashina, Genzo and Sarashina, Hikari. *Kotan Seibutsu Ki <1 Juki / Zassou hen>*
(Kotan Wildlife Vol. 1 – Trees and Weeds). Hosei University Publishing, 1992/2007

Sarashina, Genzo and Sarashina, Hikari. *Kotan Seibutsu Ki <2 Yacho / Kaijuu / Gyozoku hen>*
(Kotan Wildlife Vol. 2 – Birds, Sea Creatures, and Fish). Hosei University Publishing, 1992/2007

Sarashina, Genzo and Sarashina, Hikari. *Kotan Seibutsu Ki <3 Yachou / Mizudori / Konchu hen>*
(Kotan Wildlife Vol. 3 – Shorebirds, Seabirds, and Insects). Hosei University Publishing, 1992/2007

Sarashina, Genzo. *Ainu Minwashu* (Collection of Ainu Folktales). Kita Shobou, 1963.

Sarashina, Genzo. *Ainu Rekishi to Minzoku* (Ainu History and Folklore). Shakai Shisousha, 1968.

Kawakami Yuji. *Sarunkur Ainu Monogatari* (The Tale of Sarunkur Ainu). Kawagoe: Suzusawa Book Store, 2003/2005

Kawakami, Yuji. *Ekashi to Fuchi wo Tazunete* (Visiting Ekashi and Fuchi). Kawagoe: Suzusawa Book Store, 1991

Council for the Conservation of Ainu Culture. *Ainu Minzokushi* (Ainu People Magazine). Dai-ichi Hoki, 1970

Hokkaido Cultural Property Protection Association. *Ainu Ifuku Chousa Houkokusho <1 Ainu Josei ga Denshou Suru
Ibunka>* (The Ainu Clothing Research Report Vol. 1 – Traditional Clothing Passed Down Through Generations of Ainu
Women). 1986

Okamura, Kichiemon and Clancy, Judith A. *Ainu no Ishou* (The Clothes of the Ainu People). Kyoto Shoin, 1993

Yotsuji, Ichiro. Photos by Mizutani, Morio. *Ainu no Monyo* (Decorative Arts of the Ainu). Kasakura Publishing, 1981

Yoshida, Iwao. *Ainushi Shiryoshu* (Collection of Ainu Historical Documents).
Hokkaido Publication Project Center, 1983.

Kubodera, Itsuhiko. *Ainu no Mukashibanashi* (Old Stories of the Ainu). Miyaishoten, 1972.

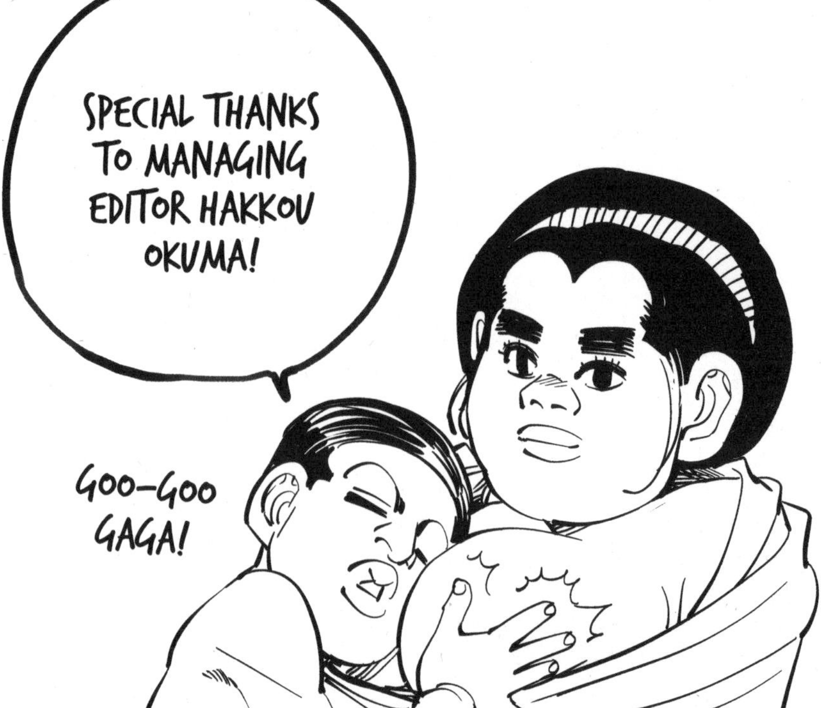
SPECIAL THANKS TO MANAGING EDITOR HAKKOU OKUMA!
GOO-GOO GAGA!

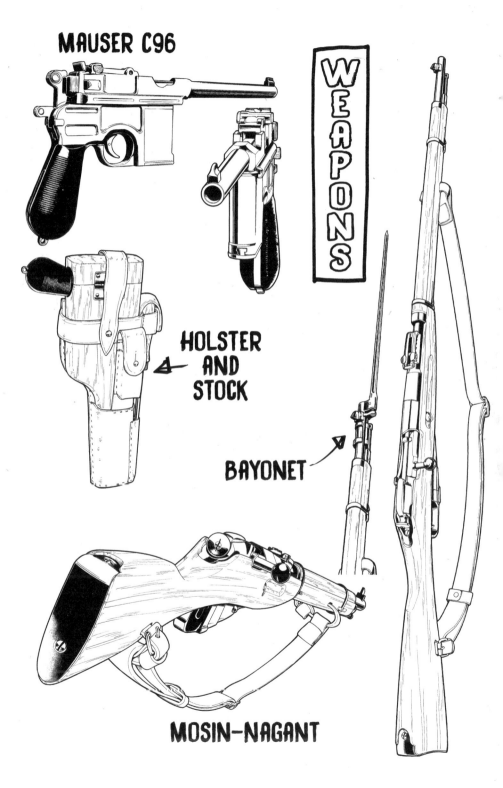

MAUSER C96

WEAPONS

HOLSTER
AND
STOCK

BAYONET

MOSIN-NAGANT

Kanto or wa yaku sak no arankep sinep ka isam.

Nothing comes from heaven without purpose. —Ainu proverb

RUUNPE

LONG, THIN PIECES OF CLOTH IN VARIOUS COLORS SEWN ONTO COTTON CLOTHES.

KIRORANKE'S CLOTHES

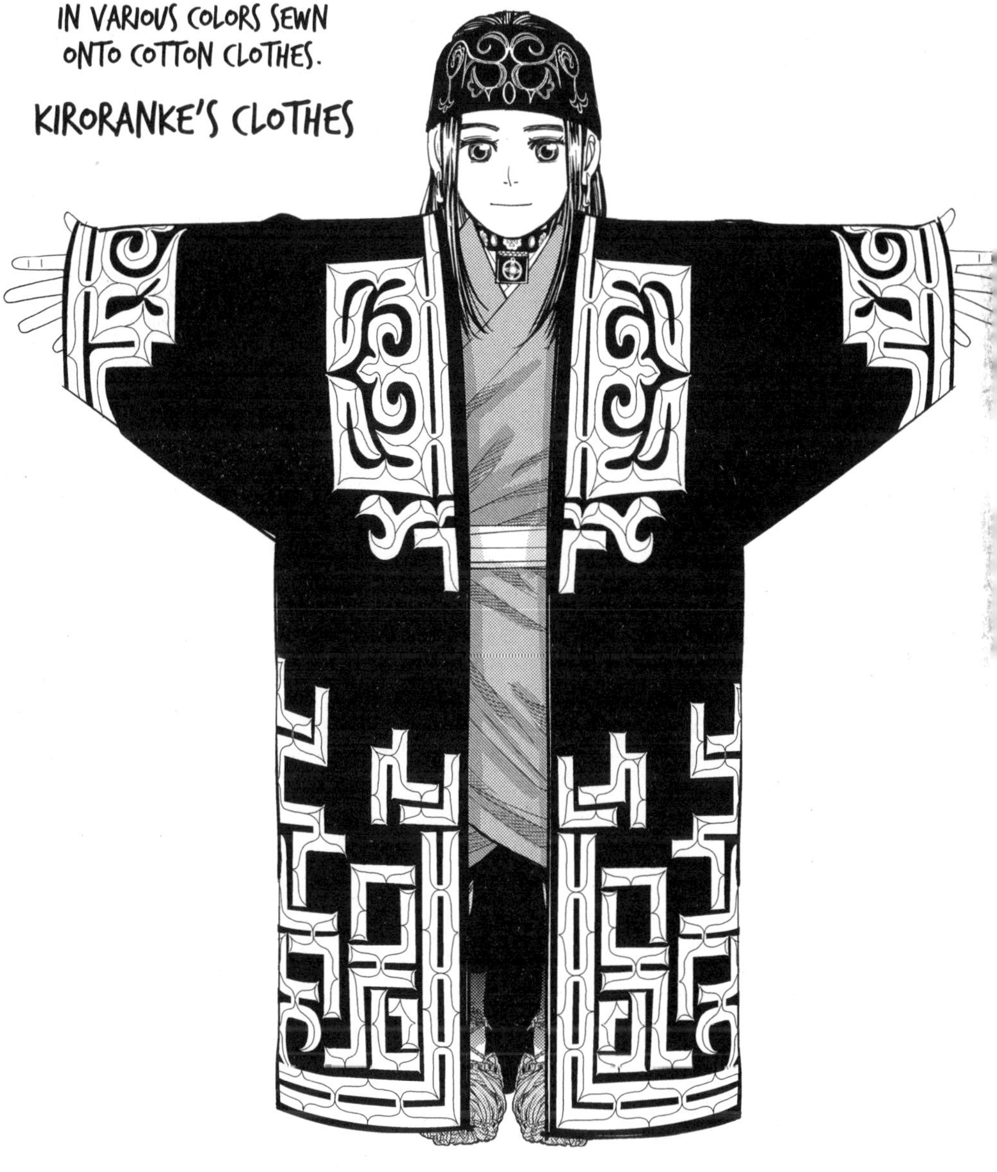

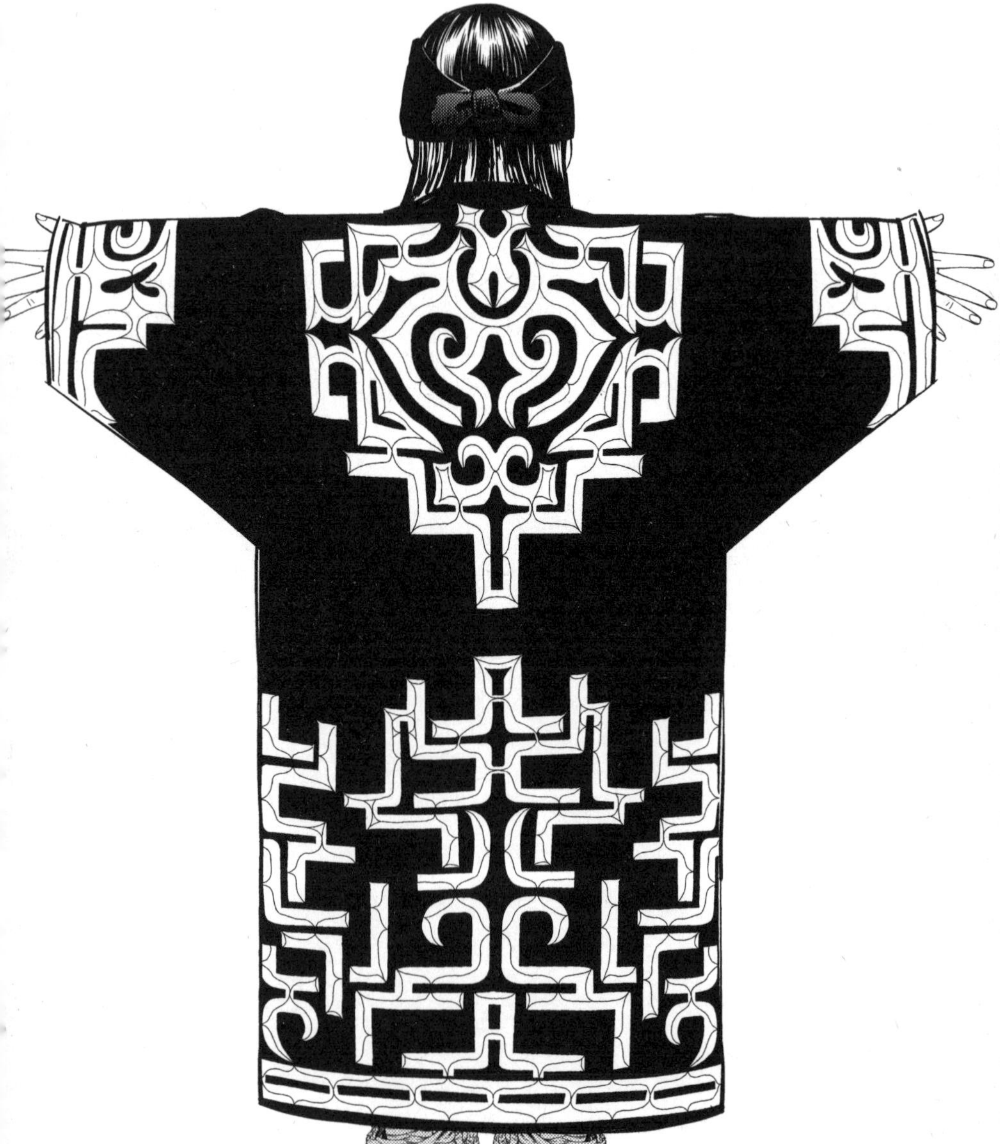

GOLDEN KAMUY

Volume 13
VIZ Signature Edition

Story/Art by Satoru Noda

First published in Japan in 2014 by SHUEISHA Inc., Tokyo.
English translation rights arranged by SHUEISHA Inc.

Translation/John Werry
Touch-Up Art & Lettering/Steve Dutro
Design/Shawn Carrico
Editor/Mike Montesa

Printed in the U.S.A.

Published by VIZ Media, LLC
P.O. Box 77010
San Francisco, CA 94107

10 9 8 7 6 5 4 3 2 1
First printing, December 2019

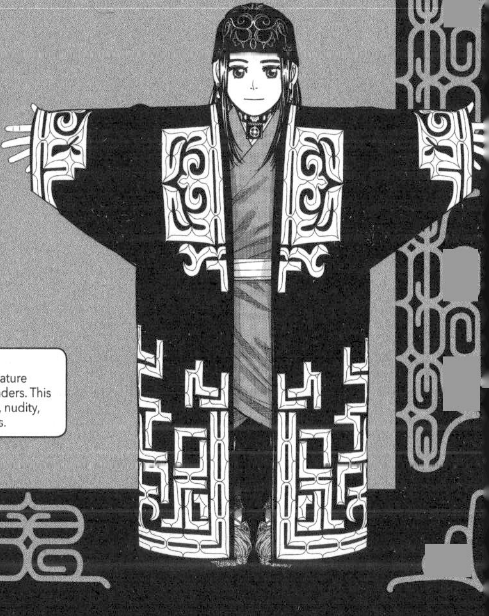

VIZ SIGNATURE

VIZ MEDIA
viz.com

ratings.viz.com RATED M MATURE

PARENTAL ADVISORY
GOLDEN KAMUY is rated M for Mature and recommended for mature readers. This volume contains graphic violence, nudity, strong language and adult themes.

THIS IS THE LAST PAGE.

GOLDEN KAMUY has been printed in the original Japanese format in order to preserve the orientation of the original artwork.

Please turn it around and begin reading from right to left. Unlike English, Japanese is read right to left, so Japanese comics are read in reverse order from the way English comics are typically read. Have fun with it!

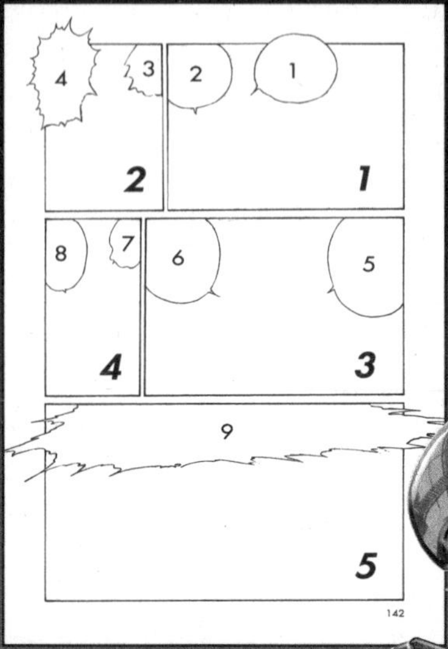

←Follow the action this way.

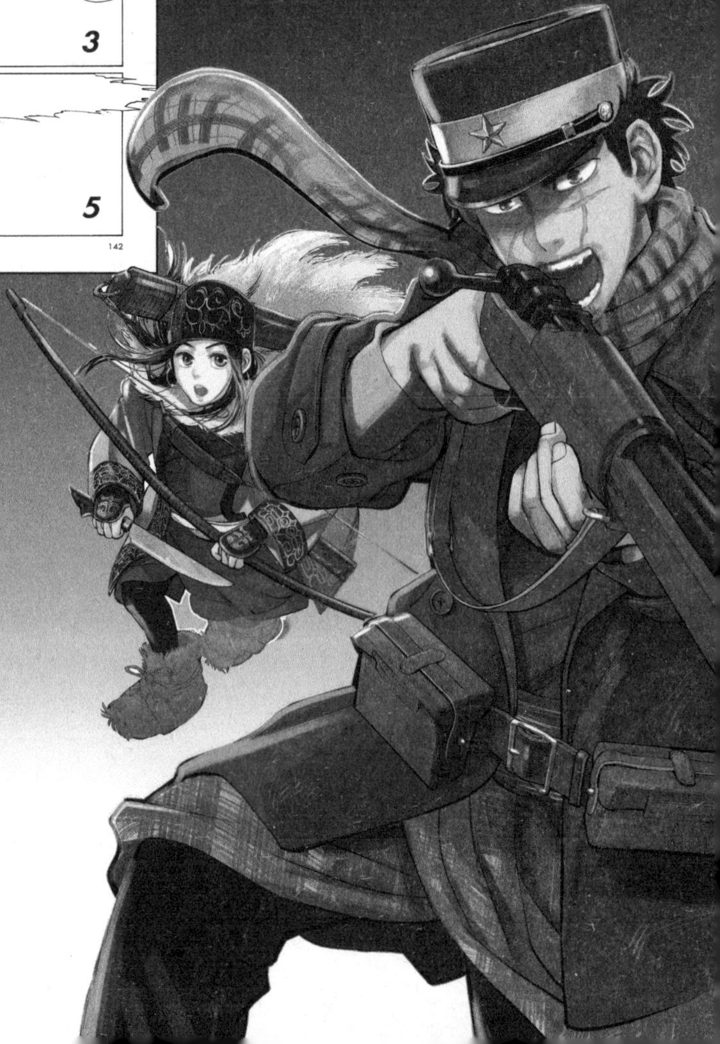